One of *Smithsonia*
Travel Books

One of *Time* magazine's
"22 Books to Read This Summer"

One of *AFAR* magazine's "8 New Books You Need
to Read Before Flying to France"

"I can't imagine a more fascinating or titillating angle to explore the history of France than this wonderful book."

—Clotilde Dusoulier, author of *Tasting Paris:
100 Recipes to Eat like a Local*

"This impressive book intertwines tales of gastronomy, culture, war, and revolution . . . with brisk wit [and] imagination."

—*The Christian Science Monitor*

"Brimming with anecdotes as surprising as they are appetizing."

—*France-Amérique*

"From the delights of French chocolate (through Portuguese Jews of Bayonne) to France's passion for plums (brought home by the Templars from Damascus), *A Bite-Sized History of France* offers satisfaction for all: tastes of history from the people who gave perhaps the world's greatest cuisine to the whole world. Why travel with a guide book on dry history, architecture, or politics when you can sink your teeth into such a delicious feast?"

—Juliette Rossant, author of *Super Chef*

"Who would have guessed forks had so much to do with bayo-nets? From the introduction of wine to Gaul by the Romans to Napoleon's pancake predictions before entering Russia, the strange dialectics of war and peas offer a fascinating means of exploring the origins of French culinary traditions. Funny and historically accurate, this delicious book will make you want to raid the fridge."

—Jean Lopez, founder and editor-in-chief, *Guerres & Histoire*

"A fascinating history of France through food [that is] excep-tionally well-researched. This culinary history is a treat for Francophiles."

—*Publishers Weekly*

"A husband and wife—he is French; she, American—move briskly through the history of France with a picnic basket full of information about the connections between history and gas-tronomy. . . . A genial journey through history that will leave readers both satiated and ravenous."

—*Kirkus Reviews* (starred review)

Stéphane Hénaut grew up in Frankfurt and Nantes, before moving to London and embarking on a wide-ranging career in food, including working in the Harrods *fromagerie* and cooking for the Lord Mayor of London's banquets. He later returned to Nantes with his family, selling obscure vegetables in a French *fruiterie*, before joining one of Berlin's finest *fromageries*.

Jeni Mitchell spent most of her adult life in Washington, DC, working as a researcher and editor in foreign affairs, before moving to London to begin graduate school. She met Stéphane on her first day in London; four years later, they married. She has a PhD in war studies from King's College London, where she is a teaching fellow specializing in civil war, insurgency, and rebellion.

A BITE-SIZED HISTORY OF FRANCE

A BITE-SIZED HISTORY OF FRANCE

Gastronomic Tales of Revolution, War, and Enlightenment

STÉPHANE HÉNAUT

and

JENI MITCHELL

NEW YORK
LONDON

Requests for permission to reproduce selections from this book should be made
through our website: https://thenewpress.com/contact.

Excerpts on pages 18–22 from *Poems to Friends* by Venantius Fortunatus,
translated and edited by Joseph Pucci, reproduced with permission from Hackett
Publishing Company.

First published in the United States by The New Press, New York, 2018
This paperback published by The New Press, 2019
Distributed by Two Rivers Distribution

ISBN 978-1-62097-251-9 (hc)
ISBN 978-1-62097-547-3 (pbk)
ISBN 978-1-62097-252-6 (ebook)
CIP data is available

The New Press publishes books that promote and enrich public discussion and
understanding of the issues vital to our democracy and to a more equitable world.
These books are made possible by the enthusiasm of our readers; the support of a
committed group of donors, large and small; the collaboration of our many partners
in the independent media and the not-for-profit sector; booksellers, who often hand-
sell New Press books; librarians; and above all by our authors.

www.thenewpress.com

Book design and composition by Bookbright Media
This book was set in Sabon and CG Coronet

Printed in the United States of America

20 19 18 17 16 15 14 13 12

For Jules

Contents

Introduction 1

1. Our Ancestors, the Gauls 5

2. The Virgin of the Kidney 10

3. Barbarians at the Plate 14

4. Ode to Gluttony 18

5. Left Behind: The Goats of Poitou 22

6. The Sweetest King 26

7. They Came from the Sea 31

8. Feudal Fare 37

9. Of Monks and Men 43

10. Fighting for Plums 49

11. The Wine That Got Away 55

12. The Vegetarian Heresy 61

13. A Papal Red 68

14. The White Gold of Guérande 73

15. Legacy of a Black Prince 78

16. The Vinegar of the Four Thieves 84

17. The Cheese of Emperors and Mad Kings 90

18. La Dame de Beauté and the Mushroom Mystery 94

19. Fruits of the Renaissance 99

20. The Mother Sauces 105

21. Conquest and Chocolate 110

22. The Culinary Contributions of Madame Serpent 116

23. A Chicken in Every Pot 122

24. The Chestnut Insurgency 128

25. The Bitter Roots of Sugar 134

26. The Liquor of the Gods 139

27. The Crescent Controversy 145

28. War and Peas 148

29. The Devil's Wine 153

30. An Enlightened Approach to Food 159

31. Revolution in the Cafés 163

32. Pain d'Égalité 169

33. The Potato Propagandist 174

34. The Pyramid Provocation 180

35. The Man Who Abolished the Seasons 186

36. The Fifth Crêpe 189

37. The King of Cheeses 193

38. A Revolutionary Banquet 197

39. The End of the Oyster Express 203

40. Revelation in a Bottle 210

41. The Curse of the Green Fairy 215

42. Siege Gastronomy 221

43. The Peanut Patrimony 228

44. Gastronomads on the Sun Road 233

45. A Friend in Difficult Hours 238

46. A Mutiny and a Laughing Cow 244

47. "Bread, Peace, and Liberty": The Socialist Baguette 249

48. Couscous: The Assimilation (or Not) of Empire 254

49. The Forgotten Vegetables 262

50. Canon Kir Joins the Resistance 268

51. France and the United States: From Liberation to
Exasperation 274

52. Conclusion 282

Acknowledgments 287
Bibliography 291
Notes 293
Index 321

be referring to the luscious dish of snails dripping in garlic butter, but rather to a style of protest—*going at a snail's pace*—frequently used by French farmers. Among their grievances is the imposition of common European standards on French agriculture, which they see as destroying their traditional way of life. As we will show, in many parts of rural France, the production of food and wine remains true to methods crafted in centuries past.

You are probably also familiar with French protests against McDonald's. But despite the disdain for the American behemoth so frequently expressed among the French cultural elite, France is the second biggest overseas market for McDo, as it is affectionately known here. As we will see, this gulf between the elites and the common people is nothing new in France.

Unfortunately, the use of food to define French identity has become a favored tactic of the French far right since the 1990s, and it has increasingly seeped into mainstream politics in the past decade as well. In the 2012 presidential election, for example, both Marine Le Pen and Nicolas Sarkozy framed halal meat as a threat to French cultural values and agricultural tradition. A number of towns run by right-wing councils have removed pork-free options from school menus. Nationalist rallies feature tables laden with pork dishes and wine, both of which have become totemic within right-wing narratives that posit a France under threat from its Muslim communities and immigrants. The subtext is rarely subtle: to be French, one should eat and drink as French people have always done. And yet one of the clearest messages to emerge from French history is that French gastronomy is an amalgam of tastes and customs from all around the globe: its vineyards bequeathed by the Romans, its most famous pastry a gift from Austria, and the birth of the café unthinkable without that fabulous Turkish import, coffee. Chocolate? From Mexico. Provençal cuisine? Imagine it without tomatoes, another American import. In short, our narrative will show how ludicrous it actually is to claim there is a "pure" and unchanging French cuisine.

Food and society and politics are interlinked here in France in ways that are constantly evolving and yet surprisingly consistent in their basic dynamics. The ways in which politics, economics, and culture intersect with food have become known as "foodways," and they can reveal a great deal about a country and its people. By exploring the foodways of France from its earliest days, we hope to reveal some of the enduring patterns that explain its rise upon the world stage as well as its lowest depths of suffering, its terrible conflicts and its marvelous innovations.

The history of France is intimately entwined with its gastronomic pursuits, whether one considers the food scarcities that begat revolutions, the wars and conquests that introduced new culinary elements, or the radical changes in religious and philosophical thought that remade the diets of millions. Some of the most transformative innovations in human history have their roots in French food, as we shall see when we consider giants such as Pasteur and Appert, and some of the most inspiring political philosophies of the modern era were nurtured in the French café. European imperialism transformed the global order and caused immense suffering around the world, a tragic history whose depths may be plumbed by considering the patterns of exploitation that emerged in food and agriculture. From the gastronomic legacies of the Gauls to the forgotten vegetables of World War II, we will share a compelling and often surprising story of France from the Roman era to modern times.

Food is also an essential ingredient in the evolving and overlapping identities of the peoples of France, as revealed in everything from the interrogations of the Inquisition to the Cold War crusade against Coca-Cola. It has been successfully deployed as a marker of social status and wealth across the centuries, and the enduring gulf between the eating habits of the rich and the poor reveals much about the society they reside within. In the end, we will see that however distinctive French cuisine may be, it also reveals some fundamental commonalities between Americans and the French that belie the antagonism that sometimes erupts between our two countries.

Each chapter is short—a series of bite-sized stories best told over a nice meal. Our hope is that you are already starting to feel a tad hungry, and a bit curious about the French foods and wines you may not be familiar with. We will be pleased if this book makes you want to travel to France and wander through its markets, towns, and countryside. But if at the end of this book all you do is go out and buy a bottle of French wine, some fresh bread, and a French cheese of your liking, and enjoy them with a new appreciation that you are not just eating food but also enjoying a part of France's rich history, then we will consider our mission accomplished.

1

Our Ancestors, the Gauls

Most French people would doubtless agree with François Rabelais, the great Renaissance humanist, who declared that "from wine, one becomes divine."[1] He may have been frequently accused of obscenity and heresy in his day, but it was not for this indisputable statement.

There was indeed a time, however, when wine was virtually unknown in the land we now know as France. Twenty-five hundred years ago, before the arrival of the Romans, wine was considered a foreign drink; most people in pre-Roman France preferred to drink *cervoise*, a fermented barley brew. Only the wealthier classes drank wine, shocking the Romans and Greeks by drinking it pure, not watered down, and to excess—and by allowing women the same drinking rights as men.[2] Most of the wine was imported from Italy, in apparently huge quantities.[3] Wine was cultivated only on a small scale around Marseille, the oldest French town and port, founded by seafaring Greeks from Phocaea around 600 B.C.E.

This vast territory between the Pyrenees and the Rhine, and the Mediterranean and the Atlantic, came to be known as Gaul, and it forms a natural starting point for history lessons in French schools. Most people who have survived the French education system will know at least two things about the Gauls.

First, they are "our ancestors." For many years, "Our ancestors,

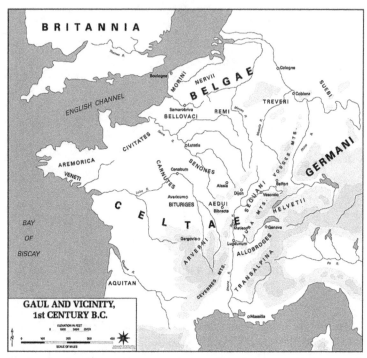

Gaul in the first century B.C.E., on the eve of the Roman conquest.
Department of History, United States Military Academy.

the Gauls," was a common refrain in history textbooks in France, somewhat willfully defying the considerably more complicated genealogies of modern French students. (This kind of approach is inevitable, perhaps, when one's idea of a "melting pot" is a fondue.)

The second thing most French schoolchildren learn about the Gauls is that they had a magic potion, made by druids, that made them extraordinarily strong. This is because French children, like all children, fall asleep during ponderous descriptions of their ancestors and much prefer to read comic books about superheroes—like Asterix, the diminutive but wily warrior from Gaul. Asterix and his friend Obelix, thanks to a magic potion supplied by their druid pal Getafix, have various adventures that mostly involve beating up Roman legionnaires, feasting on boar meat, and downing barrels of cervoise. The Asterix books have been enormously popular since the 1960s, and have even spawned a film series starring—in perhaps the most perfect case of typecasting in history—Gérard Depardieu as the drunken, boisterous Obelix.

But who were the Gauls, really? According to the Romans, they were pretty much like Asterix and Obelix: they were their noisy, drunk, uncultured, ever-fighting, banquet- and party-loving northern neighbors. As the Gauls did not provide much written history of their own, most of what we know about them comes from the Romans, so the above definition of them may not be entirely correct. Even the idea of a Gaul nation or political identity is not very accurate: they were actually Celts, a people who lived throughout most of Europe at the time, and they were ruled by many different tribal chieftains. The Gauls themselves would probably not have known that they were Gauls, but the Romans decided to call them Gauls, and so they came to be known to us.

The everyday Roman started to really pay attention to the Gauls in about 390 B.C.E., when they sacked Rome. In his *History of Rome*, Livy suggested that the Gauls had invaded Italy in pursuit "of the delicious fruits and especially of the wine," but in the end it was gold they demanded in exchange for peace—a thousand pounds of it.[4] The Romans acquiesced, but when it came time to weigh the gold, they complained that the Gauls were trying to cheat them with inaccurate weights. The leader of the Gauls used a simple yet efficient technique to shut the Romans up: he threw his sword on the scales and declared, "*Vae victis!*" ("Woe to the vanquished!"). The Romans got the message—so well, in fact, that they spent the next 350 years conquering the Mediterranean shores, and finally Gaul itself. "*Gallia est pacata,*" wrote Julius Caesar in 52 B.C.E., after his victory over the tribal chieftain Vercingetorix. "Gaul is subdued." For the next five centuries, Gaul would be one of the most important and prosperous provinces of the Roman Empire, and its people would gradually evolve into "Gallo-Romans." Nearly every aspect of their culture, from religion to language to eating habits, became blended with Roman elements. The beautiful French language we appreciate today, for example, has its roots in this Gallo-Roman marriage.

As the Gauls became more and more Romanized, they began to adopt the habits of Roman wine drinking and vine growing. New vineyards emerged throughout Gaul, producing intriguing varieties of wine that were appreciated even in Rome. In the first century C.E., Pliny the Elder noted that the Gauls around Vienne, in the Rhône Valley, were producing an excellent red wine. From the writings of

Ausonius, a Gallo-Roman poet and winemaker, we know that wine was produced in the Bordeaux region in the fourth century (one of today's finest Saint-Émilion estates, Château Ausone, is named for him). Nascent wine-growing cultures emerged in the now-famous regions of Burgundy, Alsace, and Savoy, and possibly even in the far northern region that is now Normandy.

These wines would probably not have pleased our modern palate. They were much more intoxicating, for one thing, which was why "civilized" drinkers tended to dilute them with water. They were stored and aged in porous containers and thus spoiled easily, so it was usually necessary to soften their flavor with honey or herbs. Notions of vintage and terroir had yet to be invented. Wine was appreciated not so much because of its taste but because of its disinhibiting qualities, so useful for social occasions and religious rituals, and because it was known as a disinfectant for suspect water. As we shall see in future chapters, the celebrated French wines of today emerged only after centuries of obsessive experimentation with grape varieties and winemaking techniques. Thus, the tendency for French winemakers to emphasize the ancient roots of their products should not be taken as an indication of consistent quality over the centuries. This marketing approach in fact emerged in the nineteenth century, when all sorts of gastronomic traditions were exaggerated or invented to counterbalance the dislocating effects of industrialization and urbanization.[5]

The Gauls may not have been big wine producers before the Romans arrived, but they had managed to invent one thing without which we simply could not enjoy wine and alcohol the same way we do today: the wooden barrel. It is hard to pinpoint when they invented it, but it is certain that when Caesar conquered the Gauls in the first century B.C.E., they were already using barrels—mainly for their cervoise, but also to transport items of food, such as salted or smoked pork or fish. They were thus a step ahead of the civilized Romans, who were still using amphorae to carry their goods around. Now to us, it seems easier to use something made of wood that can be rolled around, instead of a big ceramic vase with two handles. But then, the Romans had slaves to do the most backbreaking work.

Given that many of our modern tipples are aged in wooden barrels, which add some lovely flavors to the alcohol, we should really thank our ancestors, the Gauls, for making a glass of cognac, whiskey, or wine so much more enjoyable. Even the Romans, or the Italians as they are known these days, can thank the Gauls, as one of the staples of Italian food—balsamic vinegar—would not exist in its current form if not aged in barrels for months, or even years, prior to consumption.

It is not difficult to appreciate France's Gallo-Roman era today, as many cities and towns—especially in the southern reaches of the country—are still graced by buildings, aqueducts, and bridges built nearly two millennia ago. The ancient city of Arles, for example, has a remarkably well preserved collection of sites around its imposing Roman arena. Its narrow winding streets evoke both long-gone antiquity and the sunny scents of modern Provence, encouraging a perception that time does not always run in linear fashion in France. It is a land where the ancient and the modern cradle each other, creating a history that is uniquely and ineffably *French*.

The Roman arena in Arles, built in 90 C.E., hosted chariot races and gladiatorial contests for audiences of up to twenty thousand people. Today, it is a remarkably well preserved UNESCO World Heritage site. Concerts and bullfights are still held here. © Gilles Lagnel (Pixabay Photos).

2

The Virgin of the Kidney

Many of France's most beautiful cities were founded in the Gallo-Roman era—including Limoges, the historical capital of the Limousin region in southwestern France, which may have been founded by Roman emperor Augustus himself. Long before the development of its famous porcelain in the eighteenth century, Limoges was a prosperous religious and cultural center (when it wasn't being ravaged by wars, despots, and pestilence, of course). Today, the winding streets of its charming medieval quarter conceal an important clue to the history of Limoges, and to France itself: *La Vierge au rognon*, the Virgin of the Kidney. Tucked away in the small chapel known as Notre-Dame-des-Petits-Ventres, this statue of Mary holding the infant Jesus as he solemnly gorges himself on a kidney raises a score of unsettling questions. Why a kidney? Should that baby really be eating solids already? Is this some kind of sacrilegious joke? To answer these questions—well, except the second one, which is a blindingly obvious *No*—let's return to our journey in the Gallo-Roman era.

A polytheistic Celtic religion had been common among the Gallic tribes, but after the Roman conquest many of the Celtic deities merged with the Roman gods and formed a new Gallo-Roman religion. For example, the Celtic deity Grannus and the Roman god Apollo were both associated with healing and the sun, and so some Gallo-Romans eventually honored a kind of hybrid deity named Apollo Grannus. Romanized gods were often paired with Celtic goddesses, a symbolic manifestation of the broader cultural merging that was occurring. The nondogmatic nature of polytheism meant that the Gallo-Roman pantheon could be fluid and adaptive.

But everything has its limits, and this Gallo-Roman bonhomie finally met its match in Christianity. Christians, after all, believe that there is only one god, so there was never any hope of incorporating the new Christian deity into the polytheistic posse. When the first Christian missionaries appeared, condemning the false idols of the locals, they did not receive a very friendly Gallo-Roman welcome.

From the first to the fourth century C.E., they were usually either ignored or persecuted, and sometimes even martyred.

Perhaps the most famous Gallic martyr is Saint Blandina, who died in 177. She and some of her Christian companions were fed to the lions in Lyon (then known as Lugdunum), Gaul's capital city. But Blandina was rejected by the lions, either because she was very weak and did not seem much of a meal, or because God protected her (take your pick according to your beliefs). She was then tortured to make her recant her beliefs, but she never did, and she was eventually executed. She is now the patron saint of Lyon (but not its lions).

Martyrdom was always rather gruesome, but it was a very effective means of becoming a patron saint. Saint Lawrence, for example, was a deacon in Rome in the third century, known for distributing money and food to the poor. This attracted the attention of Valerian, the Roman emperor, who commanded Lawrence to bring to him the riches of his church. Lawrence brought him beggars, cripples, and orphans and said, "These are the greatest treasures of the church." The emperor was not amused and ordered that Lawrence be burned to death slowly over hot charcoal. After hanging over the charcoal for a while, Lawrence remarked to his tormentors: "This side is nicely grilled—you can turn me over now." This witty remark makes him the patron saint of cooks and broilers.

In fact, most food-related trades in France have patron saints, although not all of them met such grisly ends. Saint Martin of Tours, one of the best-known early Christian saints, died of natural causes in the fourth century. He is the patron saint of vintners (and, appropriately perhaps, of alcoholics) and is said to have introduced the pruning of vines in the region of Touraine. According to legend, his donkey chewed up some vines, and the next year the peasants noticed that on these vines there were fewer grapes, but they were bigger and tastier. Thus, thanks to Saint Martin, the wines of Touraine had the reputation of being the best in France. Another legend has it that after his death, the vintners of Touraine cried so much that their tears altered the taste of their wines, and this is how Touraine lost its spot as the best wine region of France to Burgundy and Bordeaux.

And so we come back to Limoges and the Virgin of the Kidney. Eventually, most of the food trades in France developed their own guilds, a form of cooperative association that set strict standards for participating in a trade and promoted its members' mutual interests. Guilds became very important political and social groups in the medieval era, and in France most of them adopted a patron saint to watch over them. In Limoges, the powerful butchers' guild chose Saint Aurélien as its patron saint. Aurélien was a third-century pagan priest who was originally sent to Limoges to kill its bishop, Martial, who had successfully converted many local inhabitants to Christianity. Martial asked God to protect him, and the very obliging deity struck Aurélien dead with a bolt of lightning. Martial then felt a bit bad about the whole thing and asked God to restore Aurélien to life. God, showing rather a lot of patience with his bishop, made it so. Aurélien, now convinced that there was something to this Christianity idea after all, converted and became the bishop of Limoges following Martial's death. Martial himself later became the patron saint of Limoges.

The butchers of Limoges plied their trade around the rue de la Boucherie and frequented its fifteenth-century chapel, Notre-Dame-des-Petits-Ventres (Our Lady of the Little Bellies), which became known as the "butchers' chapel." While their shops and abattoirs have long since departed the quarter, it remains a charming street of timbered houses and sunny squares. The chapel itself makes for an interesting visit, with its altar flanked somewhat conventionally by statues of Saint Aurélien and Saint Martial—and with its bizarre Virgin of the Kidney statue, whose origins are now hopefully a bit more clear. It reflects not only the old local custom of butchers giving kidneys, rich in iron, to young children and new mothers, but the marriage of commerce and religion in the medieval cities of France.[1]

The French are famously willing to eat animal parts not often seen in American supermarkets, and this tradition is particularly celebrated in Limoges, where butchers have played an important social role for centuries. You can get a good sense of the outer limits of offal gastronomy at the annual food festival sponsored by the Frairie des Petits Ventres (Brotherhood of the Little Bellies), an organization established in the 1970s to combat city plans to demolish the medieval butchers' quarter. Thankfully they succeeded, and now every October the Quartier de la Boucherie resumes its historic character with dozens of stalls offering a fascinating range of meat dishes. You might start with the relatively accessible *girot* sausage, made with lamb's blood, or try the popular sheep's testicles, sautéed in garlic and parsley. The truly brave might sample the fair's namesake dish, the *petits ventres*, which turns out to be a bit like haggis: sheep stom-

La Vierge au rognon (the Virgin of the Kidney), in the old butchers' chapel, Notre-Dame-des-Petits-Ventres (Our Lady of the Little Bellies), Limoges. © Karine Hénaut, 2017.

achs stuffed with parts of the animal you'd rather not think about. For the squeamish, there is no shame in merely sampling the more mainstream marvel of a burger made from Limousin beef, one of the best beef varieties in Europe and the region's best-known gastronomic contribution today.

The heyday of the early Christian martyrs came to a close in the fourth century, when the Roman emperor Constantine converted to Christianity; a few decades later, Christianity became the official religion of the empire. The Gallo-Romans abandoned their pagan ways in greater and greater numbers, and thus the earliest foundations of French Catholicism were laid. No doubt these early Christians foresaw a glorious future for their new religion in Gaul. Little could they know that the imperial edifice upon which it perched was already beginning to crumble.

3

Barbarians at the Plate

Few empires in history rival the Romans in terms of the sheer breadth of territory they controlled. From England to Egypt, and from Spain to Syria, nearly a quarter of the world's population lived under the Romans at the height of their power. Their technological and cultural achievements remain impressive to this day, whether we consider the roads and aqueducts that have survived all these centuries, the language that lies at the root of so many European tongues, or the poetry that continues to captivate readers around the world. Of course, the Romans also did many terrible things— they kept slaves, they fed people to lions, and let's not forget the time they razed Carthage and sowed its fields with salt. But none of this diminished their belief in themselves as the pinnacle of earthly civilization.

Roman gastronomy featured a similar duality. It included magnificent dishes and excellent wines drawn from across the empire, as well as a number of ethically and aesthetically dubious treats. Foie gras, for example, required the force-feeding of geese, while capons were the innovative result of castrating cockerels. Apicius, a well-known first-century Roman gourmand who committed suicide when his lavish budget for food ran dry, professed a taste for flamingo tongues, camel heels, and the teats and vulvas of sows.

This gastronomic diversity might lead one to think that the Romans were limitless in their affections for food. But actually, there was one practice in particular that the Romans considered so uncouth, so unimaginably foul, that it revealed a complete lack of civilization. This was, of course, the unforgivable sin of cooking with butter instead of olive oil, and it was one of the most important elements in the Roman definition of a "barbarian."

Centuries earlier, the Romans themselves had been the barbarians, from the perspective of the Greeks. But now that much of the known world was ruled and shaped by Rome, they needed their own antithesis, a vastly inferior "other" that would help define what it meant to be Roman. The various Germanic and Eurasian tribes congregating at the fringes of the empire were easily cast as the barbarian hordes. After all, they did not speak Latin or worship the Roman gods or live according to Roman law—and just look at what they ate! Food has always been a useful mechanism for demonizing populations, and it was no different in the ancient world. You knew you were dealing with uncivilized barbarians if they cooked with butter, drank beer instead of wine, and relied on meat from the hunt rather than farmed crops.[1]

Over the years, the Gallo-Roman population had generally adapted to "civilized" Roman ways, while the Germanic tribes in the north and east of what is now France adhered to their own culinary traditions. Some argue that this explains why even today there exists a noticeable divide between the north of France, where people are more likely to cook with butter and drink beer or cider, and the south of France, where most dishes are prepared with olive oil and wine reigns supreme. It would be nice if it were this simple, but such culinary divisions actually do not map this neatly onto the Roman/German divide (and as we shall see, these sorts of social preferences are rarely attributable to a single historical factor).

The Roman sense of superiority did not always correlate with the actual strength of their empire (a common historical affliction) and in the fourth and fifth centuries it was often attacked by barbarian tribes. The Romans succeeded in co-opting individual tribes, giving them land or loot if they would settle frontier territories and defend them against other barbarians, but this proved to be successful only in the short term. In the end, Gaul was swarmed by the Vandals, the Alans, the Suebi, the Burgundians, the Visigoths, and, most important for French history, the Huns and the Franks.

Attila the Hun is probably one of the few barbarian leaders whose name is familiar to most of us, with its enduring connotations of cruelty and savagery. Called the "Scourge of God," he built a mighty empire in eastern Europe, before eventually invading Gaul in 451. He sacked towns such as Metz, killing most of its inhabitants, and the terrified populace fled before him. Finally, he was defeated by the Roman army in June 451, near Paris, in the Battle of the Catalaunian

Fields, one of the bloodiest clashes in European history and the first major setback for Attila in Europe. It was not, however, a decisive victory for the Romans; Attila returned the next year to invade Italy, though he failed to reach Rome itself. He died in 453 in true barbarian fashion, choking to death on his own blood on his wedding night.

Overall, the Huns are not remembered very fondly in France. But their invasion led to a French food legend, namely that the Huns were responsible for introducing choucroute, or sauerkraut, to the parts of eastern France that they swept through, like Alsace and its capital, Strasbourg. A classic dish in French brasseries and bistros, usually eaten with pork or sausages, sauerkraut is popular throughout Germany and eastern Europe thanks to invaders from the Asian steppes (although most likely it was the thirteenth-century Mongols, not the Huns, who were responsible for its introduction). The association of sauerkraut with Germany led to a more modern kind of food demonization in the twentieth century: in Anglo-Saxon countries, "kraut" became a derogatory term for Germans during the world wars, while the French preferred to call them "choucroute eaters." During World War I, some patriotic American manufacturers of sauerkraut even renamed their product "liberty cabbage." Luckily, in the decades since, sauerkraut has lost its political stigma. Today, it is merely another trendy health food that you are probably not eating enough of.

The Franks had a much more substantial impact—not least in the fact that *France* is derived from *Francia*, the land of the Franks. The Franks were a loose confederation of Germanic tribes living in what is now Germany, Belgium, and northern France, on the fringes of the Roman Empire. After Rome fell in 476 c.e., following a prolonged period of internal decay and barbarian invasion, a man named Clovis united the Frankish tribes and became their king. As the Roman Empire disintegrated in western Europe, he conquered more and more of the province of Gaul, defeating both Roman armies and other barbarian forces.[2]

Clovis established the Merovingian dynasty, named after his grandfather Merovech, who according to legend was descended from a sea god (the Franks at that time being pagans). But Clovis married a Christian woman, and when he found himself on the losing side against the Alemanni at the Battle of Tolbiac in 496, he prayed to the Christian God, promising to be baptized if he was granted victory. The Franks turned the tide of the battle and defeated the Alemanni, and so Clovis and the Franks became Christians. This was a shrewd political move, given that by now most people in Gaul were Christian, and bishops held a great deal of power. Clovis was baptized in Reims, starting a long-standing tradition in which French kings were baptized, and later crowned, in the city. But he decided to make Paris, one of his favorite towns, the capital of his kingdom. Thus, it was traditionally said that French history started with Clovis and the Merovingians.

Theodoric, the son and successor of Clovis, had a Greek doctor named Anthimus as an adviser. Anthimus subscribed to classical Greek notions about health and the human diet, which advocated eating certain foods to ward off or alleviate illness. He wrote a culinary guide called *De observatione ciborum*, which helped Greek and Roman food customs survive within the Frankish kingdoms into the medieval era. He advised a copious use of ginger, for example, as a digestive aid, and ginger indeed came to be a prominent feature of medieval cooking. His advice was not limited to which kinds of food to eat; he instructed how they should be prepared as well. Beef should be boiled, then roasted—with a gravy of pepper, cloves, and other spices—in an earthen vessel rather than a copper one. Meat should be roasted not too close to the fire, and frequently basted. Chickpeas should be eaten only very well cooked, with a bit of salt and oil.[3] Anthimus also wrote a great deal on pork, which was very much loved by both the Romans and the Merovingians. The French have kept this love for pork and in fact have a saying that *dans le cochon tout est bon* (in the pig, everything is good).

But perhaps the lasting gastronomic contribution of the Merovingians had more to do with the way in which people ate. Men of the Roman nobility used to lie down or recline while dining; children, women, commoners, and slaves used to sit. But at a Merovingian banquet, everyone sat on long benches, and this came to be the custom in France. Indeed, the idea of not sitting properly at a table would be considered barbaric in France today.

In fact, the modern French have a lot of table manners that everyone is expected to know, which may be a bit nerve-racking for foreigners who desperately want to avoid being seen as barbarians. For example, do not smear foie gras onto toast (it should be eaten in slices). When eating salad, you should fold the lettuce into manageable bites rather than hacking it into pieces with your knife. And for god's sake, do not slice off the tip of a triangle of brie! It must be cut

The French proverb *dans le cochon tout est bon* (in the pig, everything is good) decorates the wall of Aux Trois Cochons–Le Père Fillion, a traditional *bouchon* in Lyon. Bouchons are typically family-run bistros devoted to local specialties, especially meat dishes, with reasonable prices and lively atmospheres. Unusual for France, most bouchon chefs have been women, including the famous Eugénie Brazier, known as La Mère Brazier, one of the most influential French chefs of the twentieth century. Photograph by authors, 2016.

lengthwise so that everyone has the pleasure of eating the delicious center. While you're at it, don't even think about pouring yourself an enormous glass of wine, like the Saxons (and today's Anglo-Saxons) are wont to do. Apparently, there are still plenty of ways to be a barbarian in France.

4

Ode to Gluttony

*Fate, most agreeably, has granted my wish,
my prayers deserved a savory gift
that fed the sisters, but did more good for me:*

they're sated by food while I'm nourished by love,
glittering with decency as you fashion two meals:
restoring my heart as they eat what you serve,
food feeding their bodies, love nourishing my soul—
because I need you all the more, you come a sweeter
meal to me.
In pious prayer may great God hear your petitioning
and wash over your lips an unending feast.

—*Venantius Fortunatus, sixth century* C.E.[1]

If such words do not inspire you to infuse your cooking with love and serve it to those you hold dear, you must be missing either a heart or a stomach. As we will see, the sixth-century poet and churchman Venantius Fortunatus—whom the French today call Fortunat—was lacking in neither. His platonic affection for a former queen sequestered in a convent and the divine dishes she prepared especially for him have been preserved in his poetry as a gastronomic love story for the ages.

This particular poem was written at a time when the Merovingian dynasty was often at war within itself, following the death of Clovis in 511. The Merovingian kings had the habit of bequeathing their wealth and land to all of their sons, which meant that every time a king died, the kingdom was divided again. Brothers fought each other frequently to expand their portions of the heritage. Yet somehow, despite all the family feuds, Francia remained in the hands of the Merovingian dynasty, although by the late seventh century its kings had weakened to the point of being virtual figureheads. True authority shifted to the powerful royal official known as the "mayor of the palace."

Life for the women of the Merovingian aristocracy was particularly grim. Their destiny was to marry and try to produce a male heir, and few women were lucky to live long and not die in childbirth (the life expectancy for women then was only twenty-nine years).[2] They could only inherit wealth if no eligible males still lived, and they definitely could not inherit the throne. Polygamy was not forbidden, and it was accepted that a man (especially an aristocratic man) could have more than one wife, although it was not common practice. Adultery by women was strictly forbidden and punished severely, but it was not uncommon for men to have mistresses. All in all, it was a quintessentially patriarchal society. The only option for a woman who did not marry was to enter one of the convents that began to emerge in this era. They became sanctuaries of a sort for unmarried and widowed women.

The woeful options for women at this time can be seen in the story of Radegund, the daughter of the king of Thuringia, a territory in what is now central Germany. In 531, Thuringia was conquered by two Frankish kings, Theodoric and Chlothar, both sons of Clovis. The kingdom was added to the Merovingian lands, and the eleven-year-old Radegund and her brother were given to Chlothar as tribute.

When Radegund turned eighteen, she was forced to marry Chlothar, although she felt no love for the man who had invaded her homeland and uprooted her from her family. In all her years of unhappy marriage, she never gave birth to a child. She took refuge in studying, praying, and helping the poor and the sick—so much so that it was said that the king had married a nun. But Radegund was a warm, intelligent, and extremely pious woman. Her charitable works and her devotion to God soon gave her the reputation of a saint.

Chlothar eventually allowed Radegund to live in a royal villa in Saix, a village in the Loire Valley not far from Saumur. But at some point, the king apparently tired of the arrangement and demanded that she return to his court. According to Christian legend, Radegund was saved from this fate by the "miracle of the oats." As she fled the king's men, a field of newly planted oats suddenly grew to full size and concealed her flight. Her pursuers, astounded by this miracle and not wishing to offend God, gave up the chase.

A more prosaic account has it that Radegund fled the king after he had her brother murdered, and she then convinced a few powerful Frankish bishops to make her a deaconess and threaten the king with excommunication should he try to recapture her. In any event, Radegund was now free of the king's clutches. She embraced a religious life and helped found the abbey of Sainte-Croix de Poitiers. Out of humility, she joined the abbey as a nun, not the abbess. Her lady-in-waiting and friend, Agnès, became abbess instead.

It was at the abbey that Radegund and Agnès came to know the Italian poet and traveler Venantius Fortunatus. He was originally from Treviso, Italy, but fled the city ahead of invading Goths. He eventually reached Metz, where the king of the Frankish kingdom of Austrasia had his court. Fortunat's poetry attracted many royal patrons, and he began to make a name for himself, later moving to

Paris, then Tours, then Poitiers. Fortunat loved life and food and was happy to unashamedly proclaim that he did.

How exactly Fortunat met Radegund is not clear, but he would certainly have heard about her, as her story was quite uncommon. What is clear is that a deep friendship and (platonic) love developed between him and Radegund and Agnès, and food seemed to have been a way for the two women to show him their affection. In return, he would write poems praising them and their cooking, and also sometimes send them small gifts. When Radegund and Agnès fasted as part of their religious observance, Fortunat would send them notes begging them to eat a little something. When Lent was finally over, he would send them more letters expressing his happiness that the fast could end.

At one point, it seems that our charming nuns gave Fortunat a bit too much food, and he suffered from some ailment. His doctor put him on a strict diet and he ranted about it to Agnès and Radegund, despairing that he could not see them or eat their culinary delights. He had nothing good to say about the doctor ("No meal ever satisfies him," he harrumphed).[3] But eventually Fortunat recovered, and once again received "meals dripping in honey, like the sweet combs flowing from your devoted lips."[4] Honey was a particular favorite of his.

Fortunat left behind a memorable description of the food provided by the nuns, and it also gives us a good idea of what one might eat during those "dark ages" (if one were lucky enough to be surrounded by attentive nuns, that is):

> Your sisterly concern never lets me forget
> how the meals you bring keep me alive:
> The bounty of today's supper was prime,
> at your table vegetables drizzled in honey
> ran twice up and down the board,
> the smell alone could have fattened me,
> the server could barely manage the loads,
> his feet were blistered at meal's end.
> Then a haughty mound of meat appeared,
> a mountain—with adjoining hills,
> fish and ragout girding them,
> a little garden for supper within.
> Gluttonous, greedy, I scarfed it all down:
> mountain and garden in a sluggish gut.

*I can't remember much after this, since your gifts con-
quer me.
Off to heaven, conqueror Agnes, above the clouds, fly
away.*[5]

The religious authorities must have not seen his gluttony as too terrible a sin, as he ended his life as the bishop of Poitiers and was eventually venerated as a saint in France and Italy. And perhaps unsurprisingly, he is now known in France as the patron saint of male chefs
and gourmands, absolving us from our gastronomic sins. Centuries
later, the great French chef Auguste Escoffier paid homage to Fortunat and his love of food by dedicating a recipe to him: *cochon de
lait Saint-Fortunat*. It involves cooking a whole suckling pig stuffed
with herbs, brandy, sausages, and chestnuts—the kind of dish that
undoubtedly would have sent Fortunat into a state of rapture.

As for Radegund, she too became a saint, even more well-known
than Fortunat. Her abbey was destroyed in the French Revolution,
but the beautiful eleventh-century church built upon her crypt in
Poitiers remains. It features a stunning stained glass window, with
one panel depicting the miracle of the oats; for centuries, worship-
pers presented offerings of oats to Saint Radegund. And she is now
known in France as the patron saint of *female* chefs. Whatever one
may think of the necessity of considering male and female chefs sepa-
rately, it is perhaps fitting that in this way, these two great friends
and fellow gastronomes are forever linked in the legends of France.

5

Left Behind: The Goats of Poitou

Chabichou is a delightful little French goat cheese, with a lovely
wavelike texture and a shape reminiscent of a drooping cylindrical
tower. Eaten fresh, its flavors are very floral and it has a nice creamy
texture, but after a few months its aroma becomes spicier and more
aggressive. It is exclusively made in the region around Poitiers, under

a strict set of conditions defined within its *appellation d'origine contrôlée* (AOC).* It also lends its name to the so-called Route du Chabichou, a delicious tour of the Poitou-Charentes region and its many varieties of goat cheese.

Legend says that its name comes from the Arabic word *chebli*, or goat. As it happens, Poitiers is famous not just for the lovely Chabichou, but as the site of an epic battle in the eighth century that has traditionally been seen as a turning point in European history, when the Frankish kingdom was invaded by a swiftly expanding Islamic empire. According to local legend, the armed forces of the Umayyad caliphate brought with them herds of goats, and this is the origin of the famous goat cheeses of the Poitou-Charentes region, which today accounts for about two-thirds of France's goat cheese production.[1]

Very few details of the battle are known to us. Even though French schoolchildren learn that it took place in 732 in Poitiers, it may have taken place in 733 closer to Tours. In fact, in the English-speaking world it is often referred to as the Battle of Tours. (This geographical ambiguity is absent in the Arabic name for the battle, the Balat ash-Shuhada, or "pavement of martyrs.")

Whatever the exact date, the battle took place at a time when the Islamic empire was barely a century into its existence and yet had already become a preeminent power in the Middle East and Mediterranean. Its roots lay in the nomadic tribes of the Arabian Peninsula, who were transformed by the revelations of the Prophet Muhammad and the emergence of Islam in the seventh century. In the following decades, the Arabs swept out of their homeland and conquered much of the Middle East and North Africa. In less than a hundred years, they established an empire—a "caliphate"—extending from modern-day Pakistan to Spain, in the process destroying the ancient Persian Empire and crippling the Byzantines.

The expansion of the Islamic empire across the Levant and North Africa had lasting consequences for Mediterranean cuisine. Over the

---

* The AOC framework was created in France in the 1920s and 1930s to identify and regulate geographically defined foods and wines, including many of France's best and most popular products. Each AOC defines the territory in which a food or wine must be produced, as well as the sources and methods of production. The aim is to reduce fraud and maintain standards of quality. In 2010, the AOC system was renamed AOP (*appellation d'origine protegée*), but most people continue to use AOC. A less restrictive framework for regional products also exists, known as the IGP (*indication géographique protegée*).

preceding centuries of Roman rule, a certain continuity of diet had emerged around the Mediterranean, but now its southern shores were enveloped by an Islamic culture that brought new foods from Asia— including sugar, eggplants, and citrus fruits—and forbade pork and alcohol. As a result, pork and alcohol became mostly confined to the countries north of the Mediterranean, and thus associated with an emerging European identity (a dynamic that, as we shall see, persists to this day).[2]

After the first four Muslim caliphs, and Islam's first civil war (which resulted in the schism between the Sunni and Shia sects), the Umayyad dynasty took the reins of the caliphate. Based in Damascus, the Umayyads oversaw the rapid expansion of the Islamic empire, including the conquest of Al-Andalus (the Iberian Peninsula) by an invading Arab-Berber force from North Africa in the early eighth century. The armies of the caliphate eventually crossed the Pyrenees and took several territories in western and southern Gaul, thus becoming a direct concern to the Frankish kingdom.

At this time, the Franks were still ruled by the Merovingian kings, but they had become so weak, powerless, and neglectful of their responsibilities that they were known as the "lazy kings." Real political power lay with the mayor of the palace, which at that time was Charles, son of Pepin. He already had a well-trained and experienced army under his command, and was, in fact, king in all but name.

The Umayyad invaders were led by Abd al-Rahman, the emir of Cordoba. The large army, numbering in the tens of thousands, conquered the wealthy province of Aquitaine and then advanced slowly northward toward the Loire, hoping to sack rich cities such as Tours. The Franks may have been outnumbered, and forced to rely on infantry to fight the Umayyads' heavy cavalry, but the slow advance of the Umayyad army gave Charles the opportunity to select a favorable site for the battle, on high wooded ground. In the end, this proved decisive. After a week of skirmishing, a hard-fought day of battle ended with the death of Abd al-Rahman and an Umayyad retreat. Some say it was this victory that gave the Frankish leader his enduring moniker, Charles Martel (Charles the Hammer). His decisive win was seen as a victory for Christianity itself, and he was later referred to as the "Hammer of the Infidels."

There is some debate as to the historical legacy of the Battle of Poitiers. Because it marks the furthest boundary of the Umayyad conquest in Europe, the battle has often been presented as a pivotal moment in world history, a victory that prevented Europe from falling under Islamic rule. But more recently, historians have argued that the army of Abd al-Rahman only invaded France for plunder and had no intention of lasting conquest. At any rate, the Umayyad expansion lost its momentum later in the eighth century due to internal unrest, and the forces of Al-Andalus would not have been strong enough to continue to occupy France.

Nevertheless, the Battle of Poitiers caught the imagination of the French in the centuries to come. It was said that Joan of Arc heard voices telling her to go to Poitiers and unearth the sword of Charles to help drive another invader, the English, out of France. During World War II, both the Vichy regime and the French resistance drew upon the legend of the Frankish warrior; a resistance group based near Poitiers took the name of Brigade Charles Martel.

More recently, the French far right has drawn upon the Charles Martel legend in their xenophobic campaigns. In the 1970s and 1980s, anti-Arab terrorists in the Charles Martel Group bombed a series of Algerian targets in France. The Front National (FN), France's most successful far-right political party, drew upon the symbolism of the Battle of Poitiers in the 2002 presidential elections, deploying the campaign slogan "Martel 732, Le Pen 2002." The racist message was clear: "We will defeat the new Muslim invasion." More recently, FN founder Jean-Marie Le Pen responded to the popular mantra *"Je suis Charlie,"* following the terrorist attack on the satirical magazine *Charlie Hebdo*, by declaring, *"Je suis Charlie Martel."* While most French people would see such comments as deplorable and in very poor taste, they unfortunately do appeal to a segment of the population that can no longer be called marginal. Le Pen's daughter and FN party leader, Marine Le Pen, won more than 30 percent of the vote in the 2017 presidential election.

Of much better taste is our lovely goat cheese Chabichou. Whether its origins really do lie in the aftermath of the Umayyad invasion is debatable. Goats, also known as "the poor man's cow," would have been an ideal animal to nourish an army. Goats are very adaptable, can walk on harsh terrain, and can happily just eat the grass on the side of the road while on the move. In fact, a goat will eat nearly any plant. Its milk can be drunk fresh and it is relatively easy to make goat cheese from it. It is therefore not hard to imagine that the Umayyad forces brought goats, and a tradition of goat-cheese-making, into the

Frankish lands, and left them behind as a remnant of their thwarted conquest.

Today, France produces more than one hundred thousand tons of goat cheese each year.[3] Chabichou is a delicious reminder that the meeting of different cultures and civilizations should be a source of enrichment rather than conflict. If Chabichou could talk, it would perhaps whisper, "Make cheese, not war—it tastes so much better, especially with a glass of crisp sauvignon blanc."

6

The Sweetest King

When visiting France, you may sometimes catch yourself wondering if you have accidentally traveled several decades back in time. Maybe it's the long lines at the local bakery or the vegetable shop, or the fact that hardly anything is open on Sundays. Or perhaps it's the feeling you get walking through the shopping district of any town of a decent size, where in addition to the usual national and global chains, you'll find small shops obsessively devoted to one particular item—mirrors, for example, or accordions, or typewriters (typewriters!). It all harkens back to an earlier era of consumerism, fast disappearing in many parts of the world—and even in France, where enormous *hypermarchés* sprout in ever-greater numbers throughout the countryside.

One of our favorite little shops in Nantes, on a street of old cafés and boutiques, sells honey. Only honey. Dozens of kinds of honey, with rows of sun-kissed golden jars nestled up to honeys of the darkest and thickest brown, and every shade in between. It was a bit of a shock at first—who knew bees were so multitalented? A whole new world opened up, one in which we could purchase honey by region, by flower type, by medicinal potency.

As it turns out, humans have been in thrall to honey's heavenly taste since the dawn of civilization. Some of the earliest cave paintings in Europe depict brave hunter-gatherers fighting off bees in order to collect honeycombs. The ancient Greeks thought it was the food of the gods; Alexander the Great was said to have been embalmed in it. Mixed with water and left to ferment, honey produces mead, perhaps the world's first alcoholic drink, created independently in different societies around the globe. From classical times through the Middle Ages, honey was added to many dishes, as a general preference for sweet-tasting meals endured until the Renaissance era. Even meat and fish dishes, which we tend to associate with savory flavors today, were routinely sweetened. As sugar was not available to most Europeans throughout this era—it was still slowly wending its way westward from its ancestral home in Asia—honey was the sweetener of choice. It was also celebrated for its medicinal qualities, particularly as a salve for burns, wounds, and sore throats.

One of the first things one learns, after falling into the obsessive world of honey, is that, much like wine, it is captive to its terroir: the unique characteristics of the natural environment in which it is produced.[1] Each type of honey takes on a particular flavor, fragrance, and color, depending on the flowers and pollen that its bee producers have imbibed. As with wine, the French have developed very specific labeling practices to explain the origins of their endless varieties of honey (*miel*) and to prevent fraudulent claims from cheap substitutes. *Miel de lavande*, for example, is a protected trade name for the golden lavender honey of Provence. *Miel de sarrasin* is a buckwheat honey of the darkest brown, long a specialty of Brittany, where it is used to great effect in Breton gingerbread and mead. The ancient Romans considered the honey of Narbonne, redolent with rosemary, the best honey in the world. If you want to really surrender to the French obsession with honey, you can track down obscure varieties produced by bees that visit the flowers of one specific sand dune on the Atlantic coast, such as the sublime *miel des dunes* available on Île d'Oléron.

While beekeeping and honeymaking have been practiced in France since the time of the Gauls, it was not until the eighth century that it became a more organized and respected profession. Before then, people hunted for natural beehives in the woods, or attached different kinds of man-made hives to their dwellings, whatever suited their fancy. But one Frankish ruler changed all that, setting French honey on the delicious path it treads today.

Charlemagne, the grandson of Charles Martel, was crowned king of the Franks in 768. He became one of the most powerful heads of state in history, controlling the largest landmass in western Europe since the Roman Empire. He is regularly referred to as the father of Europe, with both Germans and French claiming his heritage. Less well known is his contribution to French agriculture and, thus, to the foundations of French gastronomy.

Charlemagne's father, Pepin III ("Pepin the Short"), had succeeded Charles Martel as mayor of the palace, holding the reins of power alongside the weak Merovingian king Childeric III. Pepin took the bold leap of ending the Merovingian dynasty. He asked Pope Zacharias to intercede in his favor, and the pope declared that "whoever holds the real power should wear the crown." Pepin deposed Childeric, shipped him off to a monastery, and was crowned king of the Franks. He was succeeded by his son, Charles, whose glorious reign as Charlemagne lent its name to this new dynasty, the Carolingian, whose kings would preside over France for the next two centuries.

At that time, agriculture was responsible for the vast majority of economic and social activity in the Frankish lands, and so when Charlemagne came to power and began organizing his kingdom, he rightfully focused on farming and food. He believed that a more efficient and fair system of agriculture would revive the economy and provide stability for his kingdom. His wide-ranging reforms are evident in a document known as the *Capitulare de villis*, a collection of edicts on the management of the royal estates. The ultimate goal, according to the document, was that the estates "shall serve our purposes entirely and not those of other men," and that "all our people shall be well looked after, and not be reduced to penury by anyone."[2] Detailed instructions were given on how to manage farmland, fish stocks, and forests and how to care for vineyards and animal herds. Stewards were reminded to always have enough wine on hand and to grow and stockpile enough food to ward off famine. Surprisingly, given modern perceptions of the "dark ages," food hygiene rules were prominent, even though it would be another thousand years before anyone knew what bacteria or germs were. Sites of food and wine production should be kept especially clean, as should those workers who handled food with their hands. Wine grapes should not be crushed with bare feet.

The edicts also dictated what should be grown in the gardens of the royal estates—sixty-eight types of plants and foods in all, many of them with known medicinal properties, such as garlic. This established a template for the medieval garden, and thus played a pivotal role in spreading the cultivation of garlic throughout the Frankish realm. You can still see what a Carolingian garden looked like if you visit Melle, a small, ancient town in the Poitou-Charentes region. One of France's Petites Cités de Caractère (Small Cities of Character), Melle also hosts three impressive Romanesque churches and Europe's largest publicly accessible silver mine, which once produced currency for the Carolingian kings.

And then there were the bees. Charlemagne decreed that each royal estate should keep bees, thus expanding organized honey production in his realm. Two-thirds of the honey crop should be given over to the crown as taxes. This bee tax, or *abeillage*, endured even after Charlemagne's reign and became a key obligation of vassals during the feudal era. Beekeeping became tightly controlled; it was illegal to keep your own hive and not pay dues to your lord. There were even beekeeping officials to monitor hives and prevent honey poaching. (Though one wonders how thorough they were: there is a French proverb, after all, that avers, "He is a very bad manager of honey who leaves nothing to lick off his fingers.") While this was all most unfortunate for the population, denied unrestricted access to their beloved honey, it did help spur a more organized, innovative, and respected beekeeping profession.

Overall, Charlemagne established one of the most efficient and productive regimes since the fall of the Roman Empire. He ordered that each estate should have ironworkers, carpenters, shoemakers, soap makers, and so on. He valued education and scientific learning, although he did not know how to read and write himself, and established schools in bishoprics and monasteries. (For many years, in fact, French schoolchildren were told to appreciate Charlemagne as the "inventor" of schools, though it is not clear whether this in fact endeared the great leader to generations of bored youth.) Charlemagne attracted scholars from all over Europe to his capital in Aachen, where he built a magnificent palace, chapel, and school. No one since the Roman ages had done so much to promote knowledge: old manuscripts were perused and copied, and knowledge and science were viewed favorably. Many refer to this era as the Carolingian Renaissance, a small preview of the much greater transformation that would arrive six centuries later.

As the Frankish kingdom grew ever more powerful, it became a more attractive ally to the papacy. At that time, the pope controlled an army and levied taxes; as the political and spiritual leader of the Church, he could wage war against his rivals or excommunicate them. But the popes often needed the protection of more powerful rulers, and Charlemagne twice came to their rescue, helping them stay in power. His military campaigns also brought Christianity to previously pagan lands. Having proved such an excellent defender of the faith, he was crowned emperor by Pope Leo III in 800. This is often seen as the beginning of the Holy Roman Empire, a political entity that would play a central role in European affairs for the next thousand years. By the end of his reign, Charlemagne had extended the Frankish dominions to cover most of western Europe.

In the end, Charlemagne reigns in the French imaginary as the founder of Europe, the inventor of school, and a powerful warrior-king. His role in the proliferation of French honeymaking may not be as well known, but it was hardly less important for the generations of beekeepers who followed his reign. Today, honey remains a beloved ingredient in French cuisine, and there are still tens of thousands of honey producers throughout France, employing time-honored techniques and the kind of devotion that Charlemagne would no doubt have approved of.

But as in much of the rest of the world, France has seen a dramatic decline in its bee populations. In the past two decades, hundreds of thousands of bee colonies disappeared, and French honey production declined precipitously from more than thirty thousand tons per year in the early 1990s to only ten thousand tons in 2014.[3] While there are multiple causes of this, beekeepers argue that pesticides are a primary culprit. After twenty years of relentless campaigning, they finally won a landmark victory in 2016, when the French National Assembly banned the class of pesticides long thought to be the worst offender.

Another sizable threat to French apiculture will be harder to address. A third of French beekeepers are over the age of sixty, and very few young people are entering the trade. Increasingly, beekeeping is a side project, not a primary occupation. With these trends, we may see French honey production continue to decline even if all the other dangers are resolved—and this time, there will be no Charlemagne in place to decree a hive on every estate.

7

They Came from the Sea

England's White Cliffs of Dover, immortalized in story and song, have overshadowed their equally impressive counterpart on the far side of the Channel: the Alabaster Coast of France. Soaring white cliffs tower above pebble beaches for nearly one hundred miles along the Normandy shore between Le Havre and Le Tréport. Nestled among them, in the small port of Fécamp, is the fantastical Palais Bénédictine, a neo-Gothic palace built more than a century ago by the aptly named Alexandre Le Grand. It is here that Bénédictine, an herbal liqueur supposedly based on an old monastic recipe that includes spices from around the world, is produced.

How did this small town in Normandy come to produce such an exotic and widely sourced liqueur? It includes, after all, angelica from Scandinavia, nutmeg from Indonesia, cinnamon from Ceylon, and vanilla from Madagascar. Well, as so often in France, there is the legend and then there is the slightly more mundane version of the story. For both, we'll need to return to the ninth century and see what became of the Franks after Charlemagne.

At the time of Charlemagne's death in 814, the Franks were foolishly persisting with their tradition of sharing the kingdom among the monarch's sons. Inheritances create enough problems in normal circumstances—just imagine the problems that arise when your inheritance is most of western Europe. Fortunately, Charlemagne had only one surviving son, Louis the Pious. Unfortunately, Louis had three sons, and even before his death they came to blows.

In 843, the three brothers signed the Treaty of Verdun, which more or less established the foundations for the modern states of France and Germany. Charles the Bald received the western part of the Carolingian Empire and became the king of France. Louis the German received the lands east of the Rhine River (hence his nickname). Lothar received a long but thin stretch of territory known as Francia Media, running from Belgium and the Netherlands through eastern France and western Germany, and down into Switzerland and Italy.

If this bit of Europe sounds familiar, it may be because France and Germany (and plenty of other people) went on to fight over these lands for the next thousand years or so. So while the Treaty of Verdun helped settle a family feud, it inadvertently proved to be the seed for countless wars to come.

The war between the three brothers was highly destructive, killing tens of thousands of people, including many members of the ruling elite. This left the new French kingdom utterly unprepared for the next threat on the horizon: Viking invaders from the north.

The peoples of modern-day Norway, Sweden, and Denmark were then generally known as Norsemen, but the more adventurous sort who raided and invaded other European lands were often called Vikings in the Anglo-Saxon world. (The Franks tended to refer to them as Danes or Northmen.) The communities they terrorized saw them as primitive, violent barbarians, but they were also traders and explorers who over the next five centuries established settlements from Newfoundland to Russia, and from Scotland to Sicily.

The Vikings' European debut took place in England in 793, when they sacked the monastery of Lindisfarne and killed many of its monks. The Norsemen were not Christian, and they saw monasteries and churches not as sacred sites but as great targets for plunder, as they were usually relatively wealthy and not well defended.

At first the Vikings only attacked coastal towns in Britain, but soon they began to raid the French coast as well. The Franks were completely ill-equipped to deal with the threat. By the time news of a raid arrived, the Vikings were long gone. As time went by, the Vikings became more daring and their numbers more impressive. They sacked Rouen in 841, Nantes in 843, and Paris in 845. Charles the Bald, unable to defend Paris, only managed to repel the Vikings by paying an enormous tribute of 7,000 livres (equivalent to 7,000 pounds of silver). It was the first danegeld, or ransom, that a French king paid to the Norsemen—a useful practice in the short term, but it may have helped encourage more raids in the long run.

The Norsemen began to establish permanent bases to facilitate the plundering of cities further inland. France's impressive array of rivers, so helpful to commerce and travel in times of peace, now only helped the invaders to push ever farther into the Frankish heartland. But they remained essentially raiders, determined to acquire loot, ransoms, and slaves for the then-bustling European slave trade. They were not interested in occupying and settling the Frankish lands they raided, and so while their attacks were enormously disruptive, they did not obliterate the evolving political and cultural order of the Carolingian era.

The French had a serious leadership problem, which can best be summed up in the nicknames of the Carolingian kings at that time. Charles the Bald was succeeded by kings like Louis the Stammerer, Charles the Fat, and Charles the Simple. Yet slowly, the Franks reacted to the Viking threat and began to put up some defenses. They built fortified bridges on the rivers, and the fortifications of towns like Paris (which at the time consisted only of Île de la Cité, an island in the Seine River) were strengthened.

But in 885, the largest Viking force ever assembled in France, perhaps thirty thousand men, laid siege to Paris. Eudes, the Count of Paris, and his fellow citizens knew that assistance from King Charles the Fat, whose court was in Alsace, would take a while to arrive. They nevertheless refused to pay a ransom, and hoped that they could hold out for long enough. Attacks on the city repeatedly failed, and after a while, many of the Vikings decided to look for easier targets. Finally, after nearly a year, the king arrived with his army, but even though his men outnumbered the Vikings, he decided to let them depart. He even encouraged them to plunder the lands of Burgundy, which were currently in rebellion against him.

The Parisians and the French were horrified at the behavior of their king, and in 887, Charles the Fat was deposed by his nobles. They elected Eudes, the hero of Paris, to be the new king of France, the first non-Carolingian king since Childeric III to rule France. And while after his death the Carolingians managed to reclaim the throne, a precedent had been set.

Meanwhile, the Viking chieftain Rollo the Walker had gone off to pillage Burgundy with the French king's blessing. (He was given the nickname because he was so large, his horse could not carry him.) He then made another failed attempt to sack Paris, as well as the city of Chartres. King Charles the Simple, the Carolingian king who succeeded Eudes, finally made Rollo a surprising offer: if Rollo converted to Catholicism and paid homage to Charles, accepting him as his king, then Charles would give Rouen and the lands surrounding it to the Norsemen. In a way, Charles the Simple had found the simplest solution. Paying ransoms to the Vikings was expensive and counterproductive. While it was occasionally possible to defeat the Norsemen, they always came back. So why not let the Norsemen have the coastal lands upstream of Paris and let them worry about how to defend the place? Rollo accepted the deal. The name *Norsemen* became contracted to *Norman*, and the land they occupied became known as *Normandy*. Rollo was rechristened Robert, the first Duke of Normandy.

The Normans gradually integrated into French society—speaking French, and adopting French names and customs. They not only converted to Catholicism but, in a nice turn of events, actively aided monasteries and abbeys. This included the abbey at Fécamp, originally destroyed in Viking raids but restored as a Benedictine abbey by the Norman dukes. The first dukes of Normandy actually had their primary residence at Fécamp until the thirteenth century.

While Normandy today is a land rich in food and liquor, this cannot be attributed to the Norsemen who gave the region its name. Sadly, the Vikings did not bring a lot of exciting new food products to France. A notable exception is the plant angelica, which the Vikings brought to Normandy from Scandinavia. It was known to have various medicinal properties, and it is also one of the main ingredients in Bénédictine.

Bénédictine's other ingredients, with their origins in Asia and Africa, can perhaps be explained by considering what the Norman traders got up to after their acquisition of northern France. In the eleventh century, some highly ambitious Normans defeated the Arab rulers of Sicily and established a kingdom there that became an important site of cross-cultural gastronomic exchange. The Normans were also active participants in the Crusades, which helped expand the spice trade between Europe and Asia. In the sixteenth century, King Henry II gave the towns of Rouen and Marseille a monopoly on importing spices into France, and Norman sailors were among the first to defy the Portuguese de facto monopoly on the spice trade in Africa and Asia.

So it is not surprising that, according to legend, an Italian monk and alchemist named Dom Bernardo Vincelli, who was staying in the abbey of Fécamp, created the original Bénédictine liqueur in the sixteenth century from herbs and spices that he foraged locally. If any place in France could claim that all those ingredients were "local," it was indeed Normandy. The legend claims that the Fécamp monks continued to make Vincelli's herbal liqueur for several centuries until the French Revolution swept away all the nation's monasteries. The last monk to flee Fécamp left some precious medieval manuscripts in the hands of a local family, which seventy years later counted among its members a wine merchant named Alexandre Le Grand. He stumbled across a manuscript by Vincelli, which included his liqueur recipe, and started reproducing it under the name Bénédictine.

From the beginning, Le Grand used a very effective marketing strategy, employing well-known Belle Époque artists like Alphonse Mucha to create beautiful and distinctive advertising posters. He also marketed Bénédictine heavily abroad; today, about 75 percent of Bénédictine production is exported, with about 40 percent going to the United States alone.[1] To this day, the legend of Dom Vincelli is a bit doubtful—but it sounds true enough, and Le Grand made the most of it. He wanted to establish a liqueur empire, and for that he needed to build a castle—the Palais Bénédictine in Fécamp, a worthy seat of production for this noble liqueur. Today, the glory of Bénédictine is preserved at the palace's museum, where the story of this singular liqueur and its twenty-seven ingredients is explained.

Le Grand's granddaughter, Simone "Simca" Beck, grew up in the family business. During World War II, when her husband was a prisoner of war, she cycled around rural Normandy exchanging bottles of black market Bénédictine for food to send to him. After the war, she moved to Paris and studied cooking, and fate brought her together with an intriguing American woman named Julia Child. The two women hit it off at once, and Simca brought Julia into her circle of gastronomic devotees. They later co-authored the classic *Mastering the Art of French Cooking*. Simca devised a number of recipes that included her family's Bénédictine, its orangey sweetness making it ideal for glazing meats and adding to baked goods.

Throughout French history, the Normans proved to be some of the most adventurous and independent-minded subjects of the crown and the republic. Few things symbolize this reputation more than the purported origins of Bénédictine, which—whether true or not—reflect the region's self-identity as a land whose sailors brought the world to its doorstep.

Many of the early Bénédictine posters were produced by renowned artists and have become collectors' items. This poster was produced in 1907 by Leonetto Cappiello, known as the father of modern advertising for his contributions to the transformation of commercial art at the turn of the century. One of his innovative trademarks can be seen here: the depiction of a bold color figure against a dark backdrop. The extravagant building shown here is the Palais Bénédictine in Fécamp. Leonetto Cappiello, "Bénédictine" (1907). From the digital collection of the Bibliothèque Municipale de Lyon.

8

Feudal Fare

For more than a thousand years, French winemakers have eagerly awaited one particular fall day: the Ban des Vendanges, when their local administration decides that the grape harvest can officially begin. Traditionally, it was marked with a festival, and you can still visit Ban des Vendanges celebrations today throughout France (even in Paris, which has a small urban vineyard in Montmartre). Today the Ban des Vendanges is mainly an occasion for celebrating and promoting wine, but it remains a minor administrative hassle for vintners if they want to harvest any earlier. So, all in all, the Ban des Vendanges is very French, as France is traditionally a big producer of both wine and administrative hassles.

The Ban des Vendanges emerged during the era of feudalism, which developed in France as a result of the constant wars, internal power struggles, and foreign invasions that made the ninth and tenth centuries so anarchic. With the inability of weak French kings to defend and impose order in their realm, local lords became the dominant authority figures. They built castles, organized resistance against aggressors, and ruled their territories more or less independently. The kings could not command them and did not have the financial resources to buy their loyalty, and so they had to create new political arrangements of mutual benefit. They granted land—or fiefs—to local lords in return for their political allegiance and the provision of military forces when necessary. Over time, these grants of land became hereditary. Bishops and abbots also became feudal lords, eventually owning perhaps a fifth of France's territory.

The lords who owned these vast territories started granting land to their own vassals, who would then owe military service and allegiance to them. Thus, the feudal system was born. French society came to resemble a pyramid: At the top perched the king (who was a vassal only to God); underneath him stood the greater lords, the powerful dukes and counts of France; and underneath them were a larger number of barons, viscounts, and minor lords. A vassal was supposed to do homage to his overlord, promise to assist him militarily and financially if needed, and do him no harm. In return, the overlord promised to protect and dispense justice to his vassals. All oaths of obligation were sanctified in religious ceremonies, which in that deeply devout era carried significant weight.

At the bottom of the feudal pyramid were the peasants, who represented roughly 90 percent of the population.[1] Every peasant also had a lord, depending on whose fief they resided in. In France, most peasants were serfs, meaning they were bound to their lord on a hereditary basis, and had to provide set amounts of labor and taxes. They needed the lord's permission to marry, or to leave the land. There were also "free peasants" who rented land from their lord. These arrangements formed the backbone of the rural economy, which at that time covered most of France. Each fief, with its lord, serfs, and free peasants, strove to be self-sufficient.

In reality, feudal relationships did not always match this simplistic structure. Medieval towns were not included in the lords' fiefs and answered directly to the king. This placed them outside the feudal structure, and as towns grew in size and importance, this eventually undermined the entire political order. In addition, a lord could own multiple fiefs, each with a different overlord, and this could result in some chaotic situations. For example, the dukes of Normandy, whom we met in the last chapter, were vassals of the king of France. But when a Norman duke named William conquered England in 1066, he became the independent king of England. In that guise, he might wish to declare war on the king of France, but as the Duke of Normandy, he was technically supposed to help the king of France if England invaded. We will see later on the many headaches this created in Europe for several hundred years.

By the end of the tenth century, the feudal lords were so powerful that they decided who should sit on the throne of France. This is how Hugh Capet became king in 987, thus ending the Carolingian line and beginning the Capetian dynasty. (He made the long-overdue decision that for a dynasty to survive, it had to have one clearly designated descendant; from then on, the eldest son of the king would succeed him.) Hugh was elected king by the other dukes and counts because he was not very powerful. He only directly controlled Paris and a small area of land around it called Île de France (Island of

France). It was not physically an island, but the term aptly describes the political situation of France's royal domains. Many of the great lords controlled richer and larger tracts of land, and a weak king meant that they could maintain that strength and independence. They were also free to fight each other, a near-constant feature of feudal society. Because of this, even the most minor nobles built castles of some sort to ensure they could defend themselves.

The nobility constituted one of the three social classes, known as the three "estates." The First Estate comprised the clergy of the Catholic Church, which over the previous five hundred years had become incredibly wealthy and powerful. Aside from owning a lot of land, and dictating key aspects of daily life in this era of Christendom, the Church was allowed to impose a tithe, or religious tax, on the population. Some bishops and abbots were also of the nobility and could raise armies against their rivals.

The nobility formed the Second Estate. They could also tax the common people but did not have to pay taxes themselves. They had a host of special privileges and essentially ran the country. Despite this bounty of wealth and power, they made up only about 1 percent of the population—the original "one percenters," as it were.

Everyone else in France, from the common peasant to skilled artisans and wealthy bourgeoisie, was a member of the Third Estate, which included about 95 percent of the population. As you can imagine, they were often unhappy about their exploitation by the other two estates, and eventually this would help lead to the epochal and bloody French Revolution. But well before 1789, there were frequent peasant rebellions and urban unrest in France. Feudalism provided a rather useful social structure for those in power, but they could not completely ignore the resentment and revolts it often generated.

One way of reinforcing the increasingly rigid distinctions between the social classes was through food. During the feudal era, the eating habits of the upper and lower classes diverged enormously. Food became more than just a marker of class—it was also used to justify the rule of one class over another. As certain foods became imbued with a sense of nobility and good health, others came to be seen as base and unhealthy, and it seemed only natural that those who consumed the former should enjoy an exalted position over the latter.

The peasant diet was dominated by grains, particularly rye, barley, and oats (wheat was mainly the preserve of the upper classes). These were either cooked into a porridge or gruel, or baked into bread. Another substantial portion of the daily diet originated in vegetable gardens, which, not being taxed by landlords, were both highly desirable and ubiquitous. Leeks, onions, carrots, parsnips, and spinach were particularly common sights on the peasant table. Meat also featured occasionally, especially pork. Beef might be eaten, but only when the cow had ceased to be productive. Eggs and cheese were frequently available. The peasants enjoyed wine, or perhaps cider or beer, as much as the nobility and drank it in what we would today consider to be excessive quantities (though perhaps

This map of tenth-century France reveals the limited extent of the king's domains. From Eugène-Emmanuel Viollet-le-Duc, *Dictionnaire raisonné de l'architecture française du XIe au XVIe siècle* (Paris: Edition Bance-Morel, 1856), 136.

understandably; water was known as a potential source of disease, and milk was something that only barbarians drank straight). This was all assuming that no war was being waged and bad weather had not destroyed the harvest; food scarcity and famine could occur at any time. But overall, agricultural cultivation and production expanded enormously during the feudal era, thanks to population growth and technological improvements. This, in turn, stimulated more trade and commercial markets and helped drive the growth of towns and cities.

A noble table would look very different, and not only because the quantity of food on offer would be vastly more abundant (an easy way to show how powerful and rich you were). The nobility tended to adhere to an elaborate gastronomic code that ranked food in a hierarchy according to the four classical elements of fire, air, water, and earth. As in ancient Greece, fire was considered the noblest element, followed by air, water, and then finally the most despicable element, earth. Nobles shunned most vegetables, especially root vegetables, which grew underground. Onions and garlic were particularly offensive. Plants that grew out of the soil and reached for the sky—and were therefore closer to the second element, air—were nobler. It was therefore acceptable to eat cereals and bread, as well as fruits growing on trees.

Fish were not highly valued as food, because they were associated with the religious fasting so frequently required in those times. On Christian fast days, one could eat fish but not meat or, often, animal-derived products such as butter, cheese, and eggs. On non-fasting days, called *jours gras* (fat days), nobles would eat meat and meat and, if possible, a bit more meat. Unlike the peasantry, who usually boiled their meat, the nobility preferred their meat roasted, with no intermediary elements between the noble element of fire and the meat they consumed. In a culture where physical strength was prized, and seen as legitimizing a noble's right to rule over the population, it is no wonder meat was popular, as it was believed to be the best food for sustaining a man's strength. In some ways, it became a very symbol of power itself.[2] Disgraced knights, for example, might be commanded to not only give up their arms but also abstain from eating meat. Game was particularly desirable, mainly because it was a product of hunting, a warriorlike activity in which every lord and king partook. Beef, on the other hand, was seen as a vulgar and common meat, only good for peasants and their rough stomachs. Birds that flew in the lofty element of air were popular, including some we rarely see on tables today, such as heron, swan, and peacock. (It's also possible that medieval cooks just liked these birds because they could be presented in a grand way.) Highest on the list of noble meat were phoenix and salamander, mystical creatures who lived in fire. If only one could find them . . .

To finance their superior eating habits, as well as all their castles and wars, nobles needed money, and for that they had a very convenient power called the *droit de ban* (literally, the "right to ban"). This wide-ranging authority allowed a lord to dispense justice in his lands, to impose fines and taxes, and to force his subjects to do any work he deemed necessary, such as building or mending his castle. A lord could also force his peasants to use his mill or wine press, collecting a tax in the process. And he could also set the day on which the grape harvesting was supposed to start, hence the term Ban des Vendanges. This ensured that everyone would start the harvest at the same time and would make it easier to collect taxes on the harvest. It was also meant to ensure a better quality of the wine by forbidding people from harvesting too early. The lord could also institute a *banvin*, a ban on other people selling wine on his lands, leaving him as the only seller and giving him a monopoly on the product. In some places, the banvin lasted only a day, but it could also last nearly the whole year. (The lords who had the longest banvin were the Templars, which didn't help to make them very popular.)

So for several hundred years, the lords had a great time in feudal France. But the conditions upon which feudalism depended, such as a weak monarchy, were not permanent, and the system was gradually undermined as the French kings began reclaiming land and authority from their vassals. Strong kings such as Philip Augustus, Saint Louis, and Philip the Fair solidified Capetian control over the French state, which became more and more centralized. Better economic conditions meant that the French kings could afford to pay professional soldiers rather than relying on their vassals to provide military forces. The expanding size and wealth of towns, with their newly prosperous merchant classes, brought them considerable autonomy and increasing political influence. And by the early fourteenth century, most peasants had been given or had purchased their freedom, although they remained under the jurisdiction of their local lords. The crown had grown weary of peasant revolts and welcomed the influx of revenue from peasants purchasing their enfranchisement.

By the end of the thirteenth century, the golden age of feudalism in France had passed, although it would be several centuries before it faded completely. The last remnants of the system were finally destroyed in the great cleansing that was the French Revolution, at which time all *bans* were abolished. But communes were still allowed to issue a Ban des Vendanges if they wished, and some thought it still actually had merit—it ensured better wine quality and a more level playing field between the bigger and smaller vineyard owners. So they kept issuing the Ban des Vendanges, and to this day this very old tradition can still be found in France's wine-growing regions.

9

Of Monks and Men

Cross-cultural marriages face many tests, especially in the realm of food. Whether it's cooking the pasta too long, watering down a spicy dish, or substituting lamb for goat, there are all sorts of controversial compromises to be made in the kitchen. Sometimes, however, no compromise can be found. Take Maroilles, a distinctively square and creamy cheese with a brine-washed rind. To some, its incredibly pungent aroma is heavenly, especially when it is slathered on bread and dipped in coffee. To others, it smells like something from the depths of hell. I'll leave it to you to guess which of these people are likely to be French and which American.

The creators of Maroilles did not have to face this conundrum, as they were monks living at the abbey of Maroilles, in the north of France, more than a thousand years ago. Medieval monks were forbidden many things, but they were allowed milk, and from this they could make a huge variety of cheeses. As cheese can have various taste notes, from floral and fruity to pungent and meaty, it seems monks could not get enough of it, and some of them became expert cheesemakers. A number of classic cheeses were created by monks, such as Munster, which originated in an Alsatian monastery, and Abondance, a fruity hard cheese made in the Alps since the twelfth century. Époisses, made in Burgundy and washed with the strong local brandy, Marc de Bourgogne, is another cheese whose pungency may strain the limits of marital harmony (claims that it has been banned on public transport in France are an urban myth, yet highly believable). All these cheeses are still made today in the same areas where monks originally invented them. They serve as edible historical footprints, leading modern cheese aficionados to ancient monasteries, lost in the French countryside.

Cheese, however, is not the only reason why monasteries were important in the Middle Ages. It can be difficult for us to understand today how powerful and influential Christianity was in medieval European societies. After the collapse of the Roman Empire, the Church was one of the few institutions that could provide a sense of common social identity and a semblance of order in what was a very violent and unpredictable world. The tenets of Christianity shaped the most fundamental aspects of people's daily lives. At a time when eternal damnation was not an abstract concept but seemed a very real possibility, people strove to avoid sinful behavior, and did penance when they could not. The Church's omnipotence meant that monasteries were bound to become significant social actors.

The idea of monasticism first appeared in the third century in Egypt, when Saint Anthony decided to follow the teachings of Jesus Christ by living a life of poverty devoted to God. The first monks were hermits, but they increasingly began to live in communities as well. In France, these early monasteries mostly followed the Rule of Saint Benedict, who, at the time he wrote his monastic rules around 534, had no idea that a Norman businessman would someday name a liquor after him and his monks. By the ninth century, the Benedictine order had spread throughout the Carolingian realm.

The Rule of Saint Benedict was actually more permissive than the practices commonly followed by monks in the Holy Land, but it was still austere. Much of a typical day in a monastery was devoted to prayer, with seven sessions during the day and another in the middle of the night. Apart from praying, the monks were also supposed to work—often manual labor, but also intellectual work such as the copying of manuscripts. They were allowed to eat, but there was no breakfast, only one meal at midday; during the Easter season, a second celebratory meal might be allowed in the evening. Meat from "four-footed animals" was generally forbidden, except for the ill or very weak, and there were many days of fasting. At that time, people believed that physical health and spiritual health were inextricably linked, and these various restrictions on eating were seen as beneficial to the soul.

In practice, life in some monasteries really was not all that bleak for the monks. As shown by the saint of gastronomes, Fortunat, one could dine well in a monastery or convent. The exclusion of meat only made the monks more creative, as in their cheesemaking. And while Saint Benedict encouraged abstinence from wine, his Rule stated that "since the monastics of our day cannot be persuaded of this let us at least agree to drink sparingly and not to satiety, because 'wine makes even the wise fall away' (Ecclesiastes 19:2)."[1] He judged one *hemina* of wine per day (about half a pint) to be acceptable, although undoubtedly some monks indulged quite a bit more.

In some areas, monks also became expert in the cooking and farming of fish. The Dombes plateau, not far from Lyon, is dotted with a number of monk-made lakes that to this day produce nearly a fifth of all farmed fish in France.[2] In Lyon, *quenelle de brochet*, a type of fish dumpling made with pike from the Dombes plateau, is a local specialty not to be missed.

So while monks may have respected the strict rules regarding food, it is clear that they still believed in the importance of eating well. One indication of this is the sign language that they used to communicate when they were not allowed to speak: of several hundred signs, a large proportion referred to foods and wines. Some monasteries had up to twenty signs just for various kinds of fish.[3]

Overall, the Benedictine monks played a major role in medieval food production: they preserved traditional techniques while also inventing more productive methods of farming and new types of food, all of which they shared with the wider population. But by the twelfth century, some felt the great order had become a bit too comfortable, drifting away from the austere and devout lives envisioned by its founder. Early in that century, a group of zealous monks formed a new, more ascetic order. Originally based at a small monastery in Cîteaux, the new order came to be known as Cistercian. Within a few decades it had become one of the most prominent in

Europe, thanks in large part to (Saint) Bernard of Clairvaux, one of the most renowned medieval theologians. His intercessions in both religious and temporal politics (for example, in preaching the Second Crusade) elevated the Cistercians above other reform-minded efforts.

Bernard castigated the dissolute monks of Cluny, the most notable Benedictine abbey in France, in a lengthy rant known as the *Apologia*. Their clothing, art, and architecture incensed him, and he singled out for condemnation their excessive love of food. During meals, he huffed, "there is nothing about the Bible or the salvation of souls. Jokes and laughter and chatter are all we hear. At table, while the mouth is filled with food the ears are nourished with gossip so absorbing that all moderation in eating is forgotten."[4] He seemed offended that the cooks took such care to present an appealing variety of foods, spiced with foreign ingredients that sullied the natural foods provided by God, and drawing men into gluttony. The fact that so many different ways of cooking eggs had been devised left him particularly indignant:

> Who could describe all the ways in which eggs are tampered with and tortured, or the care that goes into turning them one way and then turning them back? They might be cooked soft, hard or scrambled. They might be fried or roasted, and occasionally they are stuffed. Sometimes they are served with other foods, and sometimes on their own. What reason can there be for all this variation except the gratification of a jaded appetite?[5]

At Cistercian abbeys, eggs were forbidden, along with fish, cheese, and milk.

It might seem strange that such a stringent order should have made a lasting contribution to French gastronomy, but part of Cistercian asceticism included a devotion to manual labor in the agricultural lands they acquired—and notably, in the vineyards of their original homeland of Burgundy. Wine had been grown in Burgundy since Roman times, but the Cistercians transformed the local varieties into the world-renowned wines they are today. Not long after the Cistercians' founding, they were given some land on the Côte d'Or and devoted themselves fully to viticulture, inventing and perfecting the techniques that would yield the best and most consistent wines.

The famous Grand Cru vineyard Clos de Vougeot is one of the best examples of their handiwork, and they are also credited with developing the first Chablis. It is perhaps a bit ironic that such delicious, even decadent wines owe their existence to ascetic monks, but it is the kind of paradox that seems to crop up all the time in France.

In the north of France, where wine was not produced locally, the monks drank beer instead. It was less intoxicating than wine and often safer to drink than water, so beer rations were usually quite generous. It was here that the Trappist order of monks could be found, and the beers they produced have always enjoyed a very high reputation in France. Unfortunately, the French Revolution and World War I pretty much wiped out the Trappist order in the region, and today there are no Trappist monasteries in France producing beer. All the Trappist beers enjoyed in France today are imported from Belgium.

An obvious question arises: how did these monks get so much land to produce food and wine? Paradoxically, the more the monks tried to pray, work, and renounce the outside world, the more they became important to that outside world. In the eyes of the laypeople, especially the nobility, monks were close to God and could, as it were, put in a good word for them so that they would not be sent to hell in the afterlife. People began to donate to monasteries or help establish new monasteries. Sometimes a condition of the donation would be that a noble's brother or nephew would become the new prior of the monastery. In this way, the nobility and the clergy began to increasingly overlap and share power and influence.

Donations could take various forms—animals, land or gold, or a relic from a saint—and some monasteries amassed huge wealth. The image of the rich and fat monk has a long tradition for a reason. Some objected to this state of affairs, even within the Church, eventually leading to the appearance of new monastic orders like the Dominicans and the Franciscans, who aimed to return to the original teachings of Christ and lived the lives of paupers.

But most monasteries continued accepting donations. When monasteries acquired land, they became the new lords of the peasants and people working on those lands. They therefore had certain rights over them and could impose taxes on them. In those days, taxes were not always paid in money. The monks of Maroilles, for example, asked their subjects to prepare some Maroilles cheeses, age them for a hundred days—the time needed for Maroilles to become really delicious—and then deliver them to the monastery. In Alsace, people could pay their taxes in Munster cheese. Obviously, this didn't always go down well with the locals, and it should not come as a surprise that during the French Revolution, the abbey of Maroilles was attacked and torn down by nearby villagers.

But getting rich also meant that the monks could become major philanthropists. They provided food and shelter for paupers and pilgrims and in effect served as the main social safety net for the poor. Convents offered a safe haven for many women. The Church tried to curb the violent excesses of the Middle Ages, successfully establishing the idea of sanctuary in churches and other ecclesiastic grounds. The Peace of God movement, which was particularly strong in southern France, tried to discourage attacks against members of the clergy, the poor, widows, orphans, or the elderly—essentially, those people who had no protection. In the eleventh century, the Church tried to impose the Truce of God, forbidding warfare on certain days of the week and all feast days (perhaps unsurprisingly, it had only modest success). Monasteries also used their wealth to promote literacy and learning, a rare thing in the Middle Ages. Until the thirteenth century and the development of universities, knowledge and the teaching of sciences was very much a monastic monopoly. Their devotion to collecting and copying manuscripts helped preserve classical knowledge and texts throughout the medieval era.

In modern France, monasteries do still exist, but their social role has eroded since the fourteenth century. They suffered greatly during the French Revolution, when most of the great monasteries were destroyed or repurposed. But monasteries still perform what they see as their social duty to the poor and vulnerable, and some of them still produce various foods, especially liquors and cheeses. The quantities produced are usually small, and the products are therefore hard to get outside of France (or even outside of the monastery's shop).

Today, the main contribution of monks to French food production seems to be of a more secular bent: images of monks are used without any scruples by the marketing departments of big food companies. Making your food product seem like it has some vague link to monks seems to be a good technique for improving sales. It is an association that may be puzzling if one thinks only of the asceticism of the medieval Church. But in the competition between the soul and the stomach, it is clear that the wondrous products of the French countryside often held the winning hand.

10

Fighting for Plums

The French have a special love affair with fruit. Each year, France produces more than 2.5 million tons of apples, grapes, pears, and the like—but even this staggering bounty is not enough to slake the French appetite for *les fruits*, with imports rising every year.[1] Many French people satisfy their cravings at specialty shops called *fruiteries*, which sell only fruits and vegetables, and with a sense of reverence that can be astonishing to outsiders. Customers must not touch the wares themselves, for example, but wait for an assistant to carefully select and bag the perfect specimens.

This French affection for fruit can be seen in many idioms of everyday life. If you want to come to a compromise over something, you must "cut the pear in two" (*couper la poire en deux*). Picking one's brain might be expressed as "squeezing one's lemon" (*presser le citron*). If you want to convey a sense of "eh" or "so-so" when asked for an opinion on something, you might say it's "half fig, half grape" (*mi-figue, mi-raisin*).

Yet there is one particular French fruit idiom that seems to make no sense at all: *ça compte pour des prunes* ("it was worth plums"). This is something you might hear when you've invested a great deal of effort in something that eventually came to naught. The clear implication is that plums are worthless, nothing to strive for. But plums are actually adored in France. So where on earth does this saying come from?

To begin, we must clear up some linguistic confusion. The juicy fruits known as *prunes* in France are what most of the Anglo-speaking world would call plums, while the dried plums known elsewhere as prunes are in France called *pruneaux*. In France, both are produced in the sun-drenched southwest, between Toulouse and

Bordeaux. The most highly prized variety of plum is the small, green, and succulent Reine-Claude. It is named for the wife of King Francis I, Queen Claude, who during her reign in the early sixteenth century was known for distributing plums from her garden to the common people. Today, their appearance in French markets every August provokes squeals of delight from gourmands, who might use them to create a sweet confit to accompany foie gras, or perhaps preserve them in Armagnac, or just gobble as many as possible while their short season lasts. The southwest region is also home to the famous *pruneaux d'Agen*, the delicious and nutritious prunes that sustained seafarers in centuries past and today continue to delight French palates. They are particularly tasty when accompanied by Roquefort and perhaps a bit of cognac.

The popularity of these plums hints at a more obscure history underlying our curious idiom. In the end, we might attribute the notion of plummy failure to God—or, more accurately, his representative here in the earthly realm of France, namely the Catholic Church.

In 1095, Pope Urban II launched the First Crusade with a ringing speech before a great crowd in Clermont, in central France. The occupation of the Christian Holy Land by the Seljuk Turks had become intolerable, and the tottering Byzantine Empire was unlikely to repel them. Pope Urban had also grown frustrated with the European nobility, who fought each other endlessly, preyed upon the clergy and the weak, and were not sufficiently obeisant to his authority. Why not find a way to channel all that violent energy toward a more worthy cause, like reconquering the Holy Land? Those who met their death, either in battle or by some misfortune on the road, would be granted admission to heaven—a powerful inducement back in those pious times. (Of course, more venal incentives, such as wealth and glory, could not be entirely discounted either.) The pope must have been pleased at the enthusiastic response to his call, as tens of thousands of men signed up for the crusade.

The armies of the First Crusade, led by some of Europe's greatest lords, departed the following year. Over the next three years they gradually conquered more territory in the eastern Mediterranean, and in 1099 they finally captured Jerusalem. Their victory was capped with a horrific massacre of the town's defenders and civilian inhabitants: "There was so much slaughter that our men put down their feet in blood up to the ankle," wrote the anonymous author of the

Gesta Francorum, one of the most important contemporary accounts of the First Crusade.[2] It was neither the first nor the last Crusader atrocity, and it evoked little spiritual angst (the primitive laws of war at the time only applied when facing Christian foes). The European forces continued to seize important towns, such as Acre, Tripoli, and Tyre, and created new European principalities known as the Crusader States (or Outremer, French for "overseas"). As it happens, the conquest was the easy part, greatly facilitated by the bitter political and religious schisms afflicting the Islamic world at the time. Holding on to the conquered lands would prove a lot more difficult.

It is commonly said that European gastronomy benefited greatly from the Crusades, due to the invaders' encounters with new exotic spices and ingredients. But in truth, this narrative is misleading. A number of spices often said to have been discovered in the Crusades, such as pepper and ginger, had graced noble tables in Europe since Roman times. Saffron, which had been cultivated in Europe in antiquity, was reintroduced by Arab invaders sometime after the eighth century. Substantial cross-cultural exchange and trade occurred long before the Crusades, especially in Islamic Spain and Sicily. So the actual culinary impact of the Crusades in Europe is more limited than commonly thought, although the late-medieval preference for sweet and fragrant dishes probably owes something to a greater appreciation of Arab and Persian cuisine. European merchants also benefited from Crusader control of Levantine port cities, which allowed them to temporarily seize a portion of the lucrative spice trade. Perhaps the greatest effect, in terms of its global impact, was the Crusaders' encounter with sugar, which Europeans began importing from the Middle East in larger and larger quantities.

It can't be said that the Crusaders bequeathed to the locals any sort of culinary riches in turn. In fact, one of the streets in a new Jerusalem marketplace servicing European pilgrims was known by the locals as Malquisinat, the "Street of Bad Cooking." It was situated between the Church of the Holy Sepulchre and the Temple Mount, where the Crusaders converted the Al-Aqsa Mosque into a Christian church.

After the conquest of Jerusalem, many Crusaders returned home, and it proved difficult for the Christian rulers to maintain security within their newly won territories and along the historical pilgrimage routes to the Holy Land. In response, a French knight named Hugh de Payns gathered a handful of fellow knights and formed a new military-monastic order in 1120, with the aim of defending Jerusalem and Christian pilgrims. As monks, they took vows of poverty, chastity, and obedience, but instead of working in the fields or copying books, they trained and fought as warriors. The popes at that time, ignoring the fact that "warrior-monk" should have been an oxymoron, not only approved of the new order but granted them special rights, and as a result they only answered to the papacy, not to any national sovereign. The king of Jerusalem gave them living space near the former Temple of Solomon, and thus they became known as the Templars.

Nobles in Europe were increasingly drawn to the Templars, who offered the opportunity to continue fighting and slaying while earning salvation. Donations also started flowing in from pious nobles and grateful pilgrims, and the Templars quickly became very rich. Much of this funding was used to support Templar forces in the Holy Land and to build the mighty fortresses that were crucial to maintaining European control in these territories where they were heavily outnumbered. But the Templars also began to dabble in monetary transactions: you could, for example, deposit money with the Templars in France and withdraw the sums when you arrived in Jerusalem. The French kings began to keep their money with the Templars—what safer place could there be than a bank guarded by warrior-monks? Later, the Templars also loaned money to the nobility, circumventing the Church's ban on usury with a series of complex financial mechanisms. (Evidently, using complex financial mechanisms to get around the rules is not a recent banking invention.)

Over time, the Templars came to own a vast portfolio of lands and properties throughout France and western Europe. They built fortresses and churches in many towns and cities, and their huge agricultural estates—known as commanderies—produced copious amounts of food, wine, and livestock. They also owned salt ponds, enabling them to produce that most valuable commodity. At their height in the thirteenth century, the Templars owned more than nine thousand forts and dwellings in Europe and the Holy Land. Most of these no longer exist, but some key sites and ruins can still be visited in France today. The Larzac plateau in southwestern France, for example, hosts several Templar villages, including the remarkably intact La Couvertoirade.

The diet of the Templars very much resembled that of other monks, but they were allowed to eat meat three times a week. It is actually thought today that their restrained eating habits, which involved lots of vegetables, fruits, and fish, were responsible for the noted longevity of Templar knights, which back then was seen as a sure sign of divine approbation.[3] The Templars were less likely to suffer from cardiovascular diseases or gout, a painful disease common among the nobility that results from too much meat and alcohol.

Unfortunately for the Templars, the whole crusading business did not end up very well for the Christians. In 1187, Salah ad-Din—the legendary sultan of Egypt and Syria, known to posterity as Saladin—defeated the Crusader armies in the famous Battle of Hattin, which allowed him to reclaim Jerusalem. (It is said that Pope Urban III dropped dead upon hearing the news.) Subsequent crusades failed to reclaim the city, and finally the rise of the powerful Mamluk dynasty in Egypt spelled the end of the Crusader kingdoms. Acre, the last Christian stronghold, fell to the Mamluks in 1291.

The expulsion of the Crusaders from the Holy Land created a problem for the French king, the strong and ambitious Philip the Fair (nicknamed the "Iron King"). When the Templars were sending their men and wealth to the Middle East, they were not a serious threat to the monarchy. But now the warrior-monks were stuck in France,

La Couvertoirade, in the heart of the Larzac plateau, is one of the best-preserved Templar villages in France. © Richard Semik (Dreamstime Photos).

and they did not answer to the jurisdiction of the king. They had been given the right to impose taxes, which they did, and they were basically a state within the French state. In the increasingly bitter confrontation between King Philip and Pope Boniface VIII over who held ultimate authority in France, they were a powerful ally of the papacy. And worst of all, Philip owed the Templars a lot of money.

In 1307, Philip had most of the Templars in France arrested on the same day, nationwide. The Templars were accused of a range of crimes, including worshipping Satan, spitting on the cross, and sodomy, and many were burned at the stake. The mighty order was essentially eliminated in France, and all of this happened with the agreement of the new pope, Clement V. He was French, and understandably more conciliatory to Philip's agenda than his predecessor Boniface VIII, who had died shortly after being attacked and arrested by Philip's troops in 1303.

In 1314, Jacques de Molay, the last Templar Grand Master, was burned to death in Paris (a plaque marking the execution site can be found near the Pont Neuf). He is said to have put a curse upon Pope Clement and King Philip, and as it happened, both died within a year. Philip's three sons then succeeded him to the throne in turn, but all died young, leaving no legitimate male heirs, and so their royal line within the Capetian dynasty came to an end. The French throne passed to the House of Valois, descended from Philip's brother, and an epic succession battle ensued that ultimately led to the Hundred Years' War between France and England. If the Templar curse was responsible for all this, as many people at the time believed, then it was a remarkably successful case of revenge.

But what about our plums? Well, in 1148, the European armies of the Second Crusade decided to attack the ancient city of Damascus, even though its Muslim rulers were allied with the Christians at the time. Their attempt at siege warfare failed, and in the end the Crusaders suffered a major defeat that doomed the Second Crusade. But according to legend, it was during this campaign that the Crusaders discovered the famous plums of Damascus on the outskirts of the city. A group of Templars apparently brought some plum trees back to southwest France, a region with a gracious climate and a substantial Templar presence. Local monks grafted the Damascus plum onto their existing plum stocks, and sensational new varieties were created. Through the following centuries, long after the Templars disappeared and the monasteries faded away, orchard keepers continued to nurture their plum crops, to the enduring gastronomic delight of the French people.

So this is what the Templars ultimately fought for: plums. Not a lot indeed. And so while the French today adore their lovely plums, and create elaborate dishes to celebrate them, they also serve as a sardonic historical reminder of how the mighty can fall.

11

The Wine That Got Away

Few gastronomic rivalries can compare to the competition between the wines of Burgundy, those fabulous descendants of Cistercian devotion, and the wines of Bordeaux, the product of more earthly incentives and innovation. It is a battle not merely for profit but for the hearts of wine drinkers worldwide. Attempts to codify their divergent tastes are often underlaid with more abstract notions of their character: the subtle, complex, somewhat unpredictable flavors of Burgundy are said to capture the bohemian soul of the French countryside, while the more dependable and polished Bordeaux wines represent the best of France's bourgeois modernity. It is an irresolvable debate, as are so many of the debates that French people love. One might adopt the position of a magistrate friend of the renowned gourmand Jean Anthelme Brillat-Savarin, who, when asked whether he preferred the wines of Burgundy or Bordeaux, replied, "That is a trial in which I have so much pleasure weighing the evidence that I always put off my verdict."[1]

For hundreds of years, there was a clear favorite in the Anglo-Saxon world: the red wines of Bordeaux, known as claret to the English upper classes. In the fourteenth century, for example, a flotilla of two hundred ships would sail for Bordeaux every spring and fall just to carry back enough wine to satisfy the enormous English demand.[2] But like so many preferences in the world of gastronomy, the affection for Bordeaux was based less on taste than on politics, business, and war. To understand the English proclivity for claret, one must begin with the life of one of the most influential, romantic, and adventurous women of medieval Europe: Eleanor of Aquitaine.

Eleanor was probably born in 1122, although records are not entirely clear about that. Her father, William X, was the Duke of Aquitaine, a vast territory in the southwest of France, extending from Poitiers and the Loire Valley in the north to the Pyrenees in the south, and from the Atlantic coast to the Auvergne in the east. Since Roman times, Aquitaine had been a distinct and mostly autonomous territory, and even though its dukes were now vassals of the king of France, they controlled a larger and more prosperous amount of land than he did. Just before William X died in 1137, the duke sent a note to the French king, Louis VI, asking him to look after his daughter, Eleanor, whom he named as his heir. Louis then had to find her a suitable husband, who would reign as Aquitaine's new duke, as it would have been unimaginable for a woman to rule in her own right. It was a fabulous opportunity for Louis, who quickly arranged for Eleanor to marry his own son and heir, Louis. (Here we have to add that French kings definitely lacked originality in naming their sons, hence the nightmare of distinguishing among the many Louis, Henrys, and Philips.)

Eleanor, about fifteen years old at the time of her wedding, was described as a beautiful and energetic woman with blond hair and green eyes. She was raised in the vibrant and joyous court in Aquitaine, where troubadours, poetry, and all sorts of entertainment were highly popular, and the court in Paris must have seemed very bland to her eyes. Her husband was around sixteen years old, the second son of the king, and had been destined for a clerical career before the death of his elder brother. He was a very pious and, some say, boring man—so much so that Eleanor later complained she had married a monk. His father died shortly after their marriage in August 1137, and so Eleanor, Duchess of Aquitaine, very quickly became queen of France as well.

Eleanor was perhaps justifiably blamed for encouraging her husband into a few fruitless military campaigns against some of her unruly subjects in Aquitaine and also against the Count of Toulouse. But what attracted the most criticism was her inability to give the king a son, which at the time was considered the main worth of a queen. In 1145, when she finally did give birth, it was to a daughter. Thus far, Eleanor was a failure in many eyes.

Relations between the king and queen really took a sour turn when Louis decided to join the Second Crusade, after Edessa fell to the Turks. Eleanor accompanied him, and in 1147 they reached Constantinople, the capital of Byzantium. There it is said that she experienced exotic dishes such as caviar, fried frogs, artichokes, and eggplant, as well as sauces redolent of cinnamon and coriander. What she must have thought of the funny Byzantine utensil called a fork, then unknown in France, is anyone's guess.

In March 1148, the Crusaders finally reached their stronghold of Antioch, which was ruled by Eleanor's uncle, Raymond of Poitiers. Raymond tried to persuade the king to reconquer Edessa straightaway, but Louis decided to go to Jerusalem first (as a pious man, he considered it to be the main objective of his pilgrimage). Eleanor sided with her uncle, and whether Louis was jealous of the complicity between Raymond and Eleanor or angry with her defiance is unknown, but there was clearly a Before Antioch and After Antioch in their relationship. When the couple left the Holy Land, after a disastrous campaign, it was in separate boats.

The pope tried to save the royal marriage. His efforts seemed successful at first, as Eleanor fell pregnant again, but she gave birth to another daughter. In 1152, Eleanor and Louis were both happy to have their marriage annulled on the grounds of consanguinity, claiming that as cousins, they should never have wed in the first place.

But Eleanor had a follow-up scheme in mind, and very shortly after the annulment she married Henry Plantagenet, who was not only the Count of Anjou through his father, but the Duke of Normandy and future king of England through his mother. (He was in fact the founder of the legendary Plantagenet dynasty in England, which would rule until the death of Richard III three hundred years later.) Henry was a decade younger than Eleanor, and a much more energetic partner than Louis. Apart from the obvious political advantages of the union, he seemed to have a genuine affection for Eleanor, and she was granted a much more active role in political affairs during her second marriage.

Two years after their marriage, Henry acceded to the throne of England (as Henry II). It was a disaster for Louis. Now the king of England, with his hereditary French lands and the acquisition of Aquitaine through marriage, controlled about half of the landmass of France and most of its coastline, from Normandy and the Channel all the way down to the Pyrenees. To add insult to injury, Eleanor, although in her thirties, gave Henry five sons and three daughters.

Louis bitterly summed up his situation to the archbishop of Oxford thus: "Your lord, the king of England, lacks for nothing: he has men, horses, gold and silk, gems, fruits, wild beasts, and everything. But in France we have nothing but bread, wine, and joy."[3]

Some of that French wine was also destined to be claimed by England. Aquitaine was now an English territory, and its wines began wending their way north in much greater amounts. Eleanor played her part in this, regularly ordering wine from her homeland, and her son Richard made Bordeaux wines the daily fare in his household, an excellent boost for the region's winemakers. But perhaps the main driver of Bordeaux wines' rocketing popularity was the fact that under the English, the city of Bordeaux became one of the great European ports. With the rise of continental trade networks, it grew into one of the largest and wealthiest cities under the English crown, second only to London. Bordeaux wine merchants were exempted from export taxes, a clever tactic for encouraging the region's loyalty to the English rather than French crown. This made Bordeaux one of the cheapest sources of wine for English drinkers, and demand exploded. Bordeaux also took advantage of its geographical position on the mouth of the Garonne River, just before the Gironde estuary and the Atlantic coast, to restrict the export of wines produced farther inland.

The medieval claret so beloved in England bears almost no resemblance to the magnificent vintages produced today. Yet the English role in building up the great port of Bordeaux and gulping down its local wines is an essential element of this success story. Of course, many others played a role, including the local nobles and merchants who built up their great estates, and the Dutch who drained the region's swamps and revealed some of Bordeaux's finest terroir (including the famed Médoc).

Credit must be given to Eleanor as well, given that it was her bold leap into divorce and remarriage that brought Bordeaux and the rest of Aquitaine into the English fold. Unfortunately, her initially happy union was derailed when King Henry began an affair with a woman named Rosamund, one that went far beyond his usual dalliances. Eleanor spent most of her time in Aquitaine governing her lands, alongside Richard (the Lionheart), her favorite son. Eventually she turned fully on Henry, supporting her sons when they rebelled against their father. Their revolt was unsuccessful, and while Henry showed mercy on his sons, he could not forgive his wife. Eleanor

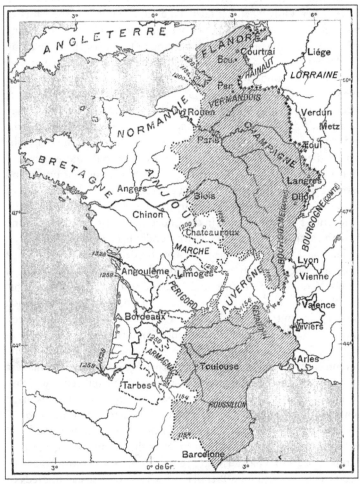

In the late twelfth century, a vast amount of northern and western France
was claimed by Henry II, king of England and Duke of Normandy;
the domains of King Louis VII of France were reduced to the shaded
territories shown here. Louis's son, Philip II (Philippe Augustus), spent
several decades dismantling the Angevin dynasty and reclaiming its
territories, so that by the mid-thirteenth century, English possessions
were reduced to Bordeaux and a large portion of southwest France. From
Élisée Reclus, *L'Homme et la terre*, vol. III (Paris: Librairie Universelle,
1905), 92.

spent most of the next fifteen years imprisoned in the royal castle in Winchester. Only when her husband died, in 1189, was she released, when Richard became king. He gave Eleanor the regency of England while he spent much of his reign fighting in France or the Holy Land.

Eleanor proved a successful regent in his absence, while also thwarting the ambitions of her youngest son, John (later known as the villain king of Robin Hood). In 1199, Richard was slain in France while besieging a rebellious vassal in the Limousin region. As he died childless, John inherited the throne. He was a terrible king, and the elderly Eleanor frequently tried to rescue him from his missteps. She finally died in 1204, at more than eighty years old, and was buried in her beloved Abbey de Fontevraud, which remains a beautiful and moving site to visit today. Not long after her death, John lost most of England's possessions in France to the powerful French king Philip Augustus. For the first time in the Capetian dynasty, the French king had an extensive amount of territory under his control.

But the English kept their grip on Bordeaux and the region of Gascony, one of the many factors that helped lead to the Hundred Years' War between France and England in the fourteenth and fifteenth centuries. When that war finally ended, Bordeaux was French once again, but the French king let the Bordeaux merchants keep their favorable export arrangements, and shipments to England continued. The nature of the English demand began to shift in the seventeenth century, when some enterprising Bordeaux winemakers created new and more expensive varieties that captured the higher end of the English market. In 1663, Samuel Pepys noted in his diary what many consider to be the "first wine tasting note in history," about a new French wine "called Ho Bryan, that hath a good and most particular taste that I ever met with."[4] Haut-Brion, the prototype Bordeaux château wine, remains one of the most luxurious products of the region, a Premier Cru Classé that costs hundreds of dollars a bottle.

Within France itself, it took a bit longer for Bordeaux wines to attain the same reputation they enjoyed in England—but today, of course, Bordeaux wines are appreciated in France as much as anywhere else, and they make up more than a quarter of all French AOC wine production.[5] But the English still have a special fondness for the old duchy of Aquitaine. In fact, many English expats have elected to live in Dordogne, an area east of Bordeaux located bang in the middle of the former duchy. (Because of this new English invasion,

The royal tombs in Fontevraud Abbey: Eleanor of Aquitaine and King Henry II (rear); Richard the Lionheart and Isabelle, the wife of King John (front). © Neil Harrison (Dreamstime Photos).

Dordogne is now regularly referred to as Dordogneshire.) In a way, it is simply the latest chapter in the centuries-long love/hate story between the English and the French. As much as these two peoples squabble and fight, they appear to be unable to live without each other, and this is true in the realm of food and wine as much as any other.

12

The Vegetarian Heresy

French people generally are not very fussy eaters and will eat many things that other peoples may be a bit afraid of—like frogs' legs or snails or calf brains. This lack of fussiness may seem a virtue, an enduring remnant of the days when most French people were peasants and could not afford to be choosy about what appeared on their tables. But unfortunately, it makes it a bit difficult for vegetarians and vegans, or those with gluten or lactose intolerance, to eat out in France. The response of many French people to any special dietary requirements usually runs along the lines of, "We have no time to tolerate intolerance." In fact, the French can be so blasé about the separation of meat and vegetable that in 2015, Cassegrain, one of the nation's leading purveyors of canned vegetables, admitted that some of its products included beef flavoring.

To be sure, it's not universally bleak. The environmental consequences of meat production have helped inspire an upsurge in French vegetarianism in the past few years, as have relatively high prices for meat. Restaurants increasingly feature vegetarian options, and leading chefs have embraced the vegetarian ethos. But still, less than 5 percent of the population is vegetarian, and most French people have probably never met a vegan. French school cafeterias refuse to offer vegetarian options on principle, believing that all French children should partake of the same cuisine.

At least today, however, the French are not burning vegans alive for their culinary heresies. Progress has been made since the thirteenth century, when, despite the uneven success of the Crusades in the Holy Land, the idea of crusading remained quite popular, and was gradually adapted for the struggle against Christian heretics within Europe itself. In France, this new form of crusade was directed mainly against a Christian heresy known as Catharism, whose adherents not only followed a radically divergent religious agenda but refused to eat the meat and dairy products so fundamental to French cuisine. Unfortunately, this dietary deviance contributed to their downfall, betraying adherents to the relentless interrogators of the Inquisition.

Much as the Gauls did not originally see themselves as Gauls, the Cathars never called themselves Cathars. They called their leaders *bons hommes* (good men) or *bonnes femmes* (good women), and they might refer to their community as *bons chrétiens* (good Christians). But their critics called them Cathars, and used the term *Perfects* to describe their leaders. The terms stuck, and so for simplicity's sake, we'll refer to them as Cathars here, as most conventional histories do.

The Cathar heresy took root in France in the twelfth century, mainly in the southwest region then ruled by the Count of Toulouse.

The beautiful city of Toulouse, known as *la Ville Rose* thanks to the pinkish hue of its terra-cotta buildings, was founded in the Roman era, and over the centuries it served as a capital for this key region linking the Pyrenees, the Atlantic, and the Mediterranean. Technically, the county of Toulouse was part of France, and the French king was the overlord of its count, but in the still-feudal system of the day, the Count of Toulouse actually controlled a richer and bigger area of France than the king—he was also Duke of Narbonne and Marquis of Provence—and could do more or less as he pleased.

Culturally and linguistically, the county of Toulouse was very different from the northern reaches of France. In the south, people spoke Occitan, known as *langue d'oc* (*oc* being the word for "yes" in Occitan), and over time the southern regions where it was spoken became known as the Languedoc. In the north, people spoke a different version of French known as *langue d'oïl*, the ancestor of modern French. Socially, the Languedoc was seen as a more open, tolerant, and cosmopolitan society: troubadour culture thrived there, for example, and women played a more prominent role in society. It is therefore not surprising that the Cathars found a greater degree of acceptance in the southern regions.

The Cathars were yet another manifestation of a curious tradition of dualist heresies that had bedeviled the Christian Church since its earliest days. The Cathars believed that our material world was actually created by the devil, and a separate spiritual world existed that was governed by God. The forces of evil and good were implacably divided and eternally at war with each other. Unfortunately, human beings were consigned to live in the evil material world, and even worse, they were doomed to be repeatedly reincarnated into it. The only hope for salvation was to lead a virtuous life and hope to be drawn by God into the spiritual world. But the Cathars argued that the Roman Catholic Church had corrupted the teachings of Christ and was working hand in hand with the devil. So it is not really surprising that the Church took a dim view of Catharism and its blatant disregard for orthodox Christian beliefs.

The leaders of the Cathars were called "Perfects," as this was what they were purported to be doing, living a "perfect life" according to their beliefs. These exemplary leaders adhered to the "rule of justice and truth," which emphasized ritual prayer, fasting, and manual labor. They were pacifists, believing that violence and war were forbidden by Christ's teachings; only God had the prerogative to take a human life. They abstained from sexual intercourse, as this only created new children who would be trapped in our evil material world. And given the importance of food in daily life, it was perhaps inevitable that they had quite a few rules about what could and could not be eaten. Eating any form of meat was bad, because there was every possibility that we might be reincarnated as an animal in the next life. Milk-based products should be avoided because they not only came from animals but depended on animals reproducing (reproduction is bad, remember). Strangely, Perfects would eat fish, as it was believed at the time that fish did not reproduce in a sexual way. They also had no problem eating fruits and vegetables (they had to eat something, after all) and therefore also no problem with wine. Ordinary followers of the Cathar faith did not have to adhere to these strict rules and could still eat meat and procreate. Both men and women could be Perfects—after all, a man might die today and be reincarnated as a woman, so there was no need for strict patriarchal segregation.

The Cathars were more or less tolerated in many parts of the Languedoc. But in Rome, Pope Innocent III was less inclined to be tolerant, eventually calling for a crusade against the Cathars. French northerners enthusiastically responded to the pope's call. After all, what was not to like? A crusade close to home, absolution of all one's sins, and the chance to win some land, loot, and glory. The Languedoc might be reduced to ashes—thus actually confirming the Cathar belief in a worldly hell—but this sort of barbarism was allowed when fighting enemies of the Church. The campaign became known as the Albigensian Crusade, for many Cathars lived around the town of Albi, and were thus sometimes referred to as Albigensians.

The crusade was launched from Lyon in 1209, and its first major target was the Cathar stronghold of Béziers, one of the oldest and most picturesque towns in the south of France. Many Catholics also lived there, and when the crusaders arrived and began besieging the town, they were given the chance to depart and escape the heretics' fate. But they refused to abandon their fellow citizens, and so before the town was stormed, the attackers asked the papal legate commanding the crusaders—Arnaud Amaury, the abbot of Cîteaux—how they should distinguish between the Cathars and the Catholics. The Cistercian abbot's infamous reply: "Kill them all—the Lord will know his own." The town was quickly taken and burned to the ground, and all of its inhabitants—about twenty thousand people—slaughtered in a horrific bloodbath.

Carcassonne was subdued next and given to the new leader of the crusade, a devout Christian warrior and veteran crusader named Simon de Montfort. For nearly a decade, Montfort terrorized the southwest, sacking towns, burning Cathars alive, gouging out the eyes of captured prisoners. He eventually met his death during the second siege of Toulouse, crushed by a stone launched from a catapult operated by a group of women within the city walls. (The celebratory cry that went up that day—"Montfort is dead! Long live Toulouse!"— was still invoked as a generator of civic pride as late as the nineteenth century.)

Despite their early victories in Béziers and Carcassonne, the crusaders actually took two decades to completely pacify the Languedoc. In 1229, an end to the crusade was negotiated between the Count of Toulouse and the crown. It is not known exactly how many people died in the crusade, but estimates of several hundred thousand are common. The crusade broke the autonomy of the southern nobles and was a key event in the gradual absorption of southern France into the central state ruled by Paris.

There were still a few rebellious holdouts after 1229 in the supposedly impregnable Cathar mountain fortresses. The most notorious of these was Montségur ("safe mountain"), a breathtaking hilltop fort in the Pyrenees surrounded by rugged cliffs and a deep gorge. Around four thousand Cathars, including more than two hundred Perfects, took refuge there in May 1243, besieged by a large army commanded by the seneschal of Carcassonne. Thanks to the difficult terrain, they were able to withstand the siege for ten months, but eventually their attackers made use of Basque mercenaries, gifted in mountain warfare, to climb the mountain heights by night and breach the fort's defenses. This surprise attack led to the Cathar surrender—but not before they allegedly smuggled an unnamed treasure out of the fort. (According to which conspiratorial website you visit, this might have been anything from a vast trove of gold to the Holy Grail.) The Perfects refused to renounce their faith and were burned together in a great pyre.

The fall of Montségur represented one of the dying gasps of Catharism, but what really destroyed it completely was the Inquisition. In 1233, Pope Gregory IX decided that the Dominican order, founded by a Spanish priest named Domingo de Guzmán partly in response to the Cathar threat, would be the perfect tool to root out the heretics. The Dominican inquisitors were judge, jury, and prosecutor combined, and after 1252, they were authorized by the pope to torture people if it would help yield confessions. They answered to no one but the pope and were feared and hated all over the Languedoc. They relied on informants and coercion, and their judgments led many people to the stake (burning people alive became a common execution method for heresy in the medieval era, with fire thought to purify as it destroys).

When poring over the records of the Cathar interrogations, the number of questions related to food is especially striking. The limited diet of the Cathars was well known, and this became a convenient way for inquisitors to identify heresy. Often one of the first questions posed to the acquaintances of a suspected heretic would be something like "Did you eat together, and what did you eat?" If the reply was "Always fish and vegetables," then the inquisitors had the medieval equivalent of probable cause.[1]

Thankfully, the worst that might happen to vegetarians or vegans

The ruins of the mountain fortress of Montségur, last stand of the Cathars. Photograph by authors, 2016.

This small stone memorial marks the spot where more than two hundred Cathars were burned to death after the fall of Montségur. Photograph by authors, 2016.

in France today is a soupçon of scorn from those who believe any nonconformist eating habit is a modern form of heresy against the nation of France. But as more and more French people embrace a meat-free lifestyle, the future for vegetarians in France appears far more promising than the fate of the unfortunate Cathars.

13

A Papal Red

Sur le Pont d'Avignon
On y danse, On y danse
(On the bridge of Avignon, there we dance, there we
dance)

—*Fifteenth-century song and children's rhyme*

Beautifully sited on the Rhône River, about fifty miles inland from the Mediterranean Sea, the town of Avignon is undoubtedly one of the most alluring locales in Provence. Underneath the towering Gothic heights of the fourteenth-century papal palace, its charming streets and squares are lined with small boutiques and cafés thrown open to the sun. Les Halles, the central food market, brims with olives, fresh herbs and spices, oysters, and an enormous variety of local cheeses, meats, and breads. In the surrounding countryside, the Côtes du Rhône wine region produces some of the finest varieties in France.

The indisputable sovereign of the southern Rhône wines is Châteauneuf-du-Pape, a strong, earthy red that was among the first French wines to receive an AOC (*appellation d'origine contrôlée*) after the invention of the classification scheme in the early twentieth century.[1] Its distinctive terroir is centered around the village that bears the same name, which translates to New Castle of the Pope. It thus serves as a viticultural legacy of a brief yet pivotal era in the history of France and the Catholic Church, known forevermore as the "Avignon papacy." It's a tale replete with fantastic castles, poisonous plots, and antipopes—legends that have endured for far longer than the complicated politics that brought them into being.

If we return to the days of Philip the Fair, in the early 1300s, we may remember it was a newly elected French pope, Clement V, who allowed Philip to suppress the Knights Templar. Clement had been elected on the strength of his skills as a diplomat, at a time when relations between France and the papacy were severely strained. As one of his main tasks was to enact some sort of reconciliation with the

French king, he decided to take up residence in Avignon. Its location on the Rhône, not far from the Mediterranean and Italian shores, made it a convenient location for traveling around Europe. A large tract of territory next to Avignon was actually owned by the papacy. And Rome was a dangerous place at that time, torn apart by power struggles among its leading families, leaving the pope extremely vulnerable. In fact, so volatile was the capital that it was not unusual then for the popes to reside outside of Rome. Clement broke new ground, however, in deciding to reside outside of Italy entirely, and in leaving a long line of popes after him in the same location. This era, in which seven consecutive French popes remained ensconced in the pleasurable idyll of Provence, is known as the Avignon papacy.

The Italians, needless to say, were not pleased by this papal abandonment. Critics referred to the Avignon papacy as the "Babylonian captivity," arguing that the papacy had been subordinated to the French kings and the spiritual integrity of the Church had been compromised. In Dante's *Inferno*, Clement V is depicted in the eighth circle of hell.

Yet this terrible sinner left a rather heavenly legacy here in the earthly realm: Château Pape Clément, produced near Bordeaux. Before becoming pope, Clement had been archbishop of Bordeaux, and there he received a vineyard in donation. He cultivated it carefully and extended its size. When he became pope, the vineyard became known as Vigne du Pape-Clément. The vineyard still has a very good reputation today, producing mainly rich and fruity wines. It can arguably claim to be one of the oldest wine-producing establishments in the Bordeaux wine region.

After Pope Clement died near Avignon in 1314, rival factions in the Sacred College of Cardinals were incapable of agreeing on a new pope. After two years, the French king essentially forced them to a vote, and they elected a frail, seventy-two-year-old French cardinal who became John XXII. Their hope was that he would have a short reign, during which each faction could strengthen its position for the next election. But their hopes were dashed, as John XXII went on to reign for eighteen years (some say his apparent ill-health had all been an act). He had previously been the bishop of Avignon and was happy to stay in place, given the continuing turmoil in Rome. His longevity was often attributed to one of his strange eating habits: he preferred to eat mainly white food products, such as milk, egg whites, white fish, chicken, and cheese. A gastronomic specialty of Avignon known as *papeton d'aubergines*, a sort of flan made with the (white) flesh of eggplants and originally shaped like the papal hat, is sometimes said to have originated during his reign.

The greatest gastronomic legacy of John XXII was not to be eggplants, however. In an effort to periodically escape the intrigues of Avignon, he established a summer residence in a small place now called Châteauneuf-du-Pape, in the Rhône Valley north of the city. Wine had been produced in this area since the Gallo-Roman era, and more recently by the Templars, but the vineyards had fallen into disuse. John XXII built a castle and brought in vintners from his hometown of Cahors, in southwest France, to restore the vineyards. They created a wine replete with the flavors of Provence, its complex character the result of more than a dozen varietals of grapes. Châteauneuf-du-Pape has enjoyed a stellar reputation for centuries, even surviving the anticlerical ravages of the French Revolution. The nineteenth-century Provençal poet Frederic Mistral, who won the Nobel Prize in Literature in 1904, famously referred to it as a "royal, majestic, pontifical wine."[2]

John XXII's other obsessions reflected the anxieties of that age. He forbade the practice of alchemy and instructed the inquisitors to investigate cases of sorcery and devil worship. This association of heresy and sorcery helped set the stage for the fervent persecution of witchcraft later in the medieval era, in which thousands across Europe were tortured and killed. After a botched assassination attempt early in his reign, involving both poison and black magic, he had developed a paranoia of both. (This may, in fact, explain his preference for white foods: they would more easily reveal poison, and the holiness associated with white might offer some magical protection.) Given the fashion for poisoning one's enemies at the time, it is not surprising that subsequent popes also developed a range of methods for detecting poisons hidden among their sumptuous feasts, from human tasters to narwhal horns to questionable mechanical contraptions.

Following John XXII's death—in the end, from natural causes—five more popes remained in residence in Avignon. Over the years, they built up the fabulous papal residence, the largest Gothic palace in the world, which still dominates the town today. The papal court in Avignon attracted scholars and artists and became one of the most important cultural centers of the Christian world. Beautiful frescoes and tapestries lined the palace walls, and its great halls hosted extravagant feasts under a ceiling painted blue as the evening sky, studded with stars. A thousand sheep might be roasted for a single meal, accompanied by thousands of gallons of wine. In fact, it was during this time that the wines of Burgundy acquired a reputation for excellence among the French elite: little known previously due to the region's inaccessibility to Paris, Burgundy wines were more easily transported to Avignon and thus consumed in great quantities there, along with the other great wines of the Rhône Valley. The chefs of Avignon turned the dining tables into a riot of expensive color with spices such as saffron and even gold leaf, and guests ate off plates of silver and gold.[3] At a time when ascetic orders, such as the Franciscans, were gaining in popularity, the decadence of the Avignon court attracted as much criticism as admiration.

Accompanying this reputation for princely extravagance were accusations of nepotism and corruption, stemming from the papal practice of promoting many members of one's family. Another enduring legacy from this era is the French phrase *Il se prend pour le moutardier du pape*, meaning "He behaves like the pope's mustard maker." It is an expression used to describe someone who, although rather stupid, thinks very highly of himself. Alexandre Dumas tells us that John XXII had a nephew too dim-witted for any responsible position, and so the pope appointed him as his grand mustard maker (John was very fond of mustard).

The sixth Avignon pope, Urban V, attempted to restore the papacy to Rome, but the comforts of Avignon proved too seductive, and many cardinals refused to follow him. It was left to his successor, Gregory XI, the last Avignon pope, to finally bring the papacy back to Rome in 1378. Now it was France that had become too chaotic and dangerous for the pope's liking, as the Hundred Years' War with England raged on, and a return to Rome would help reestablish a firm grip on papal territories and allegiances in Italy.

The Avignon era was not quite over, however. After the death of Gregory XI, the Sacred College, now back in Rome, was pressured to elect an Italian pope, Urban VI. He turned out to be very unpopular, especially among the French cardinals, who decided that his election was coerced and thus not legal. The French cardinals elected an alternative pope—or antipope—known as Clement VII, who returned to the papal residence in Avignon. He was supported by the French king and a number of other European monarchs, but many powerful states (including England and the Holy Roman Empire) supported

The majestic fourteenth-century Papal Palace still towers over the charming town of Avignon and the riverbanks of the Rhône. © Julie Mayfeng (Dreamstime Photos).

the pope in Rome instead. For nearly forty years, rival popes in Rome and Avignon divided Christendom, a period known as the Western Schism. The papal dispute created an enormous diplomatic crisis among European states, and it occasionally leached into local military conflicts as well.

The Western Schism finally came to an end with the Council of Constance and a new consensus pope, Martin V, elected in 1417. But its effects were long-lasting: this prolonged period of intrigue and conflict fed into growing antipapal sentiments, which a century later would explode into the Protestant Reformation. The extravagance and corruption of the papal courts, and their evident concern with earthly politics rather than spiritual integrity, offered ample inspiration to philosophers and clerics calling for radical reform of the faith.

The Avignon papacy, brief as it was, engendered a legacy as complex as the wines still associated with it today. While many people may only know of Châteauneuf-du-Pape as a delicious and diabolically expensive wine (and, perhaps, as a great opportunity to try out a fake French accent), it is also a surviving remnant of the titanic struggles of church and state that rent Europe seven hundred years ago. The wine that once graced the banquet tables of popes, antipopes, and kings continues to grace our humble tables today—a fairly impressive feat, given the turmoil that routinely savaged this small bit of terroir for centuries.

14

The White Gold of Guérande

On the west coast of France, in the south of Brittany, stands the medieval town of Guérande. With its imposing fifteenth-century ramparts, old cobblestone streets, granite houses, and numerous crêperies, it is truly a lovely town to wander about. One would never guess that it used to be the epicenter of a vast criminal enterprise, its signature crop craved by kings and peasants alike.

Fleur de sel, the "white gold of Guérande," may sound like a particularly elegant narcotic, but it's actually a legendary sea salt revered by gastronomes around the world. You may get a hint of its addictive properties during a stroll through the town, as you discover abundant opportunities to purchase it from market vendors and small shops. Pungent arrays of herb-and-salt mixes, guaranteed to transform even simple home-cooked dishes, are nearly irresistible. Even the strongest will in the world cannot hold out against the lure of salted caramel sauce drizzled over crêpes or ice cream.

But fleur de sel is not just any salt, as quickly becomes evident if you drive out from the town center to the salt marshes of Guérande, where the oldest saltworks date back to Roman times. Much as soil creates a unique terroir for wine, cheese, and honey, different seas lend their flavors to the salt collected from them. The Brittany coast is considered by many to produce the finest sea salt in the world, and today salt workers, or *paludiers*, harvest their crop over an area of nearly eight square miles, collecting fourteen thousand tons of salt per year.[1] A small percentage of this is the superlative fleur de sel, delicate crystals carefully collected from the surface of the seawater (often by women, who are thought to have a more tender touch for this work). But most of the salt produced here is known as *gros sel*

A *paludier* at work in the Guérande salt marshes. © Maxironwas (Dreamstime Photos).

de Guérande, a very appealing unrefined salt that is raked from the pools as the seawater evaporates; it imparts lovely sea flavors to one's cooking. (Fleur de sel, on the other hand, is best used as a final flourish over a dish, as it melts quickly under prolonged heat and its lovely flavors are lost.)

Naturally, with such a global reputation, sea salt plays a big role in the local economy. Less obvious, however, is the fact that the salt of Guérande, like many other highly addictive products, has a rich history of smugglers, insurgents, and rebellion attached to it.

Today, salt lies at the margins of everyday gastronomy, its presence cheaply acquired and taken for granted. But for much of human history, and throughout the world, salt was an essential product. In the days before canning, refrigeration, and artificial preservatives, salt was one of the few ways of preserving food for long periods, via curing or pickling. It was crucial for making cheese and helped bread rise faster and keep longer. Usually, salt was inexpensive, compared to spices, and thus was one of the few options for improving the flavor of meals for ordinary people. Like other food products, salt could be used as a currency for paying taxes or salaries—in fact, the word *salary* derives from the Latin *salarium*, the money given to Roman legionnaires to buy their salt rations. Salt has been used in religious rituals around the world for thousands of years, thanks to the symbolism of its purifying and preserving attributes; it was no coincidence that Jesus called his disciples "the salt of the earth," a phrase we still use today to describe someone honest and incorruptible.[2]

Salt is found naturally throughout the world: in salt mines, saline springs, and, of course, in seawater. Throughout history, human civilizations have devised clever ways of extracting salt from the earth and seas, and early settlements often congregated around sources of salt. France is fortunate to have ample salt resources, with its long coastlines providing a ready source for sea salt, in addition to its many inland salt mines and salt springs.

The importance of salt thus made it a key ingredient in one of the most pivotal developments of the medieval era: the expansion of trade networks throughout Europe and the growth of wealthy trading towns. Patterns of local self-sufficiency, so dominant in the early Middle Ages, succumbed to this great era of commercial and urban expansion. Now, towns might specialize in the production of certain goods—wines or leather goods, say—and use the profits from their sale to buy food and other essential goods from other locales. In this way, Guérande grew rich in the Middle Ages, its merchant ships bringing sea salt to other ports in France, England, the Netherlands, and the Hanseatic towns.

Eventually, the French kings realized that the salt market might supply them with funds for their interminable wars against rival powers, which at the time included everyone from the English and the Flemish to the Knights Templar. A new salt tax, called the gabelle, was introduced in the late thirteenth century by Philip the Fair, the Iron King. It later became permanent under Charles V (Charles the Wise) during the Hundred Years' War. Charles needed the money to ransom his father, who had been captured by the English, and to put down a rebellion by Charles the Bad, the king of Navarre. (The justifications for new taxes used to be so much more interesting.)

The gabelle became one of the most hated taxes in the kingdom, especially as the nobility and the clergy usually managed, through various dispensations, to avoid paying it (some things never change). Salt was taxed heavily—but not in the same way across the country. Brittany, which included Guérande, was completely exempt from the tax, a privilege bestowed upon the region when it was formally integrated with France in 1532. In other areas, such as Paris and most of northern and central France, salt was taxed very heavily. The price of salt could multiply by twenty just by crossing the borders out of Brittany.

Things got even worse when Jean-Baptiste Colbert, the French finance minister under Louis XIV, made the salt trade a complete state monopoly: now salt could only be bought from specific royal storehouses, which meant people had to travel, sometimes quite far, to purchase this essential commodity. They were also forced to buy a minimum amount every year, which made it a form of unavoidable direct taxation.

All of this naturally created a massive black market in salt. The rewards were potentially enormous: one successful trip, carrying salt from nontaxed to taxed areas, would bring a person the equivalent of three months' income. In 1784, the former finance minister, Jacques Necker, noted the absurd disparities in the price of a *minot* (about 107 pounds) of salt across regions: from 31 *sous* in Brittany to 591 in Anjou and 611 in Berry.[3] So it is not surprising that, by some estimates, half the people in Breton border areas were directly or indirectly living off the proceeds of salt smuggling, or that people in border towns like Vitré bought ten times as much as residents on the other side of the border.[4] While many smugglers operated on their own, or with the assistance of cleverly trained dogs or children, some salt smugglers were highly organized. The penalties for salt smuggling were among the harshest imposed by the regime; long prison sentences or even a lifetime in thrall as a galley slave awaited those unlucky enough to be caught. Children were not exempted, and they made up a good portion of those serving time in prison for salt crimes.

Obviously these smugglers were a threat to the regime, not only because of the financial loss, but also because no state likes to have armed bands roaming the countryside. A special security force known as the *gabelous* was formed in the seventeenth century to curtail salt smuggling. But the gabelous were poorly paid and often either in league with the smugglers or incompetent and violent, and they were usually loathed by the local population.

It is no exaggeration to say that the gabelle, with its punishing and unfairly applied rates, helped foment rebellion and revolution. Periodic peasant rebellions from the fifteenth century onward specifically targeted the gabelle, but they were usually put down by the regime with much force and destruction. In the Estates General assembly of

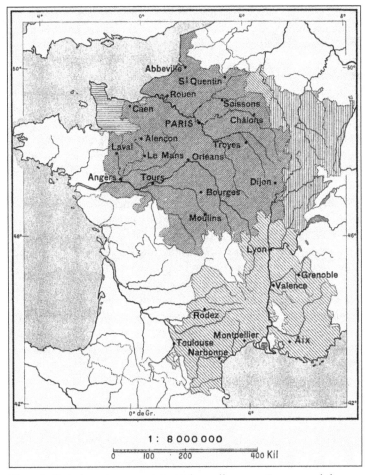

The gabelle (salt tax) was not imposed equally across France, and thus generated a robust black market. Paris and north-central France (the dark-shaded areas on this map) had the highest salt prices, twice as much as prices in the south of France and twenty times those in Brittany and the southwest. From Élisée Reclus, *L'Homme et la terre*, vol. III (Paris: Librairie Universelle, 1905), 591.

1789, on the eve of the French Revolution, all three estates representing French society agreed that the gabelle should be abolished—and a year later, following the end of the ancien régime, it was.

This made most people very happy, but it left both the smugglers and the gabelous without work. Many of them still had their weapons, however, and this is why many smugglers and royal tax collectors ended up fighting *together* in the counterrevolutionary movements that plagued the new regime during the 1790s. One of the most famous of these smugglers turned insurgents was Jean Chouan, who had previously served time in His Majesty's prisons for killing a salt tax collector. After the revolution, in his newfound unemployment, he used the peasants' discontent with forced army conscription to start a rebellion in the west of France, known to history as the Chouannerie uprising. Ultimately unsuccessful, it has achieved cultural posterity by inspiring Honoré de Balzac's first book published under his own name, *Les Chouans*.

In the end, Napoleon reestablished the gabelle—after all, he had interminable wars of his own to finance—and it was only officially abolished in 1945. But Guérande still trades and thrives, with or without the gabelle, thanks to the enduring desire for its white gold. Every year, from June to September, the harvest produces increasingly large piles of salt, destined for tables around the world. Working without the aid of machines or chemicals, the salt workers use roughly the same techniques as their ancestors did centuries in the past. Despite the tumultuous impact of repression, revolution, and war, and the innovations that have obscured salt's historic centrality, the sea salt of Guérande has maintained a niche in global gastronomy that seems unlikely to fade.

15

Legacy of a Black Prince

For more than two thousand years, the southwest of France has cradled passionate rivalries of all kinds. Its lands have been frequently ravaged by foreign invaders and the armies of the French crown, vying for local supremacy. Lost battles and doomed romances were immortalized in the songs of the troubadours, who themselves competed for lordly favor. Today, the region is riven by rivalries of a less violent nature—in rugby, for example, which is more popular here than almost anywhere else in France. But perhaps the most enduring competition features the towns of Carcassonne, Toulouse, and Castelnaudary, and its all-important motif is the question of who created and perfected the recipe for cassoulet.

Cassoulet is a legendary stew of meat and white haricot beans, cooked for many hours until it reaches molten perfection. It usually includes pork, but in Carcassonne they add mutton or partridge, in Castelnaudary they favor duck or goose, and in Toulouse they add their local sausages to the mix. Traditionally seen by the French as a peasant dish, today it is a popular comfort food, making up about a fifth of the canned meals sold in France. But no supermarket version can match the authentic cassoulet produced in the kitchens of its ancestral homeland. When Curnonsky, the famed food writer, visited Castelnaudary in the late 1920s, he found the most notable local purveyor of cassoulet—Madame Adolphine, an elderly woman—could only serve him and his party the following day, as her version of the dish required fifteen hours of cooking. She awakened six times in the night just to stir the cassoulet. (Curnonsky reported that the final product was not just a cassoulet, but *"the* Cassoulet."[1])

Indeed, Castelnaudary, a small but very scenic town on the banks of the Canal du Midi, is perhaps the most boisterous in its love of the dish, proclaiming itself the "world capital" of cassoulet. Its streets are dotted with restaurants and shops devoted to it, and every summer the Fête du Cassoulet features several days of music, games, and feasts of cassoulet for more than six hundred people. Visitors to the town are greeted by a large statue of a woman holding a *cassole*, the traditional local cooking pot from which the name *cassoulet* is derived.

The most persistent legend regarding the creation of cassoulet takes place in Castelnaudary. According to this story, cassoulet was invented when the infamous Black Prince of England laid siege to the town in 1355, during the Hundred Years' War. The inhabitants of Castelnaudary decided to put all their remaining food, mainly beans and meat, in a common pot and cook it. Thanks to the magical properties of this dish, born of necessity and solidarity, the French defenders became so powerful that they chased their attackers all the way back to the English Channel.

This legend, as lovely as it may sound to the Castelnaudary native, unfortunately is just a legend, which appeared for the first time centuries after the Hundred Years' War. The reality of that war was much grimmer for the inhabitants of Castelnaudary, and for the rest of France as well. The name Hundred Years' War is a bit of a misnomer—it lasted more than a century, and it was not one continuous war but a series of conflicts between England and France that shared similar aims and strategies. Regardless of how one labels the era, it was a devastating time for the inhabitants of France, where nearly all the fighting took place. Several million people are thought to have died as a result of this century of conflict.

We have already spoken of some of the main causes of the war, principally the continued English presence in southwestern France. As a result of the 1259 Treaty of Paris, which was meant to settle an earlier era of conflict (and, like many treaties, created the conditions for the next war), the English king had relinquished his claim to most of Aquitaine, except for the Gascony region centered on the port of Bordeaux, and agreed to pay homage to the French king, his liege lord. This was not only personally humiliating for the English kings; it also limited their ability to pursue their interests on the European stage (for example, they could not deal too favorably with Flanders, a major trading partner, because they were obliged to support the king of France, who had a frequently hostile relationship with the Flemish). Meanwhile, the English presence in Gascony was also a major irritant to the French crown, which was trying to expand its territory and authority and coveted the riches that the region produced for England. As a result of this standoff over Gascony, the two countries fought several limited conflicts in the decades leading up to the war. One of these was resolved in 1303 with the marriage of King Philip the Fair's daughter, Isabella, to the future King Edward II of England.

This marriage eventually also contributed to the outbreak of war. As we have seen, after the last son of Philip the Fair died without an heir in 1328 (possibly due to a rather effective Templar curse), the French crown passed to the House of Valois, descended from Philip's brother. The great lords of France were happy for the late king's nephew to become King Philip VI. But the king of England at that time, Edward III, felt he had a stronger claim to the throne as a direct descendant of Philip the Fair (he was the eldest son of Isabella, the daughter of Philip). French jurists and nobles rejected Edward's claim to the throne on the grounds that his succession rights came through his mother, and were therefore invalid because women could not inherit the throne. (The decision, designed to resolve this specific succession squabble, set a legal precedent that ensured that no woman ever ruled France in her own name while the monarchy lasted.) Edward did not press his claim too strongly, and so this succession squabble is often seen as more of a justification for England's going to war than a primary driver of it.

The beginning of the Hundred Years' War is conventionally dated to 1337, when Philip VI declared that England had forfeited its right to Gascony by harboring a rebellious French lord named Robert of Artois. The first major battle took place at Crécy, in the north of France, in 1346, and it was a complete disaster for the French. The English were heavily outnumbered and fighting in a hostile land, and yet in what would be a recurring feature of the war, the famous English longbows—and the unwarranted arrogance of the French knights—led to an English victory.

The English army next laid siege to the town of Calais. Their very effective blockade lasted for eleven months, and there would be no magical cassoulet to help the citizens of Calais. Their situation became desperate. People of all classes were reduced to eating not only their horses but also dogs, cats, and rats. In a letter sent to

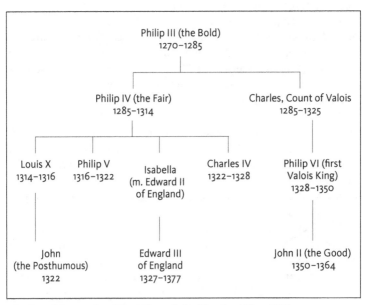

The Royal Succession Squabble and the Hundred Years' War.

the king of France, begging him to come rescue them, the governor of Calais said that "in the town there is no food to be found, unless we eat the flesh of our own people."[2] When the French king finally responded to their plea, his army found that the position of the English was too well defended, and the inhabitants of Calais were abandoned to their fate. They eventually surrendered, and Calais became an English bastion in France until 1558.

This English momentum was temporarily halted by the arrival of the Black Death, a global calamity that we will explore in the next chapter. The following years saw only limited fighting. In France, King Philip VI died and was succeeded by John II (John the Good).

But in 1355, the war picked up again, this time in the southwest of France. The eldest son of the English king, also named Edward, was known as the Black Prince because of the black armor he customarily wore. By the time he was done with the Languedoc, however, his nickname seemed apropos for other reasons.

Most of the victims of the war were not soldiers but the ordinary residents of French towns and rural villages. They were purposefully targeted not only by the brigand companies that emerged with the faltering authority of the crown, but by English forces as well. The English knew that without the food and taxes produced by regions such as the Languedoc, the French could not afford to continue fighting and would have to sue for peace. So a deliberate campaign of destruction was launched from Bordeaux in the fall of 1355, led by the Black Prince himself. He carved a seven-hundred-mile-long swathe of pillage and murder through the southwest of France, finally ending in the Mediterranean port of Narbonne.

This was the campaign that brought the Black Prince and Castelnaudary together. Unfortunately, in real life, the story did not end as nicely as the cassoulet legend would have us believe. The town was actually not besieged at all but taken rather quickly, and the Black Prince's forces departed after only two nights. They burned the town, its castle, and its churches to the ground, killing many of its inhabitants.

The Black Prince led another campaign in the Loire Valley the next year, and at the Battle of Poitiers in September 1356, the English scored another decisive victory. They even managed to capture the French king, and they demanded an enormous ransom of several million gold crowns for him. While he was still prisoner, John II signed a peace treaty with the English, the Treaty of Brétigny (1360), which ended this phase of the war. The terms restored a great amount of land to England (about a third of France), free of the obligation of performing homage. In return, Edward agreed to renounce the French crown. Overall, this first phase of the war was pretty much a disaster for France, and so unsurprisingly the fighting would soon flare up again during the reign of the next French king, Charles V (Charles the Wise).

The Black Prince continued to make his mark in France, now as the Prince of Aquitaine. In 1370, for example, he sacked the rebellious city of Limoges, killing many of its residents and sealing his own reputation for depravity. But in the end, he never ascended the English throne, dying after a long illness in 1376.

Considering the famous reputation of the Black Prince, and the damage his armies inflicted in the southwest, it is not surprising that a false but interesting creation legend of cassoulet was invented there. But it turns out that Castelnaudary has nonetheless a serious claim to be the birthplace of cassoulet. It was in a small nearby village named Issel that, in 1337, an Italian pottery maker set up a workshop and started producing a specific sort of terra-cotta bowl called a cassole. It gave a special flavor to the meat-and-bean stew that the locals cooked, and eventually lent its name to cassoulet. It was not quite the same as the modern version of the dish: one of the oldest recipes for it, in *Le Viandier*, one of the most famous French medieval cookbooks (written by Taillevent, the royal chef for Charles V and Charles VI), emphasizes mutton instead of pork and includes turnips. The white haricot beans that are now a signature ingredient of cassoulet are actually native to South America and did not arrive in France until the sixteenth century.

Cassoulet is now so important in French culture that the government decided it should be protected by legislation, and there is a law stipulating how much meat should be in canned cassoulet. But the law is silent on the great cassoulet debate. Today, most people tend to follow the conciliatory approach of Prosper Montagné, a famous French cook and writer who created the authoritative gastronomic encyclopedia known as the *Larousse Gastronomique*. He tried to settle the cassoulet war by declaring: "Cassoulet is the God of Occitan cuisine. One God in three persons: God the father is the cassoulet of Castelnaudary, God the son is that of Carcassonne, and the Holy Spirit that of Toulouse."[3] (Montagné wrote this in 1929, when such heretical allegories were much safer to engage in.) Today, cassoulet is made all over the world in nearly endless variations. It's a shame that none of these can actually empower you to rout an English army, but a warm belly full of cassoulet on a winter's evening remains rather enticing nonetheless.

16

The Vinegar of the Four Thieves

Within the average French supermarket, a few aisles are particularly perilous for transplanted expats. Accustomed to quickly choosing from a limited choice of, say, mustard or table salt or fresh yogurt, the seemingly endless varieties enjoyed by the French can prove confounding. If you come across a slack-jawed, vacant-eyed person in the cheese section at Carrefour, they are probably just trying to decide between fifty types of Camembert.

The vinegar aisle is another maze of new delights. Not here the spare display of red wine, white wine, balsamic, and malt varieties. In France, vinegar—which after all comes from *vinaigre,* or "sour wine"—is a much more interesting and diversified product. You will find it infused with herbs, fruits, or nuts, or given an extra kick by garlic or shallots. Balsamic vinegar is available in its original version or *velours,* a softer and thicker version. White balsamic vinegar is a very popular alternative. And vinegar also reigns in the cleaning aisles, which is unsurprising when you discover that most French people consider white vinegar an essential product for the home, regularly chucking it into washing machines, dishwashers, and kettles. If you're ever faced with a really unpleasant and stubborn mess in your house, a good first step is to throw some white vinegar on it (however disconcerting this may make your next encounter with salad dressing).

Yet one popular variety of vinegar, known as "four thieves vinegar," is not usually found in the standard French supermarket. It is a folk remedy, made at home, with a rather macabre legend attached to it—one that helps illuminate one of the most disastrous eras in French history.

The year 1347 was definitely a dark one for France. After losing the town of Calais to the English in the summer, the fall brought a much more devastating invasion in the south of France. At that time people called it *la peste* (the pestilence). Today, it is known to us as the Black Death, a near-apocalyptic outbreak of bubonic plague. By the time it ebbed five years later, a third of the population of France lay dead.[1]

Historians and epidemiologists continue to debate nearly every facet of the Black Death, but today it is generally thought that the plague originated in China and encroached upon Europe via the Caspian Sea region. It might have stalled there were it not for the great transformations shaping this period of early modernity in Europe. The development of markets, trading networks, currencies—all the precursors of modern capitalism—was accompanied by the building of large commercial fleets and merchant companies. With rapid population growth, the countryside was becoming more settled, and trade routes extended farther and farther into the interior. All these factors made epidemics more common, as people had higher levels of human contact, across longer distances, and as yet no understanding of bacteria and disease. Plagues were thought to be an act of divine punishment.

In actuality, the bacterium that causes bubonic plague, *Yersinia pestis*, invaded the human population in the fourteenth century via the fleas living on infected rats. As trade ships plied the waters around Europe in ever greater numbers, they were the perfect dispersal tool for plague, a deadly cargo of infected rats stowed unknowingly within their hulls.

It is thought that the disease traveled westward from the Caspian region in late 1346, after Mongol forces laid siege to a Genoese trading station at Kaffa, in Crimea. Decimated by plague, their siege failing, the Mongol attackers were said to have catapulted some of their dead into the town. When the merchants finally fled Kaffa in May 1347, it appears they brought a most unfortunate passenger with them. That summer, plague laid waste to Constantinople, before beginning its spread through the major Mediterranean trading towns.

The Black Death arrived in France through the great port of Marseille, where more than fifty thousand people died within a few weeks.[2] It spread north up the Rhône Valley to Lyon, and westward along the Mediterranean coast, ravaging the Languedoc. It followed the ancient trading routes up to Bordeaux, at that time one of the most important trade ports in Europe. From here, the plague spread easily to northern France, England, and beyond.

The plague scoured Europe with unprecedented savagery and rapidity. It tended to burn out within each locale in about a year, but in that short period of time, it might carry off a third or even half of the population. A healthy person could be infected and die within days. Contemporary descriptions of the symptoms are chilling: high fever, nausea, hallucinations, and hard swellings, or buboes, in the groin or armpit. Only a lucky few survived the disease. Its high mortality and evident agony terrified people so much that they often abandoned infected family members, even their own children. People died in such great numbers that they were tossed into mass graves. Social conventions withered under the sustained assault of death and despair: some people succumbed to all possible vices, approaching every day as if it were their last, while others embraced extreme levels of religious piety. A group of religious zealots known as the Flagellants, for example, traveled from town to town whipping themselves, trying to atone for the sins of mankind.

While many assumed the plague was some sort of heavenly curse, some people looked for more earthly scapegoats. Across Europe, thousands of Jews were tortured and killed, accused of intentionally causing the plague by poisoning wells. In Strasbourg, for example, nearly a thousand Jews were burned to death on Saint Valentine's Day 1349, before the plague had even arrived in the city. (The confiscation of their assets reveals the mercenary motives that also drove these pogroms.) Their deaths did not spare the city from pestilence, of course: more than sixteen thousand people subsequently died in Strasbourg.[3]

Over the next five years, the plague gradually enveloped much of Europe and Asia. Mortality rates varied considerably, but at least 30 percent, and perhaps even 50 percent, of the population of Europe died in this very short period of time. The plague reappeared five more times that century, albeit at somewhat less disastrous levels (the 1361 outbreak "only" killed 10 to 20 percent of the population). In part because of these and other epidemics, the population of Europe would not return to pre-1347 levels until the sixteenth century. Plague recurred with less and less frequency, but serious outbreaks continued to afflict Europe into the eighteenth century.

Over the years, the initial certitude that the plague was divinely inflicted began to yield to more secular (if still incorrect) theories, and these led people to adopt wide-ranging changes in personal behavior—including their diet. During the Black Death, the plague very obviously began in the coastal regions before moving inland, so many people believed some kind of contamination of the sea was to blame and stopped eating fish. Others noted that the plague followed the major trade routes, correctly identifying ships as an important mechanism in its spread, and began to shun spices and other imported foods. A host of folk remedies emerged as well, with people strapping live chickens or garlic around their buboes, or placing their last hopes in potions such as theriac (an ancient and expensive medicine containing snake flesh, opium, and dozens of spices, herbs, and plants).[4] Only much later did more reliable public health measures begin to be put in place, such as quarantines. In the early 1500s, Nostradamus—then a French doctor, many years before he wrote his occult prophecies—employed a "rose pill," a herbal lozenge made of rosehips, in successfully treating many plague victims, but it is likely his progressive insistence on hygiene was the actual key to his success.

During the Black Death, most doctors, not having any recourse to germ theory or other modern medical doctrine, regularly dispensed culinary advice instead. Their theories and practices were still heavily influenced by the works of classical Greek doctors, notably Hippocrates and Galen (whose advice for avoiding plague, *Cito, longe, tarde* (Leave quickly, go far away, come back slowly), could not really be improved upon even a thousand years later). The classical theory of disease began with the belief that the human body was composed of four elements (fire, air, earth, and water), four elementary qualities (hot, cold, moist, and dry), and four humors, or fluids (black bile, yellow bile, blood, and phlegm). An imbalance of humors left the body susceptible to disease, but balance could be restored by methods both benign (changes in diet) and unpleasant (leeching and purging). Thus, because a body that was mainly hot and moist had a higher risk of catching the plague, it was important to eat food that had cold and dry qualities, like roasted meat and bread.[5] Some herbs and spices were advisable (although not those on the hot end of the scale), but most fruits should be avoided.

By far the ultimate cold and dry ingredient was vinegar, which was deployed in a variety of ways against the plague. It was added to sauces or sprinkled on main dishes, and it was a key ingredient in popular plague "cures." People also washed their hands in vinegar and dribbled it around their homes. Breathing through a cloth dipped in vinegar was thought to offer protection against the miasma, or bad air, from which many contagious diseases were thought to originate.

Folk remedies such as these are fertile ground for legends, and here we come to the origins of four thieves vinegar in this early modern plague era. This vinegar is infused with a number of herbs, spices, and aromatics—everything from garlic and camphor to rosemary, lavender, and sage. Its name stems from its origin myth: during a plague outbreak in France, four thieves who were relieving the dead of their possessions were caught and brought before a judge, who at first sentenced them to the pyre. But he couldn't help notice that the four thieves looked surprisingly healthy considering their close professional contact with the dead bodies of the infected, and he made a deal with them: if they would share their secret, they would be hanged instead of burned, a much less painful death. The thieves confessed their infused-vinegar recipe, claiming to have coated their bodies with it before going about their work, and insisted this was what kept them alive.

Vinegar was already seen as a healthful ingredient for many other afflictions, and for a long time in the Middle Ages apothecaries and vinegar makers were closely linked professions, sharing the same guild. People who use four thieves vinegar today, in our mostly plague-free times, swear that it will disinfect wounds, get rid of lice, and cure mouth ulcers. It is also said to help with headaches and breathing problems.

But for the most part, vinegars are mainly used today for salad dressings. The classic vinaigrette dressing consists of oil and vinegar, usually with added mustard and herbs. In England today, it is called French dressing, possibly thanks to the efforts of an eighteenth-century French exile named d'Albignac. Brillat-Savarin tells us that d'Albignac was dining one night at a London restaurant when he was asked by a neighboring table if he would be so kind as to dress their salads (the French at that time enjoying a sterling reputation for their salad dressing skills). He obliged, and the result was so delicious that he was asked to repeat his feat at a society dinner. Eventually, he became known as "the fashionable salad maker," traveling from house to house with a servant carrying his mahogany suitcase full of ingredients, whipping up delightful salads for the upper classes. He amassed a considerable fortune, enabling him to finally return to France in comfort.[6]

Unfortunately, while vinegar may have saved d'Albignac from poverty, it did not save France from the plague. But it must be said that not all of the long-lasting consequences of the plague were negative. The drastic reduction in the labor force severely disrupted feudal arrangements: landowners had to start paying wages to those who were left to work their lands. In the cities, artisans and other workers could also demand higher wages and better working conditions. Increasingly, members of the Third Estate were able to buy land and property, their living standards rose, and new pathways of social mobility began to appear. When the upper classes tried to impose a return to previous arrangements, popular revolts ensured that the new conditions stayed in place. Thus, the Black Death is often seen as an important contributor to the erosion of feudalism in the early modern era.

The plague also undermined the strength of the Catholic Church in France, already facing much criticism due to perceived corruption during this period of the Avignon papacy. While many people clung fiercely to their faith when the plague initially hit, it quickly became evident that prayer and rectitude did not deter the implacable pestilence. Many clergy died, and religious rituals around death were abandoned in the face of such massive losses. Many people turned away from the Church, embracing mysticism and the occult, or more private forms of Christian worship, or even agnosticism. This weakening of the Church's stranglehold on the population's worldview was an important precursor to the Reformation and Renaissance eras yet to come.

And finally, the Black Death had a temporary impact on the eating habits of the French people. Initially, the collapse of agricultural production and trade meant high levels of food scarcity. But as the plague receded, leaving behind a smaller population that could demand higher wages, there was a certain amount of leveling in the eating habits of the upper and lower classes. Peasants could now afford to eat wheat bread and more meat, just like the nobles. But this more egalitarian way of eating did not last for very long. As we shall see, the upper classes rapidly set about finding new ways of differentiating themselves from the common people, and the dining table would once again become a notable front in the class struggle.

17

The Cheese of Emperors and Mad Kings

One of the jewels of French gastronomy, Roquefort is matured in mountain caves around the tiny village of Roquefort-sur-Soulzon in the remote south of France, on the vast and timeless limestone plateau known as the Causse du Larzac. This strong and salty blue cheese, the second most popular cheese in France (after Comté), may be more than two thousand years old. According to the local legend of its creation, a lovestruck shepherd abandoned his lunchtime meal of cheese and bread in a mountain cave one day in order to chase after a pretty maiden. When he returned sometime later, he found the bread and cheese had turned moldy and blue. In a further demonstration of impulsiveness, he ate a bit of the cheese and found it to be delicious, and thus the unique caves of the Combalou Rock became home to a world-renowned cheesemaking industry. Today, only cheese aged in these caves can be legitimately called Roquefort.

From the start, Roquefort enjoyed the favor of the elite. According to another folktale, Julius Caesar himself was a big fan of the cheese, which he discovered after conquering Gaul around 50 B.C.E. Another legend claims that Charlemagne encountered Roquefort—or, at least, a blue cheese that sounds very much like Roquefort—while stopping over at a bishop's residence in the south of France on his way back from fighting in Spain. It was a day of fasting, and as the bishop could not give the emperor a proper feast with meat, he gave him some of the prized local cheese. It was very moldy, which must have been a discouraging sight to Charlemagne, but being a good guest he said nothing and started picking out the blue moldy parts. The bishop protested, "No, you've got it all wrong—you are throwing away the best bits!" Having already conquered much of Europe, Charlemagne could not let a small chunk of cheese defeat him, and so he ate all of it and loved it so much that he ordered the bishop to send him wagonloads of that cheese every year.

But perhaps the most important royal figure in the history of

Roquefort was the colorful King Charles VI, also known as Charles le Fou, or Charles the Mad. His reputation for madness derived not from his love of Roquefort—no one in France is considered crazy for eating moldy cheese, after all—but from his erratic behavior during the height of the Hundred Years' War, which picked up again once the ravages of the Black Death receded.

The unfortunate King John II (John the Good), who died in English captivity after signing a treaty giving away a third of France, was succeeded by his son Charles V (Charles the Wise). Over the next fifteen years, France gained the upper hand in the war, taking advantage of clever new tactics and leadership to reclaim most of the territory it had yielded. But in 1380, Charles the Wise died and was succeeded by his eleven-year-old son, Charles VI. His reign as Charles the Mad would last more than forty years, during which France was nearly torn apart by civil war and English military victories.

The first signs of Charles's madness appeared in 1392, when he was marching to war against the rebellious Bretons. A crazed man on the side of the road told him not to ride any farther, because he had traitors in his midst. It must have affected the king quite strongly, because later that day he suddenly turned on his own soldiers and friends, shouting, "Attack the traitors, they want to hand me to my enemies!" Before he could be restrained, he had killed four people. This was the first of the forty-four bouts of madness that he would suffer in his lifetime.

Each bout lasted between three and nine months, leading to the modern medical conjecture that he suffered from schizophrenia. He would suddenly not remember his family or who he was. He might howl like a wolf or insist that he was made of glass.[1] Eventually, the madness would fade and sanity would return for a few months. But inevitably, Charles would succumb to his illness yet again.

Naturally, this created a huge problem in terms of running the country and waging the war against the English (luckily, there were long periods of truce). It became clear that Charles would have to rule mainly as a figurehead. But then who should hold the real reins of power? For the next fifteen years, the powerful dukes of Burgundy and Orléans vied for control of the crown, and their struggle finally erupted in civil war in 1407. The Duke of Burgundy eventually allied himself with Henry V, the king of England and archenemy of France.

Henry V is most famous today, of course, for his miraculous

victory at Agincourt in 1415, and for the marvelous Saint Crispin's Day speech that Shakespeare later created on his behalf ("We few, we happy few, we band of brothers . . . "). After defeating the French forces at Agincourt, he reconquered Normandy, while the Burgundians wrested control of Paris. The heir to the throne, the dauphin, who was allied to the Orléans faction, fled Paris and set up a rival court at Bourges, in central France. His political authority and territorial control were limited, and the victorious Burgundians derisively called him the "king of Bourges."

This disparagement bit even deeper when the dauphin was officially disinherited by his father in 1420, after the king agreed to the Treaty of Troyes with the English. Charles's daughter Catherine married Henry V, and he became the French king's son-in-law and new heir. It was the high point of English success in the Hundred Years' War: they and their Burgundian allies now held half of France and were in line to inherit the French throne when the mad king died. But in the end, things did not quite turn out as expected. Henry V died a few months before Charles VI, in 1422, setting in motion a new battle for the French crown. The dauphin, with a little help from a lady named Joan, would eventually become the king of much more than Bourges. But we will come to their story in the next chapter.

In the end, Charles the Mad's reign was a complete disaster for France. But the mad king did do one incredibly sane thing during his reign: in 1411, he granted the inhabitants of Roquefort the sole right to mature their particular cheese, in what is seen as the earliest historical effort at an AOC-style geographical delimitation. Through the following centuries, French monarchs renewed the royal protection of the cheese. Anyone producing a similar blue cheese ran the risk of royal sanction should they try to pass it off as Roquefort.

Nevertheless, by the nineteenth century, Roquefort producers grew increasingly worried about counterfeit products undermining their cheese's reputation. In the postrevolutionary era, royal proclamations no longer offered much protection. And once railways and refrigeration allowed cheeses to travel further distances and be enjoyed by more people, it became clear to local producers that if others could make an ordinary blue cheese and give it the legendary Roquefort label, they were doomed. So they were overjoyed when, in

1925, Roquefort became the first cheese to receive an AOC, dictating how and where it can be made. The AOC controls not just the location and means of production, but things like the breed of sheep whose milk is used and where they can graze. Any cheese that does not meet these strict criteria cannot be called Roquefort.

And yet the reputation of Roquefort is so exalted that many cannot help but attach it to any generic blue cheese product. Many Americans will have encountered the option of "Roquefort dressing" or "Roquefort sauce" when dining out, for example, but such concoctions are often made with a domestic Roquefort substitute. One should always look closely when buying Roquefort, to be sure the small print does not in fact clarify it to be "Roquefort-style."

Even more distressing is the way in which Roquefort has at times been caught up in diplomatic squabbles. Infuriated by European bans on American beef containing hormones, the United States has at times retaliated by leveling punishing tariffs on Roquefort. In 2009, in the closing days of the George W. Bush administration— not the happiest of times for Franco-American relations—an astonishing 300 percent import tax was imposed on Roquefort, making it all but unavailable in the United States. This was soon reversed, but another hurdle arose in 2014, when the FDA effectively banned Roquefort and a number of other French cheeses, claiming they contained potentially harmful levels of bacteria (a ghastly notion, easily repudiated by the millions of French people who have survived their encounters with these dangerous cheeses). New inspection regimes allowed Roquefort to trickle into the United States once again, but it remains a very expensive product. When one considers how far the love of moldy blue cheese has spread, from its tiny homeland deep inside a remote French mountain to the tables of the world, it seems altogether despicable—downright *mad*—that anyone should try to interfere with the consumption of this king of cheeses.

18

La Dame de Beauté and the Mushroom Mystery

Mushroom hunting, or *la chasse aux champignons*, is a serious and often competitive endeavor in France. Many people go every fall like clockwork, carefully guarding the location of their best mushroom patches. (If you see someone out in the woods with a flashlight in the wee hours in September, they are probably not disposing of some criminal evidence, just trying to get their share of mushroom treasure.) There are several thousand varieties of wild mushrooms in France, but most are poisonous, like the *calice de la mort* (death cap) mushroom, a single one of which can kill you. Luckily, French pharmacists are trained to identify poisonous mushrooms, so if you pick up some souvenir fungi on your woodland picnic, you can pop into your local *pharmacie* afterward and find out whether they are safe to eat.

French people also love to eat the indisputably harmless varieties of cultivated mushrooms, such as *champignons de Paris* (commonly known as button mushrooms), the most popular mushroom variety in the world. They are called *de Paris* because after the formal cultivation of mushrooms began in France in the 1600s, Paris and the surrounding regions became a popular production site. This includes the eastern Loire Valley, which is lined with hundreds of miles of caves, the scars of extensive quarrying for the beautiful white stone used to build the Loire's fabulous châteaus and cities. These ghostly caverns have been transformed into all sorts of subterranean attractions—you can stay in a four-star troglodyte hotel, dine in an underground restaurant, or even live in a cave dwelling year-round—but most delicious of all are the mushroom caves, from which tons of handpicked mushrooms emerge every year. In the small but very charming town of Le Puy-Notre-Dame near Saumur, for example, you can visit a family-run mushroom cave and learn about the history of Loire mushroom culture (and, of course, buy some mushrooms for the road). The even larger Musée du Champignon in nearby Saint-Hilaire-Saint-Florent offers several levels of underground mushroom exploration and frequent tasting events.

It cannot be said that mushrooms were always a popular element of French cuisine. They could kill you, after all, and until relatively recently they only grew in the wild, so they were an unpredictable harvest. Their earthiness placed them low on the medieval food hierarchy, and they were thought to produce unhealthy humors. But mushrooms grew increasingly popular beginning in the sixteenth century, and Louis XIV's taste for them cemented their status in French cuisine a century later. The father of modern agronomy, Olivier de Serres, pioneered methods of cultivating mushrooms in the seventeenth century, which made them a more favorable crop. So by the time the great Auguste Escoffier published his *Le Guide culinaire*, one of the bibles of French gastronomy, in 1903, it was not surprising that he included a number of decadent mushroom dishes. Interestingly, a number of them include the name Agnès Sorel: there is the classic *Velouté Agnès Sorel*, a gorgeous cream soup of mushrooms and chicken, as well as *Suprême de Volaille Agnès Sorel*, a rich dish of chicken, mushrooms, and ox tongue in Madeira sauce. Escoffier enjoyed naming his dishes after famous women; his Peach Melba, for example, was named after the famous singer Dame Nellie Melba. But who was Agnès Sorel? What did she have to do with mushrooms? As it happens, the first question is not too difficult, and the answer helps reveal how the Hundred Years' War finally came to an end. The second question, however, is a bit more complicated.

As France and England staggered into the final phase of the Hundred Years' War, things looked rather gloomy for Charles, the disinherited dauphin holed up in Bourges in the Loire Valley. The English and their Burgundian allies held Paris and the northern half of France, and it appeared entirely unlikely that Charles would ever claim the throne he had been born to. He seemed to lack the usual kingly qualities, being neither particularly charismatic nor intelligent. He began to doubt his own legitimacy and seemed very indolent and discouraged. In the end, it took two diametrically opposed women to transform this mopey little king of Bourges into Charles VII (Charles the Victorious), who went on to rule France for nearly forty years. The first of these women, Saint Joan of Arc, is one of the most famous figures in history. But the second woman, our Agnès de Sorel, remains little known outside France today. Her scandalous relationship with the king made her notorious in her own time, and facilitated her lasting mark on French gastronomy. If Joan of Arc was a saint, Agnès de Sorel was the devil in the flesh.

Briefly, for those who skipped their history lessons, Joan of Arc was a young girl who claimed to hear the voices of saints telling her to help Charles, the dauphin, reconquer his kingdom. Although the French people were deeply religious at that time, and firmly believed that France was God's chosen kingdom, it shows just how desperate Charles's cause was that Joan was believed to be an actual messenger of God. Yet they were rewarded for their faith: in 1429, a French army with Joan at its head drove the English away from Orléans, the last French-held city north of the Loire. Joan claimed victory in nine of the thirteen military engagements that followed; several dozen towns surrendered to her without a fight, so daunting was her reputation. Finally, she secured the city of Reims, the traditional coronation site for the French kings, and fulfilled her sacred mission by seeing the dauphin crowned as Charles VII.

Unfortunately for Joan, she was captured by the Burgundians the following year and then ransomed by the English, who burned her as a witch in 1431 in Rouen. Unlike many French heroic figures, Joan is not much celebrated in the gastronomic realm—perhaps unsurprisingly, as a warrior-saint with highly ascetic tendencies.

Joan helped turn the tide of the war in favor of the French. The Burgundians eventually abandoned the English and allied themselves with Charles, who recaptured Paris in 1436. Successful campaigns were fought in both Normandy and Gascony, reclaiming French towns and territory. Then in 1444, fighting was suspended for five years by the Truce of Tours. It was during this time that Agnès de Sorel appeared on the historical stage.

Agnès was probably born in 1422, to a family of minor nobility. In 1443, she caught the king's attention at court, and Charles was immediately smitten with the young woman. It seems the king found his court a bit dull, and Agnès's beauty, intelligence, and wit enlivened it immensely. Pope Pius II, a great chronicler of events in his day, wrote of Charles and Agnès: "He fell so much in love that he could not even spend an hour without her. Whether at table, in bed, at council, she was always by his side."[1] (Charles's queen, Marie of Anjou, was busy bearing and raising their fourteen children.) Charles remained devoted to Agnès until her death, showering her with wealth, and she became the first official mistress of a French king. Most notably, he endowed her with a royal castle near Vincennes named Château de Beauté, and she thus acquired the moniker *la Dame de Beauté* (the lady of beauty).

The king's public recognition of his mistress was hugely scandalous, and Agnès only enhanced her notoriety with her penchant for daring fashions that often left her magnificent bosom exposed. In the most famous portrait of Agnès, by Jean Fouquet, she is depicted as the Virgin Mary holding the infant Jesus, one breast exposed as if about to nurse him. The "breastfeeding Madonna" was a popular artistic trope at the time, and the choice of Agnès as model was justified by her reputation as the most beautiful woman in France. But it was still quite an insult to the queen, who would normally have been associated with Mary, the "queen of heaven."

Yet Agnès was much more than a source of scandal. She was a natural diplomat, said to have used her charm and wit to help the king navigate his fractious court. She took full advantage of her official status, establishing a template for the subtle exercise of power that a number of future royal mistresses would draw upon. She has been credited with transforming Charles from a lackluster king into the more vigorous and accomplished monarch who tamed the nobility and successfully reformed the French state. And according to some accounts of the time, it was Agnès who encouraged the king to renew his war against the English by telling him that when she was a young girl, an astrologer had predicted that she would be loved by the most valiant and courageous king of Christendom—and how could that be Charles, when he allowed the English to continue to occupy French territory? Perhaps Agnès was meant to be the consort of the English king instead.

Whatever the accuracy of this vignette, it is true that war resumed in 1449. The following year, Charles reclaimed Normandy, as the French outperformed the English in the gradual transition to gunpowder and cannons in warfare. The last hurdle was the conquest of Gascony, the territory in western France at the heart of so many decades of bloodshed. But finally, in 1453, after the French victory in the Battle of Castillon and the surrender of Bordeaux, the Hundred Years' War came to an end.[2] England retained Calais, but otherwise France was the clear victor, both in terms of territory reclaimed and the much more powerful monarchy that emerged. France was becoming an ever-larger and more centralized state, with the crown levying taxes across the whole of French territory and using those taxes to field a professional army.

Unfortunately, Agnès never saw the end of the conflict. In 1450, she died under suspicious circumstances, shortly after the birth of her fourth child. At the time, many thought she was poisoned—perhaps even by the resentful heir to the king, the future Louis XI. (According to one persistent legend, the dauphin took advantage of her love for *pain d'épices*, or gingerbread, and slyly poisoned a slice.) Indeed, recent scientific research on the remains of Agnès show that she died of mercury poisoning, at such high levels that the dosage was unlikely to have been medicinal.[3] The culprit, however, remains a mystery.

Agnès's short but dramatic life ensured her long-lasting fame, at least in her native France. And it is perhaps not very surprising that her name should be attached to charming and decadent dishes by chefs such as Escoffier, especially given her own attention to the art of culinary seduction. Agnès was known as a gourmand and spent considerable time in the kitchen. She hired renowned chefs and organized sumptuous feasts in the Château de Beauté. She is credited with inventing two enduring dishes, *Agnès Sorel timbales* (minced chicken and truffles in pastry, served with Madeira sauce) and *woodcock salmis* (roasted woodcock with a sauce of cognac, red wine, truffles, and mushrooms).

However, there is no evidence she created or even ate the numerous other dishes that bear her name today—and even more curious, there is no apparent reason why all of these dishes include mushrooms. Nothing indicates that Agnès was a special fan of mushrooms, which were not very popular at that time.

Yet there is no doubt that the addition of mushrooms to these particular recipes, already suffused with cognac and cream and wine, gives the dishes a warm, earthy depth of deliciousness. And it cannot be denied that mushrooms inspire a lusty enthusiasm among the French people, whether they acquire their favorites in dim forests, quiet caves, or bustling markets. So perhaps the association of mushrooms and *la Dame de Beauté* is an apt one, another example of how even common foods are elevated in France to superlative realms of appreciation.

19

Fruits of the Renaissance

As if the Hundred Years' War had not provided enough excitement for Europe, the century following its conclusion featured a frenzy of monumental historical events. The cultural and intellectual innovations of the Renaissance blossomed across the continent, as scholars and artists harnessed the inquisitive spirit of antiquity and cast aside moribund medieval traditions. European sailors found a vast American continent to explore and exploit, and circumnavigated the globe for the first time. The thousand-year-old Byzantine Empire drew its dying breath with the fall of Constantinople to the Turks. Gutenberg's printing press revolutionized the dispersal of knowledge and language to the masses, and Copernicus challenged humankind's existential foundations by insisting the sun did not revolve around the Earth. And, not unrelated to all of these events, the Protestant Reformation challenged the legitimacy and authority of the Catholic Church, spawning a vicious rivalry that left Europe soaked in blood for several centuries.

At some inexact and unheralded moment during this period, the Middle Ages came to an end, and the early modern era began in Europe, especially in France, then its strongest state. To be modern at that time essentially meant believing in human progress. People increasingly challenged ossified political and religious dogma and the medieval assumption that the boundaries of human knowledge were fixed. As new experiments and discoveries began to expand people's understanding of the world and improve their lives, the belief that human reason and ambition could yield an ever-better future began to spread widely. So while many things are associated with modernity, like strong nation-states, market economies, and the scientific revolution, they are all predicated on this gradual yet epochal transformation in how people viewed themselves and the human capacity for improvement.

No single individual better captures this transformative era than Leonardo da Vinci, a man of extraordinary and wide-ranging talents. He was the heart of the Italian Renaissance, producing masterful paintings like the *Mona Lisa* and *The Last Supper* while also inventing marvelous engineering contraptions and creating detailed anatomical studies of the human body. Perhaps less well known is that he spent the last three years of his life in happy residence at a gracious Loire Valley château, at the invitation of one of France's grandest kings. Indeed, the tomb of this Renaissance giant lies there still, on the grounds of the beautiful royal château in Amboise. The manor house he dwelt in is dedicated to his life and legacy, and you can learn here that Leonardo may have been a vegetarian, and that he encouraged moderate consumption of simple meals and watered-down wine to maintain good health.

Amboise conceals other remarkable Renaissance treasures as well. It is here, in the château gardens, that the first orange trees in France bloomed, a thousand years after the Romans first discovered that the citrus fruits of Asia and Africa could be grown on European shores in primitive greenhouses. Initially the trees in Amboise did not actually produce oranges, but cultivating the trees themselves was still considered a great success, and a kingly tradition began of constructing ever more elaborate and productive greenhouses, called orangeries. This competition culminated in the grand Versailles Orangerie, twelve hundred feet long, built for Louis XIV. Louis loved few things

Leonardo da Vinci Park, on the grounds of Château du Clos Lucé in Amboise, features several dozen large replicas of the great artist's drawings and contraptions, including this double-tiered bridge. © Aagje De Jong (Dreamstime Photos).

more than oranges and orange blossoms, and thanks to his orange-rie, he could easily enjoy them year-round. (The average commoner could not do the same until the twentieth century.) Today, France produces very few oranges compared to its southern neighbors, but they are a well-loved fruit. The French often end a satisfying evening meal not with an elaborate chocolate dessert but with a simple orange, peeled at the table.

Indeed, if one seeks the cradle of the French Renaissance, it is in Amboise and the Loire Valley that one must look. In the fifteenth and sixteenth centuries, the French kings spent much of their time not in Paris but in the beautiful royal palaces that were constructed along what became known as the Valley of Kings. In part, this was a legacy of the Hundred Years' War, and Charles VII's lengthy residence in places like Bourges and Chinon. But it was also a way for the kings to escape the intrigues and dangers of Paris, a city infested with unpredictable mobs and scheming nobles. The Parisians were, in the words of Rabelais, "upon any slight occasion so ready to uproars and insurrections that foreign nations wonder at the patience of the Kings of France."[1]

In the late fifteenth century, King Louis XI, son of Charles VII, installed his wife and heir at Amboise. Louis, who had been forced to endure his father's public dalliance with Agnès de Sorel (and was rumored to have poisoned her), did not permit women to play an influential role in his court. He was a generally unlikable sovereign, nicknamed the "Spider King" for his ruthless and manipulative ways. He was eventually succeeded by his son, Charles VIII, who was widely seen as a physical and mental weakling—and yet, in hindsight, he actually had an enormous impact on the development of France.

When Charles VIII decided to invade Italy in 1494, he could not have known that he was playing a critically important role in easing his country from the medieval to the modern. Yet while his military campaign yielded few lasting advantages—and, in fact, led subsequent French kings down a lengthy and disastrous series of Italian wars for more than half a century—it was his sojourn in Italy that kick-started the French Renaissance. Charles was captivated by the artistic and scholarly innovations he encountered during his march through Italy to the kingdom of Naples, to which he claimed dynastic rights and briefly reclaimed. While in the end he was rather ignominiously chased back across the Alps, he returned to France with a host of Italian artisans, architects, and gardeners, determined to replicate their achievements in his homeland. He installed many of them in his childhood home, the château of Amboise.

It was one of these Italian experts, a monk and master gardener named Pacello da Mercogliano, who coaxed those first orange trees to bloom in the Amboise orangerie, the first in northern Europe. A quintessential Renaissance fruit, oranges appeared frequently in the paintings of the Italian Renaissance masters (including Leonardo da Vinci, who placed a somewhat anachronistic dish of eels and oranges on the table of *The Last Supper*). Legend has it that Charles brought a host of other foods back from Italy, from melons to pasta and parmesan, but most of these tales are exaggerated: while the French entanglement in Italy did indeed have a culinary impact, as Italian foods and tastes became fashionable, it is not likely that Charles himself introduced these foods to the French court.

Charles died, rather stupidly, in 1498, after banging his head against a low doorway in the château of Amboise. As he had no living heir, he was succeeded by his cousin, the new King Louis XII (who also promptly married Charles's widow, Anne of Brittany). Louis had a series of disastrous Italian wars of his own; Machiavelli actually cites them at length in *The Prince*, in order to illustrate precisely what a ruler should not do when invading a foreign country. But Louis fared much better domestically and became fondly known as "Father of the People" after enacting some popular reforms. He was very frugal in his habits, including his diet, which was said to consist mostly of boiled beef.

King Louis and Queen Anne continued to encourage the development of Renaissance art and scholarship, but the true "King of the Renaissance" was Louis's cousin and successor, King Francis I. Indeed, the early years of his reign are recounted as among the most splendid in French history, as this young, handsome, and flamboyant king rejuvenated the court. His love of pageantry and pomp was genuine, but it was also a clever means of enhancing his popularity and royal authority. The people thronged to their new young king, especially after his first grand military victory in Italy, at the Battle of Marignano (1515), which brought the duchy of Milan temporarily into the French fold.

After his victory, Francis spent four months in his newly acquired duchy, immersing himself in the radiance of Italian Renaissance culture. It was at this time that he met Leonardo da Vinci, then sixty-four years old. Francis offered him a handsome sum to be First Painter, Engineer, and Architect of the King, an offer Leonardo could not refuse. In 1516, he departed for France, riding a mule over the Alps, the *Mona Lisa* in his baggage.

Francis remained a great patron of Renaissance arts and letters throughout his life. Humanist luminaries such as Guillaume Budé and Clément Marot were great favorites of the king—and of his sister, Margaret, a renowned writer and scholar in her own right, who offered protection to Rabelais when he was condemned by the Church and the Sorbonne. Francis founded the Collège de France, a humanist alternative to the Sorbonne, and devoted many years to building the glorious châteaus of Fontainebleau and Chambord. His personal library later seeded the Bibliothèque Nationale de France, and his art collection now graces Fontainebleau and the Louvre (including the *Mona Lisa*, which he purchased upon Leonardo's death). Much of the credit for this lifetime of artistic patronage must go to the king's mother, Louise of Savoy, who ensured that both her children received a stellar education in humanist literature, foreign languages, and the arts from a young age.

There were limits to Francis's modernity, however. While he initially showed some interest in the arguments of Church reformers, he ultimately rejected the Reformation once it became clear that it represented a political threat to his realm. After the Affair of the Placards, in 1534, when reformist tracts were posted throughout Paris and even on the doors of the king's own residence in Amboise, a brutal crackdown ensued. John Calvin, the most important French reformist theologian (and eventual progenitor of Calvinism), fled to Switzerland, while hundreds of other reformers were burned at the stake as heretics. But the Reformation was not extinguished in France. As we will see, it would eventually consume the country in a bloody decades-long civil war.

Ultimately, Francis remains a very popular French king today because he represents those qualities most celebrated by the French—he was a cultured, glamorous, and chivalrous warrior-king. But in truth, when the French remember him this way, it is mostly the first five years of his reign that come to mind. The subsequent twenty-seven years, in which Francis waged a brutal and disastrous series of wars against his bête noire, Holy Roman Emperor Charles V, are less celebrated. Francis suffered many defeats, one of which led to his imprisonment and near death in Spain, and impoverished his realm.

In the realm of food, Francis is actually slightly outshone by his reclusive, frail yet amiable first wife, Queen Claude, who sadly died young, aged twenty-four, after bearing seven children in eight years. We have already met her namesake, the succulent Reine-Claude plum. It cannot be said whether Francis enjoyed these plums as much as today's gourmands do, but he appreciated his wife's gentle and generous nature just as the public who named the fruit in her honor did (though in his case, mostly because she tolerated his predictably outrageous womanizing).

Francis himself is most often associated with a more obscure French artisanal food product known as Cotignac d'Orléans, a sweet jam made of quince (a hard pearlike fruit, much less commonly eaten today). Originally created by a pastry chef from the southern town of Cotignac who moved to Orléans, it was a medieval delicacy traditionally given to noble visitors to the great Loire city—including Joan of Arc, when she liberated it from the English. For this reason, the bloodred jam is sold in small round wooden boxes that are emblazoned with Joan's likeness. Today only one confectioner still produces Cotignac d'Orléans using the same medieval techniques, in the old village of Saint-Ay, downriver from Orléans. It is delicious eaten on its own, or with a bit of cheese.

Francis was apparently a huge fan of the jam (as was his fictitious contemporary Pantagruel, from the novels of Rabelais). Confectionary of all sorts—from candied spices and fruits to jellies and preserves—became increasingly popular among French nobles during the Valois dynasty, and even more so with the Italian influences of the Renaissance (the Venetians being at the time the undisputed masters of confectionary, thanks to their control of the still-limited supply of sugar into Europe). According to legend, Francis once brought a jar of Cotignac d'Orléans to share with his royal mistress, Anne de Pisseleu, only to discover another man, the Count of Brissac, hiding under her bed. The king left, but not before sliding the quince jam under the bed and exclaiming, "Here you are, Brissac—everyone has to live!"[2]

The Renaissance had a monumental impact upon French culture, but it did not dramatically transform French gastronomy quite yet. As we shall see, the real revolution in French food came later, in the sixteenth and seventeenth centuries, and had much more to do with other epochal changes in the early modern era. But it was still a time of new tastes and discoveries, of a burgeoning human spirit that would eventually lift France to the heights of cultural, intellectual—and indeed, gastronomical—innovation.

20

The Mother Sauces

Sauce (n.): The one infallible sign of civilization and enlightenment. A people with no sauces has one thousand vices; a people with one sauce has only nine hundred and ninety-nine. For every sauce invented and accepted, a vice is renounced and forgiven.

—*Ambrose Bierce,* The Devil's Dictionary *(1906)*

Imagine, if you will, a plateful of perfectly steamed asparagus without a spot of hollandaise, or an expertly cooked steak lacking a side of béarnaise, or a delicate fillet of fish missing its beurre blanc companion. Then again, why imagine such things at all? The French certainly don't, as they are known worldwide for their love of sauces and their great skill in inventing them. The typical French refrigerator features tidy rows of jarred sauces, little gastronomic soldiers ready to be called into action.

Many French sauces have historical legends and heated disputes attached to them. For example, one of the most useful French sauces, béchamel, was created in the seventeenth century, most likely adapted by François-Pierre de La Varenne, one of the most famous chefs of that (or any) era, from an Italian sauce. Years later, the Marquis de Béchameil (or perhaps his cook) tweaked the sauce a bit more and served it to Louis XIV, and managed to attach his name to the sauce in perpetuity. This created a fair bit of controversy at the time, as those who had been using similar versions of the sauce for years felt slighted. The unhappy Duke d'Escars protested, "He is a lucky one, this little Bechamel—I was serving chicken breast with cream twenty years before he was even born."[1]

But one aspect common to nearly all modern French sauces is their emergence after the mid-sixteenth century and the end of the medieval era. While sauces had been part of European cuisine for centuries, many were hardly recognizable as the sauces we know today. The ancient Romans loved a sauce called *garum*, for example, which was basically fermented fish guts. It was very salty and expensive, and one of the few sauces that the Romans used (the habit of lying down for eating made it messy and impractical to be overly saucy).

Sauces were much more popular in medieval France, but still fairly alien to our modern tastes. They were heavily spiced; the popular *poivrade*, for example, was made with black pepper, garlic, and vinegar, while *cameline* sauces included cloves, nutmeg, and ginger. The vibrant yellow *poivre jaunet* sauce was made with saffron and ginger. Exotic spices such as galangal, a gingerlike root from Asia, and peppery "grains of paradise" from West Africa would have been well known to a French chef of the fourteenth century. It is frequently alleged that this overuse of spice was intended to cover up the taste of meat and fish in this pre-refrigeration era, but this theory does not hold up to scrutiny: the kinds of people who could afford these expensive spices could also afford to buy fresh provisions for their table.[2] It is more likely that the heavy use of spices was due to the superior social status and wealth they conveyed, or a genuine belief that they were simply more appealing than domestic European herbs. Medieval palates had far more tolerance for heavily spiced meals, which were believed to be easier to digest, and people were fond of the brightly colored dishes that spices produced.

Medieval sauces were also very acidic, as they relied heavily on vinegar, lemons, and especially *verjus*, or verjuice, made from unripe grapes. Verjuice was probably used in more than half of the sauces at that time, though it was eventually superseded by lemon juice in those sauces requiring a bit of acidity. It did not entirely disappear from French cuisine—the distinctive ingredient in the original recipe for Dijon mustard, for example, was verjuice—but nowadays you would struggle to find verjuice in a typical French supermarket. Like many traditional ingredients, however, it is making something of a comeback of late, as cooks rediscover its usefulness as a slightly less tart substitute for wine and vinegar in sauces, marinades, and salad dressings. In several Middle Eastern cuisines, variants of verjuice have never gone out of fashion, as the enduring appeal of *husrum* in Lebanon, or *ab-ghooreh* in Iran, demonstrates.

Medieval sauces generally did not include fat, whether oil or butter. The most popular cookbooks of the fourteenth century, such as *Le Viandier de Taillevent* and *Le Ménagier de Paris*, use no butter or oil in any of their sauces. But by the seventeenth century, cookbooks such as *L'art de bien traiter* and *La Cuisinière bourgeoise* used butter in more than half their sauces and oil in another 20 percent.[3] This culinary revolution is partly explained by the Protestant challenge to Catholic proscriptions on butter, as well as to a growing inclination within French society toward more natural approaches in the arts and culture generally (butter and oil were thought to be more respectful of the natural taste of food than vinegar and spices). Modern French sauces tend to use an outrageous amount of butter or cream, so much so that one of the first sacrifices a French dieter usually makes is to eliminate sauces from the dining table. A steep price to pay, indeed.

As fats were increasingly added to most sauces, the use of vinegar and verjuice was reduced, and sauces became less acidic. Another important change was the "discovery" of locally produced herbs and vegetables, such as chives, garlic, shallots, and mushrooms, which began to be used in sauces as well. As we have seen, these common garden crops were long enjoyed by the French masses before eventually becoming accepted and popularized by the noble and wealthy classes.

Very gradually, therefore, the spicy-acidic flavors of the medieval era were supplanted by the cream, butter, and herb triumvirate associated with modern French cuisine—not only in sauces but in cooking more generally. During the seventeenth and eighteenth centuries, French chefs gradually abandoned the strong, overwhelming flavors of medieval cooking for a more natural and delicate approach. Local herbs replaced exotic spices, sauces and dressings were designed to enhance rather than overwhelm their underlying dishes, and vegetables were served fresh and crisp rather than boiled beyond recognition. For centuries, it had been culinary tradition to meld many ingredients into complex, artificial fusions; now the preference was for simpler dishes with complementary seasonings, in which the unique flavor of each ingredient could be captured and discerned.

The radical idea that "food should taste like what it is," advocated by prominent early culinary authors like Nicolas de Bonnefons, was partly inspired by broader societal changes associated with moderni-ty.[4] Some argue, for example, that the shift away from heavily spiced foods was due to the scientific revolution and the rise of modern med-ical practices, which discredited the Galenic approach to diet and its emphasis on balancing "humors." Now food could be enjoyed for its taste, not its supposedly medicinal effects. Others argue that spices became less of a luxury product in the latter half of the seventeenth century, following a massive expansion in international trade that made spices less expensive while also introducing unusual foods from newly colonized lands. Once ordinary people were able to cook with formerly noble ingredients, their appeal to the elites faded. The invention of the raised kitchen stove in the early seventeenth century enabled the cooking of sauces and other dishes that required con-stant stirring and impeccable timing, a difficult endeavor when cook-ing was done over hearth fires. Later, the spread of Enlightenment thinking in the eighteenth century led people to search for a more "authentic" lifestyle, in harmony with nature. All of these social changes encouraged the development of a simpler, more natural cui-sine, and this shift was particularly evident in French sauce making.[5]

Another important event in the evolution of French sauces occurred in the early nineteenth century, thanks to a legendary French chef named Marie-Antonin Carême. Carême was born in 1783, one of fif-teen children. At the age of ten, he was abandoned by his father, who told the young lad that he would be better off on his own (as it turned out, this was probably true). Carême found work in a tavern and learned the basics of cooking. At thirteen, he became an apprentice to Monsieur Sylvain Bailly, one of the most renowned patissiers in Paris, who encouraged Carême to study architectural drawings and construct breathtaking pastry creations. Carême's mastery of this art of *pièce montée* brought him considerable renown, and he was eventually discovered by Charles Maurice de Talleyrand-Périgord, the famous diplomat of the Napoleonic era. Talleyrand was keen to use gastronomy as a diplomatic weapon, and Carême became his general, working in his kitchens for twelve years. While cooking for the greatest men in Europe, Carême also began to refine and orga-nize French cuisine, and is thus seen as one of the most pivotal figures in French gastronomy.

Carême sought to bring order to the French sauce universe and decided that there were four basic "mother sauces" from which all other sauces could be derived: allemande, béchamel, espagnole, and velouté. These sauces might be a bit boring on their own, but the idea is that by adding a few ingredients, you can make some far more exciting "daughter sauces." Add Gruyère and egg yolks to béchamel sauce and you have Mornay sauce; add crayfish, brandy, and cream instead and you have Nantua sauce. Bordelaise sauce is nothing more than espagnole sauce with shallots, red wine, and herbs, while Breton sauce is made from adding mushrooms, leeks, and white wine to a velouté. So these four mother sauces can produce an almost endless variety of descendants, each intended to complement the specific dish they accompany (in contrast to earlier eras, where one sauce might be used rather indiscriminately with all sorts of differently flavored dishes). Talleyrand may have been inspired by Carême when he reportedly said, "England has three sauces and three hundred religions, whereas France has three religions and three hundred sauces."[6]

If you cook a bit, you may notice that all these sauces use a roux, a butter-and-flour mix that thickens the sauce, and so you may be wondering how to derive a flourless hollandaise or béarnaise from them. These sauces actually arrived later in French history, thanks to another famous chef whom we have already met, Auguste Escoffier. In the twentieth century, he decided to update the sauce categories and stated that there were *five* mother sauces. He added hollandaise and tomato sauce to the existing list and demoted allemande sauce (German sauce) to a derivative of espagnole sauce. Escoffier may not have been overly enamored of Germany, as he was a prisoner of war there in 1870. He did cook, however, for Kaiser Wilhelm II, who is reported to have been so delighted with his meal that he told him: "I am the Emperor of Germany, but you are the Emperor of Chefs."[7]

Finally, despite the tyranny of butter in French sauce making, we might remember that the French are also world famous for a sauce that uses no butter at all—mayonnaise, which relies on oil instead. There are many legends about the creation of mayonnaise, but the most often cited claims that it was invented after the French capture of the Spanish port of Mahón, on Minorca, in 1756. The Duke of Richelieu, who was in charge of the French troops, had a feast to celebrate the victory. His cook wanted to make a sauce of eggs and cream, but as he couldn't find cream locally, he used olive oil instead. *Et voilà*, mayonnaise was created!

Sauces are more than just a dollop of flavor on a favorite dish— a whole universe of gastronomic sensibilities resides within those small jars and spoonfuls. From garum to vegan mayo, they offer a

delicious glimpse into the cultural zeitgeist. So it is perhaps not surprising that they transformed so radically during the discoveries and
tumult of the sixteenth and seventeenth centuries, to which we shall
now return.

21

Conquest and Chocolate

The Basque people have dwelt in the shade of the Pyrenees Mountains for centuries, long before their region was sliced and swallowed
by the kingdoms of France and Spain. Much of the French Basque
region (Pays Basque) is rural, with agricultural traditions dating to
the far reaches of local memory. The delicious Ossau-Iraty cheese,
for example, has been made by local shepherds from mountain-
grazing sheep for hundreds of years. Every fall, the famous chili pepper known as *piment d'Espelette*—the only spice to have received a
French AOC—is harvested and hung to dry throughout the small village of Espelette, before being ground into a paprika widely used in
Basque cooking. This ambience of tradition can have the occasional
dark side: the renowned French chef Alain Ducasse was famously
chased out of the Basque countryside in 2007 after his new luxury
resort was greeted with several bomb attacks, apparently by extremists displeased with the exploitation of the Basque region by distant
French elites.

A few miles inland from the glamorous resort of Biarritz lies the
French Basque capital city of Bayonne, an ancient port on the Adour
River estuary that runs into the Bay of Biscay. There are many reasons to visit Bayonne today: its charming and colorful tall houses lining the riverside and medieval streets, the surfeit of fresh seafood and
locally produced Bayonne ham, perhaps even the annual bullfighting
tournament. But probably the most delicious reason to visit Bayonne
becomes clear each year during the Feast of the Ascension, when the
city celebrates Les Journées du Chocolat (the Chocolate Days). For as

it happens, Bayonne is home to one of the oldest artisanal chocolate-making traditions in Europe, and it attracts flocks of sweet-toothed pilgrims today. It is a story that begins with not one but two epochal conquests of the early modern era.

Given the French love for chocolate—evident in everything from the workaday *pain au chocolat* to the decadent and ephemeral chocolate soufflé—you might be forgiven for thinking that chocolate has ancient roots here. But in fact, chocolate is a relatively new addition to French gastronomy, part of what we now call the Columbian Exchange: the massive ecological transfer of crops, animals, and diseases between the Old World and the New World in the years following Columbus's fateful first voyage to the Caribbean in 1492. Two hundred million years after the continents of Europe, Africa, and the Americas physically drifted apart, human ingenuity and rapacity managed to link their ecosystems and societies together again. It was one of the most earth-shattering transformations in human history: communication and exchange finally extended around the globe, entire populations were wiped out or enslaved, and European colonialism propelled its states to world dominance. It was an era of unrivaled discovery and profit, as well as unimaginable suffering and destruction.

The first century of European colonization was driven largely by the desire to find new trade routes, either eastward or westward, to the spice-producing regions of South Asia and the Far East. New shipping routes around the African continent helped Spain, Portugal, England, and Holland amass immense fortunes. Initially, their ships only added to the existing spice trade, accommodating the increasing demand in Europe, but over time these nations began to forcefully colonize the spice lands and control production as well as trade. It was a pivotal shift in the world economy, overturning centuries of East-West trade patterns. But the French did not play a major role in the global spice trade during the 1500s, as they were too consumed by religious wars and European conflicts to engage in significant globe-trotting, and when they did begin to establish permanent colonies, it was in spice-poor locales like Canada.[1]

Westward sea voyages brought the Europeans not to the Spice Islands, as they had hoped, but to the American continent, an encounter that generated a profound and lasting impact on their respective societies and gastronomies. Without this continental exchange, Italy would not know tomatoes, nor Ireland potatoes; the Americas would be free of wheat, sugar, and oranges. (Indeed, Espelette would not know its famous *piment*.) The pace at which new foods from the Americas were adopted in Europe was varied, with somewhat familiar crops (like corn) and animals (like turkeys) being quickly adopted, while others, like the potato, took far longer to make any deep impression. The stranger the food, the longer it took to catch on. So it is perhaps not surprising that chocolate, which really had no equivalent, took more than a century to find favor.

Chocolate is derived from the pods of the cacao tree, indigenous to the Yucatán Peninsula and enjoyed by Mesoamerican civilizations for centuries before the arrival of European ships. It was ingested only as a drink, and usually heavily spiced. When Hernán Cortés and the Spanish conquistadores invaded the Yucátan in 1519, the Aztec emperor Montezuma decided on a diplomatic approach, and invited Cortés and his entourage for an extended stay in Tenochtitlan, his capital city. Thus the Spanish first encountered the bitter and spicy taste of chocolate, which they did not initially enjoy, although they noted its invigorating properties. Soon enough, diplomatic niceties failed, and the Spanish set about destroying the powerful Aztec civilization and plundering its wealth. Their superior weaponry and alliances with Aztec rivals led to victory within two years, and in the following decades, European microbes killed off 50 to 80 percent of the local population. In 1523, Cortés became the first governor of the colony of New Spain, and the Spanish systematically and ruthlessly brought much of Central and South America under their rule.

In the ensuing decades, Spanish colonists in Mexico tinkered with the native chocolate drink and found that adding sugar and vanilla (another local ingredient) made it much more pleasing to the European palate.[2] By 1600, chocolate had become a profitable trade good, and it soon conquered the hearts of the Spanish nobility (it was far too expensive for anyone but the wealthy classes to enjoy on a regular basis). Chocolate became so popular in Spain that it inspired Honoré de Balzac (who was more of a coffee addict) to later ask: "Who knows if the abuse of chocolate is not somehow responsible for the debasement of the Spanish nation, which, at the moment of the discovery of chocolate, was about to start a new Roman Empire?"[3] Indeed, after colonizing huge swathes of the world in the sixteenth century, Spain eventually was overtaken in the imperial race by the British, Dutch, and French.

It took a while longer for chocolate to make an impression in France. Its initial introduction, in fact, was the result of another sort of conquest: the Reconquista of Spain. The Islamic state of Al-Andalus, one of Europe's strongest and most enlightened states during the "dark ages," began to fragment and fall victim to Christian invaders in the eleventh century. By the mid-thirteenth century, Granada was the last remaining Islamic emirate on the Iberian Peninsula. In 1492, the same year that Columbus wandered ashore in America, his royal patrons King Ferdinand and Queen Isabella finally conquered Granada and "reclaimed" Spain for Christianity. In a diabolical encore, they expelled the entire Jewish population of Spain, numbering hundreds of thousands of people. As the fearsome Spanish Inquisition scoured the Iberian Peninsula, the neighboring kingdom of Portugal gradually banished its Jewish population as well. These Sephardic Jewish communities scattered around the known world, but many of them relocated just over the Pyrenees into southwestern France, where they continued to play an important role in the trade of products from the New World.

Most notably, a number of Portuguese Jews resettled in Bayonne and introduced the art of chocolate making. In the Saint-Esprit neighborhood, which became the Sephardic Jewish quarter of Bayonne, they imported cacao beans from the Americas and then roasted, ground, and mixed them with spices, vanilla, and sugar, creating a divine chocolate drink. For a century, chocolate making was one of the most prominent livelihoods for Bayonne's Jews, but eventually the secrets of their craft became more widely known, and they were banned from the chocolate business by the city's Christian leadership in 1691. Despite these frequent discriminatory measures, Bayonne's Jewish community maintained an important role in trade and commerce, contributing significantly to local prosperity for several centuries, before being all but destroyed during the Holocaust in the twentieth century.

The chocolate-making tradition is well preserved in Bayonne in places like its Basque Museum, or at l'Atelier du Chocolat, a working chocolate factory and shop in Saint-Esprit. The city's tourist office offers chocolate-themed tours. Wander the medieval quarter in the shadow of Bayonne's Gothic Cathedral of Saint Mary, and you'll find a number of artisanal chocolatiers still using traditional recipes; ask for a *chocolat mousseux*, a frothy hot drink of South American cocoa, milk from local Basque dairies, and vanilla or cinnamon (it may ruin ordinary hot chocolate for you forever, but it's well worth it). And, of course, the annual Chocolate Days are a fabulous opportunity to watch local chocolatiers practice their craft in the streets, and to sample endless varieties of what many consider to be the finest artisanal chocolate made in France.

This sort of chocolate indulgence would probably seem bizarre to a sixteenth-century French person, who would have been accustomed to chocolate only in drink form and, originally, as a medicinal treatment sold in pharmacies. It was very good for the stomach and digestion, warmed the chest, and gave a good boost of energy (so much so that it was considered an aphrodisiac). On the negative side, however, it was alleged to induce gossip and to cause insomnia, irritability, and hyperactivity. In 1644, the Medical Faculty of Paris recommended not drinking chocolate more than twice a day.

But during the seventeenth century, the French nobility began to appreciate chocolate as a pleasurable and fashionable indulgence, especially after both Louis XIII and Louis XIV married Spanish princesses. Queen Anne and Queen Maria Theresa both brought their love of chocolate to court, cementing its popularity. Louis XIV was not personally fond of it, complaining that it did not fill the stomach, but it was during his reign that the first French cacao plantations were built, in France's new Caribbean colonies. His successor, Louis XV, was a great fan of chocolate and liked to prepare his chocolate drink himself in his private apartments.

The Catholic Church was left rather perplexed about what to do about this new food. Priests and nuns were among the earliest and fiercest admirers of chocolate, thanks to the extensive European missionary operations in the new Spanish empire. But chocolate was thought to arouse the passions, which seemed inappropriate for Christ's servants. There was also a decades-long debate about whether one could drink chocolate on fast days. Ultimately, the Church recognized the futility of trying to ban such a popular product and went along with the old principle of *liquidum non frangit jejunum* (liquid does not break the fast). Because chocolate was only taken as a drink in Europe at that time, it could be imbibed without offending God.[4]

Until the nineteenth century, chocolate remained a luxury product, but new industrial production methods and the introduction of cacao to West African colonies helped reduce the price of chocolate and rendered it accessible to a wider audience. And once solid forms of chocolate were perfected, rendering it eatable as well as drinkable, the era of cheap chocolate for the masses could really take off (luckily for the vast labor force propelling the Industrial Revolution). In the mid-1800s, the chocolate bar was invented—a dark chocolate version in England, a milk chocolate one in Switzerland—and eventually most people were eating rather than drinking chocolate. Today, the average French person eats more than fifteen pounds of chocolate each year—only about half as much as the Swiss and Germans, but still more than just about every other country on the planet.[5]

It is possible that most French people are not aware that modern-day chocolate is the product of horrific colonial and genocidal practices. There is perhaps a bit more awareness, however, of the current controversies surrounding the chocolate trade, thanks to a sustained activist campaign highlighting the exploitative production of cacao in West Africa. More than 60 percent of the world's cacao is now grown in just two countries, Ghana and Côte d'Ivoire. Many cacao farmers earn less than $1 per day, and it is estimated that more than 2 million children labor on cacao farms, some trafficked from neighboring countries.[6] Essentially, chocolate is cheap because its labor costs are kept so artificially low, so activists argue it should actually cost much more. Since the 1980s, the fair-trade movement has tried to reduce exploitation in the cacao industry, but disagreements over what exactly constitutes fair-trade chocolate have made progress difficult.

It is a horrible irony that something so sweet and joyful has such a long, terrible legacy, but as we have seen, the history of food is often intimately connected with the worst social ills of any era. War and conquest have always shaped the human diet, and the gastronomic demands of the upper classes have consistently led to exploitation and violence. The natural antidepressant qualities of chocolate may not serve as a remedy in this regard, but one can only hope that the ever-increasing support for fairly traded chocolate will soon bring this melancholy history to a definitive close.

22

The Culinary Contributions of Madame Serpent

For decades, spinach was a reviled side dish on American tables, something that children (and many adults) forced themselves to eat under threat of a withheld dessert. The leafy vegetable does suffer from being both green and bitter, two of the most unendearing qualities any food can possess, but surely part of the problem was that Americans had not yet learned how to serve spinach the French way: *épinards à la crème*, for example, in which spinach is simmered in butter and drowned in cream, or *épinards en gratin*, spinach baked in cream and cheese. (If there is one rule of French cooking, it is that you can eat nearly anything if you smother it in butter, cream, and cheese.) Luckily, after well-known chefs started introducing and adapting French recipes for American audiences, spinach became a much more enjoyable addition to the family meal. Julia Child's creamed spinach recipe, for example, remains a classic.

The French also gave Americans the various dishes denoted as "Florentine," which always include spinach, such as the brunch staple eggs Florentine. Serving meat or fish à la Florentine is even more popular in France, which is a bit curious considering the phrase simply means "of Florence," and yet the denizens of Florence, Italy, have no more love for spinach than anyone else. While historians claim there is no definitive explanation for the Florentine label, a good case can be made that it originates in the sixteenth century, when the woman known to history as Madame Serpent arrived in Marseille to marry the future king of France.

At the time, her name was simply Catherine de' Medici, a fourteen-year-old member of the famous Medici family of Florence and niece of Pope Clement VII. King Francis I arranged for her to marry his second son, Henry, in 1533, as part of his never-ending intrigues to gain a larger French foothold in Italy. Unfortunately for Catherine, her uncle-pope died a year into the marriage, and she failed to conceive a child for more than a decade, decidedly lowering her value to the crown and leading her to fear that she might be set aside. She was devoted to Henry, but her husband preferred the company and political guidance of his beautiful mistress, Diane de Poitiers. Catherine languished in the shadows, forced to accept the humiliation of a very public ménage à trois with the prince and his mistress. Her quiet acceptance of the situation may have saved her in the end, as Diane, fearing Catherine could be replaced with a more demanding and alluring candidate, encouraged Henry to keep his pliable wife around. Eventually, Catherine bore Henry ten children, and after the deaths of Henry's father and elder brother, Henry ascended the throne as Henry II in 1547 and Catherine became queen of France.

Even after becoming queen, Catherine was forced to endure her husband's devotion to Diane de Poitiers. But this arrangement was upended when the king died of an injury sustained while jousting in 1559. Catherine exiled the royal mistress and soon became the most powerful woman in Europe, helping to rule France alongside her three young sons, who one after the other became king. (Diane died a few years later, after accidentally poisoning herself with a potion made of gold, meant to preserve her youth and beauty.)

Catherine's eldest son, King Francis II, was only a teenager when he assumed the throne upon his father's death (although he was already married to his childhood friend Mary, Queen of Scots). The sickly lad ruled for only a year, dying of an infection in 1560 and leaving his ten-year-old brother to rule as Charles IX. With Catherine as regent, Charles survived many years of religious turmoil in France, before dying without a male heir in 1574. The throne passed to his younger brother Henry III, who in the game of musical thrones then played in Europe had recently been made king of Poland. Returning to France, he reigned for fifteen years, the last king of the Valois dynasty, before being murdered by a Catholic friar.

This succession of young, weak kings emboldened the fractious nobility, who increasingly sparred with each other and with the foreign queen regent. Catherine only survived these three decades of dramatic power struggles because of her shrewd political wits (possibly inspired by her countryman and contemporary Niccolò Machiavelli). She remains a very divisive figure in French history, alternatively portrayed as Madame Serpent, an unscrupulous and murderous usurper, and as a formidable and clever ruler who had the best interests of her sons and of France at heart. (Not surprisingly, those who have wanted to discredit the role of women in high politics have usually advanced the former argument.) This discrepancy endures in large part because of her controversial role in one of the most horrific acts of violence in French history, the Saint Bartholomew's Day Massacre, in which thousands of Protestants were murdered under murky circumstances.

It was during the reign of Catherine and her three sons that France was wracked by the Wars of Religion, as the Catholic Church confronted an increasingly organized movement of French Protestants, who were known as Huguenots. It was part of an epic continental struggle between Catholics and Protestants that took several centuries to resolve, and France was a particularly bloody battleground. The Huguenots adhered to the very strict reformist doctrine of John Calvin, much like the Puritans who emerged in England. Originally a religious reform movement aimed at purifying a Christianity that had become corrupt and sclerotic, the Huguenots acquired a more overtly political character over time. By insisting that individuals could interpret scripture and achieve salvation on their own, rather than solely through the intercession of churchly representatives, the Huguenots challenged the Church's authority and, thus, the political legitimacy of the monarchy with which it was entwined. Many noble families who had grievances against the king, or objected to the increasing centralization of monarchical power, converted to the Protestant cause, which they saw as legitimizing their opposition to the crown. Royal persecution of the Huguenots, which sometimes included burning them as heretics, only increased their religious fervor. They began organizing themselves, both politically and militarily, to resist any attacks by the Church and the monarchy. They even acquired territorial strongholds, such as the Atlantic port town of La Rochelle and the kingdom of Navarre in the Pyrenees.

After the death of her husband, Catherine initially promoted a conciliatory approach toward the competing religious factions, in the hopes of preventing all-out war. But the religious schism had become irrevocably politicized, with powerful nobles lining up on either side. The first religious massacres occurred in 1562 and then spread throughout much of France. The country dissolved into civil war, as rival nobles created their own armed forces and engaged in hideous levels of violence against each other and among the population. For nearly forty years, France was consumed by frequent episodes of religious warfare—its economy broken, its people brutalized. The promise of prosperity and progress, so evident in the first half of the 1500s, lay in ruins.

In 1572, Catherine decided on a new tactic, marrying her Catholic daughter Margaret to Henry of Navarre, a royal cousin and leading Protestant noble. The marriage was meant to symbolize the possibility of religious reconciliation and peace, but instead it inflamed an already tense situation. Staunch Catholics saw the marriage as a victory for the Protestants, and the Parisian masses—mostly Catholic, and already agitated due to a sharp increase in the price of bread—were in a rebellious spirit as hundreds of Huguenots arrived for the extravagant wedding. A few days after the wedding, Catherine apparently helped convince Charles IX that it was necessary to assassinate a few dozen Huguenot leaders in order to forestall the emergence of another Protestant rebellion. But once the killing started, violence spread throughout Paris and then the regions, with Catholics believing they had royal dispensation to slaughter Protestants. Over the next week, roughly two thousand Huguenots were murdered in Paris, and perhaps thirty thousand more in the provinces, in what became known as the Saint Bartholomew's Day Massacre. Any hope of religious and political reconciliation lay dead as well, and so the Wars of Religion rumbled on.

While it's unclear exactly how much responsibility Catherine had in all this, she never expressed any remorse for the massacre, and this shocking act forms the core tale of what became known as the "Black Legend" of Catherine de' Medici (according to which she was also a poisoner and practitioner of the black arts). No doubt, it was helpful over the years for French critics to argue that the horrific massacre was orchestrated by a depraved foreign queen, but any guilt Catherine bears must be widely shared. Still, Saint Bartholomew's Day haunted her continuing efforts at reconciliation until her dying day, in January 1589.

In the gastronomical realm, Catherine enjoys a more popular reputation today, as she is credited with transforming French cuisine in many positive ways. Legends circulate around her like bees around honey. This includes, first and foremost, our explanation for *à la Florentine*. When Catherine left her home city of Florence for France, she brought with her a number of Italian chefs, confectioners, and pastry makers, who over the years introduced a number of new foods and cooking styles to the French court. At the same time, French nobles were shaking off their medieval aversion to vegetables,

The carnage and mayhem associated with the Saint Bartholomew's Day Massacre have rendered it one of the most infamous events of the decades-long Wars of Religion. Etching from the *Nordisk familjebok* (Stockholm: 1904), *999*.

and they began to embrace those that were already popular in Italy. Among them was spinach, which Catherine enjoyed and made rather popular, and thus dishes with spinach came to be designated *à la Florentine*.

Catherine and her chefs also introduced broccoli and artichokes, the latter her especial favorite (according to legend, she almost died one night from indigestion after an overdose of artichoke hearts). Artichokes were thought to have aphrodisiac qualities, which no doubt also enhanced their appeal. There is still an expression today, in fact, *avoir un coeur d'artichaut* (to have a heart like an artichoke), which is applied to people who fall in love very quickly and indiscriminately. Artichokes became very popular all over France, and today you can cook artichokes à la Parisienne, Normande, Lyonnaise, or Provençal. Catherine is also credited with bringing to France haricot beans from the American continent, supposedly a wedding gift from her uncle, Pope Clement VII. It is a plausible tale, given that many new foods from the Americas were being introduced into Europe at this time.

Asparagus, which also became very popular in France at this time, was probably not a favorite of Catherine's. Her love rival, Diane de Poitiers, ate it with every meal when available, as part of a strict diet of fresh vegetables intended to maintain her youth and the affection of the king.

Catherine's Italian cooks exercised their influence in other realms as well, bringing to France the art of making macarons, frangipane, nougat, and sorbet. In fact, nearly every imaginable confection made with sugar that can somehow be linked to this time period is credited to Catherine de' Medici and her chefs. Many of these attributions are very debatable, but it is true that at this time, sugar became the new spice. After centuries of culinary obsession with pungent spices from the Orient, sugar became the favored vehicle for flaunting one's wealth and status. Still very expensive and difficult to acquire, it was used in dishes of all sorts, even to flavor meat and fish. Henry III, on his way home from Poland to claim the French throne, attended a feast in Venice where everything from the plates to the napkins was made of sugar, a stupendous display of opulence.

In Venice, Henry also encountered the strange piece of cutlery called the fork, and he and his mother unsuccessfully tried to introduce it to the French court. People thought that forks were a bit effeminate and impractical; spoons and knives were sufficient for coping with the dishes served at that time. Some also apparently felt that the fork would incite people to sin—didn't it look a bit like a devil's pitchfork? (Forks had only two tines in those days.) The Protestants may have disagreed with the Church in nearly every spiritual and worldly matter, but on this they were united: "God protect me from forks," Martin Luther is alleged to have said.[1] These concerns failed to deter Rabelais, for one, who proudly wore his only fork, bought in Italy, on his belt. Catherine suffered from association with the sinful utensil, as her critics blamed her for bringing it into France (further proof of her satanic inclinations). Thus, one often still hears the legend that Catherine is responsible for French forks, but in truth they did not really become fashionable in France until the eighteenth century.

Overall, French cooking took a very Italian turn in the sixteenth century, but it is not accurate to attribute this solely to Catherine and her chefs. As we have seen, the French nobility had become enthralled with Italian culture some decades earlier, and Catherine herself did not become an influential force at court until after her husband's death. So the enduring tendency to credit all the new foods and tastes of this era to Catherine is a bit of a mystery.[2] Less mysterious is the French embrace of the delicious foods and cooking styles of Italy, a key step in the evolution of French gastronomy into the haute cuisine of Europe it had yet to become.

23

A Chicken in Every Pot

In the 1928 U.S. presidential election, the Republican Herbert Hoover trounced New York's Democratic governor Al Smith, who suffered the twin liabilities of being Catholic and anti-Prohibition at a time when both characteristics were highly unpopular. While much of the campaign revolved around these sorts of religious and moral questions, the plight of the common person was, as always, an inescapable political issue. Hoover's campaign promised voters "a chicken in every pot and a car in every backyard." But we all know what happened next: the stock market crash, the Great Depression, soup lines, world war, et cetera, and so on. Small wonder that today, American politicians invoke the phrase "chicken in every pot" mockingly, as an example of the kind of people-pleasing campaign promise that has no hope of ever being achieved.

In France, the phrase has a completely different connotation, because the first Frenchman to offer this promise to his people was the hugely popular King Henry IV. In fact, from his very birth, Henry was surrounded by anecdotes and legends related to food, and these helped transform him from an unpopular royal heir to the most loved king in French history.

Henry was born in 1553 in Navarre, a small kingdom straddling the French and Spanish sides of the Pyrenees. He was known for most of his adult life as Henry of Navarre, and indeed, this is how we met him in the previous chapter, as the royal cousin who wed Catherine de' Medici's daughter Margaret on the eve of the Saint Bartholomew Day's Massacre. When he was born, he was distant in the royal succession line of the Valois dynasty, as Catherine already had three living sons.

According to legend, Henry was raised simply among the common people of Navarre. (In truth, he also spent a good chunk of his childhood with his cousins in the royal nursery in Paris.) When he was born, his grandfather subjected him to a bit of medieval-style vaccination by rubbing his lips with garlic. He maintained a lifelong love for garlic in his food, which was unusual among nobles at the time because garlic, despite its medicinal qualities, was seen as a poor man's spice. But Henry exploited this food taboo cleverly to cement his reputation as a common man of the people, ingesting garlic in enormous quantities. One of his mistresses is alleged to have told him: "Sire, you are fortunate to be the king, otherwise we couldn't bear to stand next to you—you stink like a carcass."

At his baptism, Henry's lips were brushed with a bit of wine, most likely the sweet, white Jurançon wine from the region, which he also had a great liking for as an adult. Several centuries later, the poet Colette recalled: "When I was a teenager, I met a passionate prince, imperious, treacherous as all great seducers are: the Jurançon."[1] While ostensibly celebrating the flavors of this fine wine, it is also a clear reference to Henry, who developed a gargantuan appetite for women, having a true artichoke heart. He eventually fathered eighteen children by seven different women. His constant affairs and seductions brought him an endless supply of political and military problems—for example, invading unimportant locales to please the father of a current mistress. But none of this detracted from his popularity.

Henry's relationship to the ruling Valois family came through his father, Antoine de Bourbon, while his claim to Navarre came from his mother, Jeanne d'Albret. As the Wars of Religion began to roil France in the 1560s, Navarre became a Protestant stronghold, and Henry a rising Huguenot leader. He became king of Navarre when his mother died in 1572, and in August of that year wed Margaret in Paris. In the massacre of Huguenots that followed, his life was spared by his cousin, King Charles IX. But Henry was forced to convert to Catholicism, and he was kept under house arrest for several years. This imprisonment continued when Charles died and his younger brother became King Henry III.

Henry III was not popular. He was Catherine's favorite son, but he ignored much of her sensible advice and presided over a decadent court filled with frivolous young men (referred to as Henry's *mignons*, or "cuties") who engaged in constant dueling. He was often unwell, and he shunned wine for this reason, but he still hosted extravagant dinners that scandalized nobles and commoners alike. He was intelligent and not incapable, but he was widely seen as lazy and dissolute. He refused his mother's entreaties to court Queen Elizabeth I of England (she was "too old") and instead married the beautiful Louise of Lorraine, but they failed to produce an heir.

Henry III's unpopularity meant that Catholics—even his own younger brother, Francis—began to join the Huguenots in rebelling against his rule, and his reign was fraught with sedition and conflict. The situation became even more volatile when Francis died and Henry still had no children, for now the next in line to the French throne was Henry of Navarre, who had escaped house arrest, renounced his forced conversion, and was once again leader of the Protestant forces. The leading Catholic nobles, headed by the Guise family, threw all of their political, military, and spiritual resources into preventing Henry from attaining the crown. For a time there was even the ludicrously named War of the Three Henrys, fought by the armies of King Henry III, Henry of Navarre, and Henry, Duke of Guise. Eventually King Henry III turned against the Guises and reconciled with his cousin, naming him as heir. In July 1589, these two Henrys joined their forces in an effort to reclaim Paris from the Guises' Catholic League. But one evening, a Catholic friar entered King Henry's encampment, claiming to have an important message. Instead, he stabbed the king, and Henry died the next day—the first French king to be assassinated. Thus ended the Valois dynasty, after more than 250 years of rule.

Henry of Navarre was now King Henry IV, the first king of the Bourbon dynasty, but it took several more years of warfare before he could sit on his throne. In 1593, he converted to Catholicism once again, which removed the main driver of resistance against him, and he reclaimed Paris the following year. (The sincerity of his conversion cannot be known, but he is famously said to have declared: "Paris is worth a mass.") He continued to fight rebels funded by Spain for several years. Finally, in 1598, Henry signed the Edict of Nantes, which ended the French Wars of Religion. Catholicism was declared the official state religion, but important religious and political freedoms were granted to the Huguenots.

Henry IV began to rebuild his country, devastated after so many years of civil war, and he relied on his own personal popularity to restore the kind of strong personal monarchy that had benefited France in the past. He consciously strove to present himself as completely different from the last Valois kings—whereas they were weak, effete, and haughty, Henry was a rugged man of the people, who ate garlic and guzzled wine like a peasant. The previous kings had cared nothing for the common man, but Henry IV promised the French people *un poule au pot le dimanche* (a chicken in the pot every Sunday). It was a colloquial way of saying that he intended to restore peace and prosperity to the peasantry, with *poule au pot* effectively standing in for the people's basic needs. Today, *poule au pot* can be a traditional Sunday dinner in France—a whole chicken stewed with vegetables and herbs (and garlic!) for several hours—but truthfully it is not something that people eat very often these days, even if they feel rather affectionate toward it in theory.

Like Charlemagne, Henry IV understood that the backbone of the French economy was agriculture—or, as his minister Maximilien de Béthune, Duke of Sully, put it, in an expression that all French people know, "Plowing and grazing are the two breasts from which France is fed."[2] He relied on the advice of Olivier de

Serres, the father of French agronomy, who suggested growing new crops such as maize, and also mulberries, to help develop a French silk industry. Serres's wide-ranging agricultural innovations, publicized in his landmark study *Le théâtre d'agriculture* (1600), helped significantly improve productivity, and within a decade French agriculture had returned to its prewar production levels. Unfortunately, as in modern times, the French people did not literally get a chicken in every pot on Sundays, but certainly their overall well-being improved.

Henry also improved commerce and trade by embarking on major infrastructure projects (like draining marshes and building roads) and signing new international treaties. He eliminated the national debt, a feat that future kings usually failed to replicate. He promoted the development of luxury products like glassware, tapestries, and silk, and France began to develop the reputation for high-end goods that it continues to enjoy to this day. He reorganized the army and refortified France's borders, and he supported French expeditions to the New World. Above all, he sustained a period of relative peace throughout the first decade of the seventeenth century, which allowed France's natural advantages in agriculture and industry to be profitably exploited once again.

Henry must have hoped that renewed prosperity would help diminish the schism between Catholics and Protestants that had proven so destructive in his lifetime, but in the end, he was no match for the religious fervor that continued to plague France. Despite his general popularity, he was subjected to numerous assassination attempts during his reign, and in 1610 one of them finally succeeded. While the king's carriage was stopped on rue de la Ferronnerie, in Paris's Les Halles quarter, a Catholic fanatic named François Ravaillac jumped in and stabbed Henry to death. (A plaque still marks the spot today.) It was never determined whether Ravaillac was a lone assassin or in league with other conspirators, and he was eventually drawn and quartered for his crime.

Regardless of Henry's failure to literally put a chicken in every pot, he remains known today as *le bon roi* (the good king), the one who was close to his people, understood the countryside, and was not another out-of-touch Parisian noble. It is a lesson not forgotten by French politicians today, as they invariably try to reaffirm how close they are to *la France profonde*. This is why every year the French

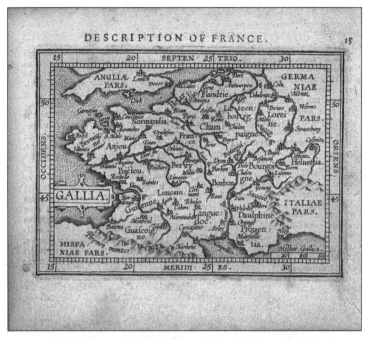

France in 1603, during the reign of King Henry IV. From the Lionel Pincus and Princess Firyal Map Division, New York Public Library. "Gallia." New York Public Library Digital Collections.

president traipses through the Salon International de l'Agriculture, the enormous agricultural trade fair that dominates Paris every February, with mixed results: Jacques Chirac was a master of the political art of *tâter le cul des vaches* (caressing the cows' asses), but Nicolas Sarkozy struggled mightily in his attempts to appear folksy.[3] Sarkozy, already unpopular for his refusal to drink wine, provoked the French electorate even further by banning the after-dinner cheese course at the Élysée Palace, apparently for health reasons. (He was not reelected.) Meanwhile, Henry IV's predilection for gluttony found an echo in the infamous last meal of President François Mitterrand before his death: several dozen oysters, foie gras, capon, and two tiny songbirds called ortolan, eaten whole (a normally illegal practice). The much less popular François Hollande, on the other hand, was most often associated with *Flanby*, a wobbly caramel custard.

Today, the far-right Front National tries to position itself as the true voice of the French countryside and frequently uses food to promote its narrow-minded ideas of what it means to be "authentically French." Nothing could be further from the legacy of tolerance that Henry IV tried to establish. "Those who follow their consciences are of my religion, and I am of the religion of those who are brave and good," the good king said, four centuries ago.[4] Unfortunately for France, her wars of religion were not quite yet concluded.

24

The Chestnut Insurgency

Louis XIII was only eight years old when his father, King Henry IV, was stabbed to death. His mother was Henry's second wife, Marie de' Medici, and she served as regent until her son came of age. At that point their relationship soured, and Louis sent his mother into exile at Blois in 1617, after which she tried to raise several rebellions against him. Louis came to rely instead on his most trusted minister, the ruthless Cardinal Richelieu (known to many as the famous villain from Alexandre Dumas's *Three Musketeers*). One of the principal aims of these two pious Catholics was reversing the progress made by Protestants in France, and in particular eliminating the Huguenot *places de sûreté* (safe havens) established under the Edict of Nantes, which Louis saw as constituting an unacceptable state within a state. This revived anti-Protestant campaign generated new Huguenot rebellions in the 1620s. La Rochelle, then the strongest Huguenot safe haven and one of France's most important Atlantic ports, was the main center of resistance—a status captured in the city's motto, *belle et rebelle* ("beautiful and rebellious").

In 1627, royal forces besieged La Rochelle, starving the inhabitants and preventing foreign powers from coming to their aid. After fourteen months, with only a few thousand inhabitants left alive, the city was forced to surrender. It was a critical moment not only for French Huguenots, who were then stripped of their territorial and political rights, but for the French monarchy, which was advancing ever further toward absolutist control over all French territory. During the seventeenth century, as religious repression continued under both Louis XIII and his son Louis XIV, several hundred thousand Huguenots fled France for Protestant states in Europe or for the American colonies. Many ended up in New Amsterdam (now New York City) and journeyed up the Hudson River to found the town of La Nouvelle-Rochelle, or New Rochelle.

Despite their near eradication in France, the Huguenots contributed some interesting gastronomic legacies. A key Protestant criticism of the Catholic Church was that it was fundamentally hypocritical and corrupt, and food turned out to be a good way of illustrating this point. The Church had dozens of fast days each year, but as we have seen, monks and clergymen nevertheless found a thousand ways to eat well on those days. The Church also sold dispensations that allowed well-off people to eat as they liked. In Normandy, for example, already famous for its delicious dairy products, many local people purchased dispensations so that they could continue to eat butter during Lent, which was normally forbidden. The so-called Butter Tower of the Rouen Cathedral, a High Gothic masterpiece immortalized in a series of Claude Monet paintings, was financed largely with butter dispensations from local Normans. Those who could not afford dispensations had to use expensive or ill-tasting cooking oils instead, which fostered considerable resentment (except in southern France, where olive oil was traditionally used anyway).

But Protestants believed there was no point in having fast days, especially when so many people got around the restrictions. Martin Luther himself railed against the dairy dispensations, arguing in 1520 that

> fasts should be matters of liberty, and all sorts of food made free, as the Gospel makes them. For at Rome they themselves laugh at the fasts, making us foreigners eat the oil with which they would not grease their shoes, and afterwards selling us liberty to eat butter and all sorts of other things . . . it is no longer easy to preach about this liberty because the common people take such great

offense, thinking it a greater sin to eat butter than to lie,
to swear, or even to live unchastely.[1]

Protestants believed that people should be allowed to eat anything, at any time, although in moderation, remembering that the purpose of eating was sustenance, not pleasure.

Fasting rules were already unevenly applied across Europe, and so when millions of Protestants started abandoning them altogether, it is not surprising that some of the least popular ones—like the restrictions on butter—faded entirely, and from the sixteenth century onward, butter became a more prominent ingredient in French cooking. Today, France is the largest consumer of butter in the world, which can hardly be surprising to anyone who has wandered into a proper French *patisserie* or *boulangerie*.[2]

As the Reformation continued to spread, and the uniform dietary rules of the Church receded, it became easier for the national cuisines of Europe to diversify. But in Catholic stalwarts like France, a number of Church rules, like the prohibition of meat on fast days, proved resilient. After Louis XIV finally revoked the Edict of Nantes in 1685, the eating of forbidden foods was a sure marker of religious deviance. Protestants no longer enjoyed any religious freedoms and were forced to choose between conversion, prison, enslavement, or exile. Some Huguenots chose to keep practicing their faith in secret, but they had to be careful not to reveal themselves by disobeying Catholic fasting rules. It would have been madness, for example, to eat *oeufs à la Huguenote* (eggs cooked in mutton juice) on a fast day.

But perhaps the most interesting Huguenot food legend has to do with the last gasp of Protestant rebellion in France, in the early 1700s. Royal troops had been dispatched throughout the provinces to eradicate every last heretic holdout. In what became known as the *dragonnades*, royal soldiers (dragoons) were forcibly lodged in Huguenot towns and homes, horribly mistreating the residents until they converted or fled. It was a very successful strategy, as many towns surrendered even before the dragoons arrived.

But some Huguenots, while seemingly converted, continued to worship in secret, even when royal administrators arrested and executed those they discovered. In the Cévennes, a mountainous and remote Protestant region in the always independent-minded Languedoc, resentment ran high against the local Catholic enforcer, Father du Chaila. His murder in 1702 was the catalyst for a rebellion among local peasants and craftsmen. They became known as the Camisards, and they successfully exploited their superior knowledge of the terrain and the support of the local population to sustain a Protestant insurgency against the crown for two years.[3] Never numbering more than a few thousand fighters, they used traditional rural guerrilla tactics, like ambushes and raids, against more than twenty thousand royal troops and militiamen. Lay preachers and prophets provided them with spiritual motivation, casting their struggle as a sacred mission to restore free worship.

As in most holy wars, both sides committed terrible atrocities. Whole villages were massacred or shipped off to royal prisons. In the fall of 1703, royal forces commenced the Burning of the Cévennes, determined to eradicate the rebellion by destroying the population that supported it (a brutal counterinsurgency approach still tragically employed today). More than 450 villages were destroyed, their residents either killed or forcibly displaced (some were even deported to Canada). It was a somewhat counterproductive move, however, as many locals then joined the Camisards.

But eventually, the crown prevailed. The Camisards were defeated or induced to surrender, and the rebellion faded away. New attempts to rouse the population continued in subsequent years but failed to take hold. Royal authority had been definitively established. The Cévennes was forced to submit to Catholic observance until the late eighteenth century, when the signing of the royal Edict of Toleration and the subsequent French Revolution granted new freedoms to non-Catholics (this period between the revocation of the Edict of Nantes and the revolution was later dubbed *le Désert*, the Desert). Today, the region is once again mostly Protestant, a rarity in modern France.

A popular belief in the Cévennes is that the Camisards would never have been able to fight the royal troops for so long if it had not been for the chestnut tree, which grows all over the region. Chestnut trees are a fabulous resource and grow well in the terraced mountainsides of the Cévennes. Each tree can provide up to seventy thousand calories of food per year, with little maintenance required.[4] Chestnuts (*châtaignes*) are very nutritious, rich in both vitamins and starch, and can be dried and preserved for off-season use. You can make a very filling chestnut porridge or a dark bread from chestnut flour or simply eat them roasted. Their leaves can also serve as fodder for sheep or goats. Medieval monks helped establish the first orchards in the Cévennes, and for centuries the trees provided the hardy locals with a considerable degree of self-sufficiency. It was said that the Cévennes never experienced famine, not even in the worst eras of food scarcity. As long as they had their chestnut orchards, their vegetable gardens, and their flocks of sheep and goats, they needed little from the outside world. So some point to the chestnut trees as an ingredient in the famous independent streak of the Cévennes people.

More prosaically, the chestnut trees became a very useful food resource for the Camisard fighters. It is easy to romanticize rebellion, with its idealistic aims and dashing fighters, but in reality, it is mundane things like food that often determine a rebellion's fate. As a nineteenth-century general later explained, in reference to Corsica, another great producer of chestnuts: "You want to subdue the Corsicans? Cut down the chestnut trees!"[5]

Today, the Cévennes is still one of the main chestnut-producing areas of France. Chestnuts are sold grilled in markets all over the country in the fall and winter, and they are particularly well loved at Christmastime. They are also a classic accompaniment to a number of holiday dishes, such as roast turkey and brussels sprouts. *Marrons glacés*, or candied chestnuts, are a specialty from southern France (marrons are a type of larger chestnut, particularly popular in confectionary). Unfortunately, chestnuts are rarely eaten at other times of the year, and over time they have gained a reputation as stodgy peasant food. The Cévennes has also been subject to the same rural depopulation as many other parts of France. So it is not too surprising that chestnut production has gradually gone down, from five hundred thousand tons per year in the late nineteenth century to only nine thousand tons today.[6]

A sublime description of the chestnut trees comes courtesy of Robert Louis Stevenson, the author of *Treasure Island*, who in 1878 spent two weeks traipsing through the Cévennes on a donkey in a fruitless effort to forget a lost love (happily, they later reunited and married). He related his adventures in the book *Travels with a Donkey in the Cévennes*, in which he included this description of the chestnut trees:

> I wish I could convey a notion of the growth of these noble trees; of how they strike out boughs like the oak, and trail sprays of drooping foliage like the willow; of how they stand on upright fluted columns like the pillars of a church; or like the olive, from the most shattered

Robert Louis Stevenson recounted his lovelorn wanderings in the Cévennes in one of his earliest works, *Travels with a Donkey in the Cévennes*. His hiking route can be retraced as the Stevenson Trail today. Frontispiece etching by Walter Crane, from the 1907 edition (London: Chatto & Windus).

bole can put out smooth and youthful shoots, and begin a new life upon the ruins of the old.[7]

Today, the Cévennes remains a relatively unexplored corner of France, but it is easy enough to follow in the author's footsteps on the Stevenson Trail, tracing ancient footpaths through the rugged hills, river valleys, and tiny villages so little changed since the time of the Camisards themselves. As in Cathar country, the distant history of rebellion and tragedy lies close to the surface in the region, a proud element of local tradition. It is another indication that the question of what it means to be "French" is not as straightforward as some may wish to believe.

25

The Bitter Roots of Sugar

André Breton, the twentieth-century French writer and principal founder of surrealism, wrote in his novel *Nadja* that Nantes was "perhaps, with Paris, the only city in France where I have the impression that something worthwhile might happen to me . . . where a spirit of adventure beyond all adventures still lives on." This ancient city, lying on the Loire River near the Atlantic coast, was also the childhood home of Jules Verne, whose splendid accounts of fantastical voyages found their inspiration in this bustling port. Today, Nantes exploits this sense of surreal adventure with an annual avant-garde arts festival and a hangar full of gorgeous steampunk contraptions (including a giant mechanical elephant that you can ride around on and a towering carousel of Verne-inspired creatures).

But there is a dark side to the adventurous spirit that has made Nantes one of the most prosperous and genteel cities in France since the late seventeenth century, one that is unwittingly preserved in some of the city's most loved food products, such as the multicolored candies known as *berlingots nantais*—and especially the rum-soaked vanilla cake called *gâteau nantais*. The city's prosperity and its dedication to sweet delicacies are a legacy of its participation in the transatlantic slave trade, which brought enormous amounts of sugar through its port for several hundred years. It is a past that has recently been acknowledged more openly in Nantes, with the city organizing several major museum exhibitions since the mid-1990s and constructing a riverside memorial in 2012. But the tragic nature of the sugar trade remains a mostly hidden strand of history to tourists and residents alike.

The giant grass known as sugarcane was gradually transplanted westward from its ancestral homeland in Southeast Asia by more than a thousand years of trade and conquest. The ancient Assyrians and Persians established a robust sugar industry in the Middle East, which was further expanded by the Arabs when they wrested control of the region in the early medieval era. (The English word *candy* derives from the Arabic *qandi*, or crystallized sugar.) By the time of the Crusades, the Middle East hosted a vast number of sugar farms and refineries, and rising powers such as Venice soon made their fortune in the sugar trade. Sugar remained a very expensive product, and as we have seen, only the wealthy classes of Europe could afford it (which only fueled elite demand).

But the rise of the Ottoman Empire in the fifteenth century gradually shut down Europe's sugar supply from the Middle East. Efforts were made to grow sugarcane in the hottest locales of southern Europe, such as Sicily and Spain, but these areas were too small to supply the European market. Colonization, however, opened up vast new lands for cultivation, and the Spanish and Portuguese rapidly established sugarcane plantations and refineries in the Canary Islands, Madeira, Brazil, and the West Indies. Sugar flooded the European market, and as early as 1600 it began to be more accessible to the general population—just in time to sweeten the new colonial drinks of chocolate, coffee, and tea. This, in turn, increased demand further, spurring ever more colonial production.

France was a latecomer to the sugar trade, after it established colonies in the Caribbean in the seventeenth century: Guadeloupe and Martinique in 1635, and Saint-Domingue (modern-day Haiti) in 1664. These islands offered ideal conditions for growing sugarcane, but harvesting and processing the cane was an extremely arduous and labor-intensive process. It proved too difficult and expensive to import Frenchmen to do the work, and the native population was rapidly dying or debilitated by new European diseases. The French turned to the same solution as other European colonial powers: the African slave trade, which had been developing since the earliest attempts to grow sugarcane in southern Europe.

In this diabolical trade pattern, ships set out from European ports with goods such as weapons, alcohol, and textiles. Once they arrived in slave ports in West Africa, or farther south in Angola, they exchanged these goods with local slave traders and filled their ships with several hundred enslaved Africans. Chained and packed into inhumane conditions and ravaged by disease, one out of every ten people usually did not survive the months at sea. Those who did were sold to plantation farmers when they reached the Americas, destined to a brutal life of often backbreaking labor. Slave traders were usually paid in sugar, coffee, or other commodities instead of currency. They then sailed back to their home ports in Europe to sell their cargo. Over the course of nearly four centuries, more than 12.5 million slaves were brought to the Americas, nearly 1.4 million of them by French traders.[1]

While sugar and coffee remained the primary imports from the Caribbean, French-bound ships also began to carry stocks of *rhum*, or rum, from the West Indies. Europeans ensconced in the "sugar islands," longing for some kind of alcoholic libation to soften the ugly reality of colonial life, invented rum by applying new distillation techniques to molasses (the syrupy by-product of sugarcane processing). French and English styles of rum emerged with distinct tastes, as the French borrowed distillation methods from cognac production, which were a bit different from English methods for distilling scotch. Rum became increasingly popular in the eighteenth century and proved a valuable side business for French sugar plantations.

As the slave trade expanded in the seventeenth and eighteenth centuries, the merchants of Nantes enthusiastically participated, and eventually Nantes became the most important slave port in France. While nearly twenty French cities participated in the trade, including La Rochelle, Le Havre, and Bordeaux, roughly 45 percent of the total French slave trade was conducted through Nantes. More than fourteen hundred slave expeditions left the city, bringing more than five hundred thousand Africans to the Americas.[2] These figures were dwarfed by the Portuguese and the English, the dominant sea powers and slave traders of the time (Liverpool, for example, organized more slave expeditions than all the French seaports put together), but it still sufficed to make Nantes a newly wealthy town. Many of the elegant white stone mansion blocks gracing the finest streets of Nantes were built with the proceeds of this barbaric trade.

At its height in the eighteenth century, Nantes was importing 40 million to 60 million pounds of sugar each year, more than any other French port.[3] Much of it required further refining before being sold, and so sugar refineries sprung up all along the Loire Valley from Nantes to Orléans. From here, sugar could easily be transported to Paris, the largest domestic market, or to export markets abroad. This central role in the French sugar industry may help explain the sweet nature of many of Nantes's most notable food products, and why the city eventually became a center of industrial food production. And it certainly accounts for the early nineteenth-century creation of *gâteau nantais*, whose unique and delicious flavor depended upon sugar, vanilla, and the famous rum of the West Indies. It remains a popular local delicacy, its provenance usually tied somewhat obliquely to colonial imports rather than to the slave trade specifically.

While Nantes is now belatedly trying to recognize its bitter past, the slave merchants at the time did not worry about trying to find moral justifications for their participation in the trade. To them, it was just a trade like any other; slaves were perceived less as people and more as private property to be bought and sold. Indeed, the French population as a whole in the sixteenth and seventeenth centuries was not overly troubled by slavery. By the late 1700s, the sugar trade accounted for about one-sixth of French export income, creating powerful economic incentives for sustaining the industry. The colony on Saint-Domingue alone produced 40 percent of the world's sugar and nearly half its coffee, and its plantations were utterly dependent on slave labor.

But in the eighteenth century, voices began to be heard condemning the slave trade. In *Candide*, written by Voltaire in 1759, a slave who has lost a hand and a leg explains: "When we work at the sugarcanes, and the mill snatches hold of a finger, they cut off the hand; and when we attempt to run away, they cut off the leg. Both cases have happened to me. This is the price at which you eat sugar in Europe."[4] Other famous Enlightenment writers and thinkers such as Montesquieu criticized the trade, although he (like the English philosopher John Locke) objected mainly to slavery within his homeland, not the colonies, and he even profited from personal investments in the slave trade.

Then came the French Revolution. Thanks to pressure from slave merchants and colonial plantation owners, the grand ideas of liberty, equality, and brotherhood were not initially extended to slaves in the French colonies. But an abolitionist movement started to gather steam, as clubs like the Société des Amis des Noirs (Society of the Friends of the Blacks) petitioned the revolutionary assemblies and distributed antislavery literature to try to sway public opinion. The revolutionary regime became more radical and less subservient to the propertied classes, especially the planters in the Caribbean, many of whom supported the overthrown monarchy. When war with Britain broke out in 1793, these royalist planters actually aligned with the British, who wanted to expel the revolutionaries in Paris, restore the French monarchy, and maintain slavery in the colonies. British forces occupied the four most important French islands in the Caribbean, including Saint-Domingue, and the transatlantic slave trade shuddered to a halt due to the war. All of this created a new set of political and strategic incentives for emancipating French slaves, and in 1794, the National Assembly voted to end slavery in the colonies. A French expeditionary force landed in Guadeloupe and freed its slave population, and the British were expelled by the end of the year. The French then fomented a series of slave revolts in the British colonial territories.

In Saint-Domingue, Toussaint-Louverture, one of the leaders of a slave rebellion that had been simmering for several years, now aligned himself with the French revolutionary regime. After six years of war, factional infighting, and diplomatic negotiation, he wrested control of the entire island of Hispaniola from his political rivals and British occupiers. The increasingly autonomous colony proclaimed him governor in 1801. But when Napoleon came to power, he was determined to regain control of Saint-Domingue, the most important and most profitable French colony, and restore slavery. A vicious war ensued, during which Toussaint-Louverture was captured and imprisoned (he died in the imposing Fort de Joux, in the Jura Mountains of eastern France, in 1803). The French committed horrific atrocities in trying to repress the rebellion, but they also suffered enormous casualties themselves and were finally defeated in the decisive Battle of Vertières in November 1803. The independent nation of Haiti was declared on January 1, 1804, after the most successful slave rebellion in history.

Napoleon reintroduced slavery in the rest of the French colonial domain, and it was only formally abolished in 1848, with the establishment of the French Second Republic. By that time, most of the sugar on French tables actually no longer derived from sugarcane but from sugar beets. European agronomists had long attempted to develop cheaper, homegrown sources of sugar from various fruits and plants; as early as 1575, Olivier de Serres had discovered the high sugar content of beets. Extraction processes remained elusive, but the maritime blockades of the Napoleonic Wars, which cut off transatlantic trade, proved an effective spur to research. In 1811, a French banker and factory owner named Benjamin Delessert perfected an industrial method for obtaining beet sugar, for which he was made a baron by a grateful Napoleon.[5] France became the largest producer of beet sugar in Europe, and today most of the sugar consumed in France is in fact beet sugar, not cane sugar.

As the food writer Maguelonne Toussaint-Samat once wrote, "So many tears were shed for sugar that by rights it ought to have lost its sweetness."[6] Nantes's attempts to acknowledge this painful history are to be commended, but they have also come under criticism from two opposing quarters: from nationalist-minded French people who object to any manifestations of regret for French colonial practices and from activist groups who argue that remembrance without justice is ultimately hollow. Of course, no one is saying that you should avoid products of the sugar trade like the gâteau nantais, which at the end of the day is merely a delicious local cake. But the question of how to acknowledge the sometimes bitter roots of French gastronomy endures, with no consensus in sight.

26

The Liquor of the Gods

For a time, in 2012, it appeared that France would soon enjoy the first theme park devoted to one of its most famous and controversial rulers, Napoleon Bonaparte. "Napoleonland," as it was dubbed by the media, was the brainchild of Yves Jégo, a French politician. The sprawling park would include daily reenactments of the Battles of Trafalgar and Waterloo, roller coaster rides through mock Egyptian pyramids, and a ski run dotted with replicas of frozen corpses, in memory of Napoleon's bitter Russian retreat. Fortunately, Jégo failed to raise sufficient funding, and the world was spared the interactive guillotine experience. Given the divisive legacy of Napoleon among French people today, it is probably for the best that he tends to be memorialized in many smaller and more abstract ways.

Even fans of Courvoisier, one of the world's most famous cognac purveyors, may not be aware that the vague silhouette on the brand's distinctive purple label is, in fact, Napoleon Bonaparte, hand tucked in coat. It is a tribute to Napoleon's appreciation for cognac: while his personal drink of choice was champagne, he distributed rations of cognac to his troops to lift their morale, and he brought along several casks of it to his final exile on Saint Helena. Today, the imposing Courvoisier Château on the banks of the Charente River, in the elegant town of Jarnac in western France, pays tribute to the little emperor with a display of some of his personal items, including a well-worn version of his famous hat.

Cognac is the name given to brandy produced in a specific wine-growing region around the town of Cognac, which lies about thirty miles inland from the Atlantic coast, between La Rochelle and Bordeaux. Its distinctive taste derives from the terroir in which its grapes are grown, the double distillation process that converts the local white wine to brandy, and, most important, the oak casks in which it is aged, which give it a glowing amber color and floral-woodsy flavor. By now you will probably not be surprised to learn that for the brandy to be called cognac, only one specific type of oak may be used (from the nearby forests of Limousin or Tronçais). The exquisite quality of cognac—the "liquor of the gods," as Victor Hugo purportedly described it—depends upon a fixed routine, one that has been refined over several centuries.[1]

Indeed, when you consider the multitude of historical coincidences that had to occur in this region in order for cognac to be invented, you might suspect divine intervention. We can thank the Atlantic waters for having once covered the Cognac region, leaving behind a special limestone and clay soil in which vines can flourish. Special tribute must go to the Gauls for inventing the wooden barrel, and to the Romans for introducing vineyards to this part of France. We must give thanks to the Arab scientists who refined ancient methods of distillation and introduced them to medieval Europe, and to Eleanor of Aquitaine's effective promotion of her beloved local wine region. And finally, we must give due to the French Wars of Religion, which helped make La Rochelle, the closest seaport to Cognac, a Huguenot stronghold with close links to the Protestant state of Holland—because, strangely enough, the Dutch played a critical role in the earliest origins of this quintessential French liquor.

For much of the sixteenth century, Holland was a small northern outpost of the mighty Spanish empire. But in 1568, the Dutch provinces rebelled, commencing their Eighty Years' War for independence from Spain. They established the Dutch Republic in 1581 and carried their war against Spain to the colonial realms. By the early seventeenth century, Holland was a powerful trading nation and commercial sea power, independent in all but name. The Dutch East India Company dominated the spice trade, raking in colossal profits, and Dutch colonies were established in Southeast Asia, the Caribbean, and on the east coast of America. Amsterdam became Europe's most important banking and commercial center for nearly a century.

Dutch traders became increasingly involved in the wine exports flowing from western France, especially from the ports of Bordeaux and La Rochelle, from the fifteenth century onward. After the English lost Gascony, the Dutch dominated the shipping of wine from the region to the rest of Europe. In the early 1600s, King Henry IV imported Dutch engineers to help drain the enormous marshes known as the Marais Poitevin, east of La Rochelle (the Dutch being renowned experts in reclaiming land from the sea). So the Dutch became quite familiar with the wines of western France, including the white wines produced around the town of Cognac. At the time, the Dutch had a reputation for being fond of drink and of life's pleasures more generally, whether food, art, or flowers.

But overall, the wine industry was suffering a serious crisis in the 1600s. Europe was wracked by wars, such as the Thirty Years' War, which killed off one-third to one-half of the inhabitants of central Europe. This seriously disrupted normal trade patterns, and French winemakers lost many of their most valuable markets even when their own lands were not affected. Demand for wine also waned with the spread of new religious movements, such as the Puritans, who abhorred alcohol, and with the rise in safer water supplies, which removed a key reason for frequent wine drinking. Wine faced stiff new competition from colonial drinks like tea and coffee, and from the new drinking establishments that sprung up to cater to their consumption. And globe-trotting peoples like the Dutch and the English faced a specific dilemma: their favorite French wines were relatively low in alcohol and spoiled easily on long sea voyages. Preservation techniques that today allow wine to be aged for decades had not yet been introduced, and at that time the upper life span of wine was no more than a year—much less if exposed to extremes of temperature and rough handling.

All of this created space for the emergence of new types of liquors: higher in alcohol, and thus easier to preserve, store, and transport, while also offering some sort of appealing new taste to consumers. The Dutch in particular increasingly began to distill wine, which involved overheating it in a special copper pot, resulting in a liquor they called *brandewijn* (burnt wine), eventually known in English as brandy. The process of distillation itself was not new, but the market for distilled spirits had traditionally been quite small. The colorless, high-octane alcohol known in France as eau-de-vie was mostly used for medicinal purposes; only the Germans had really taken to drinking it solely for intoxication. But distilled spirits began to become more popular, and the eau-de-vie produced from the Cognac wines was particularly delicious (unlike most brandies, it did not have to be distilled multiple times, and so it retained more of its original grape flavor). The liquor became a best seller in northern European taverns. At first the Dutch mainly distilled the wines in Holland, but eventually they decided to simplify things by distilling Cognac wines locally, and so the first cognac distilleries were built in the Charente region.

Of course, the Dutch do not deserve sole credit for cognac, as this early version was still quite primitive, and was usually mixed with water or fine herbs. French distillers took over and made substantial refinements—most notably, the lengthy aging of the liquor in oaken barrels, which is what distinguishes cognac from a banal eau-de-vie. This innovation took hold in the eighteenth century, and may have arisen by accident, after long delays in loading and transporting a shipment of the liquor gave it a more pleasing flavor, so it could be drunk straight. Today, cognac is aged from two and a half years to half a century before sale.

Cognac's flavors deepen the longer it ages, but there is a trade-off: about 2 percent of the liquor evaporates each year. In an indication of the quasi-religious aura surrounding cognac, this lost portion is referred to as *la part des anges*, "the angel's share." Over the course of a year, France loses the equivalent of 20 million bottles of cognac to the angels (obviously they love cognac as much as we mortals do). This evaporation process turns the walls of the surrounding chamber black, which was once an enormous help to tax collectors trying to determine who might be illegally producing and selling cognac. Today, many old buildings around Cognac still bear the black traces of drunken angels on their walls.

As cognac began to take longer to produce and improved in taste, it became less of a cheap drink for sailors and commoners and more of a special liquor for the wealthier classes. By the eighteenth century, it was already selling at a premium in Amsterdam compared to other spirits. More and more land in Cognac was devoted to producing grapes for distillation; by the late nineteenth century, an area larger than Luxembourg was cultivated solely for cognac grapes. Overproduction was a regular occurrence. Producers would have to sit on their stock and wait for supply to fall, but luckily this just meant more aging time for the cognac.

Many of the great cognac-producing families of the seventeenth century were Huguenots. Following Louis XIV's campaign of persecution, they fled to Holland, England, and Ireland but retained their ties to the Charente and thus helped spread appreciation of cognac even farther abroad. The English and Irish in particular took to the strongest varieties of cognac, and two of the most important cognac houses, Hennessy and Martell, were founded by an Irishman and an Englishman, respectively, in the eighteenth century. (Richard Hennessy was an Irish mercenary who discovered the joys of cognac while recuperating from injury in La Rochelle; Jean Martell was from the Channel Islands, a smuggler's paradise awash with illicit cognac.) Americans were not immune to cognac's charms either: during the great cocktail era of the nineteenth and early twentieth centuries, cognac anchored classic tipples like the sidecar and the stinger. And so the great cognac houses weathered several centuries of war, revolution, economic depression, and foreign occupation, all the while maintaining a reputation for luxury and refinement. During World War II, for example, German authorities requisitioned 27 million bottles of cognac alone.

But in France today, cognac is generally seen as more of an old man's drink. The French much prefer whisky, which they drink more of each year than any other country in the world. Whisky accounts for about 40 percent of the spirits market in France, with Scottish brands the clear favorite, while cognac claims less than 1 percent.[2]

Outside of France, the story is very different. In the United States, cognac was recently popularized by the American hip-hop community. Sales of Courvoisier jumped nearly 20 percent thanks to Busta Rhymes's hit "Pass the Courvoisier," and other cognac brands rushed to arrange new sponsorship deals with hip-hop luminaries like Jay-Z and Snoop Dogg.[3] In a shrewd reverse-marketing move, Martell began to sponsor a popular American blues festival in Cognac every summer. In new economic powers like China, cognac has become an increasingly popular signifier of new wealth. Rémy Martin now caters to Chinese preferences by selling the liquor in eight-sided bottles (eight being a particularly lucky number in China). These kinds of savvy and open-minded marketing techniques are typical of the cognac industry, which is considered much less fussy about how its wares are adapted and imbibed than other French producers. It is an inescapable necessity, really, given that more than 95 percent of the cognac produced in France is exported to other countries.

Of course, even cognac producers have their limits, and like most French industries, they zealously defend the cognac AOC, which prevents producers outside the Cognac region from referring to their brandies as cognac. One of their longest-running battles, curiously enough, has been with the Armenian brandy industry. In 1900, Nikolay Shustov, an Armenian brandy maker, entered a blind tasting competition during the Paris International Exposition and won the Grand Prix. He began to refer to his brandy as cognac, and Armenian "cognac" later became a beloved staple of the Soviet elite. (According to legend, Winston Churchill became a fan of cognac after Joseph Stalin gave him a bottle during the Yalta Conference.) Today, most countries defer to French AOC laws and market the Armenian liquor as brandy, but you will still find bottles of Armenian cognac throughout the former communist world. It is a reminder that however underappreciated cognac might be for the average French drinker today, it remains a most heavenly liquor worldwide.

27

The Crescent Controversy

It would be natural to assume that the recent invention and popularity of the Cronut—a croissant-donut hybrid—would send the average French person into an apoplectic rage. *"Zut alors!"* you can imagine Jacques saying. "How dare anyone disfigure our perfect morning pastry!" But by and large, the French seem more bemused than repulsed by the Cronut. As all kinds of croissant mutations spread around the world, the French simply shrug their shoulders and pop out to the local boulangerie for a *croissant ordinaire* (the stereotypical crescent, made with margarine) or even more sublime *croissant au beurre* (usually a straighter shape, made with butter). To add even a swipe of jam or butter to a freshly baked croissant seems superfluous, let alone sugar, ham, cheese, or anything else. You may, however, dunk your croissant in coffee without shame.

The croissant may be one of the most iconic French foods of all time, and yet it is fairly well established today that its origins are not very French at all. Its most likely ancestor is the *kipfel*, a crescent-shaped pastry made in Austria. According to well-traveled legend, the first chapter in its journey to fame commenced in 1683, with the Ottoman siege of Vienna. Early rising Viennese bakers foiled an Ottoman attempt to tunnel under the city's walls, allowing the defenders to hold out until Polish king Jan Sobieski arrived to drive back the invaders. To celebrate their role in saving the city, the bakers created a crescent-shaped pastry, a gloating reference to a favored symbol of the defeated Ottomans.

Naturally, the truth is somewhat less tidy than the legend. The kipfel actually dates back to the thirteenth century, and it was more of a dense roll than a fluffy pastry. Some versions of the tale place the pastry's origins in earlier sieges of Vienna, during the sixteenth century, or in an entirely different Ottoman siege of Budapest. And an implicit assumption in all the legend's iterations is that the French would share the Austrian Hapsburgs' enthusiasm for a pastry celebrating victory over the fearsome Turks. Yet in fact, France enjoyed a 250-year alliance with the Ottoman Empire and was less than thrilled when the Turks failed to capture Vienna, the capital of France's most noxious European rival. Louis XIV had not only refused to send aid to the beleaguered city but reputedly had encouraged Ottoman grand vizier Kara Mustafa Pasha to attack Vienna in the first place.

The Franco-Ottoman alliance was controversial from the start. The Ottoman Empire had been encroaching upon mainland Europe since the late fourteenth century, gradually acquiring more territory in Greece and the Balkans while also extending its control over much of the Middle East. It was a multiethnic empire noted for its religious tolerance; when the Wars of Religion began to tear Europe asunder, many Protestant exiles found sanctuary in Ottoman lands. New Ottoman cities in Europe, such as Sarajevo, hosted Muslim, Catholic, Orthodox, and Jewish communities. But the sultans were devout Muslims, and however tolerant their religious rule, the expansion of their Islamic empire into Christian Europe sent shockwaves throughout a population that still possessed strong religious identities and worldviews.

So when King Francis I signed a treaty of alliance with Suleiman the Magnificent in 1536, it might have made perfect sense from a Machiavellian perspective—the Ottomans were seizing ever more territory from his Hapsburg rivals, advancing well into Hungary—but it was seen as a shocking betrayal of the Christian European cause. Nevertheless, the alliance endured for more than two centuries, with the two powers cooperating in military campaigns against shared European rivals and enjoying favorable trade arrangements. The relationship allowed French scientists and linguists to visit Ottoman lands and greatly expand their knowledge of astronomy, mathematics, botany, and Eastern languages. And a remarkable cultural exchange occurred, as Turkish art, architecture, music, and literature became fashionable in French circles. The trend for "Turquerie" gradually spread throughout Europe, especially after the Ottoman defeat at Vienna, commonly seen as the turning point in their European fortunes (over the following two centuries, they lost all the European territories they had conquered before 1683). As the perception of the Ottoman Empire as a military threat diminished, it came to be seen more as a source of exotic objects and strange practices, selectively appropriated by European elites eager to show off their worldliness and self-perceived superiority. Such patterns of European engagement with Eastern cultures—commonly grouped by critics within the concept of Orientalism—grew and expanded over the following centuries.

Perhaps unsurprisingly, one of the enduring legacies of the Franco-Turkish alliance can be found in the realm of gastronomy. In 1669, the new Ottoman ambassador, Suleiman Aga, presented himself to Louis XIV at Versailles and inadvertently offended the Sun King by wearing a plain set of clothes and refusing to bow before him. He was thus packed off to Paris, where, undeterred, he set about winning over the nobility—particularly, the female members of the aristocracy—with extravagant displays of hospitality and wealth. Most notably, he served the still somewhat exotic beverage of coffee to his noble visitors, and evidently acquired a fair amount of intelligence on French political affairs from his caffeinated and overstimulated guests. Coffee gradually became fashionable in Paris, especially with the creation of the first cafés later in the century, although it did not really conquer Versailles until the time of Louis XV, when the royal mistress, Madame du Barry, imposed her taste for coffee upon the court.

This mutually beneficial alliance came to an end in 1798, when Napoleon invaded Egypt, then part of the Ottoman Empire. It is not clear whether, at this point, some version of the kipfel had been popularized in France. Another set of legends claims that Marie Antoinette, homesick for her native Vienna after becoming queen of France in 1774, introduced a crescent-shaped pastry to the French court. But there is little historical evidence to support this tale.

In fact, many historians today believe that the true origins of the croissant lie in a Viennese bakery established in Paris in 1838 by a former Austrian army officer named August Zang. At the time, French bakeries did not actually enjoy a stellar reputation, and Zang found their bland bread and pastry offerings disheartening. He opened his Boulangerie Viennoise on rue de Richelieu and attracted hordes of Parisians with his delightfully buttery, sweet Austrian pastries, which came to be known in France as *viennoiserie*. His kipfel proved to be particularly popular, and when it began to be made with puff pastry around the turn of the century, the modern croissant was born. Some unknown baker eventually had the idea of wrapping the same pastry dough around a chunk of dark chocolate, and thus the *pain au chocolat* joined the croissant in the pantheon of French breakfast treats.

Today, the Sunday morning trip to the boulangerie for freshly baked croissants is a common French ritual. They really must be eaten fresh—if you were to suggest picking up some croissants the night before so you can sleep in, you would be met with looks of incomprehension or horror. Yet there is an ongoing controversy over croissants today, as it turns out that more than half of the croissants sold at French bakeries are industrially made and then reheated from frozen rather than baked on site.[1] (Boulangeries can get away with this outrage because the law requires them to bake only their own bread, not pastries.) More and more often, croissants are made with margarine instead of butter. And in other European countries, the American trend of using croissants for sandwich bread continues to grow.

So the superficially simple tale of the croissant, that beloved French cliché, turns out to be a bit more complicated than it first appears. It still has a more straightforward story than the pain au chocolat, which has virtually no origin legend at all, and which the residents of southwestern France insist on calling a *chocolatine*. Recently, the pain au chocolat became caught up in political controversy when the right-wing politician Jean-François Copé claimed that a French schoolchild had a pain au chocolat snatched from his hands by a street gang enforcing the Ramadan fast—an anecdote that, while probably apocryphal, served as a transparent metaphor for right-wing narratives of the threat posed by Islam and immigration.[2] The French boulangerie might seem like it should offer a warm and cozy escape from social and political ferment, but as it turns out, all sorts of anxieties and agitation can be manifested in humble baked goods.

28

War and Peas

In the annals of European monarchy, no other ruler outshines Louis XIV, whose reign lasted a staggering seventy-two years, until his death in 1715. Small wonder that millions of tourists from all over the world visit the Palace of Versailles each year to gaze upon Louis's most monumental work.

Yet Versailles is more than just the château and its beautiful gardens; it is also a town in its own right, which grew alongside the fabulous château. Today, it is a well-heeled suburb of Paris, popular among Anglo expatriates. And for its residents, it is another of Louis XIV's creations that remains the most beloved treasure of Versailles: the Place du Marché Notre-Dame, which hosts one of the largest and best food markets in the region. Three days a week, the square fills with stalls offering every imaginable product: rare fruits and vegetables, artisanal cheeses, local wines, olives, candies, and spices. Small food trucks sell crêpes and piping hot escargot swimming in garlic butter. The covered market surrounding the square is open every day (except Monday, *bien sur*) and holds a luscious array of meats, fresh fish, and oysters.

But for a true glimpse of the intersection of French gastronomy and royalty in the seventeenth century, visitors are well advised to seek out the Potager du Roi, the king's vegetable garden, located just outside the château gates. A triumph of early modern science and ingenuity, it serves as an enduring testament to the Sun King's imperious demands for everyday transcendence, and the innovations he spurred among his most loyal courtiers.

Louis XIV became king in 1643, at the age of four, after his father (that pious persecutor of Huguenots, Louis XIII) died of tuberculosis. His mother, Anne of Austria, served as regent, assisted by her legendary chief minister, Cardinal Mazarin. After Mazarin's death in 1661, Louis ruled in his own right, gradually solidifying his total control of the nobility and the state. He initiated far-reaching economic and military reforms that transformed France into an ever more centralized, wealthy, and modern state. *"L'état c'est moi!"* Louis once famously declared. "I am the State!" Louis adopted the sun as his royal emblem, blatantly invoking its divine and omniscient qualities as he fashioned himself into an absolute monarch of unprecedented power.

While the decadent and romantic escapades of Louis's court have been the subject of much pulpy pop culture over the years, the Sun King's true passion was diplomacy and war. At that time, what Louis termed the *métier de roi*, the kingly craft, was consumed above all else with foreign affairs, and especially with defending and expanding one's territorial domain. To the extent that a king troubled himself with domestic affairs, it was largely in the service of strengthening the state so as to make it more powerful on the European stage. Louis brought a more aggressive stance to French foreign policy, pursuing numerous wars of conquest. He had been gifted a large and effective army, the perfect tool for expanding France into a more impressive and defensible territory—for example, by seizing Alsace and moving the French border to the Rhine. Louis was particularly fond of fighting the Dutch, then a preeminent power, and extended French territory to the north and east in a series of campaigns.

France's military strength and aggressive foreign policy provoked the English and the Dutch to ally themselves with France's traditional adversary, the Austrian Hapsburgs. This led to the War of the Grand Alliance, or Nine Years' War, which was fought not only along French land borders but in the American colonies, Ireland, West Africa, and India (making it one of the earliest "world wars"). The tail end of Louis's reign was taken up by the War of the Spanish Succession, in which Europe's major powers fought for control of the Spanish throne and its vast global empire after the death of the last Spanish Hapsburg king. After a long and brutal war, the Spanish crown passed from the Hapsburgs to the House of Bourbon, as a grandson of Louis XIV became the king of Spain. But overall, the war was not a great success for France, as it was forced to relinquish a number of colonies and territories. England, on the other hand, won a raft of new colonies and commercial arrangements, and the war is commonly seen as marking the beginning of England's ascendancy over France and Spain on the global stage.

All these wars were costly, and French debt soared in the final decades of Louis's reign. The French people tired of their Sun King, with his endless wars and heavy taxes. This public discontent with the monarchy was not mollified by Louis's successors, and it would culminate later that century in the French Revolution.

Yet Louis cared little about earthly annoyances like debt and discontent, and he spent many years and millions of livres transforming his father's hunting lodge at Versailles into the splendid palace we know today. His motivations were not purely decadent: he also used the luxurious château to seduce and pacify the historically mutinous French nobility. Rather than scheming rebellion, the court at Versailles became obsessed with fashion and luxury, gossip and trends, and competing for the king's favor.

In Versailles, the Sun King maintained a strict routine, timed to the minute, as a way of maximizing efficiency and enjoyment. The rules and rituals surrounding food were among the most important, and the kitchens at Versailles employed five hundred cooks and servants to fulfill the king's culinary expectations. The king was often seated alone at his table, either *au grand couvert*, in a large hall in view of the entire court, or *au petit couvert*, in his own rooms with high-placed courtiers lurking about. Unlike the traditional banquet, with its elaborate seating arrangements reflecting gradations of privilege and power, the *couvert* emphasized the absolutism of Louis's reign, in which even his closest family members dared not approach him.[1]

Louis was known to have a ferocious appetite; his sister-in-law, Princess Elizabeth Charlotte (known as the Princess Palatine), noted that she "often saw the king eat four full plates of various soups, a whole pheasant, a partridge, a big plate of salad, two big slices of ham, mouton in gravy and garlic, a plate of pastries, and also fruits and boiled eggs."[2] Perhaps unsurprisingly, it was discovered upon the king's death and autopsy that his stomach was three times larger than that of a normal adult. Yet despite chronic digestion and dental issues, the king persevered with his feasts, determined to maintain a public façade of good health even when suffering mightily. In the words of the nineteenth-century French literary critic Charles-Augustin Sainte-Beuve, "if the man in reality was so often ill, the King always appeared well."[3]

Dr. Guy-Crescent Fagon, the royal physician, was rather vexed by the king's gluttony, and in particular his love of vegetables, which were thought to worsen his digestive issues. Of particular concern was the king's love of green peas, on which he apparently gorged whenever they were in season. Peas first became fashionable at Versailles in 1660, when a courtier returning from Italy presented a basket of peas to the king in January, far ahead of season. Initially a novelty, a serious green pea craze ensued. The court became so enamored of peas that they appeared on the menu every evening, in multiple dishes. Madame de Maintenon, the mistress and later second wife of the king, wrote,

> The chapter of peas still lasts: the impatience to eat some, the pleasure of having eaten some, and the joy of eating them again are the three points which our princes have been talking about for the last four days. Some ladies, after having supper with the king and eaten well, find

peas at home to eat before going to bed, at the risk of having an indigestion. It is a fashion, it is a furor.[4]

The Sun King had a great affection generally for *les primeurs*, the "new vegetables" grown just ahead or at the very beginning of their usual season. (They tend to have a fresher taste; *carottes primeur*, for example, available in May and June, are sweeter and crunchier.) So he eventually ordered his gardener, Jean-Baptiste La Quintinie, to defy nature and produce his favorite fruits and vegetables out of season. La Quintinie was a renowned gardener, but even he must have been daunted by the task set before him, especially when he saw what was set aside for the new vegetable garden: a swampy patch of land on the edge of the château grounds. Yet he had the benefit of limitless funds and manpower, and between 1678 and 1683, the land was drained and a system of terraces and walls built up, creating multiple levels at which plants could be grown. By manipulating these levels and their exposure to the sun, La Quintinie could create various microclimates within the twenty-five-acre garden. He also built greenhouses and experimented with new pruning methods. His dedication and ingenuity eventually paid off, and he was able to produce for the king asparagus in January, strawberries in March, peas in April, and so on. He planted dozens of varieties—fifty types of pears and sixteen kinds of lettuce, for example—so fresh produce could be served to the king year-round. A new *figuerie* housed seven hundred trees to provide the king with his beloved figs, and the demand for asparagus was so high that it was eventually given a larger plot outside the garden (the *clos des asperges*, or asparagus enclosure). La Quintinie himself was enamored of a winter pear, the Bon Chrétien (Good Christian), which could satisfy the court's fruit cravings until the spring blooms. Louis sent these pears as gifts to European notables.

Louis XIV was delighted with his *primeurs* and with his new garden. He enjoyed walking in the Potager du Roi and admiring his miraculous vegetables and fruits, and he often showed it off to foreign dignitaries. He ennobled La Quintinie for his efforts and rued his death in 1688 as a "great loss." After bending the aristocracy to his will and reshaping the map of the world with his armies, Louis must have been pleased that he could also force nature to bear its fruit earlier for him.

Somehow the king's vegetable garden survived the French Revolution and two world wars, and it is now used by the École Nationale Supérieure du Paysage to train future landscapers. It still produces fruits and vegetables, which can be bought in the garden shop. La Quintinie's achievement may not seem so miraculous to our modern sensibilities, with globalization bringing us virtually any type of food year-round, but his garden reminds us that for most of human existence, the diets of even the most powerful and divine kings were subject to nature's rules. For all the immense power that the Sun King accumulated, he could not in fact call forth his favorite vegetables with his own brilliance. It was science that came to the rescue, and not for the last time.

29

The Devil's Wine

All of the great revolutions in human affairs we have encountered thus far—the Renaissance, the Reformation, the decline of feudalism, and the discovery of the New World—culminated in the most epochal transformation of this millennium: the scientific revolution. The belief that experimentation and reason could explain the world around us, rather than ancient texts or God's mysterious ways, irrevocably ushered in the modern era.

French scientists—or as they were known then, "natural philosophers"—were among the most pivotal figures of this age. The philosophical arguments of René Descartes, captured in the famous phrase "I think, therefore I am," helped establish the very modern notion that humans could use their own reason in pursuit of truth, rather than depending on divine revelation. Descartes was also one of the leading mathematicians of the early seventeenth century, developing the initial principles of analytic geometry. Pierre de Fermat, another legendary mathematician, invented differential calculus and, with yet another Frenchman, Blaise Pascal, formulated the theory of probability.

Naturally, this era of rapid innovation and experimentation

featured advances in the gastronomic world as well. Better under-standing of chemical and anatomical principles gradually displaced the emphasis on balancing "humors" within one's diet, and prefer-ences of taste began to be prioritized over medical advice.[1] But if there is one product that captures the shift from serendipity to sci-ence in French gastronomy, it is champagne—one of the most beloved wines of France, and indeed the world, but only because of decades of obsessive tinkering and experimentation.

As with many French wines, we would not recognize the earliest versions of champagne, produced in the region of the same name in northeast France. Lying on the extreme edge of possible winemak-ing terrain, its vineyards historically produced a thin, pale pink wine. Local vintners strove to compete with the renowned wines of nearby Burgundy and benefited from the royal tradition of staging coronations—with all the excessive drinking they entailed—in Reims, the central city of the Champagne region. For hundreds of years, wine from Champagne was highly valued in both France and England—but as *still* wine, not the sparkling beverage we know today.

In fact, throughout the medieval and early modern eras, bubbles were seen as a major flaw in Champagne's wines. They were a quirk of the region's northerly climate: after the fall harvest, the fermen-tation of the wine during the winter months could be prematurely halted by the excessive chill. Then, as temperatures rose again in the spring, the fermentation would restart and produce an excess amount of carbon dioxide. For several weeks, the wine would churn and froth in its barrels, until the gas completely leaked out and the wine settled into a still form, ready to be distributed.

But beginning in the sixteenth century, winemakers and mer-chants throughout Europe began storing and selling wine in bottles instead of barrels. This proved problematic for champagne because if it was bottled before the second fermentation began, the carbon dioxide had no way to escape, and the bottle would often randomly explode into bits.[2] The wine acquired the nickname *vin du diable*, "the devil's wine," in keeping with the traditional inclination to attribute misfortune to otherworldly agents. Vintners at the time made use of fermentation without actually understanding the chemi-cal processes at work, and so they did not know how to prevent these calamities.

Those bottles that survived the winter intact yielded a wine with a bubbly, sparkling quality that drove the vintners of Champagne to despair. But the English upper classes took a liking to fizzy champagne and were the first to recast it as a glamorous indulgence. It was actually an English scientist, Christopher Merret, who first presented a paper to the eminent Royal Society in London, in 1662, on the practice of adding sugar to wine during fermentation in order to intentionally produce sparkling wine. French products were very fashionable in London in the 1660s, following the Restoration of King Charles II and his nobles, who had spent a lengthy exile in France. The wines of Champagne and Bordeaux profited a great deal from his return to the throne.

Perhaps unsurprisingly, the French legends surrounding champagne tend to omit these English contributions and focus instead on the colorful character of Dom Pierre Pérignon. He was a Benedictine monk at the abbey of Hautvillers, in the Champagne region, who coincidentally was born and died in the exact same years as Louis XIV (1638–1715). He was in charge of the abbey's vineyards, and according to legend he had an amazing superpower: he could taste a grape and tell you exactly which vineyard it had come from. Some say this was thanks to his extremely limited diet, or perhaps it was because he was blind.

Dom Pérignon originally sought to prevent the secondary fermentation thought to be so ruinous to champagne, but by the 1670s, as the sparkling variety became more popular in both England and France, he embarked on a series of innovations intended to make the winemaking process more predictable. He is credited as the originator of *la méthode champenoise*, the "traditional method" of champagne making, which vintners continue to use today. He developed a new white wine blend for the initial fermentation, produced from red grapes via a new pressing method. According to the French, it was Dom Pérignon who discovered the trick of using sugar to intentionally induce secondary fermentation, after observing the effects of using sweet beeswax to seal wine bottles. Legend says that he got the idea of using cork to plug the bottles, which helped them resist the intense pressure building up inside them, from a pair of traveling Spanish monks (but like many elements of his legend, this may be purely apocryphal). He built wine cellars deep within the chalky soil of his abbey to limit temperature variations. By the time of Dom Pérignon's death, champagne making was still a volatile and not fully understood process, but it had progressed considerably down the road to modernity. In the nineteenth century, his vineyards at the abbey of Hautvillers were acquired by Moët & Chandon, who later gave his name to one of the world's finest champagnes.

Champagne was introduced to Versailles in the late seventeenth century, but it became more widely popular in France during the Régence, or Regency, after the death of Louis XIV in 1715. Louis had ruled for so many years that his sons and grandsons had preceded him to the grave, and so the crown passed to his five-year-old great-grandson, Louis XV. The old king's nephew, the Duke of Orléans, ruled on the child's behalf until 1723. The Regency was a more relaxed era, when the French people—and especially the nobility—felt liberated from the stifling autocracy they had endured under the Sun King. The court returned to Paris, with the regent ensconced at the Palais-Royal, and the famous Parisian salons became popular gathering places for political and cultural discussion. The upper classes reveled in extravagant celebrations, and the bubbly sparkle of champagne seemed to fit the zeitgeist perfectly. Its popularity continued into the reign of Louis XV—his mistress Madame de Pompadour famously declared that "champagne is the only wine that leaves a woman beautiful after drinking it"—and on into the present day.

The Regency is also when the Enlightenment, known in France as *le siècle des Lumières* (the century of lights), is commonly held to have begun, as the revolutionary thought of philosophers and scientists crescendoed in a broad movement advocating liberty, religious tolerance, and human progress through reason. The roots of modern liberalism were planted here in the eighteenth century, with Paris as an epicenter of intellectual rebellion against the political and religious dogmas of the day. Montesquieu developed the idea of the separation of church and state, and Jean-Jacques Rousseau put forward his vision of the "social contract," in which a ruler's legitimacy is derived not from God but from the consent of his people to be governed. Voltaire, one of the greatest writers of this or any period of French history, suffused his philosophical and literary works with a quintessentially modern belief in religious tolerance and human progress, and advocated passionately for the abolition of torture and other barbaric punishments of the time.

Voltaire was also an enthusiastic devotee of champagne. He wrote, in 1736:

> A *wine of which the pressed foam,*
> *From the bottle with sleek force,*

Painting by Jean-François de Troy, *Le Déjeuner d'huîtres (The Oyster Lunch)*, 1735. On the far left, a bottle of champagne has been opened, and several diners admire its cork flying upward—perhaps one of the earliest representations of the "devil's wine" in action. From the collection of the Musée Condé, Chantilly.

> *Like a thunder made the cork fly;*
> *It lifts off, we laugh; it strikes the ceiling.*
> *The sparkling froth of this fresh wine,*
> *Is the brilliant image of our French.*[3]

Unfortunately for the makers of champagne, their homeland in northeast France lay astride one of the best invasion routes into the country. But one of the most famous innovators of champagne found a way to turn this to her advantage. Barbe-Nicole Ponsardin had married François Clicquot, the head of a small champagne-producing enterprise, in 1798. After his untimely death in 1805, she took over the family business and renamed it Veuve Clicquot Ponsardin (*veuve* meaning "widow" in French). She introduced a number of techniques to champagne production that produced an exceptional wine, considered by some to be the first truly modern champagne.

Disaster loomed, however, with Napoleon's defeat at Moscow and slow retreat back to France, pursued by a coalition of Russian, Prussian, and Austrian armies, which entered Champagne in 1814. Most of her fellow producers buried their wares and fled, but the widow Clicquot decided to take a different approach, offering her wines freely to the occupying troops before the looting began. She was betting that the Russians, in particular, would develop an affinity for her brand, famously declaring: "Today, they drink. Tomorrow, they will pay!" And sure enough, when she undertook a massive gamble the following year and shipped several thousand bottles of champagne to Russia, she found the aristocracy already clamoring for it. The tsar himself, upon sampling her best vintage, declared that he would drink nothing else, and the Russian obsession with Veuve Clicquot endured as long as the tsars themselves.

Eventually, in the nineteenth century, a young French chemist named Jean-Baptiste François figured out how to calculate the right amount of sugar to add to champagne, thus making it easier to control fermentation and limit the damage caused by exploding bottles. The great Louis Pasteur, in his studies of beer and wine, discovered exactly how the fermentation process worked. And so finally, the apostles of science managed to subdue the devil's wine, making its production safer and more predictable.

They could not, unfortunately, protect champagne from the ravages of nature and humankind. In the late nineteenth century, the region's vineyards were virtually wiped out by phylloxera, a microscopic pest inadvertently imported from North America. After a long struggle to rebuild the vineyards, World War I broke out, and the front line ran directly through the Champagne region. Women and children struggled to harvest the grapes as artillery attacks and ground offensives swirled about them, and in the end perhaps 40 percent of the region's vineyards were destroyed. With the end of war came the double whammy of the Bolshevik Revolution and American Prohibition, which destroyed two of the wine's biggest markets. Yet the producers of champagne prevailed, rebuilding their vineyards and focusing on other markets—in particular, the British, who preferred a drier version of the wine and thus permanently altered the predominant style of champagne produced. In 1936, an AOC was awarded that meant no wine grown outside of the region could be called champagne (a rule the French have been trying to get foreign producers to respect ever since).

Over the years, many notable figures have professed a love for champagne. There is some controversy over whether it was Napoleon or Churchill who first said, "In victory, you deserve champagne; in defeat, you need it," but there is no doubt that both adored the wine, along with millions of others around the world. Today, more than 300 million bottles of champagne are produced annually to satisfy the world's thirst for extravagance.[4] It may be the quintessential French product: passionately grown, elaborately curated, imparting an evanescent joie de vivre and sense of liberating escape from the travails of everyday life. Thanks to the stubborn efforts of vintners and scientists, champagne has truly escaped the devil's clutches and lodged itself firmly within the pantheon of French gastronomy.

30

An Enlightened Approach to Food

Nothing is more insipid than early fruits and vegetables.

—*Jean-Jacques Rousseau*[1]

After eight years of the Régence, Louis XV came to power in 1723, at the tender age of thirteen. He would sit on the throne for more than fifty years, presiding over a gradual decline of French power and prosperity. He tried to emulate his great-grandfather's autocratic rule, but this Louis was no Sun King. He was not particularly bright, nor forceful, nor ambitious. France spiraled into disorder while the king indulged in a life of languor and vice, with the court reensconced in the decadent environs of Versailles. The king was a profligate spender and notorious for his many mistresses and his predatory pursuit of women. Whispers of a royal "harem" of young beauties swirled scandalously about the court for years.

In the spring of 1744, Louis was encouraged by one of his young mistresses to take a more active role in the plodding War of the Austrian Succession, another French attempt (this time, allied with Prussia) to cripple their Hapsburg foes. While preparing to invade the Austrian Netherlands, he fell ill for some months in the city of Metz, of some kind of unspecified fever. This may have been the only time Louis XV was truly popular among his subjects, as the French people prayed fervently for his recovery. Thousands of candles were lit at Notre-Dame for Louis "le Bien Aimé" (the Well Loved). Louis vowed that should he survive, he would build a new church dedicated to Saint Genevieve, the patron saint of Paris. He eventually recovered and commissioned the church to be built on a hill overlooking the Seine, in the Latin Quarter of Paris. By the time the fabulously ornate church was completed in 1790, the French Revolution had dimmed enthusiasm for religious projects. The building instead became the magisterial Panthéon, a secular mausoleum dedicated to the most transcendent citizens of the Republic.

Among those buried in the Panthéon is Jean-Jacques Rousseau, a giant of the Enlightenment whose radical political philosophy enormously influenced the American and French revolutionaries of the late eighteenth century. Relatively less attention has been given to his unorthodox ideas about food and the human diet, which also epitomized the broad challenge to dogma and authority that characterized eighteenth-century France.

Rousseau believed that early man had been born free, in a "state of nature," but over time had become corrupted and enslaved by the social conventions that arose with the progress of civilization, and especially with the emergence of private property. One manifestation of this fall from innocence was the eating of meat, an unnatural practice that symbolized man's abandonment of harmony with nature for a world of cruelty and competition. He wrote: "All savages are cruel, and it is not their morals which cause them to be so. This cruelty comes from their food. They go to war as to the hunt and treat men like bears . . . Great villains harden themselves to murder by drinking blood."[2]

Unlike most people at that time, who saw the ever-increasing diversity and sumptuousness of food as a sign of the progress of civilization, Rousseau disapproved of complicated and luxurious foods. They transformed the act of eating from one of survival to one of prestige, and they provided yet more evidence of man's increasing detachment from nature. And Rousseau was particularly appalled by the "new vegetables" so painstakingly produced at Versailles: "It takes effort—and not taste—to disturb the order of nature, to wring from it involuntary produce which it gives reluctantly and with its curse."[3]

Clearly, if eating meat, fancy foods, and unnaturally early vegetables took mankind away from the benevolent state of nature, harmony might be encouraged by avoiding such foods and adhering to a simple diet of bread, eggs, dairy, fruit, and conventional vegetables, which is exactly what Rousseau advocated. He was particularly fond of omelettes, and apparently considered himself something of a specialist in preparing them.

Rousseau enjoyed wine, but not to excess. Interestingly, while he saw drunkenness as a failing, he did not assume it was worse than many other vices; an honest drunk was worth more than a duplicitous sober person. He wrote, "In countries of bad character, plots, treasons, adultery, one fears the state of indiscretion when one can show his heart without thinking about it. Everywhere, people that loathe drunkenness the most are those that have the strongest interest to avoid it."[4] He described three categories of wine. *Vin du cru* was the regular *vin de pays* enjoyed by ordinary people, those who embraced good food without pretension. This was the best wine, of course, the most natural and authentic. *Vins fins* was the luxury wine of the elites, and *vin frelaté* was the adulterated wine sold by unscrupulous innkeepers.[5]

While Rousseau was an extreme voice, his devotion to authenticity over artificiality was shared by a number of other thinkers at that time.[6] The famous *Encyclopédie* edited by Denis Diderot and Jean Le Rond d'Alembert, for example, revealed its bias toward authenticity in its entry for "Cuisine," noting that there existed "about a hundred different ways to disfigure the foods that nature gives us, which thereby lose their good quality and become, if one can say so, pleasing poisons that destroy tempers and shorten lives."[7] Gradually, more and more people came to see the virtue of simplicity and tradition. The kind of rustic cuisine long scorned by tastemakers became seen as thrifty and virtuous, contributing to a more moral lifestyle. Moderation in diet was increasingly seen as vital for good physical health, too, as scientific understanding of the human body progressed. Fresh food, prepared simply, was appealing after so many years of elaborate, heavy dishes. New cookbooks appeared to help the bourgeois classes adapt aristocratic recipes to their own capabilities.

Even Louis XV, hardly a progressive thinker, favored a more natural and intimate style of dining than his predecessor. He enjoyed having meals at a round table in a small *salle à manger*, or dedicated dining room, a concept just then becoming popular among the aristocracy. He even cooked for himself sometimes, and a number of his courtiers were keen gastronomes. Louis's most notable mistresses, Madame de Pompadour and Madame du Barry, plied the king with his favorite foods, creating or inspiring a number of dishes (*filets de sole à la Pompadour*, for example, features Madame's beloved truffles; *crème de chou fleur à la Dubarry* is a creamy cauliflower soup, as pale as its namesake's skin).

Louis gradually spent less and less time at Versailles, preferring the conviviality of Paris. But this did not limit his carousing and spending, and the royal debts piled higher and higher. The luxurious tastes of Madame du Barry also cost the crown millions of livres (she would eventually be sent to the guillotine, in 1793, during the Reign of Terror). Louis also engendered serious diplomatic and military reversals for France, embarking on a disastrous alliance with Austria and losing French dominions in Canada and India to the British following the Seven Years' War. By the end of his reign, French power had substantially evaporated, and popular dissatisfaction with the monarchy was evident everywhere—in provincial assemblies, among philosophers and writers and artists, in the cafés of Paris. In his final years, the king did not dare appear in public.

Louis XV died of smallpox in 1774. Only three candles were lit in Notre-Dame for the previously Well Loved, a sign of how far he had fallen from favor.[8] So great was the popular hostility to the monarchy that only a truly splendid king could have snatched it from its looming fate. Instead, Louis's grandson assumed the crown as King Louis XVI, the last king of the ancien régime.

31

Revolution in the Cafés

The fourteenth of July is France's national holiday. In English-speaking countries, this holiday is usually called Bastille Day, marking the liberation of the Bastille prison in Paris on July 14, 1789, which is commonly seen as the opening event of the French Revolution. But this is not how most French people refer to it, and a few people might find it slightly offensive. Technically, the holiday is meant to commemorate the Fête de la Fédération, the nationwide celebration held on July 14, 1790, upon the establishment of a constitutional monarchy in France—a far loftier achievement than storming a prison. The French themselves usually refer to the fourteenth of July as *la fête nationale* (the national celebration) or even just *le quatorze juillet* (the fourteenth of July).

While much of the country shuts down for the day, many cafés do stay open, which seems only fitting given that the cafés of Paris played an important role in nourishing the ideas and ideologues of the French Revolution. Sometimes the café makes a dramatic appearance in the revolutionary narrative—witness Camille Desmoulins, one of the foremost agitators of revolution, leaping upon a table at the Café du Foy to incite insurrection among the Parisians two days before the Bastille fell. But their overall influence was more subtle, as throughout the eighteenth century, cafés gradually acquired a social function that went far beyond the provision of coffee, wine, and snacks.

We have already seen, in a previous chapter, the introduction of coffee to the Parisian elites by the Ottoman ambassador. But it was an Armenian entrepreneur named Pascal who first supplied the ordinary people of Paris with the new beverage, selling coffee at his lemonade stands and setting up a temporary Turkish coffeehouse at Saint-Germain's annual fair. In 1672, he decided to open a more permanent version near the Pont Neuf, which he called a *café* (the French word for coffee). It attracted meager crowds, mostly those who had lived or traveled in the Orient and were already fond of coffee. He eventually went broke, closed the coffeehouse, and sailed for London, where coffee was more popular.

But his efforts were not forgotten, and some years later, another immigrant entrepreneur named François Procope, from Sicily, tried a different tack. After working at one of Pascal's lemonade stands, he decided to open an eponymous coffeehouse in a more propitious location in Saint-Germain-des-Prés in 1686. Soon after, the Comédie-Française, the celebrated theater company, moved across the street, providing Café Procope with a readymade theater and literary crowd that cemented its reputation and profitability. Many years later, the café was transformed into a restaurant, and it remains a popular (if perhaps slightly overrated) tourist destination today.

Cafés flourished during the Enlightenment, offering a convivial space for writers, artists, and intellectuals of all sorts to work, exchange ideas, and enjoy the vibrant Parisian zeitgeist. Voltaire fed his impressive caffeine addiction at the Café Procope, reputedly drinking several dozen cups a day of coffee mixed with chocolate. Benjamin Franklin was also a patron during his charm offensive in Paris, trying to win French support for the American revolutionary cause. Jean-Jacques Rousseau and Denis Diderot sparred at the chessboard in the Café Maugis, although Diderot usually labored over his *Encyclopédie* at the Café de la Régence (the *Encyclopédie* eventually tried to capture the rousing atmosphere of cafés by describing them as "manufactories of mind, whether good or bad"). By the 1780s, there were hundreds of cafés in Paris. Some of the most popular, such as the Café du Foy and Café de la Régence, were tucked into the arcades of the Palais-Royal, a den of gambling, prostitution, and febrile political discourse. Originally intended as mere coffeehouses, the cafés began serving wine and a bit of food as well, as they do today.

The men who would lead France to revolution were great patrons of the cafés. Maximilien Robespierre preferred the Café de la Régence, when he wasn't devouring oranges at Café Procope; Danton was fond of the Café Parnasse, so much so that he eventually fell in love with and married the café owner's daughter, Antoinette-Gabrielle Charpentier. The cafés provided a space for political debate and agitation, for sharing the latest news and rumors, and for crafting plots and alliances. Their importance only increased as political turmoil grew ever more fervid.

By 1789, financial crisis and food scarcity had generated unprecedented levels of anger and resentment among the French people, particularly in the traditionally unruly environs of Paris. King Louis XVI decided to convene, for the first time since 1614, the Estates General, a meeting of representatives of the traditional three estates (the clergy, the nobility, and the common people). He hoped this would allow him to enact a number of measures to stabilize the country's finances, but the members of the Third Estate in particular developed overoptimistic expectations about potential reforms, hoping that their concerns would finally be addressed. As in previous eras, the vast majority of French people were members of the Third Estate, but now the bourgeoisie was the financial motor of France, and they were increasingly resentful of their lack of political and social power.[1] The French population was one of the most heavily and unequally taxed in Europe. The clergy and nobility were still exempted from most taxes, while the Third Estate faced a seemingly endless variety of them—not just the personal taxes levied on each family, but the salt tax, tithes to the church, customs duties, and one-off taxes to pay down the huge national debt. Tax collectors were often corrupt, and the entire system was ridiculously inefficient. Popular grievance simmered ever closer to the boiling point.

Fueled by the ideas of Enlightenment thinkers, the members of the Third Estate who attended the Estates General in May 1789 were determined to achieve fundamental change. The situation was well summed up by Emmanuel-Joseph Sieyès, a clergyman and influential political activist: "What is the third estate? Everything. What was it until now in the political sphere? Nothing. What does it want? To become something."[2] In June 1789, the representatives of the Third Estate declared themselves to be a National Assembly, the true voice of the nation, and vowed to write a new constitution that would govern the affairs of France.

King Louis eventually acquiesced to the creation of the Assembly, but he also positioned several thousand troops around Paris, heightening tensions in the capital. The catalyst for revolt was the king's firing of the popular finance minister on July 11, which appeared to herald a crackdown on the Assembly and brought angry Parisians into the streets. Desmoulins's rabble-rousing speech at the Café du Foy on July 12 helped transform the simmering unrest into actual riots, and the barricades were raised. As the mob took control of Paris, they burned down a primary target of popular anger: the *barrières*, or toll booths, that surrounded the city and imposed a toll on all the foods and wines that entered the capital.[3] Rebellious

Camille Desmoulins incites the crowd to revolution at the Café du Foy on July 12, 1789, with the legendary appeal, *"Aux armes, citoyens!"* ("To arms, citizens!"). A statue of Desmoulins leaping upon his café chair was raised in the spot on the centenary of the revolution but removed and melted down by the Vichy regime in 1942. From the French Revolution Digital Archive, a collaboration of the Stanford University Libraries and the Bibliothèque Nationale de France. Unattributed. *Camillus Desmoulins predigt Aufruhr in dem Palais Royal: den 12 Jul. 1789*, produced in Germany between 1794 and 1820.

militias also seized thousands of guns from the Hôtel des Invalides, and this may have provided the actual motivation for storming the Bastille, which was not only a symbol of royal despotism but a storage space for gunpowder. It was captured and its governor executed, his head paraded on a spike through the streets. The citizens of the capital prepared for a royal onslaught, but faced with this turmoil, the king withdrew his troops. The Marquis de Lafayette, the hero of the American Revolution now supporting the French revolutionary cause, took command of a new "Bourgeois Militia," soon renamed the National Guard, which seized responsibility for law and order in Paris away from the royal guards. (Lafayette later gave the original key to the Bastille to George Washington, and it remains on display at Mount Vernon.)

We tend to think of the French Revolution as a unitary event, but it was really a series of political uproars that extended over many years. In this earliest phase, those advocating the transformation of France into a constitutional monarchy won out, while the more radical voices clamoring for a republic were forced to wait a few more years. In August 1789, the National Assembly formally abolished all feudal rights and structures, which were seen as the underlying basis for social inequalities, and announced the Declaration of the Rights of Man, an astounding manifestation of liberal Enlightenment ideals.

The cafés continued to house political intrigue in the following years, even as some of their most ardent patrons went to the guillotine: Desmoulins and Danton were consigned to death in April 1794 by Robespierre, who followed himself a few months later. The French politician Narcisse-Achille de Salvandy noted that even as the cafés became more moderate in the postrevolutionary era, "one does not govern against the cafés. The revolution took place because they were for the revolution; Napoleon reigned because they were for glory." Small wonder he defined them as "one of the branches of legislative power in the free nations."[4]

The revolution also generated a sea change in the capital's restaurants. With the fall of the Bastille and the ugly public mood surrounding it, many wealthy nobles decided (probably correctly) that emigration might be a safe course of action. As they fled, they left behind their household staff, including their chefs, many of whom were talented and ingenious cooks. A number of these unemployed chefs decided to open their own restaurants, in which anybody with sufficient funds could dine in style.

Restaurants had existed before the revolution, but they were a fairly new invention and suffered from competition with the various food guilds that had existed since the Middle Ages. Every type of food business had its guild, and each guild had its privileges. It was not possible, for example, to go to a single purveyor for a wide range of meat. *Traiteurs* served cooked meat dishes and stews, while *rôtisseurs* sold roasted meat, and *charcutiers* served cured pork products like ham, rillettes, and sausages (for raw meat, a trip to the butcher or poulterer was required). Bar owners and wine sellers could sell drinks but they were not allowed to sell food. Prior to the revolution, restaurants—from the French *restaurer*, "to restore"—were limited to selling restorative bouillons, which were technically distinct from the meaty stews that only traiteurs could serve. But as French cuisine developed, the medieval rules imposing a neat division of food types became more and more difficult to enforce. Already, in the decade prior to the revolution, restaurants were pushing the boundaries of the guild rules and offering full menus of elaborate dishes. Instead of the common table available at traiteurs and taverns, they offered small private tables, where individuals and small groups were served by elegant waiters.

Restaurants were still limited in number until 1791, when the Assembly voted to abolish the guilds and their sales privileges. Restaurants could now legitimately sell anything, and this led to a rapid expansion in their numbers and quality. It was a great advance for the capital's dining scene, although not everyone immediately appreciated the restaurant concept. A contemporary writer, Louis-Sébastien Mercier, complained about the idea of a menu with fixed prices that you received upon entering: unlike the more honest traiteur, who displayed the food and price at the same time, restaurants demanded high prices without any view of the food on offer. When the plates did arrive, the meals were always very small, like a "sample of future meals to come."[5]

On the plus side, the growth of restaurants enabled local specialties from various regions to be discovered by Parisians. Les Frères Provençaux, whose chefs originated from Marseille, offered a cuisine with a strong Provençal influence and is credited with popularizing tomatoes in Paris (although another legend claims that tomatoes came to Paris alongside "La Marseillaise," the national anthem, when prorevolutionary troops from Marseille came to Paris in 1792).

Restaurants very quickly became a landmark feature of Paris and helped define its identity. Less political than the cafés, they served all segments of society: rich and poor, manual workers and students, lawyers and artists, everyone could find a restaurant adapted to their needs. In 1801, shortly after restaurants invaded Paris, Joseph Berchoux coined the term *gastronomie*. Writers such as Grimod de la Reynière and Brillat-Savarin—who advised not on how you should cook but on what food you should enjoy—became popular. The cuisine of the ancien régime, like so many other elements of royalist rule, had been delegitimized by revolution, and this created space for the nation's finest chefs and restaurateurs to steer classical French cuisine in new directions.

Most of the restaurants and cafés of the revolutionary period have disappeared from Paris. Yet if you visit a café anywhere in France on

July 14, you are likely to get a sense of what made them so beloved and influential those many years ago. The sense of camaraderie, wit, and enjoyment of life's pleasures that so infused the cafés from their earliest days has survived intact, and they are as good a place as any to celebrate the birth of modern France.

32

Pain d'Égalité

Paris has risen, once again, like the Ocean-tide; is flow-ing toward the Tuileries, for Bread and a Constitution.

—*Thomas Carlyle[1]*

Queen Marie Antoinette, the notorious wife of Louis XVI, is best remembered for an expression she never uttered. According to leg-end, when Marie Antoinette was told that the people of France had no more bread to eat, she replied, "Let them eat cake!" In the French version of this tale, she actually instructs them to eat brioche, a very buttery and sweet loaf. In truth, there is no evidence that she ever said anything remotely like this, but it became a useful shorthand for the apparent callousness and ignorance of the French monarchs.

Kings and emperors have long understood the danger of ignor-ing the public's need for their daily bread. Roman emperor Augus-tus famously bribed the masses into quiescence with free grain and bloody spectacles, later cynically dubbed "bread and circuses." The French monarchy itself had previously tried to regulate the supply of grain through stockpiling and sales restrictions. So the idea that the queen either did not understand the importance of bread, or did not care, was a particularly effective bit of character assassination.

It helped that Marie Antoinette was deeply unpopular to begin with. She had married the future Louis XVI in 1770, at the age of fourteen, and was described as a very charming but frivolous young woman. Her union with Louis began unhappily, and it took eight years for their first child to be born. She was Austrian, at a time when France had only recently allied with its historic enemy. And her obvious preference for luxurious clothes, fine jewelry, and expensive food and furnishings, at a time when France was already sinking into debt thanks to poor governance and ruinous wars, made her an obvious target for public anger.

Marie Antoinette was known to have a sweet tooth, even baking cakes and pastries herself. One of her specialties was a lovely light meringue. She also liked fresh vegetables and had built for herself a small idealized peasant village on the grounds of Versailles. It was a place where she could pretend to be a shepherdess and experience the "rustic life." But it was also a working farm that supplied the kitchens of Versailles.

Her rustic village did not endear her with the masses, who saw it as another waste of money by a monarchy who did not appreciate their problems. This smoldering resentment intensified in 1788–89, when the price of bread rose due to bad weather and poor harvests. Bread was typically the cheapest way for people to fill their bellies; for the poorest classes, bread (or gruel made from the same grains) might furnish up to 95 percent of daily caloric intake, with people eating one to three pounds of whole-grain bread per day.[2] More than half the average household budget was spent on it. So when the price of bread doubled, things became quite desperate for a large part of the population, and this eventually helped fuel the motor of revolution.

Marie Antoinette received much of the blame for the food shortage; the king was still seen as a sort of decent but doltish buffoon, in thrall to his arrogant and decadent wife. So when Paris experienced a complete lack of bread in October 1789, three months after the fall of the Bastille, a crowd of perhaps ten thousand women walked from Paris to Versailles, determined to obtain bread for their families and bring the king back to the capital. Away from the bubble of Versailles, forced to confront the poverty and hunger in Paris, Louis would hopefully sympathize with his subjects and make sure bread was available. The marchers arrived at Versailles peacefully enough, and the king promised to provide grain, but overnight the crowd turned violent and invaded the palace. The queen nearly lost her life, only narrowly escaping the furious mob who attacked her chambers. Calm was restored when the royal family agreed to return to Paris, alongside fifty wagonloads of wheat and flour. The women accom-

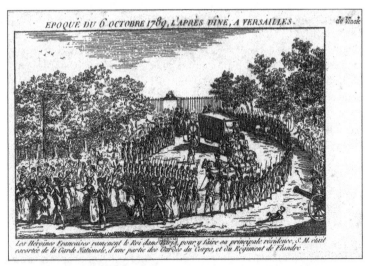

EPOQUE DU 6 OCTOBRE 1789, L'APRÈS DÎNÉ, A VERSAILLES. de Vinck

Les Héroïnes Françaises ramènent le Roi dans Paris, pour y faire sa principale résidence, S. M. était escortée de la Garde Nationale, d'une partie des Gardes du Corps, et du Régiment de Flandre.

Thousands of women escort the royal family—"the baker, the baker's wife, and the baker's boy"—back to Paris in the hopes of ensuring a daily supply of bread. From the French Revolution Digital Archive, a collaboration of the Stanford University Libraries and the Bibliothèque Nationale de France. Unattributed. *Epoque du 6 octobre 1789, l'après diné, à Versailles les héroines françaises ramènent le roi dans Paris, pour y faire sa principale résidence* (1789).

panied them all the way, shouting, "We won't lack bread anymore: we've brought back the baker, the baker's wife, and the baker's boy." The royal family took up residence in the Palais des Tuileries, essentially hostages to the goodwill of the revolutionary Assembly and the Parisian mob.

This became an increasingly fraught prospect, as the Assembly issued ever more radical decrees. All noble titles and ranks were abolished, and local *parlements* (courts) disbanded. The Catholic Church in France was subordinated to the state and no longer allowed to collect the tithe; monasteries were shut down and all Church property confiscated and sold to pay down the national debt. France's patchwork of idiosyncratic regions was replaced by a new system of eighty-three *départements*, with uniform administrative structures, enabling greater centralization of political authority. Guilds, trade monopolies, and internal tariffs were abolished in order to liberalize commerce and expand economic opportunities.

Fearful of what might come next, the royal family tried to flee Paris in June 1791. But the escape was badly executed and they were caught in Varennes, well short of their intended destination of Montmédy, where a royalist army waited. There are a number of legends around this escape: one holds that the gluttonous king fatefully delayed his flight by stopping at the town of Sainte-Menehould to try its famous pigs' trotters, while another claims he tarried to enjoy some Brie de Meaux. These are probably just embellishments, but it is true that the royals journeyed through the countryside at a glacial pace, which made their recapture inevitable.

The king was returned to Paris, and shortly afterward the Assembly approved the first French constitution. It empowered a new Legislative Assembly with sweeping political powers, while the king retained a veto. But this epic achievement was met with severe economic crisis and growing social unrest. Peasants, defrocked clergy, and émigré nobles fomented rebellion, and other European monarchs grew increasingly hostile. Finally, the king and the revolutionaries could agree on something: the best recourse for France was war (the king thought this was his best chance to restore the absolute monarchy, while the revolutionaries believed victory would entrench and spread the revolution). In April 1792, France declared war on Austria.

The war went badly. Austrian and Prussian forces menaced Paris, which only inflamed the situation further. In August, a mob attacked the Palais des Tuileries, and the royal family fled to the Legislative Assembly for protection—but the Assembly caved to popular pressure and voted to arrest the king. It also decided to hold new elections, with universal suffrage, for what would now be called the National Convention. In September, the Convention ended the constitutional monarchy and proclaimed France a republic, and French armies began winning victories in the field. The revolution had been saved.

Louis and Marie Antoinette, however, were doomed. Imprisoned in the towering Temple fortress with their two children, in conditions that left them ill and weak, they clung to scant hopes of rescue from faithful friends or foreign armies. Instead, the king was put on trial and sent to the guillotine in January 1793. Marie Antoinette followed him that October. Their young son died in the Temple prison two years later; only their daughter survived.

The killing of the king marked an irrevocable moment for the revolution. After regicide, there was no going back. All efforts were directed at building and sustaining the republic, which was threatened by foreign armies, counterrevolutionary uprisings, and social and economic unrest. More than twenty thousand people died in the cruel repression known as la Terreur, or the Reign of Terror (1793–94), but the revolutionary government also understood the need to provide for its citizens, both to contain opposition and to reform society according to republican ideals. Robespierre himself wrote, in 1793, "When, then, will the people be educated? When they have enough bread to eat . . . "[3] Price controls were instituted on a range of basic foodstuffs, including bread.

Another decree stated: "Because wealth and poverty shall disappear in the new egalitarian regime, there shall no longer be made a bread of fine flour for the rich and a bread of bran for the poor. All bakers shall, on the penalty of imprisonment, make only one good type of bread, the bread of equality."[4] This *pain d'égalité* was a very dense and unappealing bread, three-quarters wheat and one-quarter rye, and a great disappointment to a populace who had hoped social equality would mean aristocratic white bread for everyone. The real reason for the decree was a severe grain shortage, as price controls led French farmers to grow less grain and war with Britain impeded grain imports, but it was a nice bit of revolutionary rhetoric. Policies such as these make Robespierre a controversial historical figure: the embodiment of pure evil to conservatives, perhaps of necessary evil to some liberals, but altogether admirable to some Marxists.

Bread is still an essential and emblematic food for the French, but it is consumed far less than during the revolutionary era. Today, the average French person consumes about 120 grams of bread daily, which is four to ten times less than during the eighteenth century.[5] This does not mean that bread has become unpopular—virtually every French person eats bread—but it is a sign that food habits are evolving and diversifying. Still, the importance of bread can be seen in the countless small villages of France, where the last independent business to survive is usually the bakery; even towns without a post office or supermarket will manage to keep a bakery afloat.

In short, there is a reason that the French believe the "holy trinity of the table" includes not only wine and cheese but bread.[6] Had the royal heads of France only recognized this simple truth, the history of France, and indeed of liberal democracy, might look very different indeed.

33

The Potato Propagandist

The French Revolution did not just overthrow a hated regime: it laid waste to an entire social order, one that had been constructed over the course of a thousand years, and its destruction left an immense vacuum. Fueled by a utopian mélange of egalitarianism, nationalism, and scientific innovation, the new French ruling class embarked on a radical remaking of society. We have already seen some of their dramatic measures: the declaration of legal equality for all men, the subordination of the Church, the establishment of a republic. These far-reaching reforms were buttressed by social tinkering in many aspects of daily life, all of which were intended to reinforce the dramatic revolutionary project now under way.

For example, the radicals' fondness for decimalization led not only to the introduction of the first metric system of measurement but to a new calendar, which was followed for about twelve years. The new year now began on the fall equinox, and the twelve months were given new names like Vendémiaire (from *vendange*, or grape harvest) and Fructidor (from the Latin *fructus*, or fruit). Each month consisted of three ten-day weeks, with each day reconfigured into ten hours. Previously, each day of the year had commemorated a different Catholic saint, but this was adapted into a more appropriate form of worship: each day now celebrated a different element of French agriculture, such as its fruits and vegetables, its crops and livestock, even its soils and farm implements.

In this new calendar, 11 Vendémiaire (previously known as October 2) celebrated the humble *pomme de terre*, or potato. Certainly to the French today, it is a crop worthy of worship: rich in vitamins and antioxidants, easy to grow, and almost infinitely malleable, whether fried, boiled, mashed, sautéed, or baked (and it even produces pretty flowers). The potato is the most widely eaten vegetable in France, fashioned into an endless variety of gratins, soups, purees, casseroles, and pancakes. And yet shockingly, this love for potatoes is surprisingly recent, only emerging in this era of revolutionary cataclysm— and mostly as a result of the tireless propaganda efforts of one man, Antoine-Augustin Parmentier.

The ancestral home of the potato is the Andes Mountains, in modern-day Peru and Bolivia. Wild varieties were domesticated more than seven thousand years ago, and were eventually discovered by Spanish conquistadores during their destruction of the Inca civilization in the sixteenth century. The Spanish introduced the potato to Europe, but unlike some of the more successful transplants we have already encountered, the potato met with considerable resistance. It seemed dangerous to eat: the greens were poisonous, it belonged to the same toxic family of plants as deadly nightshade, and people also came to believe potatoes caused leprosy. Potatoes were not mentioned in the Bible, which gave them a suspect air. They also had a bland taste. So they were mostly used as animal feed, and this cemented their status as food not fit for humans.

But by the eighteenth century, potato consumption increased in other parts of Europe, including Italy, Britain, and the Low Countries. Frederick the Great of Prussia issued fifteen royal decrees promoting potato cultivation as a means of combating famine, and he was largely responsible for their growing popularity among Germans. For this he is sometimes called *der Kartoffelkönig*, the Potato King, and to this day people leave potatoes on his grave in Potsdam.

It is thanks to the Prussians that our hero, Monsieur Parmentier, became fascinated with the humble spud. Parmentier served in the French army as a pharmacist during the Seven Years' War (1756–63) and was captured by the Prussians. During his lengthy captivity, he ate potatoes for the first time. To his surprise, his new diet did not give him leprosy, and it actually kept him in decent shape. He returned home with a mission: to convince the French to eat potatoes. It proved to be a long and arduous campaign.

Parmentier had some early success, in 1772, when the academy of Besançon awarded him first prize in a competition on "the study of food substances that could mitigate the calamities of famine." The very existence of such a competition indicates the severity of food scarcity in this era. For Parmentier, the pursuit of the potato was not just a scientific endeavor but a moral quest to solve the enduring problem of hunger and famine. In his Besançon essay, he wrote:

> Without taking away the gratitude that we owe to the Aristotles, the Descartes and the Newtons, whose genius shed light on the universe, would not it have been

desirable that one of them, instead of gliding over the most elevated heights, dropped down to consider the primary needs of his fellow men? What does it matter to the ordinary man the course by which the stars follow their path, if during this very time they die of hunger?[1]

Yet potatoes were still slow to catch on. Many people focused on trying to use them to make bread, a logical goal at a time when the population was overly dependent on this one food item. But it was actually very difficult to make bread solely with potato flour, which lacks gluten, and the final product did not taste very good. Only gradually did people realize it was best to mix potato flour with traditional grains. Voltaire became a cheerful potato supporter, extolling the virtues of half-potato/half-wheat bread.

Parmentier remained undeterred and decided the best way to get the general population to embrace potatoes was to promote them to the aristocratic and wealthy classes first. Throughout history, foods that were seen as rare, expensive, or popular among the elites eventually became fashionable among the masses as well, so this was a fairly shrewd tactic by our potato propagandist. On the advice of Benjamin Franklin, an early convert, he organized an elegant potato dinner for prominent Parisians, in which every course featured a different potato dish.

But Parmentier's greatest marketing coup was to win the support of the royal family. In 1785, he approached King Louis XVI and Marie Antoinette at a royal banquet. He carried with him a bunch of potato flowers and somehow charmed the king to put one in his buttonhole, while the queen placed some in her wig. Thus the flower became a new fashion accessory, and the king became aware of the nourishing potential of the potato. He gave Parmentier a piece of land near Paris to cultivate potatoes, and according to legend said to him: "France will one day thank you, for having found the bread of the poor." (Unfortunately for the king, this day did not come soon enough to save his own head.) Parmentier cleverly exploited this royal gift by placing guards around his potato field to fend off intruders, leading locals to imagine that the crop planted there must be extremely valuable, and thus raising the potato's reputation higher.

Still, by the time of the revolution, the potato had made only slight inroads into popular tastes. Parmentier was not in favor with the new regime, and he left Paris for a time. But the hour of the potato had come, for the revolutionary leadership well understood that the food scarcity that had helped bring them to power could just as easily cast them out again. A malnourished population would be more inclined to criticize and resist their radical reforms and to support the royalists and counterrevolutionaries threatening the fragile republic.

In December 1793, the revolutionary government distributed ten thousand copies of Parmentier's memoir on the cultivation and consumption of potatoes. As it turned out, the potato was an ideal revolutionary food: it was a novel staple crop at a time of unprecedented innovation and transformation; it was cheap to produce and thus democratic, suiting rich and poor alike; and because it was heavier and bulkier than cereals, it was more difficult for treasonous speculators to hoard them and drive up prices.[2] Its humble character was a welcome antidote to the immoral luxuries of ancien régime cuisine.

The potato cause was also helped along by the publication of a recipe book called *La Cuisinière républicaine* in 1794. It was the first French cookbook attributed to a woman, Madame Mérigot, and it consisted solely of potato recipes. These were fairly simple: for example, *pommes des terres au champignons*, a mix of potatoes, mushrooms, shallots, and chives in a vinegary bouillon. She also had a very simple recipe for a potato salad: "After the potatoes are cooked, slice them and season with oil, vinegar, herbs, salt, and pepper. Instead of oil you can use butter or cream: this salad can be eaten hot or cold."[3] Simple, cheap, and nourishing: a food fit for the new men and women of the revolution.

As people learned more delicious ways of consuming potatoes, and scarcity continued to encourage substitute food sources, they became ever more popular, especially in Paris. The magnificent Tuileries and Luxembourg Gardens were planted with potatoes, and the balconies of the capital were dotted with potato plants. A few years later, as revolutionary ardor receded, the government's enthusiasm for promoting the potato waned. But its practical benefits had become evident, and cultivation gradually increased throughout the country. By 1803, France was already producing 1.5 million tons of potatoes per year; by midcentury, that figure rose to more than 10 million tons. Parmentier's mission was complete: the potato finally found a lasting place in French cuisine.

Parmentier was among the first recipients of Napoleon's new Legion of Honour, and he was appointed director of the national health service. When he died in 1813, he was buried in the famous

Père Lachaise Cemetery in Paris, his grave surrounded by potato flowers. In 1904, the Parmentier station was opened on the Paris Métro Line 3, and it remains a wonderfully effusive shrine to the great man: a detailed history of the potato runs alongside the platform wall, and a large statue of the noble Parmentier handing a potato to a kneeling peasant captures his popular legacy. His name also lives on in a number of potato recipes, most notably *hachis Parmentier,* a casserole of mashed potatoes and minced beef.

Today, France still produces more than 5 million tons of potatoes every year, and the average French person consumes more than 110 pounds of fresh or processed potatoes annually.[4] The country that once considered potatoes only fit for pig feed now showcases a range of delicious varieties, such as the flavorful Belle de Fontenay new potato, popular since the late nineteenth century; the Ratte fingerling potato, with a slight chestnut flavor; and the deep purple Bleue d'Auvergne, which pairs well with the cheese of the same name.

The Parmentier Métro station in Paris features a statue of a noble Parmentier giving a potato to a hungry peasant. © Lillian Hueber, 2016.

Of course, one of the most popular uses of the potato in the world today is the french fry, but it is not entirely clear whether the French can claim credit for this invention. The Belgians take particular pride in their *frites* and claim to have been eating them since the seventeenth century, when villagers in the harsh winter months would fry potatoes instead of fish when the rivers froze over. According to this narrative, American servicemen are to blame for the dish becoming known as French instead of Belgian: during World War I, American GIs encountered frites in southern Belgium, where French is spoken, and so brought them back to the United States as "french fries."

According to an alternative narrative, the French began eating frites in the 1780s, and it appears that an early French version of the fry—*pommes de terre frites à cru en petites tranches* (small slices of raw potato, deep-fried)—was brought back to the United States by none other than Thomas Jefferson, who served as American ambassador to France. They became known as "French-fried potatoes," but they did not really become popular in the United States until the twentieth century, when the name became shortened to "french fries." Regardless of which narrative is more accurate, McDonald's and other American fast-food empires helped transform the fry into a global favorite later in the twentieth century.

Today, the French eat frites with many dishes—the classic *steak-frites* springs to mind—but they are not quite as obsessed with them as the Belgians, who have been trying to acquire UNESCO cultural heritage status for their frites. When U.S. congressmen spearheaded a move to rename french fries "freedom fries," after France refused to support the 2003 invasion of Iraq, the French basically shrugged and pointed out that fries were Belgian anyway. (Their sangfroid was probably a bit more tested by reports of bottles of Dom Pérignon being poured down gutters, which just seems sacrilegious.)

But the French remain greatly enamored of potatoes generally. In fact, if a French person is feeling in great form, he or she might say *"J'ai la patate!"* ("I've got the potato!"). It's not clear where this expression comes from, but it's another indication of how positively French people now feel about a food they once demonized.

34

The Pyramid Provocation

The small town of Valençay, on the edge of the Loire Valley, is rather well known in France despite its diminutive size (historically, around three thousand inhabitants). This is partly due to the delicious wines and cheese that bear its name; in fact, Valençay is the only locale in France to have won an AOC for both its wine and its cheese. Few things are more sublime in the French summertime than sharing a bottle of crisp Valençay sauvignon blanc alongside the distinctive Valençay goat cheese, which is shaped like a cropped pyramid and coated with a salty charcoal ash.

There is a well-known legend explaining how Valençay cheese came to have this unusual flat-topped pyramid shape, and it has to do with the other notable feature of Valençay: its enormous and elegant Renaissance château, which draws thousands of visitors each year.

Valençay's striking shape has spawned a revealing legend about the remarkable duo of Napoleon and Talleyrand. © Pipa100 (Dreamstime Photos).

Among the most popular attractions at the château are the extensive kitchens, in which the finest chefs of France once performed exquisite gastronomic feats. Today, the château bears homage to their talents by presenting monthly gourmet dinners, drawing upon the delectable bounty of the Loire Valley.

The Château de Valençay was built in the sixteenth century, but its most famous occupant did not take up ownership until 1803. Charles Maurice de Talleyrand-Périgord, known familiarly to history as Talleyrand, bought the château and its lands with a little financial help from Napoleon Bonaparte, whom he was then serving as foreign minister. It was purportedly thanks to his purchase of the château that the local goat cheese acquired its famous shape—an incident that reveals a good deal not only about Napoleon's fiery temper but about the skilled diplomat who orchestrated French and European affairs so cunningly during one of the most tempestuous periods of the modern era.

Talleyrand's diplomatic skills are evident in his record of support for, consecutively, the monarchy, the revolution, the Directory that replaced the faltering revolutionary government in 1795, and the coup d'état that eventually brought Napoleon to power. He had a superb knack for supporting a political order until the moment it became untenable, and then finding a suitable position in the new regime. (He once justified his opportunism with the cynical quip, "Treason is a matter of dates.") Born into an aristocratic yet poor family, he had amassed a large fortune through shrewd business deals, and this facilitated a life of luxury that, while indulgent, was also strategic. While serving as a French ambassador and then foreign minister, Talleyrand deployed the best of French culture and French gastronomy to win over rivals, flatter potential allies, and craft artful compromises that seemingly benefited all parties. He was an unparalleled practitioner of what today we call "soft power," explicitly taking advantage of the reputation of French cuisine—regarded as the most refined in Europe since at least the mid-seventeenth century—to pursue core national interests.[1] He is famous for saying to the king, upon departing for negotiations at the Congress of Vienna that would reshape European politics: "Sire, I have more need of saucepans than instructions."

Talleyrand had a long and complicated relationship with Napoleon, who rose to power in the 1790s as the revolutionary project began to unravel. Napoleon had also been born into a noble but relatively poor family, in Corsica, in 1769. Like many impoverished young French noblemen, he embarked on a military career, and he began to find fame in the early years of the revolution. In 1793, he reclaimed the key port city of Toulon from a counterrevolutionary force of royalists backed by the British navy; two years later, he put down an attempted royalist uprising in Paris. He was given command of the French army in Italy and won a series of improbable victories there, displaying the innovative and dauntless war-making style that would eventually help him conquer much of Europe. This made him a popular hero, and also essential to the revolutionary government, as the plunder he amassed in Italy was desperately needed to stave off national bankruptcy.

The revolutionary regime was in desperate straits, beset by financial calamity, wars with European rivals, and internal rebellion. In 1795, the National Convention was superseded by the Directory, a panel of five men appointed by two elected assemblies. But the Directory fared little better and was constantly assailed by both royalist and radical factions. Concerned over Napoleon's growing popularity, the Directors persuaded him to embark on a new challenge: the conquest of Ottoman Egypt. France was at war with Britain, but its navy was too weak to confront the British directly. The French invasion of Egypt was intended to indirectly harm Britain by disrupting its quickest trade route to India, which was then falling under British control. It might even give France a platform for challenging British imperial dominance in South Asia.

Napoleon, already envisioning himself as a new Alexander the Great, sailed east in 1798 with more than thirty thousand men. At first, he enjoyed a string of successes. He evaded the British navy in the Mediterranean and captured Malta and then the Egyptian port of Alexandria. After marching two weeks through the desert, he defeated the fearsome Mamluk army in the shadow of Cairo's pyramids, the modern weapons and tactics of the French army overwhelming the fiercest soldiers of the Ottoman world. Napoleon dreamed of conquering a vast eastern empire, later writing that he saw himself "marching into Asia, riding an elephant, a turban on my head and in my hand a new Koran that I would have composed to suit my needs."[2] But these visions of grandeur were crushed by Admiral Horatio Nelson of Britain, who finally caught up to the French fleet off the coast of Egypt and sunk nearly every ship. Napoleon was trapped, with no way to return home or resupply himself. He

This contemporary cartoon depicts Admiral Nelson's victory in the Battle of the Nile. Each crocodile represents a French ship that was captured, blown up, or managed to escape. From the French Revolution Digital Archive, a collaboration of the Stanford University Libraries and the Bibliothèque Nationale de France. Drawing by James Gillray (1798). *Extirpation of the Plagues of Egypt; Destruction of Revolutionary Crocodiles; or, The British Hero Cleansing Ye Mouth of Ye Nile.*

still clung to hopes of conquest, mounting a doomed expedition into Syria, but his army was plagued by disease and poor morale.

In the end, Napoleon abandoned his soldiers in Egypt and returned to France, then threatened by war with Britain, Russia, and Austria (his Egyptian army eventually surrendered to the British in 1801). He and his political allies fomented a coup, replacing the ill-fated Directory with a Consulate of three leaders. Napoleon was first consul and, for all intents and purposes, now dictator of France. Talleyrand supported his coup and became foreign minister.

Napoleon acquired the nickname "the Corsican Ogre," thanks to his monstrous talents for conquest and bloodshed in the ensuing years. He revolutionized European warfare, which throughout the preceding century had been conducted in a very limited way, with correspondingly indecisive results. Tactics and weaponry in the

1700s required well-trained soldiers, and so European armies tended to be rather small and expensive to maintain, and were thrown into battle only when absolutely necessary. They relied on massive supply lines, which restricted their mobility. Generals tried to outwit their adversaries rather than annihilate them on the battlefield, and statesmen focused on achieving victory at the diplomatic table. Some saw these limitations on war as an indication of heightened civilization.

The French Revolution changed everything for the French army. With the nation under attack from within and without, a small army of professional soldiers was inadequate. The state had endowed French citizens with new political rights and now demanded from them new obligations: the French people themselves should defend their nation and the revolution, either by fighting or by contributing economically to the war effort. In 1793, the *levée en masse* was decreed by the revolutionary regime, a forced military conscription of hundreds of thousands of young men. Their lack of training meant that conventional tactics had to be abandoned, and there was not enough food to supply them, so they had to forage off the land. But this actually made the army more mobile and allowed innovative French officers to experiment with new tactics and improved artillery. When Napoleon came to power, he was able to wield an enormous and highly mobile army against European forces still wedded to the old way of things, and this disparity largely accounts for the sensational victories of the first half of his reign. A new era of offensive warfare—of "total war"—had been introduced to Europe.[3]

But "Ogre" was an apt nickname for Napoleon's eating habits as well: he was prone to scarfing his meals down in minutes, paying little attention to what he was eating. When he was on campaign, he would not waste time sitting down to eat, instead eating on horseback. Among the most numerous victims of his reign were chickens, a particular favorite; his cooks grilled a new chicken every half hour, day and night, so there was always a fresh meal available at whatever time he might decide to eat. Perhaps unsurprisingly, one of the most famous recipes linked to his name is *poulet Marengo*, made using the ingredients his chef could forage after Napoleon's victory over the Austrians in 1800 at Marengo, Italy. According to legend, the original dish featured crayfish, eggs, and brandy in addition to the usual chicken, but today poulet Marengo is generally just chicken sautéed with tomatoes, garlic, parsley, and white wine. (The delicious napoleon pastry has nothing to do with the diminutive Corsican; its name is actually an unfortunate mutilation of *napolitain*, reflecting the pastry's origins in Naples.)

Talleyrand, of course, more than made up for his patron's failings in the gastronomic realm. His table was known to be one of the best in Europe, and he employed great chefs like the legendary Antonin Carême. Talleyrand did not eat very much himself, but he could talk about food and wine for hours, as if it were the most important subject in the world. Having charmed his guests with his genial manner and a sumptuous meal, Talleyrand could then discuss affairs of state in a most agreeable atmosphere of conviviality.

After purchasing the château in Valençay, Talleyrand naturally began serving its delicious goat cheese at his dinner parties and banquets. According to legend, at that time the cheese was shaped like a proper pyramid, triangular with a pointed top. One day, someone unwisely served the cheese to Napoleon himself, who flew into a rage upon seeing this reminder of his failed Egyptian campaign. Leaping to his feet, he drew his sword and sliced off the top of the unfortunate cheese. And so, to avoid further offending the mighty ruler of France, Valençay was made with a flattened top from that day forward.

An alternative legend explains that Talleyrand himself ordered the cheese to be flattened, before Napoleon could ever see it, anticipating how provocative its shape would be to his short-tempered ruler. And really, considering how skillfully Talleyrand survived one of the most murderous eras for politically engaged Frenchmen, this story seems far more likely.

Talleyrand is generally seen as trying, and usually failing, to moderate Napoleon's tendency toward excess. This became even more difficult after 1804, when Napoleon crowned himself emperor of France, effectively abolishing the First Republic and ending the revolutionary era. Napoleon continued remaking French society: he issued nearly eighty thousand decrees during his reign, reforming nearly every aspect of state administration and daily life. The Napoleonic Code, the civil code enacted in 1804, was widely imitated and still serves as the core legal code in France today. Napoleon rebuilt a strong, centralized French state, and then tried to export the revolution across Europe via his massive armies. He was more or less constantly at war until his final defeat and exile in 1815. As we shall see, this era of unparalleled destruction also yielded a revolutionary change in the human diet—and offered Talleyrand one final chance to save the French nation at the banquet table.

35

The Man Who Abolished the Seasons

Napoleon is famous not only for his legendary military and political exploits but for his many profound and provocative aphorisms. One of the best-known sayings attributed to Napoleon is probably *Une armée marche à son estomac* (An army marches on its stomach). As it turns out, he may not have ever actually uttered the phrase; some attribute it to Frederick the Great instead. But Napoleon understood perfectly that a well-fed and amply supplied army was essential for victory, and as he spent most of his time trying to conquer Europe, he rightly prioritized the search for new means of feeding his enormous Grande Armée. At its height, he had more than half a million men under his command. His armies were forced to forage for their own food supplies while on campaign, which usually left the countryside devastated and soldiers underfed. In 1795, the Directory had offered a prize of twelve thousand francs to anyone who could manage to find better ways of food preservation; but as Napoleon's armies traversed the lengths of Europe, the prize remained unclaimed.

The reward had piqued the interest, however, of a Frenchman who was already pondering a new process that would revolutionize food production and supply forever. His name was Nicolas Appert, and his discovery of a new means of food preservation irrevocably altered a central culinary assumption across the ages: that one must rely, for the most part, on foods that are local and in season. A nation that a mere century earlier marveled at the creation of early vegetables in the gardens of Versailles could now entertain the notion of eating fresh vegetables at any time, for years after harvesting, far from their original source. It was a radical shift in the human diet and a key step in the gradual industrialization of food production.

Appert was born in 1749 in Châlons-sur-Marne. His father owned an inn, which is where young Nicolas learned how to cook, and also how to bottle champagne. As an adult, he worked as a private chef for a noble family in Germany, before moving to Paris in 1784 and becoming a confectioner. He opened a shop on rue des Lombards, a street described as *le chef-lieu sucré de l'univers* (the sweet capital of the universe) by Grimod de la Reynière, the star gastronomic critic of the day. Confectioners not only sold sweets but also utilized some of the relatively limited methods of food preservation available at that time. Appert would have been expert in the preparation of syrups and jams as well as in the preservation of cherries and other fruits in alcohol.

Appert became obsessed with expanding the options for food preservation. All the traditional methods—smoking, salting, sugaring, alcohol—were expensive and changed the taste of the food, and they were not always completely effective to boot. In his initial experiments, he used champagne bottles (which were made more solidly than regular bottles to help contain the explosive force of the devil's wine). The method he developed was simple enough: place the food in the bottle, hermetically seal it, and boil it in a bain-marie (a double boiler) for a set length of time (usually several hours). *Et voilà*, the food would remain preserved within the bottle for years. Appert did not precisely understand at that time why this process worked. It is only thanks to Louis Pasteur's subsequent microbial discoveries that we now know that "appertization" essentially sterilized the food, killing the microorganisms responsible for decomposition. Nevertheless, because of his revolutionary invention, Appert is known today as the father of canning.

Appert first applied his method of heat sterilization to green peas. The pleasure the Sun King's courtiers found in eating early peas could not compare to the astonishment of Appert's guests, offered peas in December. As the *Courrier de l'Europe* later reported: "Monsieur Appert has discovered the art of fixing the seasons: in his home, spring, summer, and fall live in bottles, similar to those delicate plants that the gardener protects under glass domes against the intemperate seasons."[1]

Appert started preserving foods on a larger scale in 1802, when he opened a small factory in Massy, in the Parisian suburbs. He planted a fruit and vegetable garden next to the factory so that he could bottle his produce as soon as it was picked, thus offering the freshest and healthiest product possible. Soon, his bottled foods were appreciated by the Parisian elite and newly prominent gourmands.

One of Appert's key problems was that his bottles were expensive. This made his products exclusive, and therefore desirable, but like other food innovators at the time, Appert wanted his inventions to benefit humanity more widely. He thought his bottled foods would particularly benefit sailors, who at the time were still afflicted by scurvy and other deadly forms of malnutrition on their long voyages. In the prerevolutionary era, one out of twelve sailors died every year from disease.

In 1803, the French navy ordered some of Appert's bottles so that they could be tested. The reports were very positive: one of them stated that after three months at sea, "the beans and the green peas, both with and without meat, have all the freshness and flavor of freshly picked vegetables." But unfortunately for Appert's ambitions, in October 1805, British admiral Horatio Nelson once again thwarted Napoleon's grand schemes, crippling the French navy in the legendary Battle of Trafalgar. There would be no French invasion of England, nor a grand French fleet to rule the waves. Appert's hopes of churning out bottles of vitamin-rich vegetables for the navy came to naught. He continually struggled to keep his business afloat.

In 1810, the government finally decided to award Appert the sum of twelve thousand francs, the equivalent of twelve years' average salary, if instead of patenting his invention, he published a book explaining his preservation methods. Appert accepted the offer and published *Le livre de tous les ménages, ou L'art de conserver pendant plusieurs années, toutes les substances animales et végétales.* The book was intended to be of use for all households (*tous les ménages*), in line with Appert's aims of helping ordinary people. As a businessman, he was an utter failure, but Appert wanted the world to benefit from his invention. The book was a rapid success in France and was eventually translated into other European languages as well.

Appert's preservation method was more than just a way of offering fresh food year-round. Ideally, it would eradicate food scarcity entirely, because foods could be prepared and stored in anticipation of shortages. Large institutions—not only the navy and army but humanitarian organizations like hospitals—could better meet their food needs. He foresaw the rise of new food trades and industries, with countries able to import and export all sorts of local specialties. To a large extent, his visions did indeed come to fruition. While food scarcity is an enduring problem, today this is more a matter of politics and logistics rather than practical or technological problems.

Appert never really solved his bottle problem, and indeed it was left to France's archenemy, the British, to invent a solution. In 1810, a new British patent was awarded based on Appert's method of sealing and boiling, but using tin cans instead of glass bottles. From 1813 onward, the British navy supplied its ships with canned food. Appert could not immediately emulate this development, as his factory was destroyed by occupying troops in 1814. In the end, the Grande Armée never benefited from his marvelous invention. By the time Appert recovered and started canning food himself, the Napoleonic Wars were over. Britain took the lead in tin can manufacturing, so much so that when the French army and navy finally decided to extensively use canned food in the Crimean War (1853–56), most of the cans had to be purchased from British manufacturers.

Appert never managed to make a real success of his business, and in 1836 he retired. He died poor and was buried in a mass grave in 1841—hardly a suitable fate for someone whose invention so enormously benefited humanity. Today, Appert is barely known outside France, and he is not even really a household name in his native country either. It is an astonishing level of obscurity for someone who so radically expanded the limits of the human diet.

36

The Fifth Crêpe

Like many Christian holidays, the French celebration of la Chandeleur, or Candlemas, has its roots in pagan traditions: in this case, the Roman fertility rites that were held as the depths of winter began to recede and farmers started preparing their fields for planting. The pagan rites were abolished in the fifth century and replaced with candlelight ceremonies in Christian churches, in celebration of some important religious event that most French people today would probably not be able to explain to you. Despite France's longstanding

Catholic identity, only 10 percent of its population still regularly attends church.

But Candlemas, celebrated on the second of February, remains a popular holiday, no doubt in part because it doubles as an annual celebration of a French food favorite: the crêpe. For hundreds of years, people have celebrated Candlemas with these thin and delicious pancakes, and have attached various superstitions to the practice of flipping them in the air during cooking. For example, farmers long believed that a crêpe that was flipped without breaking or falling on the floor on Candlemas was a sure sign that the next harvest would be successful. Today, everyone knows that if you flip your crêpes properly with one hand while holding a coin in the other, you will be lucky and successful for the next year. Otherwise, well, don't expect life to treat you very nicely until the next Candlemas.

Napoleon was thought to be, like most Corsicans, overly superstitious. He believed his first wife, Josephine, brought him good luck, and he tried to avoid any adventures or battles on Fridays and on the thirteenth of each month. June 14 and December 2, on the other hand, were lucky dates, when he had won the Battles of Marengo and Austerlitz, respectively. He believed he was guided and protected by a lucky star, which appeared at all the great moments of his life.

By 1812, there was every reason for Napoleon to feel pompous. His astounding military successes, alongside the skillful deployment of family members onto European thrones, had given the First French Empire control of most of western and central Europe. He'd enjoyed triumphal marches through the streets of Vienna and Berlin, after breathtaking victories against the Austrians and Prussians. The Hapsburgs had dissolved the Holy Roman Empire rather than let him seize that crown, bringing to an end the thousand-year-old line. Russia, the great imperial land power on the other side of Europe, had been contained within a cagey alliance with France since being defeated by Napoleon at the Battle of Friedland in 1807.

There were challenges, to be sure. Britain, with its mighty navy and colonial realm, protected by the English Channel, was a constant and exasperating enemy. Austria and Prussia, humiliated in postwar settlements, were keen to regain lost territory and status. European armies were adapting to Napoleon's unique style of warfare. Rebellions emerged in various parts of the empire, notably in Spain, where irregular forces proved such a challenge that they lent their name to what we still call guerrilla warfare (from the

Spanish *guerrilla*, or "little war"). In 1812, a British army drove French forces out of Spain entirely. Napoleon's relatives and advisers were increasingly disobedient or treacherous; even Talleyrand was dismissed, after seemingly collaborating with the Austrian ambassador in Paris, a brilliant young diplomat named Klemens von Metternich. Napoleon's rule in France turned increasingly despotic, with censorship, arbitrary detention, and rule by personal decree all corrupting the republican ideals that France supposedly fought for.

It was at this point that Napoleon committed the single greatest blunder of his life: he decided to go to war with Russia. The Franco-Russian alliance soured in 1811, when Tsar Alexander I reneged on his agreement to participate in the continental blockade of Britain, which had proven ruinous to the Russian economy. Napoleon sent the Grande Armée into Poland and built it into one of the largest armies ever assembled, with more than 600,000 men drawn from throughout the French empire. His initial plan was not necessarily foolhardy: he believed his numbers were so great that he had simply to engage the Russians in a single decisive battle, and victory would be his. Then the Franco-Russian alliance could be restored and attention returned to the enduring confrontation with Britain.

But given his superstitious tendencies, Napoleon may have been a bit unsettled by what occurred on Candlemas, while he was preparing his campaign. According to legend, Napoleon celebrated Candlemas by flipping his own crêpes. He flipped one crêpe and said, "If I turn this one, I will win my first battle!" And the crêpe was successfully turned.

Then came the second crêpe and again: "If I turn this one, I will win my second battle!" And again, the crêpe survived intact.

Then came the third . . . and the fourth . . . and all was fine.

Then came the fifth crêpe . . . and this one fell into the ashes.

Despite this ominous portent, Napoleon proceeded with his *campagne de Russie* in June 1812, marching in the enervating summer heat across the plains of eastern Europe. But the Russians did not play along: in the face of such an immense army, they dared not directly engage in battle and instead retreated farther and farther east, setting the countryside aflame as they went. This was the worst possible scenario for the French. The farther they pursued the Russians, the lower their supplies ran, and the vast army could not sustain itself on the scorched earth. As the weeks of blistering heat continued, more and more men fell to sickness and desertion. Before a single battle was fought, Napoleon had lost more than 150,000 men.

The Russians finally stood their ground in early September, as the French approached Moscow. At the famous Battle of Borodino, on September 7, more than 25,000 men died in fifteen hours of utter carnage. Napoleon later wrote, "Of the fifty battles I have fought, the most terrible was that before Moscow." Neither side won decisively, but at the close of battle, the Russians withdrew. Moscow had apparently fallen to Napoleon.

But again, Napoleon's hopes were dashed. Upon his triumphal entrance into Moscow, he discovered the population evacuated, along with their food stores. No Russians remained to negotiate a peace, and his army had nothing to eat. Even worse, after midnight, flames began to rise within the city, soon turning into a giant conflagration that lasted three days and destroyed two-thirds of the city. (While the causes of the fire will never be known with absolute certainty, many historians agree that the Russians themselves set fire to Moscow, the desperate culmination of their scorched-earth tactics.[1]) When Napoleon saw the city on fire and realized that his army was isolated, in winter, without proper supplies or shelter, in the heart of Russia, he purportedly cried out to his aides: "It's the fifth crêpe!"

Tsar Alexander refused to capitulate, and the Grande Armée was forced to abandon Moscow on October 18 and retreat westward. A few weeks later, the Russian snows began. The depths of misery suffered by the retreating French troops were almost unimaginable: starving, freezing, mercilessly attacked by Cossacks, as they trudged hundreds of miles on foot. The French still call a crushing defeat a "Berezina," in reference to the crossing and the battle of the Berezina River during the retreat. Of the mighty force that had departed for Russia, only around forty thousand soldiers returned to France.

Whether doomed by an unlucky crêpe or not, the Russian campaign was the beginning of the end for Napoleon. All the European powers were united against him now, and his aura of invincibility was no more. "My star was fading," Napoleon later recalled. "I felt the reins slipping out of my grasp, and could do nothing to stop it." Throughout 1813, he fought fiercely against the united armies of Europe, still winning some key battles but losing ever more territory. In early 1814, France itself was invaded. Napoleon fought desperately, but his army was badly outnumbered, and in March it was the turn of his enemies to march triumphantly through the streets of Paris. Napoleon abdicated the throne and accepted exile in Elba, an idyllic island in the crystal blue Tyrrhenian Sea off the coast of Tuscany.

Yet Napoleon's adventures were not quite concluded. As we will see, he decided to defy the Candlemas curse one last time, and once again it would be left to Talleyrand to salvage the fate of the French nation.

37

The King of Cheeses

So many Americans know and love brie that this classic French cheese has almost become passé, as people increasingly seek out more obscure and intriguing cheeses. But most Americans may not be aware that the brie sold in the United States is a pale imitation of the real thing, thanks to strict import laws requiring pasteurization and the unfortunate market dominance of industrial brie. Unlike many French cheeses, plain old "brie" is not protected by an AOC, and today most brie is produced in factories outside its region of origin. The brie sold in the United States, whether by American or French brands, tends to be creamy and buttery—pleasing, but inoffensive. So it can be a real shock to try one of the two AOC-protected varieties, Brie de Meaux or Brie de Melun, which fairly ooze onto your plate once you slice through the white rind, and assault your senses with their overwhelmingly pungent fall flavors. Sadly, these proper Bries are so threatening to the American authorities that you'll have to leave the country to sample them.

For centuries, the French have referred to brie as the "cheese of kings," in part because it was traditionally produced in the region of Brie, between the Seine and Marne river valleys, not far from Paris. Charlemagne apparently liked brie so much that he asked for it to be sent twice yearly to his palace in Aachen. Henry IV, that incorrigible womanizer, is said to have forgotten to visit his mistress whenever his wife brought out the brie. As we have seen, Louis XVI was said to have lost his last chance for freedom when he tarried too long on the road from Paris to enjoy a Brie de Meaux. Brie's popularity was not limited to royalty; as a deputy in the Assembly declared during the revolution, "The Brie cheese, loved by the rich and the poor, preached equality before we thought it possible." But it has maintained a sort of royal reputation through the ages, long after the monarchy itself disappeared.

There was a time, however, when brie was known not only as "the cheese of kings" but "the king of cheeses"—all thanks to the wily Talleyrand and his desperate efforts to restore French honor after Napoleon's dramatic fall.

With Napoleon exiled to Elba, it was left to the victorious Allies—Britain, Russia, Austria, and Prussia—to bring stability back to Europe. Napoleon's conquests had massively disrupted the old political order, and Europe's patchwork of principalities had to be reconstituted and parceled out among the major powers. A decade and a half of war had also altered the relative strengths of the leading states. A new balance of power needed to be agreed upon and consolidated among the great powers if peace was to be sustained. The European monarchs were also keen to return the revolutionary genie back to its bottle, and prevent any republican zeal from emerging in their own nations. So the victors gathered in Vienna in September 1814 for what became known as the Congress of Vienna, a months-long diplomatic tussle over how to rebuild the European political order.

Talleyrand, having fallen out with Napoleon, helped negotiate the restoration of the French monarchy, not out of any royalist affinity but because he saw it as the only viable option for a defeated France. The Bourbon heir to the throne since the death of the little prince in the Temple prison was the brother of Louis XVI, and he now ascended the throne as King Louis XVIII. He sent Talleyrand to Vienna to represent France in the negotiations, although he was expected to have little influence given France's absolute defeat. But Talleyrand did a remarkable job of exploiting the victors' rivalries, as well as their desire to permanently quash the contagion of revolution with a successful monarchical restoration. His diplomatic maneuverings helped preserve France's status as a major power and most of its territorial integrity; in the final peace treaty, France was forced to surrender only those lands acquired after 1791, although it did have to pay a staggering indemnity of 700 million francs to the victors.

The original peace terms were even more generous to France, but naturally, Napoleon scuppered the deal with one last grasp for glory. As the months rolled by during his forced retirement on Elba, the former master of Europe grew bored and restless. When reports arrived of discontent and unrest under the restored king, Napoleon saw a chance to escape his dreary exile. In March 1815, he landed with a small force of a thousand men on the southern French coast in a last campaign known as the Hundred Days. The French army had not been purged of Bonaparte loyalists, and they now rallied to their general, who proceeded to Paris. When the armed forces in the capital defected as well, Louis XVIII fled, and Napoleon briefly reclaimed his rule of France. But in June, the forces of Britain and Prussia dealt Napoleon his final defeat, in the legendary Battle of Waterloo.[1] Having learned their lesson, the victors now exiled Napoleon to a barren rock in the middle of the South Atlantic Ocean. He died there, on Saint Helena, in 1821.

It is a testament to Talleyrand's immense diplomatic capabilities that even this outrageous Napoleonic aggression did not completely derail his campaign to save France. As in his previous career as foreign minister, he employed every gastronomic tactic possible to seduce and sway his European counterparts—a more vital and yet difficult mission than ever before, given the weak hand France had to play. Luckily, the participants in the Congress were as fond of the luxurious life as Talleyrand, and there were ample opportunities to deploy his gifts at banquets, concerts, and balls. In fact, the frequent socializing was one reason the conference took months to reach accord; in the words of Prince Charles de Ligne, a charming Austrian field marshal, *Le congrès danse beaucoup, mais il ne marche pas* (The Congress dances a lot, but it does not move forward).

Talleyrand lodged at the Kaunitz Palace, and with the help of his favorite chef, Antonin Carême, he transformed the space into a gastronomic paradise. Talleyrand's elegant dinners were intended to make his counterparts more receptive to his suggestions, but he also used them as a sort of culinary espionage tool. Knowing that fancy food and wine often loosened tongues, he instructed his service staff to listen in on his guests' conversations and report details back to him.

One night, at yet another Viennese dinner party, the assembled diplomats began talking about their respective national cheeses, growing increasingly boastful as they proclaimed the virtues of

Stilton, Limburger, and Gruyère. Talleyrand, of course, maintained that no cheese could equal Brie, the "cheese of kings." So a dinner was organized to judge the matter, and ultimately fifty-two European cheeses made it to the table. In the end, Brie was announced the winner, and thus earned the new title of the "king of cheeses." (After the dinner, one guest remarked of Talleyrand and brie: "This is the only prince he will not be able to betray.")

This little cheese victory helped remind the assembled diplomats of the enduring riches of a vanquished power. Indeed, it was a lesson already being learned back in France, as the hundreds of thousands of occupying troops discovered the pleasures of French cuisine. According to Brillat-Savarin, Paris became

> an immense dining hall. These intruders, they ate at the restaurants, the traiteurs, the cabarets, the taverns, the street stalls, and even in the streets. They stuffed themselves with meat, fish, game, truffles, pastry, and especially our fruits. They drank with an avidity equal to their appetite, and always asked for the more expensive wines . . . The true French laughed and rubbed his hands saying, "They are under the spell, and tonight they will give us back more money than the public treasury gave them this morning."[2]

There is a myth that the term *bistro* originates in this period, with the Russian soldiers shouting at the French waiters, "быстро, быстро" (*"bistro, bistro"*—or "quick, quick"). It is true that a French bistro is a nice place to grab a relatively quick meal, but this tale is probably apocryphal.

And so the Napoleonic era came to close, with France a fallen but quiescent power, stripped of its glory but still possessed of great cultural and gastronomic wealth. The revolutionary project appeared to be dead but in fact was merely slumbering, biding its time until the doomed French monarchy finally slipped into historical oblivion.

38

A Revolutionary Banquet

After more than twenty-five years of revolution and war, France settled down to a long era of reconstruction. More than a million people had died in the maelstrom of political violence, and French society remained deeply divided. France lagged behind other powers, especially Britain, in exploiting the potential of the Industrial Revolution and international trade. The French economy, especially its rural economy, had to be rebuilt. All of these challenges were managed for a bit more than thirty years by the restored kings of France, until the rash decision to ban a banquet finally extinguished the French monarchy for all time. Royalists who had become accustomed to depriving the French people of their political and civil rights neglected to consider the danger in encroaching on an even more fundamental liberty for the French: the right to share a meal with one's friends and neighbors.

Banquets had long been a serious business in France, and not just because they were an enjoyable way to eat and be merry. They had performed various social functions since the Gallo-Roman era, implicitly conveying identity, social norms, and power relationships.[1] This was even more true during the revolutionary era, when banquets became a useful means of encouraging *fraternité* among the different social classes. For the Fête de la Fédération in 1790, for example, more than fifteen thousand people from all three estates feasted in the Parc de la Muette in Paris. In the ensuing years, smaller banquets were organized by local communities across France, so that citizens could socialize with one another regardless of class, share their food and wine, toast the revolution, and sing the new revolutionary songs. Robespierre made great use of outdoor banquets during the Terror, but not everybody shared his enthusiasm. Louis-Sébastien Mercier explained: "Under the threat of being a suspect, or to declare oneself the enemy of equality, everybody came to eat with his family next to the man he detested or despised."[2] Grimod de La Reynière abhorred the "fraternal meals staged in the gutters of every street, where the prevailing tone, as signs on every building proclaimed, was one of 'fraternity'—presumably that of Cain and Abel, since there was never less liberty or equality in France than when signs on every wall proclaimed those virtues."[3]

Banquets remained popular under the restored monarchy, and they began to be held in newly fashionable restaurants. In an era of unbridled factionalism, they continued to serve a political function, offering the royalist and republican camps a chance to converse and socialize with their fellow adherents. Sometimes things went too far, as in May 1831, when two hundred republicans attended a banquet at the restaurant Aux Vendanges de Bourgogne. During the banquet, Évariste Galois, a brilliant young mathematician and activist, offered a toast to King Louis-Philippe—a glass in one hand, a knife in the other. This regicidal reference caused a huge and mostly approving uproar, but it unsettled some of the guests, including Alexandre Dumas (in his memoirs, he claims to have escaped out of a restaurant window into the garden to avoid being implicated in the incident). Galois was arrested the next day but later acquitted. He died in a duel the following year at the mere age of twenty, thus securing his status as one of the most romantic figures in the history of mathematics.

To understand why Galois and his republican friends were so agitated about the king, we should return to the manner in which Louis-Philippe ascended the throne in the first place. The first restored Bourbon, Louis XVIII, died in 1824 and was succeeded by his younger brother, Charles X. While Louis had been a relatively moderate ruler, allowing some republican liberties to remain in place, Charles was an ultraroyalist who wanted to erase all traces of revolutionary reform. As he grew increasingly despotic, raising the specter of the absolutist ancien régime, popular discontent grew. Charles tried to improve his reputation by invading Algeria, thus commencing a long and torturous history between the two nations. Algiers and the coast were swiftly taken, but it took more than fifteen years to defeat the Algerian insurgency, as its skilled commander, Abd al-Qadir, exploited the vast interior terrain and the popular support of his people.[4] French methods of suppression were brutal and led to the deaths of hundreds of thousands of Algerians over the course of two decades.

By then, Charles was long gone. In July 1830, his government suspended the freedom of the press, dissolved the legislative assembly, and further restricted the already small number of people who had the right to vote. This triggered an uprising known as the July Revolution, which ended when Charles abdicated and his cousin Louis-Philippe claimed the kingship.

Louis-Philippe was essentially a compromise between reformers and royalists: the monarchy was preserved, but the new king was more amenable to guaranteeing political liberty and reinstating a constitutional monarchy. Louis-Philippe was the son of Philippe Égalité, Duke of Orléans, who had been a revolutionary hero (even voting for the execution of his cousin Louis XVI) before being sent to the guillotine himself. Louis-Philippe had also supported the revolution, but he was forced to flee France after being associated with a counterrevolutionary plot (a key reason for his father's arrest and execution). During his exile, Louis-Philippe traveled and made a living as a teacher throughout Europe, and he even moved for four years to the United States. In 1796, he lived and taught on the second floor of a building in Boston that later housed the Union Oyster House, the oldest continuously operated restaurant in the United States (est. 1826). He returned to France only after the fall of Napoleon, and while he recouped his family's wealth, he continued to live a "simple" bourgeois life. This made him rather popular at the beginning of his reign, and he was nicknamed the "Citizen King."

During Louis-Philippe's reign, France embraced the great advances in production and transportation that were transforming European commerce and society. The French textile, metallurgy, and banking industries were developed, the railroad was introduced, and more roads and canals were built. Freedom of the press was granted and newspapers flourished, a great benefit for the ongoing republican opposition to the king, which occasionally flared into small-scale revolts (as in the June 1832 Parisian uprising, memorialized in Victor Hugo's *Les Misérables*). As the 1840s progressed, the republicans were joined on the left by the emerging socialist movement, which found great inspiration in the tumultuous Parisian scene. It was in Paris that Engels met Marx, in 1844, at the old Café de la Régence in the Palais-Royal. During his two years living in Paris, Marx developed much of his theory on the class struggle, then so evident in the French political landscape. Three years after leaving Paris, he and Engels published *The Communist Manifesto*, on the eve of a tremendous revolutionary surge across Europe.

By the mid-1840s, the Citizen King was no longer so popular. In the opposition press, he was caricatured to resemble a pear (*poire*), which is what the French call someone who is naïve or simpleminded.

Charles Philipon, manager of the newspaper *La Caricature*, and Honoré Daumier created this image of the king transforming into a pear (*poire*). Its publication caused an uproar, but Philipon managed to avoid imprisonment. He sparked another furor with his drawing of a proposed monument titled *Expia-poire*: a giant pear on a pedestal in the Place de la Concorde. The title is a play on the French word *expiatoire* (atoning), and its setting is a clear reference to the execution of King Louis XVI. Philipon rejected charges that he had published a provocation to regicide, arguing that it was at most a provocation to make marmalade. Caricature by Charles Philipon and Honoré Daumier, in Arsène Alexandre, *L'art du rire et de la caricature* (Paris: Libraires Imprimeries Réunies, 1892), 169. Courtesy of the Bibliothèque Numérique de Lyon.

He was not royalist enough for the royalists, nor reform-minded enough for the republicans. The bourgeoisie chafed at their continued lack of political power and the corruption afflicting the regime. The working class and the poor suffered from deplorable living and working conditions. To make things worse, poor cereal harvests in 1845–46 led to bread riots, and economic crisis in 1847 left hundreds of thousands of people out of work. Increasingly violent demonstrations were punctuated with cries of "Work and bread!"

This was the context for the "banquet campaign," which began on July 9, 1847, with more than a thousand people attending the Banquet du Château-Rouge in Paris. At the time, meetings of more than twenty people required approval from the authorities, which was never granted to political meetings critical of the regime. But a banquet was not a meeting. How could the authorities possibly forbid a gathering of friends over a delicious meal? And so these banquets became the most effective way for critics of the regime to legally meet and sustain their cause. They were fairly expensive to attend, so they excluded the poorer classes of society, and women were still not welcome in the political sphere. In its early stages, the banquet campaign was a vehicle for the male bourgeoisie.

A series of seventy banquets was organized in 1847–48, throughout France, and more than twenty thousand people attended.[5] Banquet organizers originally focused on reform of the electoral system, as voting was still limited to landowners and the very rich. Not everyone wanted universal suffrage, a truly radical idea—some merely wanted voting privileges expanded to their own class. But as the banquets continued, they grew more radically populist in their goals and membership. This disparity became evident in the toasts that were given: the toasts of the moderate reformist might include "to the revolution of 1830," "to national sovereignty" or "to the parliamentary and electoral reform"; the radicals toasted "to the sovereignty of the people," "to the workers," or "to the improvement of the working class."[6]

There was a certain risk in the banquet campaign, as noted by Alexis de Tocqueville, then serving as a parliamentary deputy for Valognes, in Normandy. In *Recollections*, his vivid firsthand account of the events of 1848, he explains, "I refused to take part in the affair of the banquets. I had both serious and petty reasons for abstaining." The petty reasons, which he admits to be "bad reasons," were the "irritation and disgust aroused in me by the character and by the tactics of the leaders of this enterprise."[7] More seriously, he argued that as the banqueters increasingly appealed to the masses, they risked alienating the middle class, who would then renew their support for the regime. There was also the possibility that populist agitation would spiral out of control, to unpredictable extremes. By his account, even the banquet organizers worried over the latter scenario, and indeed their fears would come to pass.[8]

After more than six months of banquets, the last one of the campaign was scheduled for February 22, 1848, in Paris. The date was not accidental: it coincided with the birthday of George Washington, a revered figure for republicans in France. But the regime decided that enough was enough and rashly banned this particular banquet. The press called for demonstrations, and barricades went up in the Parisian streets. Louis-Philippe remained stalwart, saying, "The Parisians know what they are doing; they are not going to trade the throne for a banquet."[9] But two days later, as violence and rebellion spiraled, Louis-Philippe did what he felt best for the country and abdicated. He was the last king of France.

This new French revolution in 1848 helped kick-start what became known as the Spring of Nations, when republican revolts broke out across Europe. In most countries, a combination of reform and repression contained the rebellions, which proved to be a false spring for the pursuers of democracy and socialism. European monarchism endured.

In France, however, a provisional government declared the establishment of the Second Republic. At first, things looked promising: universal suffrage was instituted; slavery and capital punishment were abolished; and freedom of the press, assembly, and religion was guaranteed. Socialists won the concession of a "right to work," although dissatisfaction with government efforts to assist the unemployed led to another small rebellion in June. The Second Republic would be led by a popularly elected president, who would hold office for four years and serve only one term.

The political banquets continued in these unsteady days and became more inclusive. They were organized to be cheaper so that the lower classes could attend (although people complained that this only made the food more disappointing). Women began to be admitted to some of the banquets, usually those hosted by socialists. But even on the left, not everyone was happy to allow women into their privileged political spaces, and so some socialist women started organizing their own banquets. This threatened traditionalists even more, and they directed vitriolic propaganda at these depraved women, whom they labeled (in a nice bit of wordplay) *les femmes saucialistes*.

But this revolutionary banqueting was reaching its end. In December, the first presidential election was won by Louis-Napoleon Bonaparte, one of the late emperor's nephews, in a victory for conservative forces. Over the next four years, the initial achievements of 1848 were rolled back, and authoritarian rule restored. Finally, in 1852, Louis-Napoleon crowned himself Emperor Napoleon III, and the Second Empire was born. For nearly twenty years, he would preside over a vast project of modernization and foreign adventurism. But republican and socialist opposition endured, and as we shall see, it was only a matter of time before the Second Empire followed the First into obsolescence.

39

The End of the Oyster Express

I love oysters: it's like kissing the sea on the lips.

—Léon-Paul Fargue

The Emerald Coast, named for the stunning blue-green waters lapping the shores of northern Brittany, is one of the most beautiful stretches of France's two-thousand-mile-long coastline. From the stark beauty of Cap Fréhel to the splendid walled city of Saint-Malo, from the white sandy beaches of Val André to the towering majesty of Mont-Saint-Michel, the Brittany coast offers an intoxicating mix of natural beauty and historic charm. Gourmands will enjoy the incredible varieties of mussels, langoustines, and scallops available across the region, alongside traditional Breton specialties like galettes, *kouign-amann* pastries, and sparkling apple cider. And for shellfish aficionados, one small town on the Emerald Coast is a bull's-eye destination: Cancale, the oyster capital of Brittany. Every year, thousands of visitors descend on this picturesque seaside town to sample some of the finest oysters in the world. They have their choice of quayside restaurants, but perhaps the most romantic option is simply to select a platter of oysters—at unbelievably low prices—from the small oyster market perched at the foot of the town pier. Few gastronomic delicacies can be more satisfying than sitting on a seawall on a sunny day, savoring fresh oysters nearly as large as your hand, plucked from the massive array of oyster beds in the sea below.

Humans have been gathering and eating oysters from the sea since prehistoric times, and Gaul was already blessed with miles of natural oyster beds along its coasts when the bivalve-loving Romans arrived. They delighted in the oyster harvests around Marseille and the Médoc, shipping hordes of Gallic specimens back to Italy. The barbarian invasions put an end to the oyster trade, and they became once more merely a ready source of food for local inhabitants. Indeed, for much of the oyster's history, it has been a staple food for poor people on the coasts rather than a luxury treat for distant elites. It was not until the Renaissance period that oysters reappeared on

Fresh oysters from the market at Cancale, Brittany. Photograph by authors, 2017.

noble tables, with a number of recipes in the earliest cookbooks. And it was only in the eighteenth and nineteenth centuries, thanks to a series of transportation innovations and industrial transformation, that oysters could be enjoyed at any real distance from the coastline.

A perusal of early cookbooks reveals that until the seventeenth century, oysters were mostly eaten cooked; raw oysters were seen as unhealthy and indigestible. But both medical and gastronomic experts began to advise eating oysters raw, as cooking only destroyed all of their healthy, salty juices and thus actually made them harder to digest. Raw oysters also became known as an aphrodisiac, which no doubt enhanced their appeal. The famous seducer Giacomo Casanova was, naturally, devoted to oysters, which he only ate with champagne; Louis XIV could eat dozens of oysters in one sitting. When *Le Cuisinier françois* was published in 1651, cooked oyster dishes were still the norm, but by the time Menon published his *La Cuisinière bourgeoise* in 1746, oysters were usually eaten uncooked.[1]

The preference for raw oysters was not a problem for those living by the sea, but for those residing in Paris or the Loire Valley, it posed a major problem. For oysters to be eaten raw, they need to be fresh, and in those days transport was nowhere near as fast as it is now. The closest place for saltwater fish or oysters was the Normandy coast, more than 120 miles away. Usually, the coastal catch had to be salted for the journey inland.

This changed with the emergence of the *chasse-marrée* in the early modern era.[2] Chasse-marrées were convoys of light carts that carried fresh fish and oysters, on ice, from the Channel coast to Paris and Versailles. The carts usually stopped every twenty miles for a short ten-minute break, to change horses and take advantage of strategically located icehouses. By this means, Paris could be reached in twenty-four to thirty-six hours.[3] Oyster criers began to roam the streets of the capital, laden with heavy wicker baskets, hawking their wares at relatively inexpensive prices.

The chasse-marrées were also a godsend for the noble residents of Versailles and the other châteaus that hosted the Sun King on his royal visits. But perhaps their most famous appearance in food lore is actually a tragic tale of delivery gone wrong. In 1671, François Vatel, maître d'hôtel at the Château de Chantilly, had the immense responsibility of hosting a large banquet for Louis XIV on a Friday, and thus required a large amount of fresh fish from the chasse-marrée. When it failed to arrive at the expected hour, Vatel was despondent, believing he would have nothing to serve his imperious king, and he took his own life. Unfortunately, just then the chasse-marrée arrived, full of fish and oysters, and so the banquet went ahead as planned.

The rule that one should not eat oysters in the months without an *r* (from May to August) is partly a consequence of the chasse-marrées and the popularity of oysters during the reign of Louis XV. Oysters had become such a favored indulgence that it was not unusual to eat several dozen as an aperitif, to open up the appetite for the main course. Overconsumption began to threaten the oyster supply, and so Louis wisely decreed that during their summertime reproduction period, they should not be eaten. These were also the hottest months of the year, when even the chasse-marrée could not always outrun spoilage.

Both Louis XIV and Louis XV devoted considerable resources to the construction of the best national road system since Roman times, with more and more royal roads snaking out from Paris to the provinces. It was easier than ever for people—and oysters—to move about France. But within a hundred years, the chasse-marrée became obsolete, a victim of the tremendous technological and societal transformation that accompanied the Industrial Revolution. As French industry and trade developed, the need for faster means of transport became ever more evident. In 1827, the first railroad line in France was completed, between Saint-Etienne and Andrézieux, linking the Saint-Etienne coal mines and the Loire River. It was very primitive: only thirteen miles long, and with the wagons pulled by horses (on downhill slopes, they let gravity take over). A few years later, the first passenger train line in continental Europe began operating between Saint-Etienne and Lyon.

French railways developed much more slowly than in countries like Britain and Germany; by 1842, only 353 miles of rail had been placed. This was partly due to the country's lagging industrial development, as well as fierce opposition from the existing transport companies running France's extensive canal, river, and coastal shipping networks. An entire infrastructure of trade and profit was bound up in waterborne transport, and these interests did not want to see it scuttled by a shift to rail transport. There was also a measure of sociocultural opposition to the railways, as rural residents throughout France were horrified at the idea of serene pastures and forests torn up by the iron engines of progress. The Rouen Chamber of Commerce, for example, objected to the construction of the Paris-

Rouen railroad in 1832, arguing that it would disrupt traditional ways of life and damage the existing trade and transport networks the city depended upon.

Nevertheless, in 1842 the government approved plans for a national rail network, with five great lines connecting Paris to the most important regional cities. The private companies that built the railroads also constructed the monumental train stations of Paris, such as Gare de l'Est and Gare du Nord, that are still in use today. Steam locomotives, imported from England, were introduced, with then-astounding speeds of 75 miles per hour. The worst fears of the canal operators were realized, as their freight traffic declined precipitously.

Railroad development did not proceed smoothly. The private rail lines did not connect with each other, only with Paris, which created a great deal of inefficiency. The network's shortcomings were revealed in the 1870 war with Prussia, when the German railway system played a major role in the rapid Prussian mobilization and eventual victory. But by 1914, France possessed the most developed

One of the great Paris rail stations, Gare du Nord (North Station) was built by the rail company Chemins de Fer du Nord and opened for service in 1864. Today, with more than 200 million travelers each year, it is the busiest rail station in Europe. From the Miriam and Ira D. Wallach Division of Art, Prints and Photographs, the New York Public Library. "Gare du Nord." New York Public Library Digital Collections.

rail network in the world, extending to more than 37,000 miles of track.

The development of the rail network had an enormous effect on all sorts of food trades in France. Normandy cheeses like Camembert, for example, were introduced to Paris, and fruit and vegetable farmers in the sunny south of France could supply more far-flung locales. The southern vineyards of the Languedoc now had access to a huge new market in the northern cities and were increasingly planted with inferior varieties that produced cheap, light wines (called *petit rouge*) for the working classes. By the end of the century, the Languedoc had become France's most productive wine region, supplying 44 percent of national production.[4] This new availability of cheaper southern wines sent northerly vineyards like those around Chablis into decline. The invention of the refrigerated railcar made it possible to transport fresh meat and fish over incredible distances. Regional cuisines became better known as a growing wave of tourists explored the provinces. At the same time, the old network of roadside inns that dotted the French countryside began to disappear as travelers increasingly chose the train over the coach.

And of course, the railroad had an immense impact on the oyster trade in France. It was now possible for residents of Paris and central France to get oysters in less than a day, and not only from Normandy but from other renowned oyster production sites in Brittany, the Bay of Arcachon, and the Mediterranean. In Charente-Maritime, south of La Rochelle, a railway line opened in 1876 with the explicit purpose of transporting oysters. It was called the *train des mouettes* (seagull train), for obvious reasons, and while it eventually ceased operating, it was reopened in the 1980s as a tourist train—the oldest French steam train still in use.

The railroads were also responsible for one of the great touristic transformations of the nineteenth century: the rise of the seaside resort. The extensive coastlines of France had long attracted noble and wealthy visitors, but such getaways were not accessible to the middle and working classes until railroads made it possible to reach the coast more quickly and cheaply. As railroads snaked their way to the French Riviera, or the Atlantic beaches, tourists from all over France—indeed, all over Europe—discovered the sublime benefits of coastal living. This usually included fresh local oysters, available in nearly all French seaside towns. And so raw oysters became more popular across Europe, and France cemented its reputation as the world's supreme purveyor of oysters, a status it continues to hold today.

Even with the expansion of the modern oyster farming industry in the nineteenth and twentieth centuries, oysters retained intense parochial loyalties. Like so many other products we have discussed thus far, oysters have their own distinct terroir (or as some wags refer to it, a *merroir*), which grants unique flavors to each locale. Oysters from Normandy are more delicate than those from the Vendée; Arcachon oysters are a bit saltier than those from Brittany. To boost the terroir effect, it's a good idea to pair your oysters with a dry white wine from roughly the same region—a sauvignon blanc from Bordeaux, for instance, or a Loire Valley Sancerre—although, of course, champagne remains the ideal paramour. Some people swear that Guinness stout pairs delightfully with oysters, but we must confess to not having dared attempt this combination yet.

The French oyster industry has suffered many tragedies over the years and remains extremely vulnerable to environmental disaster. The original native variety, the *pied de cheval*, or flat oyster, was virtually wiped out by overharvesting and disease and today makes up only a small percentage of the tens of thousands of oysters farmed each year. The Portuguese oyster gradually replaced the flat oyster all along the French coastline, but an apocalyptic disease struck this variety in the 1970s, virtually eliminating the French oyster industry. Fortunately, the Pacific oyster (sometimes called the Japanese oyster) was successfully introduced to French oyster beds, and the world's oyster lovers breathed a sigh of relief. But since 2008, French oysters have again been suffering from disease and pollution, possibly exacerbated by a changing climate, and overall production has nearly halved. There is no tranquillity for the oyster producers of France.

France is still the leading oyster producer in Europe, and also its leading oyster consumer; more than 90 percent of French oysters are eaten domestically. About half the yearly crop is consumed just in the Christmas period, as oysters are a traditional holiday treat, often served as an appetizer for the Christmas Eve feast. They are still usually served raw, with perhaps a bit of lemon or a light vinaigrette made of red wine and shallots. Of all the gastronomic blessings that France enjoys, few rival its exceptional oyster harvests.

40

Revelation in a Bottle

A bottle of wine contains more philosophy than all the books in the world.

—Louis Pasteur

The Jura region of France is draped over a chain of mountains on the border with Switzerland, not far from the mighty Alps. The unique geology of the Jura Mountains attracted nineteenth-century scientists seeking to develop a chronology of Earth's history, and in 1829 the French geologist Alexandre Brongniart dubbed the second period of the Mesozoic era the Jurassic period in their honor. Despite its great beauty and its fossil-hunting possibilities, the Jura is one of the quieter and less-visited regions of France, which makes it easier to peacefully enjoy its wooded slopes and sky-blue mountain lakes, its ancient small towns, and its sublime local gastronomy. Comté, the most popular cheese in France, is produced here; a top tourist attraction is the enormous bunker beneath the former military fort of Saint Antoine, now known as the "cathedral of Comté," where more than one hundred thousand giant wheels of cheese gradually acquire their distinctively earthy flavor. *Poulet de Bresse* is the only chicken to be protected by an AOC, reflecting its reputation as the most delicious poultry in the world. Its succulent flavor is attributed to a combination of terroir and careful free-range breeding practices, which aim to keep the chickens as happy as possible during their short lives.

But perhaps the most intriguing gastronomic discovery in the Jura is its wonderfully unusual wines, which have captivated French wine drinkers for centuries.[1] The charming town of Arbois, for example, provides a congenial introduction to the region's range of AOC wines (including a delightfully oaky chardonnay) and to the unique *vin jaune* (yellow wine), a golden-hued and intense wine that is produced only in the Jura. Vin jaune is aged for six years, three months in an oaken cask, and its flavors are so complex and unequaled that it has acquired near-mythical status.

Yet Arbois has made a far greater contribution to humanity. It was the childhood home of Louis Pasteur, and its local wines helped him revolutionize our understanding of disease and decay. His story serves as another reminder that the modern world we so often take for granted is actually of rather recent vintage.

Before Pasteur, the wide-ranging effects of microbes were experienced without really being understood. We have already seen, for example, how devastating plagues were attributed to a plethora of fanciful causes, and how processes of fermentation and food decomposition were manipulated without genuine understanding of their exact workings. The scientific revolution produced copious new theories, but the basic idea that specific microbial organisms caused disease and decomposition would have seemed fanciful for most of scientific history. Indeed, even Pasteur, in the mid-nineteenth century, faced furious opposition from doctors and biologists devoted to long-held alternative theories like spontaneous generation (a faulty notion that Pasteur finally debunked for good). Luckily, his tireless experimentation won out, and his scientific innovations would eventually save untold millions of lives.

The role of food and wine in the evolution of Pasteur's research was evident early on. Arriving as dean of the faculty of sciences at the University of Lille in 1854, he developed an academic program that encouraged students to apply their scientific research to the realities of food and alcohol production, a major industry in this booming northern city. In his first lecture at Lille, he said: "But I ask you, where will you find in your families a young man whose curiosity and interest will not immediately be awakened when you put into his hands a potato, with which he may produce sugar, with that sugar alcohol, with that alcohol ether and vinegar?"[2]

Pasteur himself was asked to practice what he preached when he was approached by Monsieur Bigo, a local producer of beet alcohol. Some of his enormous vats were producing sour beet juice instead of alcohol, and he asked Pasteur to investigate. Thus began Pasteur's revelatory research into the process of fermentation. His microscope revealed the presence of microbes that were killing the yeast that normally drove fermentation, and producing lactic acid instead. He was not able to devise a method for killing the microbes, but he advised

Bigo to clean the spoiled vats thoroughly and take precautions to prevent the reintroduction of harmful microorganisms. The following year, he published two papers on fermentation, thus inaugurating the field of microbiology.

In 1860, Pasteur published his landmark study on fermentation. His experiments showed more precisely how yeast microbes caused fermentation by converting sugar into alcohol, while different microorganisms were responsible for the contamination that produced soured wines or vinegar instead. By developing methods to limit the effects of these harmful microbes, it finally became possible to scientifically adjust the fermentation process to improve the quality, not just the quantity, of alcoholic beverages. Alcohol production had long been considered an art, not a science, but Pasteur's empiricism made a persuasive case for rethinking this stance.[3]

As a result of these studies, Pasteur was asked by the French government to investigate widespread problems with French wines, now the second-largest agricultural product (after cereals) and a major export. Winemaking had expanded greatly since the French Revolution, which had removed many controls on wine production and allowed many inexperienced vintners to join in. The transport opportunities generated by the railroads encouraged the overproduction of popular varieties, and new industrial methods were used to increase the speed and quantity of production. All of this led to a greater incidence of disease and contamination, to the point where the reputation of French wines was suffering internationally. Emperor Napoleon III asked Pasteur to investigate.

Pasteur, naturally enough, returned to his hometown of Arbois, having grown up among its vineyards and long appreciated the virtues of the local wines. Over the course of three summers, he experimented on Jura wines and further developed his microbial theories. Local vintners began coming to his house with their spoiled bottles of wine, seeking advice from the "wine doctor," and this gave him a ready supply of problem wines to investigate. Contrary to existing belief, Pasteur showed that the souring of wine was not accidental, or inevitable, but the result of external contamination from microbes. He thus recommended limiting exposure to contaminants throughout the winemaking process, but more important, he developed the process of "pasteurization," which in this case involved briefly heating young wines to 120 to 140 degrees Fahrenheit, which would kill harmful microbes. (This was not quite the same thing as "appertization," which involved boiling bottles for much longer at even higher temperatures.) Today, pasteurization is used on a wide variety of foods, most notably milk and dairy products. There is no telling how many lives have been saved by this ingenious method of preventing food contamination.

Pasteur's experiments and advice are credited with saving the French wine industry, a feat he repeated in the 1870s when he developed similar techniques to improve the quality of French beer. In this endeavor, he was driven by his ardent patriotism, recently inflamed by France's humiliating defeat in the Franco-Prussian War (1870–71). Pasteur became virulently anti-Prussian, refusing to travel in Germany or to allow his works to be published in German—he even refused to drink German beer, then among the most popular in Europe and a major German export. France was known more for its wine than its beer, except in regions such as Alsace and Lorraine, which were lost to Prussia in the war. And so Pasteur saw it as a matter of national honor to elevate the French beer industry, both to enact a measure of revenge on the Prussians and to demonstrate how science could help France best its rivals. He devoted several years toward developing what he called the "beer of revenge," a product that could match the taste and longevity of German lagers. He disseminated his new production techniques throughout Europe (except, of course, in Germany), and they were widely adopted, immeasurably improving the European beer market. But despite his best efforts to keep the results of his research out of his enemy's hands, German beer producers eventually followed his recommendations as well, and Germany remained one of the top beer-producing nations for many years. France would obtain a measure of revenge against Germany in the years to come, but never within the realm of beer.

Pasteur even managed to save a French industry he knew nothing about: the profitable and prestigious silk industry in southern France. When silkworm growers across Europe despaired over an unknown disease afflicting their little producers, Pasteur spent several years investigating their plight. He eventually discovered multiple microbes responsible for the crisis and invented new techniques for limiting their access to healthy silkworm eggs.

His experience with silkworms ushered Pasteur into the field for which he is most gratefully remembered, as he began applying his microbial theories to the study of infectious disease. At the time, the idea that disease arose from invisible organisms that could be spread by human contact seemed absurd, but Pasteur doggedly set out to prove the principles of "germ theory" against the hostility of the medical profession. He was an early proponent of medical hygiene, arguing that doctors were actually infecting healthy people by not washing thoroughly enough between patients (this argument only antagonized the medical profession further). He invented vaccines for animal diseases such as anthrax, and then developed a successful treatment for rabies, a horrific disease that was previously a death sentence. This work helped demonstrate the even more radical idea that specific microorganisms were responsible for specific diseases. Pasteur's research helped launch the field of immunology, which no doubt would have pleased him, as he lost two daughters to typhoid fever (now preventable with a vaccine). It is thanks to Pasteur, and other early proponents of germ theory, that the field of medicine embarked upon an era of radical discovery and innovation, saving untold numbers of lives. The full sum of his scientific contributions remains unmatched, and so it is not surprising that Arbois continues to celebrate his legacy, hosting a museum in his childhood home, a Pasteur walking tour, and a number of reverential memorials.

Ironically, pasteurization is not as popular in France as it is in other parts of the world. We have already seen that many French cheeses are not pasteurized, which gets them into trouble when they try to cross the American border. (Pasteur, who unsurprisingly became a major germophobe, would probably agree with the U.S. Food and Drug Administration on this question.) French wines, the earliest recipients of pasteurization, are today usually unpasteurized, as vintners became convinced that the process did in fact alter the taste. On the other hand, while it is possible to buy normal pasteurized milk in France, many people also buy UHT milk, which has been subjected to even higher temperatures in a process of "ultra-pasteurization." UHT milk can actually sit for months unrefrigerated in your kitchen cabinet, but it also has a slightly "cooked" flavor that may take a while (or never) to get used to.

Comté is an unpasteurized cheese, but luckily it is allowed into the United States because it has been aged for more than sixty days (legally, to meet the requirements of its AOC, it must be aged at least four months). And it is increasingly possible for Americans to enjoy France's favorite cheese with its partner in terroir, the wines of the

Jura. The intensity of this cheese-and-wine pairing is perhaps incongruous with the calm beauty of the Jura, but it symbolizes rather well the ferocious obsessions of its favorite son, another towering legend of French achievement.

41

The Curse of the Green Fairy

Paris and the other great cities of France usually manage to snare the lion's share of attention among those fascinated with French politics and culture, but within France itself there is a visceral attachment to what is known as *la France profonde*, the French countryside. It is a phrase that captures a widely held belief that the deepest, most profound elements of the French nation are to be found in its rural retreats, where time seems to pass more slowly and tradition wields a tighter grasp. Like all national myths, the idea of *la France profonde* contains both truth and imagination. But it is the reason why French presidents traipse through the enormous agricultural show in Paris every year, complimenting cows and attempting repartee with skeptical farmers; it is why there is so much media attention on the decline of small towns and agricultural trades.

This affinity for *la France profonde* has much to do with the concurrent attachment to the foods and wines that emerge from its depths. Perhaps one of the best expressions of this dual affection are the numerous gastronomic trails snaking through the French countryside, celebrating specific local products. We have already encountered the Route du Chabichou, a network of rural goat cheese producers in Poitou-Charentes. Each summer, horse riders and hikers re-create the Route du Sel, or historic salt trade routes, through the Languedoc region. And on the French-Swiss border, a mountainous hiking trail known as the Route de l'Absinthe extends for thirty miles of stunning pastoral scenes, with frequent tastings of absinthe, the notorious local specialty known as *la Fée Verte* (the Green Fairy).

The Absinthe Trail begins in the picturesque mountain town of

Pontarlier, the site of the first French absinthe distillery, built in 1805 by a Swiss man named Henri-Louis Pernod. He and his father-in-law adapted their herbal distilled liquor, with its distinctive flavor of anise, from a medicinal potion patented by a French doctor named Pierre Ordinaire, who had fled to Switzerland during the French Revolution. Pernod's French distillery was successful, and the absinthe business gradually became the lifeblood of little Pontarlier. At its height, a century later, there were twenty-five absinthe distilleries around the town, producing nearly 30,000 liters of absinthe per day.[1]

Among the earliest fans of absinthe were members of the French army, as Pontarlier also hosted at that time a training camp that brought thousands of artillerymen to the town each summer. During the extended conquest of Algeria, absinthe rations were given to the troops there to purify their water supplies and hopefully prevent malaria and other fevers. It was a popular and seemingly effective policy, and absinthe became a consistent feature of colonial conquest throughout Africa and Southeast Asia.

The soldiers continued to enjoy absinthe upon returning home and made it popular among the bourgeoisie during the gilded era of the Second Empire. Absinthe became the perfect aperitif, traditionally drunk before dinner (to drink absinthe all night would have been incredibly gauche in mainstream society). It became so popular in Paris that the aperitif hours between five and seven p.m. became known as the "green hour." The adding of water to the drink made it seem very refreshing and light, and the ritualistic serving of absinthe (slowly poured into a glass through a bit of sugar placed on a specially made spoon) made it attractive to a crowd in search of a new sensation.

Absinthe attracted a more bohemian reputation as the century wore on. Writers and artists in the Belle Époque, including Van Gogh, Verlaine, Baudelaire, Rimbaud, and Toulouse-Lautrec, believed the Green Fairy sparked their creative spirit. (Not all writers succumbed to absinthe's charms; Proust famously needed only a madeleine to liberate a lifetime of memories in *Swann's Way*, the first volume of his epic *In Search of Lost Time*.) Picasso, Degas, and Manet painted absinthe drinkers with varying degrees of approbation. Absinthe also became popular among the working classes in the 1870s, in part because lax regulations enabled the proliferation of cheaper, inferior versions.

Absinthe became ever more popular despite—or perhaps because of—its reputation for causing hallucinations, euphoria, seizures, and violent tendencies. Interestingly, recent pharmacological studies have shown that wormwood, thought to be the source of absinthe's hallucinogenic effects, could not have been the true culprit; more likely, the extreme intoxication associated with absinthe was the result of its absurdly high alcohol content (around 70 percent), or toxicity due to haphazard distillation methods. Nevertheless, the appeal of absinthe was also strengthened when wine, the usual vehicle for French intoxication, suffered an apocalyptic crisis thanks to an accidental and most unfortunate American import.

Phylloxera is a nasty little louse that feeds on the roots of vines, causing them to swell. The infected roots are rejected by the vine, sap stops circulating, and within three years the entire vine dies. Phylloxera was native to the United States, and the long sailing times on maritime voyages effectively quarantined the pest to its home continent. But the nineteenth-century steamship allowed the Atlantic to be crossed in ten days instead of several weeks, and somehow phylloxera hitched a ride to France, now helpfully crisscrossed with ever-faster railways. Its first victim was a vineyard near Arles in 1863. Bordeaux was infected in 1866, followed by Cognac, Burgundy, and the rest of France. French wine production fell from 84.5 million hectoliters in 1875 to 23.4 million hectoliters in 1889—a monumental calamity.[2] Champagne was the last major region to be infected, at the end of the nineteenth century.

The loss of the French wine industry was unthinkable, and every effort was expended to find an end to the crisis. Unfortunately, eliminating the pest by fumigation was too expensive and labor-intensive for most producers. An alternative path was proposed by French scientists, who rationalized that this American problem must have an American solution. Vines in America had adapted to phylloxera and were immune to its effects, so the obvious answer was to graft resistant American vines onto European vines. As you can imagine, the idea of introducing American vines to French winemaking sent some producers into apoplexy, and the French government did not approve the plan for nearly nine years. But after a great deal of trial and error, the experiment worked, and French vines slowly began to recover.

However, the traditional French wine producers returned to a much-changed market. During the phylloxera crisis, the French population coped by drinking imported wine, or watered down wine, or even fake wine made from raisins. (It was only as a result of the phylloxera crisis that France finally enacted a legal definition of wine, in 1889.) The vineyards of Algeria, which had produced wine even before the French conquest, expanded sixfold in the last two decades of the nineteenth century, and viticulture became an increasingly important sector of the colonial economy. Some people had stopped drinking wine entirely, turning to alternative liquors like absinthe.

And so French wine producers entered into an unholy alliance with the temperance movement. As in the United States, the French temperance movement blamed the excessive consumption of alcohol for the most pernicious ills of modern society. The French had become the largest consumers of alcohol in the world, with the average person consuming more than forty gallons of wine per year by the 1860s.[3] Alcohol was increasingly blamed for a whole raft of social problems: physical and mental illness, criminality, political radicalism. *Alcoholism*, a term that had not even been coined until 1849, became seen as a national problem, not an individual one. Rising alcoholism was then—as so often now—largely blamed on the poverty, urban misery, and questionable morals of the lower social classes. The conditions that propelled radical workers' movements were thought to also cause alcoholism, and so the two phenomena became closely linked in the minds of those who lived in dread of both. (By contrast, French socialists argued that alcoholism was encouraged by the bourgeoisie to keep the working class in thrall, and so it was yet another social ill that would disappear after the glorious workers' revolution.) But in truth, the rise in alcohol consumption was more likely due to France's increasing prosperity, with more people having the disposable income to afford alcohol, as well as the scientific innovations in alcohol production that led to new and cheaper forms of alcoholic drink.

The average French person still drank far more wine than any other alcohol, and French temperance activists were unique within the global temperance movement in tolerating, or even advocating the consumption of wine. It was a "natural alcohol," like beer and cider, and moderate consumption was acceptable. Indeed, wine had long been thought to have medicinal benefits, especially for digestion. It was the "industrial alcohols" that were seen as the primary driver of alcoholism, and among these, absinthe was seen as particularly noxious, causing madness, perversity, criminality, and death.

So as long as the French temperance movement had its sights set on industrial alcohols, it was supported by the wine industry. In fact, the Ligue Nationale Contre l'Alcoolisme (National League Against

Alcoholism), which campaigned to ban absinthe, was co-founded by a wine producer named Émile Cheysson. During the massive wine protests of 1907, when hundreds of thousands of people across the Languedoc protested the importation of cheap Algerian wines, one of the recurring slogans was "All for wine, and against absinthe." The emotional resonance of wine drinking in France was captured in a statement by the archconservative writer Léon Daudet: "I am for wine, and against Absinthe, like I am for tradition, and against revolution."[4] This tactical alliance of temperance activists and vintners was ostensibly pursued for social and humanitarian reasons, but it must be admitted that wine producers would also benefit materially from the elimination of rival alcohols.

In August 1914, with the outbreak of World War I, the French government banned the sale and later the production of absinthe, part of a wider campaign against social practices seen as undermining the country's military and moral strength. (France was not alone in this: in the same year, Russia made the shocking decision to ban the production of vodka.) Other industrial alcohols were subsequently banned, but by contrast, each serviceman in the French trenches received a daily ration of wine.

In France, a total prohibition on alcohol, as in the United States, was never seriously considered, although efforts to reduce alcoholism continued. As late as the 1950s, alcoholism was still a leading cause of death in France, but the creation of the national health service, better understanding of treatment methods, and government determination to reduce the social and economic costs of alcoholism finally led to a dramatic change in French drinking habits. Between 1960 and 2010, average annual consumption was cut in half, although it remains high relative to the United States and other western European countries, and it is a continuing source of concern for French public health authorities.

In the wake of the absinthe ban, the distilleries of Pontarlier managed to successfully convert to the production of pastis, an alternative anise-flavored liquor that did not contain wormwood, the supposed cause of absinthe's malevolence. But in 2010, the French government reversed its absinthe ban, and Pontarlier joyously embraced the Green Fairy once again.

French winemakers, meanwhile, remain a powerful and combative force, especially in regions where they constitute the dominant economic sector. More than a century after the 1907 wine protests,

This dramatic poster was apparently distributed to bars around France following the ban of absinthe. It depicts the president of France, Raymond Poincaré, standing victoriously above the mortally wounded "Green Fairy," while a World War I battle rages in the background. *La fin de la Fée Verte* © David Nathan-Maister, 2017. Courtesy of the Musée Virtuel de l'Absinthe.

the Languedoc continues to seethe with frustration over government wine policies and rival producers. Their main antagonist today is the bulk wine industry, both Spanish and French, which floods French supermarkets with cheaper wines at the lower end of the market, the traditional selling point for small Languedoc producers. Most protests are nonviolent, but the militant group Comité Régional d'Action Viticole (CRAV) has claimed responsibility for numerous incidents of arson and sabotage since the 1970s, as well as more recent propaganda efforts like emptying Spanish tanker trucks full of thousands of liters of wine after they cross the French border. The French government's countercharge is that the Languedoc wine industry needs to evolve in tandem with industry trends and be more innovative: French people today drink less wine, of better quality, and there are more non-European producers than ever to compete with. But such arguments fall flat in a region with unemployment rates of up to 20 percent and what they see as insufficient government investment.

It is a mark of how vitally important the French alcohol industry is—not just economically but socially and emotionally—that the question of what people should drink has been so all-consuming and furiously politicized throughout the modern era. It is a dynamic that is unlikely to disappear anytime soon, as the combined effects of globalization, climate change, and evolving drinking habits will force some of the most powerful economic interests in France to adapt or perish. The consequences of failure for the French countryside would be *profond* indeed.

42

Siege Gastronomy

One of the worst Christmases in the history of Paris arrived on December 25, 1870, the ninety-ninth day of a brutal siege by the Prussian army. France had stupidly stumbled into a war with its German neighbors, and now the capital was paying the price. Most of its

residents were starving. Emperor Napoleon III was a Prussian captive and the Second Empire had fallen. The French nation had been
humiliated on the European stage once again.

Yet there is a curious continuity throughout the history of war,
and that is that even in the most dire situations, the wealthiest strata
of society usually manages to lead a more charmed life than the famished masses. And so on Christmas Day 1870, some of the richest
denizens of Paris sat down to a feast legendary for its gothic innovation. The acclaimed chef Alexandre Étienne Choron had acquired a
number of former residents of the then-shuttered Paris zoo and fashioned them into one of the most famous menus in French culinary
history—one that would have horrified diners a few months earlier
but now seemed unbelievably decadent.

The Christmas Day meal at Voisin, Choron's restaurant on rue
Saint-Honoré, began with a stuffed donkey's head, an inelegant successor to the usual porcine centerpieces of prewar banquets. The soup
course included elephant consommé. This was followed by kangaroo
stew, rack of bear in pepper sauce, and roasted camel *à l'anglaise* (a
cheeky reference to what the French saw as the plainness of English
cuisine). The main course included *le chat flanqué de rats* (cat flanked
by rats) and *cuissot de loup, sauce chevreuil* (wolf in deer sauce), a
wry inversion of the natural order. A terrine of antelope and truffles
invoked a fast-disappearing age of luxury. The feast ended relatively
normally, with a cheese course of Gruyère, and was accompanied by
some of the finest wines still in stock (an 1846 Mouton Rothschild,
an 1858 Romanée-Conti, and an 1827 Grand Porto). The ingenuity
and absurdity of this macabre siege menu immediately cemented its
place in French gastronomic legend.

The feast also serves as an excellent illustration of the disaster and
folly of the short Franco-Prussian War, which destroyed the Second
Empire and laid the seeds for a later global conflagration. France was
essentially goaded into declaring war by Prussia's wily chancellor,
Otto von Bismarck. He dreamed of uniting the different German
kingdoms into one powerful German state, dominated by Prussia.
He correctly predicted that a French war of aggression would draw
the recalcitrant southern German provinces into his unification project, and so he engineered a diplomatic dispute over the Spanish royal
succession into a French declaration of war. It was a further sign
that the European balance of power crafted at Vienna in 1815 was
beginning to fray. Prussia was a rising power, having already bested

The animals of the Paris zoo were sacrificed during the siege, as the caption to this dramatic illustration explains: "For many months, no food came into Paris, besieged by the Prussians. To feed the 2 million souls that were in the capital, soon dogs, cats, and even rats were sacrificed! Finally the administration, bowing to the situation, handed over some animals of the Jardin des Plantes for consumption. The elephant, because of its mass, was one of the first to be sacrificed and served as food to the most famished." Elie Haguenthal, Pont-à-Mousson, "1870—La Guerre—1871 Siége de Paris. Abattage de l'Elephant" (1871). © Musée de l'Image–Ville d'Épinal/cliché H. Rouyer.

Austria in the Seven Weeks' War of 1866, and was now targeting the military might of France, the grande dame of Europe.

Napoleon III's Second Empire had been a prosperous and transformative era for France, a triumph of bourgeois interests and modernizing zeal. But by 1870, the emperor's popularity had declined amid economic crisis and continued opposition from republicans and socialists. A limited program of liberal reform in the 1860s was merely a façade for an essentially authoritarian regime, and many aspects of modernization—including the radical redevelopment of Paris spearheaded by Georges-Eugène Haussmann—benefited the wealthy purveyors of bourgeois capitalism, at the expense of the poor and working classes. As so often in the past, the scent of rebellion could be detected in the Parisian streets. In fact, one of the motivations for Haussmann's *grands boulevards* was to replace the narrow streets of central Paris, so easily barricaded and held by small groups of urban revolutionaries, with wide roads more conducive to control by imperial armed forces.

Napoleon III believed a quick victory over Prussia would restore his popularity and insulate his regime from political challengers. He failed to take into account Prussia's military advantages, such as its superior troop strength, the entrepreneurial flair of its officers, and its impressive mobilization capabilities. The well-planned German railroad network brought 380,000 soldiers and a mountain of equipment to the front in less than three weeks, while French forces struggled to organize and equip themselves.

Quite predictably, the Prussian army won several pitched battles in August, before delivering a knockout blow at the Battle of Sedan on September 1. The emperor himself, who had been commanding the troops, surrendered to the Prussians, along with one hundred thousand of his soldiers. The rest of the French army was pinned down in Metz and would eventually surrender in October. The war was effectively over at this point, but the French capital had yet to be taken. On September 19, the Prussian siege of Paris began.

With the emperor captured, a provisional government had taken control in Paris and proclaimed a new Third Republic. One of its primary considerations was how to keep the capital's population of 2 million civilians and 200,000 National Guardsmen alive for what was anticipated to be a relatively short siege.[1] Unfortunately, it lasted longer than expected: French negotiators would not agree to the Prussian demand to surrender Alsace and Lorraine, and attempts to raise French provincial armies and lift the siege failed.

Supplies had been laid in before the snare closed completely. The parks of Paris, including the Bois de Boulogne and Jardin du Luxembourg, hosted tens of thousands of sheep, cows, and pigs. Massive quantities of rice, potatoes, corn, flour, cheese, wine, and other food items were laid in store. But already in October, butchers began to sell the meat of horses, donkeys, and mules. The rationing of meat was instituted, first at 100 grams per adult per day, but quickly dropped to 50 and then 33 grams. Fish was still being caught in the Seine, but it was usually destined only for high-end restaurants. Adventurous people went foraging for vegetables in fields near the enemy lines. The famous cafés and boulevards of Paris were dark and quiet by ten p.m.

Eventually, one journalist declared, "we will end up going through the whole of Noah's ark," and he could not have been more right. In November, butchers started to sell cats and dogs. The butcher stalls in Les Halles indicated if they were selling bulldogs, terriers, or basset hounds. The meat of a rat was supposed to be tender and delicious, and it was valued much more than dog meat, which was seen as too tough.[2] Because they were so expensive, vegetables were sold in half or quarter units. "How much for half a carrot?" became a frighteningly common new shopping phrase. People waited for hours in the freezing cold for the mere chance of meat or decent food. Municipal canteens provided only the most meager sorts of rations.

Of course, not everybody was suffering to the same degree. The upper classes still usually managed to procure enough food, and high-end restaurants remained open, if sharply curtailed in their provisions. Auguste Blanqui, one of the most prominent socialist revolutionaries, divided Parisian society into two classes, "the fat and the thin," noting that "the fat particularly look after their favorite good, their belly . . . they lounge on their table, drinking, laughing, eating, each one with a triple chin and an abdomen that rebounds on their knees."[3] So it is not particularly surprising that when the Paris zoo was forced to close in late December, its most exotic and expensive animals were consumed by the capital's wealthiest citizens.

Food prices became stratospheric during the siege, even as the average French worker still only earned a few francs per day. In a remarkable journal recounting those days, Edmond Pascal describes the worsening situation on December 22:

> The rich . . . still find ways to live and maintain their habits of good food, they can pay 30 fr. [francs] for a chicken, 35 fr. for a rabbit, 70 fr. for a goose, 25 fr. for a pound of butter, and 18 fr. for a pound of Gruyère cheese, but my mother cannot buy a leek to make soup, because it would cost her 1 fr. 25 . . . Everything that can be eaten has in the past few days increased by 50 percent on the already excessive prices being asked. I will give you a small example by saying that a sparrow, a vulgar sparrow, is sold for 2 fr.[4]

On January 1, 1871, Pascal reported: "Our situation with regard to food becomes more and more critical, a cauliflower is 7 fr., a cabbage 8 fr., and butter is now 40 fr. per pound, and yesterday I saw a crow bought for the price of 2 fr. 50."[5] Bread was becoming darker and darker, as unknown substances were used to bulk up the grains. It was an intolerable situation, and the people of Paris grew increasingly malnourished and ill. Infant mortality soared.

The final straw came when Prussian forces began bombarding the capital in early January. After several weeks of shelling, with virtually no food of any sort left in the city, Paris surrendered, and the war came to an end. The Prussian victory transformed Bismarck's dream into reality, with the proclamation of the German Empire on January 18, 1871, in the Hall of Mirrors at Versailles. Germany was now the ascendant power on the continent. The peace settlement transferred Alsace and part of Lorraine from France to Germany, a wretched loss with a number of lingering consequences, including in the gastronomic realm.

For instance, while Alsace had long been the most Germanic region of France, the harsh imposition of a Prussian regime and the influx of more than 100,000 German settlers led one out of every eight residents to flee to other French provinces. This exodus helped the brasserie, a type of Alsatian restaurant that served beer and choucroute, become popular throughout the rest of France. Brasseries were more informal and open for longer hours than typical French restaurants, and for a while they popularized beer drinking in previously wine-devoted regions. Over the decades, their association with brewing faded away and they lost their overtly Alsatian flavor. But something of their original spirit can be seen in the revival of the craft beer industry in France, which is slowly attracting more interest from French drinkers.

Alsace is an ideal wine-growing region, with the Vosges Mountains creating a cool and dry microclimate for the production of white wines. At the time of the war with Prussia, Alsace produced some exceptional Riesling and Gewürztraminer wines, often considered superior to those produced by German winemakers. But after annexation, the region was tasked with delivering inferior varieties in bulk for the domestic market, thus removing a key competitor for German wines from the international market. Further catastrophe ensued with the arrival of phylloxera in Alsace in 1890, and the local wine industry did not recover its former status for many decades.

But perhaps most important, the loss of Alsace and Lorraine was a humiliation deeply felt throughout France, leaving an emotional scar that was preserved by successive French governments. French schoolbooks began to emphasize the nation's Gallo-Roman heritage over its Germanic-Frankish roots.[6] France never really accepted the German annexation, although residents of the provinces gradually resigned themselves to their political fate. More than four decades later, the unwavering French desire to reclaim Alsace and Lorraine became a critical dynamic in the causes and course of World War I.

As for Paris, the lifting of the siege brought much-needed food supplies into the capital. But stability remained elusive, as leftist and working-class activists in Paris objected to numerous policies of the conservative postwar government and feared plans were afoot to restore the monarchy once again. When the government attempted to disarm Parisian National Guard units in March 1871, the city rose in insurrection. A diverse coalition of radical republicans and socialists established the famous Commune of Paris, a revolutionary municipal government that during its ten-week existence attempted to implement a left-wing program, with some success. Karl Marx considered it the first great proletarian uprising and wrote a pamphlet called *The Civil War in France* to dissect its lessons for the socialist cause. Lenin also wrote at length about the lessons of the Commune, and it became a beacon of hope and inspiration for leftists throughout Europe for decades.

The French government, of course, could not allow the Commune to continue, and Paris was once again gradually besieged, this time by French government forces. On May 21, they moved into the capital, and over the course of the following week drove the Communard defenders farther and farther inward. A last stand ensued in Père Lachaise Cemetery, with the final resisters shot against the Mur des Fédérés (Federalists' Wall), a leftist pilgrimage site ever since. As many as fifteen thousand Communards were killed in the fighting or executed on the spot during the so-called Bloody Week.[7]

The fall of the Commune was a staggering blow to the French left, but it may have helped save the Third Republic and prevent a royal restoration. By cracking down on the Commune, the republican government firmly set itself on the side of law and order, thus reassuring conservatives and monarchists of its moderate intentions. Over the next two decades, the Republic slowly became more stable and institutionalized, with a range of political freedoms restored. A free press returned, trade unions were allowed to form, and the state education system was secularized. But sharp political divisions and opposition remained, both among leftists eager for more radical reform and among the increasingly nationalist and authoritarian right wing. Extremists within the new anarchist movement married their utopian vision with the recent invention of dynamite in a terrifying campaign of bombings and assassinations. France was on the verge of one of its most fabled and prosperous eras, but beneath the glamour of the Belle Époque lay deep social divisions and the rumor of approaching war.

43

The Peanut Patrimony

Peanut butter can usually be found on the regular shelves of larger French supermarkets, but typically only one kind is offered, of a brand unknown to any American (although it will usually have a large American flag billowing across its label). A tiny jar can cost four euros, a painful toll for homesick expats. The French have not really embraced peanut butter, which is a shame considering how lovely their jams and breads are. Peanut butter sales amount to only $30 million a year, compared to more than $300 million in annual revenue in the United States.[1]

But curiously, the French consume more peanut oil than virtually any other country in Europe. In part, this is because it is especially suitable for deep frying—crucial for producing those popular *frites*—but the French also use peanut oil in light vinaigrettes and dressings (except in the southern reaches of France, where olive oil still reigns supreme). This atypical affinity for peanut oil has deep historic roots in the second major era of colonial expansion, when France sought to cement its great power status with a global empire.

As we have seen, the French participated in the first European rush to empire in the sixteenth and seventeenth centuries, but with mixed results. France was never the naval power that Britain and Holland were, and its rulers tended to be more preoccupied with continental affairs than far-flung possessions. During the eighteenth and early nineteenth centuries, many colonies were surrendered to other Euro-

pean powers after French defeats in war. Haiti was lost to rebellion
and Louisiana sold to the United States. Throughout the world, the
British Empire was in the ascendancy.

But a second wave of empire-building commenced in the nineteenth century, focused especially on Africa and East Asia. France
began its conquest of North Africa by taking Algiers in 1830, and
under Napoleon III a massive effort to enlarge the French empire
was undertaken. New colonial armies were formed, and the expansion and modernization of the French fleet made France the second
greatest naval power in the world. The colonies became ever more
entwined with the economic and political affairs of mainland France
(also known as Metropolitan France, or la Métropole). They provided vast amounts of food and natural resources, as well as soldiers
and laborers, and a "colonial lobby" gradually became more influential in French domestic politics. At the same time, French interests
dictated the development of each colonial territory. Local political,
social, and economic patterns that had endured for centuries were
swept aside by whatever best suited France, whether that meant
replacing hostile leaders, enforcing the planting of particular crops,
or drawing boundaries that ignored ethnic and tribal divisions. The
human costs of imperial despotism were staggering and continued
well beyond the colonial era, as the now-independent nations of the
developing world struggled to escape the ties of dependency so carefully constructed by the colonial powers.

This pattern of displacement and exploitation was evident in the
French subjugation of Senegal, one of the earliest targets of colonial expansion in the nineteenth century. France had first established
trading posts on the Senegalese coast in the early seventeenth century. It captured the island of Gorée, well known today for its haunting memorial to the horrors of the transatlantic slave trade, from the
Dutch in 1677. The slave trade in West Africa preceded the European
presence, but it had traditionally flowed north, across the blazing
Sahara. When the Europeans arrived, seeking vast amounts of labor
for their American colonies, captives from the interior were increasingly diverted to trading posts on the western coast of Africa. The
Senegal River was a key transit route, and the slave trade became one
of the most dominant economic activities in the region.

The slave trade began to decline in Senegal in the late eighteenth
century, and France formally abolished slavery in its colonies in
1848. This necessitated a turn to alternative commodities and trade,

at the same time that France was keen to enlarge its territorial reach in West Africa (as always, in competition with the British). Over the next few decades, France gradually expanded its presence from the Senegalese coast. French governors constructed a series of forts on the Senegal River and built roads and railroads inland so they could directly control economic activity in the interior rather than relying on local traders. Kingdoms that had existed in the area for hundreds of years were forcefully subjugated if they could not be co-opted. A large new port was built at Dakar, which became one of the most important cities on the African coast and the capital of French West Africa.

Undoubtedly, French military might and violent coercion were a decisive factor in its expanding control of Senegal. But French commercial interests also played an important role, as the economic hegemony they helped establish for France in the region bolstered its political control as well. This is perhaps best illustrated by examining the history of Senegal's most important crop: the peanut.

Peanuts are actually legumes and grow below ground beside the roots of the peanut plant. Native to South America, peanuts were introduced to West Africa by Portuguese traders as early as the 1500s. Because they were similar to the Bambara groundnut already grown in the region, but more nutritious and easier to harvest, they were accepted rather easily and cultivated widely. They became a staple ingredient of West African cuisine, often ground into a paste used in soups, stews, and sauces. But they were not of much interest to European traders, as they were grown mostly in the remote interior and still primarily a basic food crop.

This all changed with the wide-ranging innovations of the Industrial Revolution in the nineteenth century, when peanut oil became a hotly demanded product. Europe's ever-increasing mechanization required huge amounts of lubricants and industrial oils, and advances in chemistry revealed new uses for tropical oils in soaps, waxes, and other products. The legendary soap industry in Marseille, for example, preferred using peanut oil in its soaps because it did not affect their color. Peanut oil was increasingly used in French kitchens as well, supplanting olive oil in dressings and driving a new taste for fried foods.

At first, the peanut trade was controlled by local Senegalese merchants, who used their existing trade networks extending into the interior. France encouraged the export of unshelled peanuts by keep-ing taxes on them low, so that their processing into peanut oil mostly took place in the ports of Metropolitan France.[2] This practice of restricting commodity production in the colonies to raw crops, while the processing that greatly increased their value was reserved for the colonial mainland, was common. Local oil mills in Senegal only began exporting small amounts of peanut oil in the late 1920s.

As French interest in the peanut grew, Senegalese farmers increas-ingly began planting peanuts to the exclusion of other crops. The creation of giant peanut plantations was actively encouraged and funded by French colonial interests, and gradually peanuts became the dominant cash crop in Senegal. As French control of the interior expanded, merchants from Bordeaux and Marseille gradually took over the peanut trade. In essence, French commercial interests drove the Senegalese agricultural economy in the direction most beneficial for themselves, and then reaped most of the benefits by monopolizing the trade of the most important commodity.

French economic hegemony in Senegal helped bolster its imperial-ist claims vis-à-vis its main rival in the region, Great Britain (which, incidentally, preferred the palm oil produced by its own West Afri-can colonies). The European competition for African colonies grew more and more intense throughout the nineteenth century, as indus-trialization and great power rivalry fueled an insatiable greed for resources and territorial expansion. Advances in transportation, communication, and tropical medicine rendered previously inac-cessible regions of the continent open to European intrusion. For much of the century, what is sometimes called "informal imperial-ism" prevailed, whereby European powers enjoyed economic and military dominance over various African territories, but their direct governance was limited to coastal areas and trading centers. But the 1884–85 Berlin Conference, an attempt to regulate European rivalry in Africa, established a new principle of "effective occupation" that drastically transformed the continent. In setting out rules for the division of Africa, it was determined that states could only claim specific territories if they directly administered them. While inter-pretations of the rule varied, it is seen as a primary driver of the "Scramble for Africa," the rapid colonization of the entire continent. By 1914, every African territory had been claimed, save for Liberia, Ethiopia, and part of modern-day Somalia. Most of the north and west of the continent was part of the French empire, now the second largest in the world.

The French established a colonial administration throughout West Africa that presumed Africans to be subjects, not citizens. The only exception was in Senegal, where residents of four coastal communes were subjected to a greater degree of enforced assimilation and given the same political rights as French citizens. While some effort was made to improve health and educational opportunities for local populations, there was never any doubt that France's primary colonial incentives derived from political and economic self-interest. And so Senegal continued in its role as peanut provider to France, rather than developing a more diverse and robust economy that would benefit its own people.

This was more or less sustainable as long as Senegal was simply one part of French West Africa, but it created enormous problems once Senegal achieved its independence in 1960. It was now one of the largest peanut producers in the world, but it was almost completely dependent on this one cash crop. Peanuts did not command high prices, and demand fluctuated significantly, especially as the popularity of other oils grew. Meanwhile, Senegal had to import food that it used to grow itself, before the peanut had swept everything aside. It is a familiar story for many African states that have struggled to escape colonial bonds of dependency and exploitation.

Today, Senegal continues to try to diversify its economy, even as it finds major new markets for peanuts in China and India. It is an uphill battle: more than a third of the country's arable land is devoted to peanut farming, which remains Senegal's most important cash crop. France retained enormous influence in Senegal for many years after its formal independence, and it is still one of Senegal's most important trading partners. So in the end, the French affinity for peanut oil is not that strange after all. It is yet another example of how conquest and colonization transformed the French culinary and economic landscape, and how enduring the habits of imperialism have proven to be.

44

Gastronomads on the Sun Road

The most celebrated road in the United States is undoubtedly Route 66, immortalized in song and film for more than seventy years now. The French equivalent is the legendary Route Nationale 7, with an even longer lineage of appreciation. The Romans built the first roads connecting Paris to the Mediterranean, and these were periodically developed over the centuries by modernizing rulers like Louis XI, Louis XIV, and Napoleon. In 1871, the modern Route Nationale 7 was established on these ancient byways. It became the main travel route from Paris and Lyon to the Côte d'Azur, traversing some of the most beautiful regions of France before arriving at the dazzling Mediterranean coast. It acquired even greater significance in the twentieth century, as the development of mass tourism and the invention of the automobile brought unprecedented crowds to *la route du soleil* (the sun road). The French affection for the road is evident in the classic Charles Trenet song "Nationale 7," which evokes its summery pleasures and closes with the joyful proclamation, "We are happy, Nationale 7."

To be sure, the Nationale 7 did not always instill happiness in travelers. It was famous for its traffic jams and accidents, especially during busy holiday periods. But these were made more tolerable by the gastronomic delights found along its path, and indeed the Nationale 7 played a critical role in the emergence of the "gastronomad," or gastronomic tourist—a very modern sort of traveler that unsurprisingly flourished in the bounteous French countryside.

Farmers' stalls, *traiteurs*, and restaurants peppered rural France along the six hundred miles of the Nationale 7, offering delicious sustenance to weary travelers. Patisseries enticed hungry voyagers with local delicacies, such as the sweet white nougats of Montélimar or the *calissons* (almond sweets) of Aix-en-Provence. The melons of Cavaillon were so legendarily succulent that they were sold for miles along the roadside. (Alexandre Dumas famously gave the Cavaillon library a copy of every one of his published works in exchange for a lifetime supply of melons.) As the highway curved toward Nice, the classic flavors of Provence could be found in a slice of *pissaladière*, an intensely fragrant tart of onions, black olives, and anchovies. Menton, the last French town to be graced by the Nationale 7 before it crossed into Italy, was the largest producer of lemons in Europe, thanks to a splendid seaside microclimate.[1]

Wine lovers could visit some of the most celebrated vineyards in France, as the road threaded the Upper Loire Valley, glided down the Rhône River, and crossed southern Provence. Where there is wine, there is cheese, and many a good cheese was produced near the Nationale 7. In the Loire, a small, very strong goat's cheese called Crottin de Chavignol was popular, despite *crottin* meaning "dung" (which the cheese somewhat resembled in appearance). Further south, one of the mildest of blue cheeses appeared, Fourme de Montbrison (it remains an excellent choice today for gratins and vegetable dishes). In Lyon, it would have been a shame not to try the ridiculously creamy Saint-Marcellin, or the herbed cheese dip called *cervelle de canut*, literally "brains of the silk weaver." Lyon had long been a leading producer of silk, one of France's most important luxury products, but the workers operating the industrial silk looms were subject to poor pay and working conditions.[2] Their usual working lunch was a humble mélange of soft cheese, herbs, and shallots, which eventually became a local staple.

The introduction of the automobile massively expanded the potential audience for these local delicacies. The French were among the earliest pioneers of automotive technology, and in fact they consider the Frenchman Édouard Delamare-Deboutteville to be the inventor of the first automobile, in 1884 (a controversial claim due to the significant problems he experienced in actually producing and running his vehicles). By the end of the 1890s, Armand Peugeot and the Renault brothers had built and sold their first cars, and France quickly became the largest automaker in the world, producing nearly half the global total. By the eve of World War I, 100,000 cars were traversing the roads of France, a number that would rise to 2 million by the time of World War II.[3]

The automobile opened up all sorts of opportunities for new industries, and perhaps no one grasped this chance more successfully than the Michelin brothers, Ándre and Édouard. They owned a rubber factory in Clermont-Ferrand that already sold tires for bicycles, and they quickly developed a pneumatic tire for the first automobiles in the 1890s. Their company would go on to become one of the leading tire and rubber manufacturers in the world.

The Michelin brothers realized that if they could help expand popular demand for both automobiles and tourism, they would sell more tires. They published the first Michelin guide in time for the Paris world's fair in 1900, and distributed 35,000 free copies to drivers. It listed sites throughout France where one could stay overnight, find something to eat, refuel the car—and, of course, find a garage to change one's tires. It was only much later, in 1926, that the guide began awarding stars to the best restaurants, eventually settling on a formula whereby a two-star restaurant was "worth the detour" while a three-star restaurant was "worth a special trip." This contributed significantly to the growth of reputable restaurants outside of Paris, and some of those along the Nationale 7 became famous, including La Pyramide in Vienne, La Maison Troisgros in Roanne, Maison Pic in Valence, and La Mère Brazier in Lyon. For a long time, finding a three-star Michelin restaurant that was not in Paris or near the Nationale 7 was an anomaly. Restaurateurs began anticipating the next Michelin edition with a mixture of fear and hope, as they do to this day.

Following the successful launch of the Michelin guide for France, similar guides were produced for the neighboring states of Europe, and for Algeria and Tunisia as well. Publishing was suspended during World War I, but not before the release of a new edition for western Germany in early 1915. At that time, it was still hoped that the French would be swarming into Germany imminently, and so with typical entrepreneurial optimism, Michelin decided to produce an up-to-date guide for the area (ultimately, an unwarranted one). More useful were the "battlefield guides" of the Western Front that Michelin began publishing in 1917, while the war was still ongoing, which included haunting photographs of trench wastelands and before-and-after shots of ruined landmarks. Later, during World War II, Allied forces relied on Michelin guides during their invasion and occupation of France, as their maps were considered to be the most accurate.

In the interwar period, Michelin sponsored a number of publications that encouraged French drivers to explore the countryside, using regional cuisine as an effective lure. One of the most renowned contributors to this literature was Maurice-Edmond Sailland, who

A LA MÉMOIRE
DES OUVRIERS ET EMPLOYÉS DES USINES MICHELIN
MORTS GLORIEUSEMENT POUR LA PATRIE

La deuxième
bataille
de la Marne

MICHELIN & Cie — ÉDITEURS — CLERMONT-FERRAND

Copyright by Michelin & Cie 1919

Tous droits de traduction, d'adaptation ou de reproduction totale ou partielle réservés pour tous pays.

A Michelin battlefield guide from 1919: "The Second Battle of the Marne." It is dedicated to the Michelin workers who "died gloriously for the homeland." Michelin, *La deuxième bataille de la Marne* (1919). Courtesy of the Bibliothèque Nationale de France.

wrote under the pseudonym Curnonsky. Following in the tradition of bons vivants like Brillat-Savarin and Grimod de la Reynière, Curnonsky wrote copiously on French gastronomy in humorous yet devoted fashion. In addition to penning short articles for Michelin, he wrote dozens of books celebrating the diverse regional cuisines of France (including, with Marcel Rouff, *Le Tour de France gastronomique*, a twenty-four-volume survey of France's culinary wonders and gastronomic history). He obsessively explored local traditions and specialties, not just the haute cuisine of the nation's premier kitchens, and argued passionately for their preservation as industrial food production expanded its universalizing grip.

Unlike earlier gastronomic writers, Curnonsky was able to explore *la France profonde* by car (he did not drive himself but was fortunate to have a number of friends happy to serve as chauffeurs). He recognized the transformative impact of the automobile, writing that it "allowed the French to discover the cuisine of each province, and created the breed of what I have called 'gastro-nomads.'"[4] Today, we have come to take for granted the many food enthusiasts who cross the globe in pursuit of obscure and tasty dishes, but the concept of a gastronomad was still novel in the early twentieth century. Curnonsky was one of the most influential voices promoting this development, writing that "in France, tourism and gastronomy . . . are inseparable. Due to the incomparable diversity of its landscapes, its picturesque sites, and its thirty-two cuisines . . . France will always be the paradise of gastronomic tourism."[5]

It remains an enduring paradox in France that while economic, political, and cultural power is overwhelmingly concentrated in Paris, most gastronomes would agree that the true heart of French gastronomy lies not in the capital but in the regions. For example, while it is common for foreigners to extol the culinary treasures of Paris, the average French person would probably consider Lyon the true food capital of France (Curnonsky even dubbed it the "world capital of gastronomy"). Many of the best-known French dishes are in fact regional specialties, including cassoulet, bouillabaisse, coq au vin, and foie gras, to say nothing of the hundreds of cheeses and wines linked to a specific terroir. The cuisines of Provence, Burgundy, Normandy—in fact, virtually every French region—are treasure troves of delicious and intriguing dishes, and their popularity today owes much to the dedicated wanderings of the first gastronomads.

The final heyday of Route Nationale 7 was undoubtedly the 1950s and 1960s, when French citizens acquired longer paid vacations and more affordable cars came onto the market. But sadly, the Nationale 7 has suffered a fate similar to Route 66, as the construction of faster highways since the 1970s has diverted much of its traffic. Many stretches have been downgraded to local roads and relabeled with new route numbers, making it difficult to follow the original road in all its glory. But those who opt for its slow-moving charms will continue to be rewarded, as many of the restaurants, markets, and small towns that made the Nationale 7 so beloved are still there. The *route du soleil* may have been partially eclipsed by impatient modernity, but the delectability of the French countryside remains undimmed.

45

A Friend in Difficult Hours

There is no lack of remembrance of World War I in France, where much of the war was fought and where more than 1.3 million French soldiers lost their lives. It was the first mass industrial war of the twentieth century, and the introduction of machine guns, modern artillery, tanks, and eventually airpower led to far greater casualties than had ever been seen before. Indeed, the Western Front generated such an unprecedented level of carnage that contemporary observers believed the conflict would be "the war to end all wars," and a number of haunting memorials reflect the horrific battles that occurred there. Perhaps the most symbolic of these for the French is the Battle of Verdun, which more than any other event represents both the heroism and the futility of the war from a modern French perspective. More than 800,000 French and German soldiers were killed, wounded, or went missing during more than three hundred days of fighting at Verdun, in one of the longest and deadliest battles in human history. These horrors are movingly captured in a collection of museums and monuments around the former battlefield.

Remembrance of this terrible war is not limited to large battlefield memorials but endures in the heart of virtually every French town and village, however small. In traveling through the French countryside, it becomes impossible to miss the poignant sculptures anchoring the town squares, carved with the names of local boys who never returned from the trenches. Even in tiny hamlets, the list can be surprisingly long. Twenty percent of France's population, amounting to more than 8 million men, was mobilized during the war, and more than 70 percent of these men were killed, wounded, or presumed dead. It is therefore not surprising that the war touched almost every community in France, even those far from the front lines.

This near-universal involvement of French communities in the war had some unexpected consequences for French gastronomy. Most notably, it was thanks to the Western Front that French soldiers, and then the French people, and then the entire world came to know and love one of the quintessential French cheeses: the intense yet comforting Camembert. It was merely one of a number of regional Normandy cheeses prior to 1914, albeit with a reasonable following

Memorial to those lost in World War I from the town of Cancale, Brittany. Similar memorials can be found in nearly every small town and village in France, which lost nearly 1.3 million men in the war. Photograph by authors, 2017.

in Paris as well. But it was during the war years that Camembert became a national treasure, one of the few bright spots in an otherwise dismal era.

No one anticipated this vast universe of suffering when the war began in the summer of 1914, after the assassination of Archduke Franz Ferdinand of Austria triggered a diplomatic crisis among Europe's great powers that escalated into all-out war. It was a conflict long in the making, as great power rivalry in the Balkans, an escalating naval arms race, and imperial competition gradually undermined the European balance of power. Tension and distrust had grown to the point where the killing of one nobleman could serve as a catalyst for continental war. France entered the war in alliance with Russia and Great Britain, forming the Triple Entente against Germany, Austria-Hungary, and the Ottoman Empire (the Central Powers). Additional countries, including the United States and Italy, later joined the Entente, and became more widely known as the Allied Powers.

Throughout Europe, politicians and populations alike believed the war would be short and decisive. In France, the mood was more of resignation than enthusiasm, although the possibility of reclaiming Alsace and Lorraine helped make the general mobilization a bit more palatable. One might have expected the socialists and communists, at least, to oppose the war, reluctant to fight their fellow workers in Germany on behalf of French bourgeois capitalism. But even on the left, defeat to militaristic Germany appeared a worse fate than temporary alliance with capitalism, and opposition was limited. One of the few exceptions was Jean Jaurès, a leading socialist who frantically tried to persuade politicians of the folly of this war. His efforts were in vain, and he was assassinated in the Café du Croissant in Paris by a French nationalist.

As France quickly became more nationalist and anti-German, food became an easy way to express this new mood. Bars, brasseries, and shops that had even a hint of German association were attacked by mobs (anything along the lines of *Brasserie de Munich* could expect major trouble). Alsatians who had relocated to France but still spoke with a German accent were looked at with suspicion. Léon Daudet and the archnationalist Action Française accused a range of food businesses with supposed links to Germany of acting as a sort of fifth column inside France. After the German invasion of Belgium, the *café viennois* (coffee topped with whipped cream and chocolate) was rebaptized as *café liégeois*, after Liège. The name has stuck and now *liégeois* is generally used to order that drink.[1]

The Germans marched through neutral Belgium relatively quickly and then invaded France in late August 1914. It initially appeared their maneuver would be successful, as they closed upon Paris, but a French counteroffensive drove them back. By December 1914, the lines of the Western Front had more or less stabilized, snaking through the northeastern French countryside. Over the next four years, the Allies and Germany would all launch offensives that killed hundreds of thousands of men yet failed to significantly shift the battle lines. The war gradually spread beyond the confines of Europe: to the Atlantic, where submarine warfare eventually drew the United States into the conflict; to the Middle East, where the Arab Revolt helped finally topple the Ottoman Empire; and to Africa, where the colonial powers fought each other and fended off local rebellions. On the Eastern Front, the Russian Revolution in 1917 led to the country's withdrawal from the war and the eventual establishment of the Soviet Union.

These momentous events reshaped the world order, but for the average French infantryman (or *poilu*), the war took place within a very limited sphere of action, in the trenches and forward positions of the Western Front. Much has been written over the years about the horrors of trench life, and while it is true that the average soldier spent much less time within the trenches than is commonly assumed, their nightmarish qualities continue to resonate in the popular imagination. There were so many ways to die: if you stayed in your trench, you might be blown up by enemy shells; if your unit was ordered to attack, you might be shot a few steps into no-man's-land. Chemical weapons made their terrible debut, with the most common acquiring the name "mustard gas" due to its smell. Diseases such as tuberculosis and pneumonia stalked those who survived the perils of battle.

These dangers would have been fearsome enough on a full stomach, but this was not always the case for the poilus. True to stereotype, their rations mostly consisted of bread, wine, and cheese. Their wine rations increased as the war went on, from a bottle every three days in 1914 to nearly a bottle a day in 1916. Very rarely, they might be given a stronger type of grain alcohol known as *gnôle*, but this was not actually appreciated very much, as the men usually assumed it meant a new offensive on the morrow. More substantial meals, including meat, potatoes, and beans, were sometimes available, although rarely hot by the time they arrived at the trenches. The meat was sometimes canned, and of dubious quality, and was nicknamed "monkey meat."[2] Food production in France fell by a third during the war, with so many young men at the front, and the civilian population throughout France had to endure shortages and rationing as well. Nevertheless, soldiers sometimes received packages of food from family and shared them with their fellow trench mates, who hailed from all over France. Thus the foods of Brittany, Savoy, Normandy, Provence, and many other regions found new fans, as soldiers held their little potluck dinners on the dreary front.

But it was the inclusion of cheese in the daily rations that eventually had one of the most long-ranging impacts on French gastronomy. At the beginning of the war, the French army bought massive supplies of Gruyère, and later Cantal: hard mountain cheeses with long shelf lives that could be transported and eaten easily. But these cheeses soon faced new rivals, as other producers saw the serious amount of money and marketing that inclusion in the rations could bring and began lobbying the army for contracts as well. Among the most persuasive were the Normandy producers of Camembert.

According to legend, Marie Harel "invented" Camembert in 1791, on the advice of a priest who had fled the anticlerical purges of the French Revolution and was hiding on her farm. The priest came from the region where Brie is produced and suggested to Marie that she make her Livarot cheese, a traditional round cheese from Normandy, using similar techniques. Unfortunately for this narrative, accounts of a cheese called Camembert predate Marie's birth, so at best she merely improved upon an existing product. But it is true that she passed her methods down to her children, who founded one of the largest Camembert companies in Normandy.

With the outbreak of World War I, Camembert producers adopted a hearty patriotism and festooned the distinctive wooden Camembert boxes with French flags, the French cockerel, and images depicting a victorious France. But the producers were not satisfied with propaganda efforts alone and became determined to acquire an army contract to provide Camembert in the soldiers' rations. After several years of lobbying, and offering the cheese at very competitive prices, they succeeded. Camembert became the daily cheese of the French soldier, most of whom had never encountered it before. By 1918, the army was requesting 1 million Camemberts each month, a quantity producers struggled to supply.[3]

For the poilus, their daily morsels of Camembert came to represent something much more than mere food. Its strong, earthy flavors were a reminder of the rural France that most of them called home. Pierre Boisard, author of a popular history of Camembert, has suggested that the startling white and round Camembert, combined with the deep red of the daily wine ration, reminded the overwhelmingly Catholic soldiers of the Eucharist and wine offered at mass, "a patriotic equivalent to the Catholic rite of communion."[4] Its creamy, comforting texture became associated with the calm moments when rations could be eaten. Georges Clemenceau, the French prime minister at the end of the war, reportedly called Camembert the "friend of man, in difficult hours."[5]

The poilus who survived the war returned to their home regions with a newfound taste for this strong northern cheese. This should have been a gold mine for the Normandy producers of Camembert, but in those days before AOC protection, there was nothing to stop cheesemakers from other regions from labeling their own products as Camembert. Soon, new Camembert cheeses were appearing all over France, and they were eagerly snapped up by a newly appreciative population. The French government officially declared *Camembert* a generic term, one that anyone in the world can use. Only Camembert de Normandie, a raw unpasteurized cheese made of milk from Normandy cows, has ever received an AOC, in 1983.

And so, just as France would eventually win the war but lose the peace, the original producers of Camembert won the hearts of the French nation but lost the chance to be the sole financial victors from it. It may have been some consolation to the descendants of Marie Harel that she continued to receive adulation from a grateful clientele around the world, as evidenced by the arrival in the town of Camembert of an American doctor named Joseph Knirim, in 1926. He was convinced that Camembert had cured his digestive disorder, a notion that Normandy cheesemakers would probably have agreed with (the virtues of bacteria-laden, unpasteurized cheeses are practically gospel in Normandy). He was so grateful that he sponsored the raising of a statue of Madame Harel in nearby Vimoutiers, which the local residents gladly accepted. At a time when the provenance of Camembert had become so diffused, it was helpful to have a small reminder of its origins.

Unfortunately, during World War II, Vimoutiers was heavily bombed by the Allies, decapitating the statue. After the war, the

244 I A Bite-Sized History of France

chairman of Borden, one of the largest cheese producers in the United States, offered to replace the statue, and company employees raised $2,000 to pay for it. The residents of Vimoutiers gladly accepted, and it appeared a happy ending to the sad tale was imminent. But when it came time to unveil the statue, the residents of Vimoutiers erupted in anger at the proposed sign to be attached:

THIS STATUE WAS THE GIFT OF THE BORDEN OHIO CAMEMBERT FACTORY.

Sacre bleu! Were the creators of Camembert supposed to accept that the Americans were not only producing Camembert on an industrial scale, but flaunting this fact in its very birthplace? To make matters worse, the United States had recently banned the importation of raw-milk Normandy Camembert. So there was a mighty uproar, but eventually things were smoothed over and the new statue was erected, without the offending sign. The new text read: THIS STATUE IS OFFERED BY 400 MEN AND WOMEN MAKING CHEESE IN VAN WERT OHIO USA. A copy of the Marie Harel statue was later erected in Van Wert as well.

World War I had enormous consequences for nearly every aspect of French society, many of them much more noticeable and important than the elevation of one cheese from Normandy. But it is hard to overstate how beloved Camembert is among the French people, or the extent to which it has come to symbolize French gastronomy in such a short space of time.

46

A Mutiny and a Laughing Cow

The terrible conditions in the trenches of the Western Front were exacerbated by the most enervating factor of all: the slow passage of time, with almost nothing to show for the immense human suffering being perpetuated. World War I was a war of attrition; once both sides settled down into defensive positions in late 1914, decisive battles became near impossible, and the only real option was to wear down the enemy until he had no choice but to surrender. Long periods of inactivity were punctuated with intense artillery bombardments and optimistic offensives against well-fortified lines, both of which generated incredible levels of casualties. By early 1917, more than 1 million French soldiers had been killed, to no obvious benefit.

Morale in the French army plummeted as spring 1917 arrived. Another failed offensive in April seemed to steal the last reserves of strength from the *poilus*. News that the United States would be joining the war was welcomed, but spirits sank again once it became evident that American troops would not be jumping into the trenches for many months yet. The audience for socialist and pacifist arguments against the war grew ever larger, especially after the Russian Revolution in March 1917 boosted antiwar forces in that country. French soldiers were weary, sick, and frustrated, as their continued suffering at the front seemed to have no purpose.

And so in the first week of May, the mutiny began. French infantry units simply began to refuse orders, whether to fight or to go to the front. Thousands deserted. In some locations, protests and violence occurred. It is estimated that more than 40 percent of the frontline units experienced some level of mutiny and insubordination. Shockingly, the Germans did not realize or take advantage of the fact that the French army was in such serious disarray (news of these events was not revealed even within France until the 1960s).[1] By June, authorities had suppressed the mutinies with mass arrests and courts-martial. Several thousand men were sentenced to death or hard labor, but it appears only a few dozen were actually executed. Army commanders did not want to inflame the situation any more than necessary.

Indeed, the new commanding general, Philippe Pétain, instituted a range of policies designed to improve morale and save the French army from disintegration. First and foremost, he decided to forego large-scale, suicidal offensives until the Americans arrived and the revolutionary new tanks being built by Renault were ready for the battlefield. He dealt firmly with cases of insubordination and desertion, but he also began to give soldiers longer leaves away from the front. He listened to soldiers' complaints about conditions at the front and encouraged officers to devise some new ways to keep up the spirits of the poilus. And as a result, the world would eventually experience the peaceful invasion of the laughing cow of France.

Among those mobilized for the war in August 1914 was a young cheesemaker from the Jura named Léon Bel. His father had founded a *cave d'affinage*, a central site for maturing cheeses, and Léon helped oversee the aging of wheels of Comté, Gruyère, and Emmental. Like most soldiers, he probably expected to return home to his business within a few months, but in 1917 he found himself still on the Western Front. He was assigned to the RVF (Ravitaillement en Viande Fraîche), the large supply unit responsible for delivering fresh meat to the front.

As part of the morale-boosting program, it was decided that each unit should have its own emblem, something that would encourage good cheer and camaraderie. After a small competition, Bel's

La Wachkyrie, the RVF B.70 emblem created by Benjamin Rabier during World War I. Courtesy of Les Amis de Benjamin Rabier, Valençay, France. © The Heirs of Benjamin Rabier.

RVF B.70 section chose a design by Benjamin Rabier, who had been an illustrator before the war. His emblem depicted a laughing cow above the inscription LA WACHKYRIE, a characteristic example of French wordplay. Phonetically, *La Wachkyrie* sounds like *la vache qui rit*, the cow that laughs, but it also calls to mind *La Walkyrie (The Valkyrie)*, the famous Richard Wagner opera so beloved in Germany. The Germans actually used the image of the flying Valkyrie, the fierce women warriors of Norse mythology, in their war propaganda. So *La Wachkyrie* was essentially a mocking rejoinder to the Germans.

Thanks to these and other efforts, the morale of the French army was gradually restored by early 1918. The Americans had finally arrived, and the Russians had left the war. The collapse of the Eastern Front allowed Germany to launch a new offensive in the west in March, which initially appeared successful but could not be sustained, and Allied forces launched a counteroffensive that encroached upon German territory. By fall, the threat of invasion and the draining force of attrition made German defeat all but certain. The successful Allied blockade had led to famine inside Germany, and revolution was brewing among its sailors and workers. In the waning days of the war, the German monarchy was overthrown and a democratic republic (later known as the Weimar Republic) was established. The new government shouldered the blame from right-wing forces for the German surrender in November 1918, generating the infamous "stab in the back" myth that helped catapult the Nazis into political success in the next decade.

The November armistice allowed the gradual demobilization of the French army, and Bel returned to his family's cheese business in 1919. He found that Swiss cheesemakers had invented a new type of processed cheese that could be kept for extended periods in tin cans, and he decided to modernize his own business with a similarly new product. Using leftover bits of cheese from the *cave d'affinage*, he invented in 1921 a creamy processed cheese that, for the first time, was packaged in individual foil triangles. It was easily portable and kept for long periods of time.

When it came time to market and sell his new cheese, Bel remembered the joyful *Wachkyrie* of the trenches and named his product La vache qui rit, which is how it is still known in France. In the 1930s, he began exporting it to other countries under the brand name

Laughing Cow, which is how you will normally find it on American shelves. He tracked down Benjamin Rabier and asked him to adapt his original emblem for the new cheese.[2] Rabier produced a near copy of the original laughing cow but added some attractive earrings on the advice of Bel's wife. Rabier was later asked how he managed to draw such an unnaturally smiling cow. He replied:

> My job is harder than people think it is. How to make a cow laugh! I spent many sleepless nights to achieve it. From my dairy farmer I borrowed a cow and its calf. I started with the calf, thinking he would be more receptive as he was younger. But quite the opposite happened. It was the mother who laughed first, so happy was she to see me playing with her young one.[3]

That joyful cow was destined to be a global success. Today it is sold in 136 countries, and 10 million portions are sold every day. It has joined that small coterie of global brands that are seemingly available anywhere in the world, offering travelers a small slice of familiarity in strange lands. The Bel Group is now the third largest cheese company in the world.

In France, it cannot be said that processed cheeses are particularly respected, but because La vache qui rit is a popular choice for *goûter* (children's afternoon snacks) many French adults still associate it with happy childhood memories. Sometimes one needs a break from the rich and complex foods of adulthood, or the unfamiliar cuisines encountered when traveling, and a simple bit of Laughing Cow offers a nice respite. It is ironic that such a pleasurable food should emerge from the horrors of war, but as we saw with Camembert, this is not an altogether unusual occurrence. Unfortunately for France, the coming years would offer renewed opportunities for wartime innovation to occur.

47

"Bread, Peace, and Liberty:" The Socialist Baguette

One cannot overstate the importance of a good *boulangerie* to a French person. This became evident during our relocation from London (not exactly known for its bakeries) to Nantes, when Stéphane decided there was no point viewing flats more than a ten-minute walk from a boulangerie. "What is the point of moving back to France if you can't get a fresh baguette in your own neighborhood?" he asked, quite reasonably. Luckily, we found a flat one block away from one of the best boulangeries in town. Early in the morning and at lunchtime, the queue for fresh bread and simple sandwiches stretched around the corner. We learned to pop in during quiet times, when the ladies behind the counter would have time to coo over our toddler and slip him a *chouquette*, a small pastry fluff studded with pearl sugar.

Our boulangerie produced excellent baguettes, which was fortunate as we slipped into the French habit of buying one daily. So we were understandably dismayed, a few months after our arrival, to visit the boulangerie one day and find it would be closed for three weeks. There was no bankruptcy, no massive oven fire, no disaster of any kind. It was simply time for the employees to take their annual holiday, a somewhat mystifying turn of events for those unaccustomed to the sanctity of the French summer vacation.

French labor laws guaranteeing limited working hours and ample paid holidays have achieved almost mythical status in other countries, generating a stereotype of a French worker who barely works at all. In truth, this is highly exaggerated. It is more difficult these days to obtain the permanent contracts that include generous leave policies, and companies can skirt some working regulations by offering overtime. Most full-time employees work close to forty hours per week, and French productivity levels remain high relative to other developed economies. So the stereotype of the lazy French worker is well overdue for retirement.

That said, it is true that compared to the United States, French workers enjoy a much better work-life balance thanks to limitations on their working hours. A French proverb argues that *Si de beaucoup travailler on devenait riche, les ânes auraient le bât doré* (If working hard made one rich, donkeys would be covered in gold), and the French belief that working too many hours is deleterious to one's health and happiness is well known. What may be less well known, however, is that the same labor laws that improved life so markedly for the French worker also helped bring about the relatively recent popularity of the baguette—and also help explain why so many French people have to make do without their local boulangerie each summer.

We have already seen the intimate relationship French people have with their daily bread, and today the bread most associated with the French is certainly the baguette (which in French means "stick" or "wand"). The classic *baguette ordinaire* has, by law, only four ingredients: flour, yeast, water, and salt. Many prefer the more rustic *baguette tradition* or *baguette campagne*, distinguished by their pointier ends. A proper baguette does not stay fresh for more than a day, which is why French people have made a habit of the daily trip to the boulangerie or, if they are lucky, having their baguettes delivered to their door. (In the countryside, the baker himself might make deliveries, and in the cities a host of new food delivery services have emerged in recent years.) It is customary to serve some slices with lunch and dinner, and not just to be slathered with butter or cheese. A chunk of baguette is the ideal implement to *saucer* your plate after eating—in other words, to mop up any delicious remnants of sauce or dressing (note: not to be done in formal settings, unless you wish to look like a barbarian).

The baguette is such a routine part of life in France that it is somewhat shocking to discover that its popularity stems only from the 1920s. Prior to that, a variety of long, thin breads existed, but they were not overly popular, and they were not yet called *baguettes*. In the nineteenth century, the steam oven arrived in France, apparently brought by August Zang, the inventor of the croissant. This oven allowed bread to be baked with a crisp exterior and soft interior, and it eventually became the typical means of producing baguettes. Wheat also became cheaper and more readily available in the nineteenth century, thanks to a series of agricultural innovations and new import markets, and so ordinary citizens were finally able to partake of the noble white bread on a regular basis.

Working in a bakery has always been a tough and physically demanding job, with long and irregular hours. French bakers had to start working in the middle of the night in order to have fresh bread ready at opening time. Many bakery owners had no compunction about making their employees work seven days a week, even the apprentices, who were as young as twelve or thirteen. Bakers were called the "white miners," because they shared the same appalling work conditions as coal miners but were left coated in white flour rather than dark coal dust.

During the Paris Commune of 1871, the radical city government created a new law which forbade bakery employees from working before four a.m. This particular law disappeared along with the Commune, but in the early twentieth century, trade unions actively campaigned to outlaw nighttime work. A law was eventually passed in 1919 that outlawed employing people in bakeries between ten p.m. and five a.m., although it was not universally followed. But it is commonly believed that this law is responsible for the rise of the baguette, which could be produced more quickly than traditional breads, thus allowing bakers to comply with the new law but still offer fresh bread in the mornings.

In truth, there were probably other factors at work in the sudden popularity of the baguette, but it is not surprising that most French people believe this story given that the interwar years are usually associated with a number of progressive reforms. These were tumultuous years for France, which had been left victorious yet severely weakened following the end of World War I. Its finances were shattered, and they were further crippled by the worldwide depression of the 1930s; its population was battered by wartime deaths, injuries, and deprivations. Conditions were ripe for the spread of authoritarian ideologies on both the right and the left, with the Soviet Union, Fascist Italy, and Nazi Germany emerging during this era as influential models for disaffected factions within France. Throughout the 1920s and 1930s, control of the government shifted back and forth, from right to center to left, as the leading parties struggled to address the severe challenges facing the nation.

Some of the earliest social reforms were enacted under conservative governments, such as those between 1928 and 1932 that established a social insurance system for employees (which covered periods of illness, for example) and paid allowances to families. But an even greater momentum for change occurred with the electoral victory of the left-wing coalition known as the Popular Front in 1936. Its agenda was to fight "against misery, war, and fascism and in favor of bread, peace, and liberty." Its victory encouraged a wave of strikes throughout the country, as optimistic workers saw an opportunity to negotiate better pay and working conditions. Even the famous cafés and restaurants of Paris were affected by striking cooks and waiters. One can understand why from George Orwell's classic *Down and Out in Paris and London*, which describes his time working as a *plongeur* (dishwasher) in the Hôtel X near the Place de la Concorde:

> The hours were from seven in the morning till two in the afternoon, and from five in the evening till nine—eleven hours; but it was a fourteen-hour day when I washed up for the dining-room. By the ordinary standards of a Paris *plongeur*, these are exceptionally short hours . . . Our cafeterie was a murky cellar measuring twenty feet by seven by eight high, and so crowded with coffee-urns, breadcutters and the like that one could hardly move without banging against something. It was lighted by one dim electric bulb, and four or five gas-fires that sent out a fierce red breath. There was a thermometer there, and the temperature never fell below 110 degrees Fahrenheit—it neared 130 at some times of the day . . . The food we were given was no more than eatable, but the *patron* was not mean about drink; he allowed us two litres of wine a day each, knowing that if a *plongeur* is not given two litres he will steal three.[1]

The Popular Front government negotiated with the trade unions, and the resulting accord raised salaries by up to 15 percent. A series of reforms reduced the workweek to forty hours, gave workers fifteen days paid annual leave, and enshrined the right to strike without retaliation. The impetus for such reforms was not purely altruistic: it was hoped that reducing working hours would boost the employment rate, for example. In the end, they did not do very much to improve economic conditions, but they were very popular among the working classes.

The socialist experiment was short-lived, as the Popular Front was increasingly assailed on all sides. Its own communist cadres objected to its decision not to intervene on behalf of the Republican faction in the Spanish Civil War; centrists grew frustrated with the lack of economic progress. Right-wing nationalists accused the government of weakening the country, and far-right fascists hurled anti-Semitic invective against Léon Blum, the first Jewish and the first Socialist prime minister of France. By 1938, the Popular Front's brief moment in the sun was over. A new government was formed under former prime minister Édouard Daladier, leader of the Radical Party (which, despite its name, was really more of a centrist party). The forty-hour workweek was rescinded, but paid holidays endured, and family allowances were increased even further. This program of social reform was interrupted, however, by the outbreak of World War II the following year.

Paid holidays and baguettes both survived the war, and so today French people continue to queue for their daily bread, except for the few weeks each year when their boulangerie workers drive off into the sun. Modern-day Paris has not forgotten the lessons of 1789, however, and by law boulangeries are only allowed to close in July and August, and they are corralled into two groups that alternate holiday periods, thus ensuring that there is never a complete bread blackout in the capital.

While baguettes remain the most popular reason to visit a boulangerie, today many French people buy them at supermarkets and chain bakeries, which sell industrial versions made with frozen dough. This has led to a sharp decrease in the number of independent boulangeries operating in France, down from more than 37,000 in the 1990s to about 28,000 in 2015.[2] There is also a never-ending commentary on the "baguette crisis," encompassing both complaints about the quality of the modern baguette and concerns over diminishing bread consumption. Younger generations tend to see bread as optional rather than a staple, and new fast-food options have replaced the traditional lunchtime *jambon beurre* (ham-and-butter baguette sandwich).

But even as worries about the baguette and the boulangerie mount, French baked goods have become increasingly popular in overseas markets, especially in Asia. The South Korean bakery chains Paris Baguette and Tous Les Jours, for example, have hundreds of outlets worldwide supplying Asian-accented French baked goods (such as a *croque-monsieur* served on fluffy Japanese milk bread). There is also a big push within France to train a new generation of bakers, to ensure the survival of France's bread traditions. So the future is not wholly pessimistic for the baguette. Its peak popularity may have receded, but it has secured a spot in the hearts of the French people, one that is unlikely to disappear altogether.

48

Couscous: The Assimilation (or Not) of Empire

Marseille has been one of France's most important gateways since the pre-Roman era. Like many ports, it suffers from high rates of crime and economic inequality, which have given it a seedy reputation, one that is not entirely deserved. Visitors today will discover a lively city of museums, markets, and seaside promenades—and some of the best food in France. Many of the world's historic port cities feature phenomenal local cuisines, rooted in local seafood and flavored by their diverse populations, and Marseille is no different. One of its oldest and best-known specialties is bouillabaisse, originally a simple fisherman's soup designed to use up all the leftover bits of the daily catch but today a much pricier and elaborate affair. Luckily, there is a panoply of seafood to be enjoyed at more reasonable prices, just as local residents have done for centuries—steamed mussels, fresh oysters, octopus stew, grilled sardines. The pleasures of Provençal cuisine are here to be enjoyed as well: rich, garlicky aioli; anchovy-suffused tapenades and tarts; artichokes *à la barigoule* (braised in white wine and olive oil). And there is a robust Italian influence, one that is unsurprising given several centuries of Italian migration to the city. It may sound ridiculous to visit France and order pizza, but all doubts will be dispelled after tucking into the Marseille version, crisp and wood-fired, topped with a hearty tomato sauce, anchovies, and olives.

But one of the highlights of a gastronomic tour of Marseille is undoubtedly its Maghrebi cuisine, which became permanently ensconced in the city as migration from North Africa expanded in the interwar period.[1] At its pinnacle stands couscous, a dish of Berber origin so revered in the Maghreb that in some locales, such as Algiers, it is simply referred to as *al taam* (the food). The story of couscous in France sheds light on the horrific impact of French imperialism, the complex dynamics of migration to and from the Maghreb, and the ongoing struggle to reconcile different cultural identities within one French nation. France has become Europe's largest consumer of couscous, and surveys suggest it is now the third-favorite dish of the French people (after *magret de canard* and *moules-frites*).[2] Yet debate continues as to whether this is evidence of enlightened cosmopolitanism or a mere fig leaf for enduring antagonism.

The single word *couscous* encompasses a pleasingly flexible array of meanings. It refers both to the tiny grains that are painstakingly rolled and steamed before consumption and to the entire dish that is served upon them, which varies according to region, season, and occasion. Traditionally, the grains are accompanied by a spiced meat and/or vegetable stew, with a seemingly infinite number of local variations; within each country, there may be dozens of versions of the dish. Yet couscous retains a universal appeal to residents across the Maghreb: it is the food of one's home and family, of celebration and mourning, of comfort and belonging. It is often compared to pasta in Italy, or rice in China. Its central place in the cuisine of the diaspora is therefore not surprising.

The first written evidence of couscous in France appears to be courtesy of a traveler named Jean-Jacques Bouchard, who wrote that he sampled the dish in the southern port of Toulon in 1630. But the real encounter began in the nineteenth century, with the French conquest of Algeria (1830–47). Throughout the colonial era, the coastal regions of Algeria were administered as part of Metropolitan France, with the creation of the three *départements* of Alger, Oran, and Constantine.[3] This meant that unlike other overseas territories, Algeria was seen as part of France itself, and this helps explain why its eventual struggle for independence was particularly brutal and bloody. It is also why there was such significant migration between the two territories, in both directions. Algerians usually went to France for work, as colonial practices destroyed the traditional economic fabric that had previously sustained their communities. Unusually, a large number of French people also migrated to Algeria, where they (and their descendants) became known as *pieds-noirs* (black feet). Always a minority, they nevertheless occupied a privileged position in Algerian society, and they became a powerful political force both there and in mainland France.

Traditional Algerian cuisine features elements of Berber, Arab, and Turkish cooking, reflecting the country's history of occupation and adaptation. The French added another gastronomic layer, as seen in the continuing Algerian affection for baguettes and European cheeses. But the French colonists were also influenced in turn, as the pieds-noirs adopted many local dishes, including couscous. By the early twentieth century, French manufacturers in Algeria had developed a mechanized process for preparing couscous, in place of the laborious handmade methods.

As we have seen, European colonization of Africa accelerated in the late nineteenth century. France seized Tunisia from the crumbling Ottoman Empire in 1881 and subdued the independent state of Morocco in 1912, establishing protectorates in both territories. The French embarked on programs of modernization and economic development across the Maghreb, as part of a "civilizing mission" that in fact entailed enormous costs for local residents. They were not granted the same civil and political liberties as French citizens yet were expected to adopt the French language and cultural values. Local economies were reshaped for the benefit of France, and the most profitable industries were controlled by Europeans. The best land was appropriated and given to French settlers, causing significant displacement and disrupting the traditional social order. Maghrebis were taxed at higher rates than colonists, even as their opportunities for work and education shriveled. All of this ensured that various forms of everyday resistance to colonial rule endured, sustaining a base of opposition that would be drawn upon in later decades. French control of the Maghreb—indeed, of all its colonies—was never as absolute as might be assumed from color-coded maps of empire.

During World War I, the French colonies played an important role in sustaining France's military efforts in Europe. Manpower shortages at the front and in the factories were filled with nearly 300,000 men from Algeria, Tunisia, and Morocco. After the war, labor migration from the Maghreb continued, becoming an enduring component of the French economy. Tens of thousands of Algerian men, for example, took up factory jobs in the industrial north and east of France, or in large cities like Paris, Marseille, and Lyon. As is the case with so many labor migrants today, most of them worked temporary jobs, and their earnings were devoted to supporting their families and villages back home.

The shortages and devastation that France experienced during and after the war helped spur a renewed devotion to the imperial project, in particular by the so-called colonial lobby (those living in and/or profiting from the colonies). Colonial enthusiasts strove to convince the French political class and the wider public that the empire was essential to the sustenance of the French nation, and that the costs of preserving and defending it were well justified by the benefits it brought to the metropole. Food became an important part of this narrative, as France struggled to repair its agricultural sector and cope with food shortages. All sorts of colonial products, previously unknown or rarely consumed, were now promoted in France: curries and spicy sauces, tropical fruits, rice from Indochina, canned meat from Madagascar. Yet these efforts found mixed success, as French consumers tended to reject products that were overly strange or too associated with "inferior" colonial peoples.[4] Rice, for example, was mostly imported for animal feed in the interwar period, unable to dent the French attachment to bread and pasta. Yet the French accepted elements of colonial cuisine that could be adapted into French recipes, such as curry sauces, or that had an air of exotic prestige, such as tropical fruits. For the first time, ordinary people could enjoy bananas and pineapples.

Couscous was not embraced by the French population in the interwar period. It was a staple food, lacking the sense of exoticism or rarity of other colonial products, and it was flavored with ingredients unappealing to the French palate. It was traditionally prepared by women, an obvious negative given the sensibilities of culinary writers at that time, even those who extolled the virtues of other foreign dishes. But this did not mean that couscous was entirely absent from mainland France during this time. Maghrebi migrants helped root their cuisines in the localities where they settled in increasing numbers—especially in Paris, where they bought up a large portion of the city's bistros and began serving couscous alongside traditional French dishes. (Today, the *couscoussières* of Paris are generally well regarded as sources of authentic couscous.) Yet somewhat ironically, it was not until the nations of the Maghreb gained their independence from France that couscous emerged as an increasing favorite among the French people.

This newspaper was published during the 1931 International Colonial Exposition in Paris, an elaborate attempt to highlight the contributions of empire to the French nation. Algeria was represented by a traditional mosque, minaret, and bazaar. The United States (the only non-European colonial power) also contributed a pavilion, a replica of Mount Vernon. In keeping with the loathsome imperial practice of putting living people on display in so-called human zoos, a Sioux chief and his companion were dispatched to Paris as well. *Le Journal de l'Exposition Coloniale*, no. 3 (Paris: June 1931). Courtesy of the Bibliothèque Nationale de France.

The principles of national self-determination and anti-imperialism increasingly suffused the colonial world in the twentieth century, but it was World War II that really doomed the European empires. The French surrender to Germany, coupled with the economic devastation it endured during the war, greatly diminished its authority and capacity to govern overseas territories, and this breathed new life into nationalist movements. The stunning success of Mao Zedong in China provided an insurgent template that was emulated by resistance movements around the world. The creation of the United Nations and the emergence of the United States as a global superpower formed the basis for a new international order, one in which the old imperial arrangements were increasingly anachronistic. The costs of maintaining an empire were staggering, especially as revolts and resistance grew. In the two decades after the end of World War II, most of the world's colonies gained their independence, either through force of arms or negotiated agreement. The era of direct imperial rule was over, to be replaced by new forms of coercion and influence (collectively referred to as "neo-imperialism" by critics).

In Indochina, France experienced one of the most humiliating defeats among the imperial powers, as the ingenious Vietnamese insurgent commanders Ho Chi Minh and Vo Nguyen Giap waged a successful guerrilla war against French forces trying to rebuild their Asian empire. In 1954, after the stunning loss at Dien Bien Phu, the French essentially conceded defeat and turned the problem of Vietnam over to the Americans (who would fare no better in the end). By 1960, nearly all of the French colonies in Africa had gained their independence, including Morocco and Tunisia in 1956.

Algeria was a special case, however, given its greater level of integration into Metropolitan France. The French could accept the loss of an overseas colony, but the secession of French départements was a different matter. When the Front de Libération Nationale (FLN) launched an armed insurrection in 1954, the French government was determined to quell the rebellion and preserve the status quo. Algeria suffered eight years of brutal warfare, in which hundreds of thousands of Algerians died. French security forces abducted and tortured thousands of people and herded entire villages into detention camps in an effort to break the insurgency. Instead, these harsh methods drove the Algerian population to support the insurgency and delegitimized the war in the eyes of the French public. While the

FLN also engaged in urban bombings and massacres, its overall aim of independence garnered more legitimacy at home and abroad.

In 1958, a coalition of frustrated army officers and pieds-noirs perpetrated a military coup in Algiers, and the ensuing political crisis led to the fall of the French government and the end of the Fourth Republic.[5] Charles de Gaulle, the hero of French liberation in World War II, assumed the presidency of France, and the era of the Fifth Republic began. De Gaulle already understood that Algerian independence was inevitable, and he eventually arranged negotiations and a referendum on self-rule. The Algerians voted in favor of independence, which was finally granted in 1962.

Two large-scale waves of migration in the post–World War II era help explain the status of Maghrebi communities—and their cuisine—in France today. Labor migration from Algeria, Morocco, and Tunisia resumed after the end of the war, and by the time these countries gained their independence, hundreds of thousands of their citizens were living and working in France. Many of them were still only working temporary jobs and frequently returning home to their families, but this became less viable once their countries were formally separated from France. Increasingly, entire families relocated to France and settled permanently. This expanded and entrenched Maghrebi cuisine, and especially couscous, which was traditionally prepared by women.[6] As families adjusted to their radically different lives in France, their culinary traditions became an important means of sustaining community and identity.

But there was another migration that also contributed to the newfound popularity of couscous. With Algerian independence, about 1 million pieds-noirs returned to France.[7] They were repatriated through the southern ports of France, including Marseille, and many chose to stay in this region. They remained a distinct community within France due to mutual hostility with the metropole population, who blamed them for a long, bloody, and unpopular war (for their part, the pieds-noirs were angry at being "abandoned" by the French nation). This antagonism sustained the separate identity of the pieds-noirs, who despite ostensibly returning to their own country, clung to the cultural practices—and especially the food—of their lost home. Their attachment to staples such as couscous also expanded its popularity in the regions where they resettled.

The pieds-noirs remained a potent political and social force within France for decades, even to this day. Emmanuel Macron was delivered a sharp lesson on their enduring influence during the presidential campaign of 2017, when he was forced to apologize to an audience of pieds-noirs in Toulon after characterizing the French colonization of Algeria as a "crime against humanity." His comments were condemned by Marine Le Pen, the candidate for the far-right Front National (FN), which has traditionally done well in the southern regions of France with a substantial pied-noir population. Jean-Marie Le Pen, her father and the founder of the FN, was a paratrooper during the Algerian war, and he explicitly courted the so-called couscous vote during his political career.[8]

French manufacturers were also repatriated from Algeria, including those who operated couscous factories, and many of them settled around Marseille and established a new couscous industry there. Over time, the broader French population came around to the appeal of this modern version of couscous, which was noticeably different from the traditional Maghrebi style. Industrial couscous was bought prepackaged, either dried, canned, or frozen, and could be ready in minutes. Instead of a lovingly prepared communal meal, it was an easy comfort food, which could be topped with traditional French meats and vegetables. This assimilated version is now very popular in France, but no one—neither Maghrebi nor French—really sees it as authentic couscous.

It is this lack of authenticity that dictates caution in trying to read too much into the popularity of couscous in France today. It is not so much an embrace of a foreign cuisine and its people as it is a selective appropriation from a cuisine still seen as inferior to French cuisine and a population still held at arm's length in so many ways. Racial and cultural tensions are still rife in French society. When it comes to multiculturalism, the French generally adhere to the idea of laïcité (which can be translated, somewhat imperfectly, to "secularism") and to a strict separation of private and public identities. In essence, people are free to indulge their cultural and religious traditions at home, in the private sphere, but the public sphere and the state itself should be a neutral ground, a place where French republican values predominate. Long promoted by the left, laïcité is now increasingly used by the right as a bulwark against the expression of Islamic beliefs and practices that they perceive as threatening. Some argue that laïcité is no longer about a neutral secularism but has been hijacked to promote white Christian French values. This dynamic has been seen in the fierce debates over the banning of the niqab in France, and particularly in the realm of food, such as with the controversies over halal meat and pork on school menus. The FN has also railed against the proliferation of kebab shops in city centers.

Couscous has not really been at the forefront of this rhetoric. While it is undoubtedly associated with the Maghrebi diaspora, it is not really associated with Islamic practices, nor with something alien to French values, and therefore it seems to be less polarizing.[9] It is also unlikely that the FN would attack couscous when it is a favorite of their pied-noir supporters.

Yet the history of couscous in France shows that it has always been tied to broader political and social currents. Today, it is not certain exactly what the future holds for Maghrebi communities in France, given the relative popularity of right-wing sentiments, divisive counterterrorism policies, and severe economic challenges. Our chapters thus far have revealed the repeated absorption of diverse cultures into the French nation throughout history, but they have also shown that this process is never uniform or simple—and indeed, some regional and cultural identities have remained remarkably resilient over the centuries. So it is likely that Maghrebi cuisine will continue to reveal important insights into the evolution of identity and cultural exchange in France.

49

The Forgotten Vegetables

Certain vegetables have been having a bit of a comeback in France lately: the so-called *légumes oubliés*, or "forgotten vegetables." At food markets, *fruiteries*, and hip restaurants, the unceasing search for new tastes has revived attention to vegetables not popularly consumed for decades—including the Jerusalem artichoke, which in French is called the *topinambour*. It is actually from North America, not Jerusalem; its name is a mutation of the Italian *girasole*, or sunflower, the family to which the plant belongs. The edible root of the plant is not an artichoke but a tuber, like a potato, although it has a slight artichoke taste that might explain its name.

Not that long ago, however, this vegetable was decidedly *not* forgotten in France. During World War II, most French people had to learn to live under Nazi rule—and with topinambour.

The horrors of World War I did not, in the end, prevent the recurrence of another, even more terrible war. Throughout the interwar period, the French worried that Germany would one day recommence hostilities, and this appeared even more likely with the ascension of Adolf Hitler and his escalating aggression: the resumption of armament production, the remilitarization of the Rhineland, the annexation of Austria. France's preparations for a potential new war were constrained by economic weakness and domestic politics, with left-wing governments preferring an army of short-term conscripts rather than a larger professional army that could potentially back a reactionary coup.[1] By the late 1930s, French military doctrine was largely defensive, based upon an elaborate series of fortifications known as the Maginot Line, which the French army could presumably hold against a German invasion for an extended amount of time. German forces would hopefully be worn down in fruitless attack, and eventually France and her allies could launch a counteroffensive and repel the invasion.

In 1938, Hitler moved to annex the Sudetenland, the heavily German region of neighboring Czechoslovakia, which France had enjoyed an alliance with since 1924. French prime minister Édouard Daladier and British prime minister Neville Chamberlain met with Hitler and Benito Mussolini in Munich to negotiate the crisis. Daladier was under no illusions as to Hitler's true intentions, presciently arguing that if Hitler were allowed to dismember Czechoslovakia, there would be no end to his continental conquest. But there was no appetite in France for war, and Chamberlain pushed hard for compromise, which Daladier eventually acceded to. He returned to France despondent, only to be greeted with cheers and accolades for avoiding a new conflict. *"Ah les cons, si ils savaient!"* he supposedly remarked to an aide: "Ah these fools, if only they knew!" His fears indeed came to pass, as Hitler annexed the whole of Czechoslovakia, signed a nonaggression pact with the Soviet Union, and prepared for all-out war.

The beginning of World War II in Europe is conventionally dated to September 1, 1939, with the German invasion of Poland. Both

France and Britain then declared war on Germany, but eight months of "phony war" followed, during which France could do little but wait for the inevitable German invasion. This arrived in May 1940, with an astoundingly effective "blitzkrieg" offensive that utilized tanks, airpower, and innovative maneuver warfare tactics to smash through the Low Countries and the most vulnerable section of the Maginot Line. The British Expeditionary Force was evacuated from France in the great rescue operation at Dunkirk. The French army was unable to prevent the Germans from marching into Paris on June 14, a humiliating military defeat that left lasting scars on the French psyche. Two million French soldiers were taken as prisoners of war, and millions of French civilians fled south ahead of the German armies.

From London, General Charles de Gaulle urged the French people to resist the invaders, but in Bordeaux, the hastily evacuated French government decided to seek an armistice with the Germans. Under its terms, France remained a formally independent country, but it was divided into two zones: the northern half of France and its entire Atlantic coast was occupied by the Germans, while the southern half was ruled by a new French government headed by Marshal Philippe Pétain, the hero of World War I. Pétain headquartered his government at the spa town of Vichy, which gave its name to the extreme right-wing regime that replaced the Third Republic. Political parties and the free press were banned; Jews and communists were increasingly persecuted. In 1942, French collaboration in the Holocaust began in earnest, as both French and foreign Jews were rounded up and held in French concentration camps such as Drancy before being deported to the east. Conditions grew even worse at the end of 1942, when Germany occupied the whole of France. More than 75,000 Jews were deported from France, including more than 11,000 children. Most of them died at Auschwitz; it is thought that only about 2,500 of those deported survived.[2] The last deportation train left France in August 1944, with the Allies on the brink of liberating Paris—an indication of the fanatical Nazi commitment to the Holocaust, even at the expense of German military efforts.

Germany instituted a harsh system of exploitation during its rule, using France's considerable resources to fuel its mammoth campaign on the Eastern Front, its ongoing occupation of Europe, and the needs of its own citizens in Germany. The Nazis remembered the lessons of World War I, when a starving population supported the over-

This memorial plaque in Temple Square, Paris, bears witness to the 11,000 children deported to Auschwitz by the Nazi regime, in collaboration with the Vichy government. Among them were 500 children from the 3rd arrondissement. The names listed on the plaque are those of the 87 toddlers who were deported, before they had even grown old enough to attend school. © Lillian Hueber, 2016.

throw of the monarchy and the German surrender, and their efforts to keep the German population well fed and happy were largely designed to prevent another "stab in the back," as they referred to it. More than 3.5 million French people were deported to Germany to work as laborers, in a work scheme called the STO, or Service du travail obligatoire. This led to a significant drop in the production of food and other goods in France at the same time that the country was expected to contribute materially to the Nazi war machine. The excessive requisition of food, combined with the drop in production and imports, meant that there was less and less food available for the local population, although this varied considerably by region.[3] Wealthier citizens fared somewhat better, but even the well connected struggled to maintain a peacetime diet. In a postwar *Life* article on the state of French gastronomy, it was noted that Curnonsky, the "Prince of Gastronomers," had dropped from a robust 277 pounds to 181 thanks to the deprivations of war.[4]

To control the situation, the government issued ration tickets.

An adult person living only on these ration tickets would consume between 1,000 and 1,300 calories a day, far below the necessary average of 2,400 daily calories.[5] As the war went on, the rations became smaller—especially in the lead-up to D-Day in 1944, when the Germans wanted to make sure that they would have enough food to feed their army during the long battles ahead.

And as if rationing wasn't bad enough, simply having ration tickets did not mean that you would actually be able to get food. Especially in towns, stores could remain empty for quite a while due to a lack of supplies. A massive black market *(marché noir)* developed, as farmers and tradesmen tried to sell as little as they could on the official market, where prices were set artificially low. Some sold their products at extortionate prices and became rich, at the expense of their social legitimacy. Others kept prices reasonable, with their primary aim merely being to reserve food for hungry French people rather than the Germans (this informal exchange was often called the gray market, or *marché gris*). In an intriguing reversal of the usual dynamic, city dwellers were now much worse off than rural residents. Many survived only thanks to food packages sent from relatives in the countryside, or through trips (usually by bicycle) to the country to buy or barter products from farmers.[6]

This difficult situation was described in a remarkable remnant from those years, a small booklet titled *Instructions for British Servicemen in France 1944*, produced by the Foreign Office for troops participating in the Allied invasion.

> Remember that continental France has been directly occupied. In consequence it has been stripped of everything by the Germans. Almost all French civilians (including French children) are undernourished, and many have died from exhaustion and hunger, because the Germans have eaten the food. The Germans have also drunk the wine or distilled it into engine-fuel . . . You have known something of rationing at home, and seen temporary shortages of various things to which you were accustomed to. But you have never known, as the French, thanks to the Germans, have known, a lasting dearth of the commonest articles. Food, drink, clothes, tobacco—everything has been rationed, but to have a coupon has not meant to get even the meagre ration.

Women have queued up daily for vegetables from four
in the morning till the market closed at 8.30—and gone
away without any because the Germans had robbed the
lorries on the way. Bread has often been unobtainable
and often nearly uneatable.[7]

The only positive aspect of rationing (if one could use the term
positive in those dark times) was that people could not smoke or
drink as much, as tobacco and wine were rationed. Thus, the number
of deaths from smoking- and drinking-related diseases fell during the
war years.

Even with a vibrant black market economy (who said the French
have no word for entrepreneur?), food remained scarce. People started eating pigeons and crows instead of chicken; some people ate cats.
They would make mayonnaise without eggs, if you can imagine.
People strove to find substitutes for what was lacking, and as the
French language has a sense of black humor, a German word for
this phenomenon seemed appropriate, and so these substitute products were called *ersatz*. It was a particularly traumatic situation for a
nation whose gastronomy was such an important element of identity,
a marker for the superior civilization they felt they possessed.

This is when topinambour had its moment of gastronomic glory.
It had never really caught on with the population after being introduced from America in the seventeenth century and was considered
a food for the poorer classes.[8] But now this vegetable was not being
requisitioned by the Germans and was not rationed (unlike potatoes,
which were meticulously seized by the occupying forces). And as it is
also a vegetable that grows in poor soil and with little care, suddenly
people were growing Jerusalem artichokes everywhere and eating
them a lot. It was a filling vegetable, and its leaves could also be used
as ersatz tobacco (although it was not a very nice ersatz). Unfortunately, as topinambour is not very easily prepared or digested, it did
not make for a very pleasurable substitute.

Other overlooked foods were resorted to as well, such as the rutabaga. Previously used only to feed animals, it was now grown in
the Jardin du Luxembourg in Paris and throughout the countryside.
The Germans had no inclination to requisition rutabagas, perhaps
because they reminded them of their own experience of wartime
famine, the *Steckrübenwinter* (rutabaga winter) of 1916–17.

While France was not as harshly occupied as other countries, it

was still a miserable era, and after the war, all the dire food products that had sustained the population were put aside. As an elderly
lady once said to Stéphane, when he was working at a Nantes *fruiterie* that began selling topinambour: "Really, topinambour! We had
them all the time during the war. I could not eat a bite of it now
even if you paid me." In fact, they were not being given away for
free—they were actually four times as expensive as potatoes, due to
their recent hipster-food quotient. They remain best eaten as a potato
substitute—mashed with plenty of butter and salt, or lurking in winter soups—but the distinct artichoke flavor remains off-putting to
some diners. Only time will tell if topinambour will be forgotten
once again.

50

Canon Kir Joins the Resistance

World War II remains the deadliest conflict in modern history, with
roughly 60 million people perishing across its multiple fronts. What
remains so unsettling about the war is not simply the enormous number of casualties, but the way in which modern technology and industry were so ruthlessly deployed to perfect the machinery of killing.
Airpower introduced a "third dimension" to warfare, and soon sent
combatants hurtling down the path toward total war, with entire
cities incinerated in a night's bombing. Tanks and armored vehicles
gave armies a new mobility and lethality, and by the end of the war
two colossal million-man armies were sparring across the length of
eastern Europe. Scientists bent their attention to developing the most
efficient gas chamber and inventing the atomic bomb. Against such
massive forces and technological superiority, ordinary people were
often helpless to resist.

And yet, resistance movements did emerge in every country affected by the war, along a broad spectrum of size and effectiveness. In
Denmark, the entire population secretly cooperated to evacuate the
country's Jews before the Germans could deport them. In Poland, the

Home Army fought a fierce but ultimately futile two-month battle to liberate Warsaw in 1944. Throughout Europe, sympathetic diplomats and government officials risked their lives to provide papers and escape routes to populations at risk. Resistance to the Nazis was extremely dangerous: not only the resisters themselves but local civilians were often killed in retaliation. In one of the most memorialized incidents of the war, virtually the entire population of the French village of Oradour-sur-Glane—more than six hundred men, women, and children—were massacred by a Waffen-SS unit after reports of local partisan activity.

Among all the European resistance movements, perhaps none have been so romanticized—or have caused so much controversy—as the French resistance. It is difficult to know exactly how large or pervasive the French resistance really was, and its impact has often been overstated. A great many French people openly collaborated with the new order, whether within the Vichy government or in the notorious Milice paramilitary units. Probably the overall stance of most of the population was neither collaboration nor resistance, but what the French call *attentisme,* a sort of "wait and see" position. This popular passivity benefited the Nazi and Vichy regimes early on but shifted to the advantage of resistance groups as they grew in strength later in the war. The French Communist Party (Parti Communiste Français; PCF) stepped up its clandestine activities after the German invasion of the Soviet Union in 1941, and after the Service du travail obligatoire forced labor scheme was imposed in 1943, thousands of men fled deportation and joined rural resistance groups. The *Instructions for British Servicemen in France 1944* booklet stated: "We need not doubt the goodwill of the vast majority of the people of France . . . The small, astoundingly brave minority who have led *active* resistance within the Mother Country, have had behind them a growing proportion (lately up to 95 percent) of the French people, who have *passively* resisted the Germans and their Vichy stooges."[1]

The complexity of the decision whether to resist, and the various forms that resistance could take, can be seen by looking at specific locales within France—such as Dijon, the historic capital of Burgundy. As it happens, the story of Dijon's resistance helps explain the popularity of the *vin blanc cassis,* a classic aperitif better known as Kir, named for a popular resistance hero.

Dijon is often described as the gateway to the famed Burgundy wine region, but it is perhaps best known worldwide for the spicy mustard that bears its name. Mustard is made from the seeds of the mustard plant, which has been cultivated in Europe since antiquity, making it a relatively inexpensive and thus popular condiment for centuries. In the mid-fourteenth century, the first large-scale mustard industry grew up around Dijon, and it was here that the firm of Grey Poupon was established in the nineteenth century by the inventor of the steam-powered mustard mill. Today, Grey Poupon is an American company and its mustards are impossible to find in France. But there is no shortage of other options, as mustard is by far the most popular and inexpensive French condiment, flavoring all sorts of dressings and sauces, and a preferred accompaniment to sausages, hamburgers, and other meat dishes. Dijon mustard is the most common style, but it is also worth trying *moutarde à l'ancienne*, a much grainier variant. Curiously, Dijon does not enjoy an AOC for its namesake mustard.

Another local specialty is black currants, a tart purple berry that is virtually unknown in the United States because it was banned in the early 1900s after it was discovered that its shrubs spread a fungus deadly to pine trees. Most Americans will only know the berry via crème de cassis, a black currant liqueur invented in Dijon in the mid-nineteenth century. About half a century later, local cafés began serving a cocktail of crème de cassis and dry white wine (ideally, aligoté from Burgundy). They called it a *blanc-cass*, and its refreshingly crisp, sweet flavor made it a splendid aperitif.

Dijon has a long history of prosperity, serving as the seat of the powerful dukes of Burgundy before the region was incorporated into France, and enjoying renewed success with the nineteenth-century expansion of railways and roads into the region. It was occupied by the German army a few days after Paris fell in June 1940, and it lay within the northern occupation zone that was created after the armistice. The mayor of the city fled, and so a group of prominent locals took on key municipal responsibilities, such as ensuring food distribution and the continued operation of hospitals and schools.

One of these local notables was Félix Kir, a Catholic priest then in his sixties. As a conservative parish priest, he was not wholly unsympathetic to the new regime of Philippe Pétain and its motto of *Travail, famille, patrie* (Work, Family, Fatherland), which replaced the republican *Liberté, égalité, fraternité* during the war years. Kir was also ideologically pleased with the French regime's staunch anticommunism. But he could not understand nor forgive Pétain's submissive collaboration with the German invaders, and from the start of the occupation, Canon Kir adopted a different posture. A number of legends detail his supposed repartee with the German authorities. According to one, when the German troops arrived and asked Kir to surrender on behalf of the town, he replied, "No, sir, because surrender is not French." When Nazi officials came to the town hall and demanded one hundred tons of hay, Kir protested that they were in the town hall, not a farm—they were welcome to shoot him and turn him into *saucisson*, but there was no hay available. And when the Nazis requisitioned all the best Burgundy wines, he pretended not to care and declared that blanc-cass was the official drink of Dijon anyway.

Kir's resistance to the Germans went beyond rhetoric. When a prisoner-of-war camp was opened at Longvic, near Dijon, he used his official position as a de facto town leader to arrange personal visits. He smuggled in extra food rations, and his car regularly had more passengers on the way out than on the way in. Dijon was not very far from the demarcation line and unoccupied France, and Kir provided travel permits to escaped prisoners that allowed them to cross into unoccupied territory. According to legend, he and the local resistance helped more than five thousand prisoners escape the camp.

The term *French resistance* encompasses a wide spectrum of groups and activities. There were people like Kir, who used their official duties to help others escape France or shield locals from the full brunt of occupation. Underground activists printed newspapers and leaflets denouncing the occupation. More organized groups emerged in the countryside and became known as *maquis* or *maquisards*. They sabotaged factories and rail lines, greatly impeding the production and shipment of military supplies and food to the Germans, and helped downed Allied airmen escape France. They supplied critical intelligence to Allied forces and received airdrops of supplies and advisers. The maquis groups were often organized according to ideology or identity, so there were distinct communist resistance groups, a Jewish resistance network, and local groups that also sought regional autonomy. Cooperation among them increased over time, so that by the end of 1942, the Comité Français de Libération Nationale under General Charles de Gaulle served as an umbrella organization for all the resistance groups in France. Their effectiveness improved greatly, and by 1944 they comprised perhaps 100,000 people. They played a key role in preparing for the Allied D-Day invasion and hindering the German response to it.

Burgundy was a key locale for the resistance, as it lay astride the demarcation line and featured large swathes of inaccessible terrain, such as the Morvan Forest, an excellent haunt for the maquis. The Germans were naturally determined to crush resistance activities, and in Dijon they grew suspicious of Canon Kir. He was eventually arrested and sentenced to death. But a senior German commander was reluctant to execute a popular priest and town official, and after several months in jail, Kir was released on the condition that he refrain from any official duties going forward. He continued with his covert resistance activities until 1944, when he was shot by a pair of French collaborators and nearly arrested by the Gestapo. He decided to flee and went into hiding about sixty miles from Dijon.

Shortly after the Allied invasion of Normandy in June 1944, it was determined that a second front needed to be opened, and Operation Dragoon commenced that August. In this lesser-known invasion, American, British, and French forces landed on the Mediterranean coast, along the Côte d'Azur, and pursued a weak German army northward up the Rhône Valley. The offensive was greatly aided by local resistance groups, who damaged German communication and transportation lines and thus hampered their defense. The Germans attempted to hold their ground at Dijon but were pushed back to the Vosges Mountains, where a new front stabilized. The entire south of France had been liberated in a little more than four weeks. Allied troops from the southern landing met up with those who had fought their way in from Normandy, and plans were made for the final push into Nazi Germany.

As the Allied troops proceeded toward Dijon, Kir returned to his town, purportedly walking all the way back. He entered Dijon at the same time as the Allies and was instantly recognized and celebrated as one of the town's liberators. Thanks to his wartime popularity, he was elected mayor of Dijon, a position he held until his death in 1968, and also became a parliamentary deputy for the town. He was an enthusiastic propagandist for the town's main products, including crème de cassis, with which he greeted visitors to the town hall. When several producers asked if they could use his name to sell the liqueur, he happily agreed. After his death, the producers ended up in court fighting over who had the true right to his name, but by then the blanc-cass was commonly being referred to as a "Kir," as it is today throughout France and the rest of the world.

There are many variations of the Kir cocktail. Perhaps the best known is the Kir Royale, which is made with a dry sparkling wine instead of still wine, but there are many additional regional variations in France. Crème de cassis mixed with cider is a Kir Normand or Kir Breton; in Nantes, it is mixed with the local wine, Muscadet, and called a Kir Nantais. Crème de cassis mixed with red wine is either a Kir Communard or a Kir Cardinal, depending on your ideological inclinations.

The barmen of Dijon also created a cocktail called the KK, for Kir Khrushchev, in honor of Father Kir's efforts to promote peace during the Cold War through cultural exchanges with the Soviets. (Unsurprisingly, it is made with crème de cassis, white wine, and vodka—a combination sure to make adversaries forget their political differences.) Premier Khrushchev even visited Dijon during his tour of France in 1960, but unfortunately he was not able to meet Canon Kir: the Catholic Church called Kir away from Dijon on some pretext, apparently worried he might adopt a too-friendly posture toward the godless Soviets. In his memoirs, Khrushchev notes his regret at not being able to meet the resistance hero but expresses delight in the warm welcome he received from the people of Dijon.[2]

Like many tales of the French resistance, it is difficult to separate fact from fiction in the legend of Canon Kir. But it is noteworthy how well traveled his legend became, in part thanks to the delicious drink that bears his name, and what it indicates about enduring French beliefs about their wartime experience. Since World War II, the French have enjoyed one of their longest periods in history without foreign aggression. And yet, this extended period of peace did not erase the scars of defeat and occupation for many years. There were new battles to be fought within France itself.

51

France and the United States: From Liberation to Exasperation

The liberation of France began on June 6, 1944, when an Allied force of more than 150,000 American, British, and Canadian troops invaded the northern shores of Normandy. Most French people were happy to see the Germans driven out and grateful to the Allied soldiers who arrived in their place bearing food, coffee, cigarettes, and other staples not enjoyed for years. Scenes of ecstatic crowds welcoming Allied forces with cheers and embraces established an iconic template of liberation. The cities and towns of France savored their restored sovereignty, even as they counted the terrible costs of the offensive that brought it about.

D-Day has remained an emotionally resonant event on both sides of the Atlantic. Every year, millions of tourists visit the landing sites and nearby towns, which are dotted with museums, memorials, and the hauntingly enormous graveyards of the fallen. Most of these sites lie within the French *département* of Calvados, home to four of the five D-Day landing beaches (Omaha, Gold, Juno, and Sword). As the landing forces moved inland, they encountered the small towns and villages of rural Normandy, and their interactions with the locals make for particularly interesting reading in the many war memoirs from that time.

One Normandy specialty comes in for special mention in many remembrances: the fiery apple cider brandy also named Calvados. It was historically called *eau-de-vie de cidre*, indicating that it was a distillation of the local apple cider, a tradition that appears to have begun in the sixteenth century. Proper Calvados is aged for a minimum of two years in oak barrels, taking on a golden-lit hue and smoother flavor. American troops took a great liking to both cider and Calvados, although they had to be careful with the latter given its potency (it is usually around 85 proof). Rumor had it that Calvados could be used to fuel the GIs' cigarette lighters, a reasonable enough suspicion given that in both world wars, armies had requisitioned Calvados for use in the armaments industry. It was this mistreatment of their beloved brandy that drove Calvados producers to seek an AOC for their product, which was granted in 1942, thus preserving the brandy for its originally intended purpose.

Unfortunately, the celebratory mood and newfound bonhomie did not last very long. Even in the early weeks of liberation, some American forces received less friendly welcomes, and American military commanders became exasperated with their French counterparts. In 1945, the U.S. military published an extraordinary booklet for American soldiers stationed in France, titled *112 Gripes About the French*. It lists a fascinating range of common complaints from servicemen—the French are ungrateful, arrogant, cowardly, too cynical, too dirty, too garlic-scented, and so on—and offers robust rebuttals to each one, reminding Americans not only of the extreme deprivations of occupation but of France's historical contributions to world civilization. An entire section is devoted to debunking the idea that the apparently more efficient, cleaner, and braver Germans would be more natural allies for America, an indication that even at this early date, trouble was brewing for postwar relations. Interestingly, there are no gripes about French food, except that soldiers were not being offered enough of it.[1]

After the German surrender in May 1945, a new era of Franco-American prickliness ensued, as the challenges of recovery and the emergence of Cold War politics complicated the relationship across many realms. One of the most visible was the gastronomic, which took on an exaggerated symbolic importance as political tempers frayed, resulting in periodic spats and controversies.

One of the earliest occurred in 1950, when it appeared that France might actually ban Coca-Cola. Thanks to a long history of aggressive marketing and its patriotic efforts during World War II, Coca-Cola had become one of the foremost symbols of the United States and all it stood for—capitalism, free markets, and staunch anticommunism. The company did not shy away from politics; its chairman of the board, James Farley, proclaimed in 1950: "The time has come for Americans to challenge the aggressive, godless, and treasonable practices of totalitarian communism."[2] This overt stance made the drink deeply unpopular among European communists, who joined forces with local beverage producers worried about competition as Coca-Cola began trying to establish a foothold in Europe after the war.

In France, the Communist Party was the largest party in the National Assembly, with enduring support from about a quarter of the population. This made France a key battleground in the emerging Cold War, as the United States and the Soviet Union competed for the loyalties of European populations. French Communists deplored the outsized influence of the United States in postwar France and began to refer to this creeping Americanization as "coca-colonization," after Coca-Cola's plans for establishing bottling plants in France were revealed in 1948. In this view, Coca-Cola was just another symptom of the American effort to subjugate France, a sort of cultural subversion that underlay more obvious schemes like the Marshall Plan and NATO. America's newfound hegemony in the political, military, economic, and cultural realms was increasingly assured, an anxiety-inducing state of affairs for one of Europe's oldest great powers.

The Communists were not the only ones opposed to Coca-Cola. French producers of wine, juice, and mineral water worried about unfair competition, and public health activists accused the drink of being addictive, possibly even poisonous. In 1950, this coalition of opponents arranged a vote in the National Assembly on the matter. The Communist proposal to ban Coca-Cola outright was defeated, but a more moderate proposal was suggested that would grant the government the authority to ban "nonalcoholic beverages made from vegetable extracts" (in other words, Coca-Cola). This motion passed, but it had no real effect as it did not directly mandate a ban.

After several years of legal wrangling and appeals to government officials on both sides of the Atlantic, Coca-Cola was finally able

Previous page: In spring 1945, a U.S. Army medic named Victor Kobas arrived in Paris for a posting of several months. He collected a number of postcards and photographs during his time there, as well as this helpful brochure produced by the U.S. Army, filled with maps and tourist tips for the liberated capital. He passed his collection on to his son, and the brochure was rediscovered during the writing of this book by his granddaughter, Jeni Mitchell. The illustration reveals American assumptions about the cultural highlights to be enjoyed in Paris, while also incautiously depicting the towering position of the United States that so infuriated many French people in the postwar era. Courtesy of George Kobas and Linda Grace-Kobas.

to proceed with its operations in France. It was not wholehearted-ly embraced by the French public, however, and even today France (along with Italy) has the lowest rate of Coca-Cola per capita con-sumption in Europe, about a third of U.S. consumption rates. Yet as in other countries, it still came to symbolize a kind of carefree and youthful pleasure seeking. In his 1966 film *Masculin Féminin*, Jean-Luc Godard characterized the young people of France as "the children of Marx and Coca-Cola."

The American press and public were not happy with French oppo-sition to Coca-Cola, and in their reaction we can see the rhetorical strains of many future clashes over gastronomic trade. Farley thun-dered, "Coca-Cola was not injurious to the health of American sol-diers who liberated France from the Nazis so that the Communist deputies could be in session today."[3] Others called for the United States to ban the import of French wines. The crisis was resolved before such drastic measures came to pass, but new controversies would arise over the years whenever the United States decided to ban French products, whether on grounds of public health or politics.

One of the more frequently banned items, as we have already seen, has been cheese. Before World War II, the United States had very few regulations about cheese at all, but in 1949 it banned the import of cheeses made with unpasteurized raw milk if they had been aged less than sixty days. This encompassed a whole swathe of the French cheese industry, notably the producers of Camembert in Normandy. Later, in the 1990s, the FDA came close to banning all raw milk cheeses, but it eventually backed off. In 2014, however, it lowered the acceptable bacteria levels in raw milk cheeses, effectively ban-ning some of the best French cheeses, like Roquefort, Saint-Nectaire, Morbier, and Tomme de Savoie. New inspection regimes eventually lifted this ban, but an atmosphere of resentment and uncertainty remains. French cheese producers remain bewildered by American bans. Is this simply a cultural difference, with Americans exhibit-ing more squeamishness over the idea of raw milk anything? Or are these bans actually driven by political and economic motivations? In any event, it is difficult for the French to retaliate in kind, as France imports hardly any American cheeses at all (with the exception of processed cheese products, like Cheez Whiz, for the benefit of home-sick expats).

Sometimes the motivations for these American hit jobs on French cheeses are not mysterious at all. Roquefort has been subject to several U.S. tariff hikes as part of explicit retaliatory measures for European bans on the import of hormone-treated beef from the States: a 100 percent hike in 1999 and a crippling 300 percent hike in 2009, during the last days of the George W. Bush administration, which also included higher duties on French truffles and foie gras (this was thankfully reversed by the Obama administration). This focus on Roquefort is a bit curious, given that only a few hundred tons of the cheese are usually exported to the United States, perhaps 2 percent of total sales. It seems that much like Coca-Cola functioned as a symbol of the United States in the postwar years, Roquefort has become emblematic of France in the "cheese-eating surrender monkey" era.[4]

The 1999 Roquefort tariff hike produced one of the most celebrated acts of food activism in modern France, when a Roquefort sheep farmer named José Bové dismantled a McDonald's under construction in Millau. Bové, a longtime local food activist, wanted to call attention to the new tariff's harmful effects on the Roquefort region, as well as to the fast-food chain's use of hormone-treated beef globally. He claimed his campaign was not anti-American per se, but part of a broader antiglobalization stance, in keeping with his long-standing opposition to the industrialization of agriculture and the destruction of local food traditions. He spent six weeks in jail for the crime, but it propelled him into national politics, and he was twice elected to the European Parliament. He ran for the presidency in 2007 and received more than 400,000 votes. His political activities have made him a figure of intense controversy in France, but his views on food are not particularly extreme to many people.

From this episode, and considering the rise in French anti-Americanism over the years, Americans might be tempted to think that most French people would never set foot in a McDonald's. Surely, this must be the epitome of *malbouffe*, a terrible French insult applied to "bad food," or what we would usually call "junk food."[5] But in fact, the second most profitable market for McDonald's worldwide is France, where it is affectionately known as McDo. To be clear, a French McDonald's is worlds apart from the American version. The company has astutely adapted to French tastes, offering everything from croissants and baguettes to Roquefort burgers and Le Croque McDo. The beef comes from grass-fed cows, and the chicken has not been washed in chlorine (another American habit banned in the European Union). Many of the franchises are designed to look more like cafés than fast-food joints. So it becomes a bit more understandable that French people would deign to eat in McDonald's, even if its popularity still seems out of place given the usual clichés about French habits and tastes.

McDonald's only expanded to France in the 1970s, around the same time France was exporting to the United States a food trend at the opposite end of the gastronomic spectrum: nouvelle cuisine. The roots of this new approach to cooking can be traced in part to the tumultuous year of 1968, when France, like the United States, experienced serious social unrest and cultural upheaval. The unpopular American war in Vietnam was a source of anger and protest among French youth as well, married to a deeper resentment over the increasingly authoritarian and conservative government of Charles de Gaulle. The traditional opposition parties on the left had collapsed, leaving fewer outlets for effective political expression. In May 1968, student protesters demanding radical reforms were joined by the trade unions, and for several weeks France was paralyzed by general strikes and demonstrations. Barricades and riots roiled the Latin Quarter of Paris, and the prospect of revolution seemed tantalizingly close. In the end, the government cajoled the trade unions and the middle classes away from revolt, mixing the offer of new elections and limited concessions with an implied threat to restore order by force. The protests wound down, but "Mai 1968" retained an enormous resonance within French society, representing a generational shift toward antiestablishment approaches in politics, literature, film, academic theory, and many other facets of life.

This broad challenge to conformity and stasis within the social and cultural realms echoed within the gastronomic world as well, where food critics like Henri Gault and Christian Millau and talented chefs like Paul Bocuse, Jean and Pierre Troisgros, and Roger Vergé were already challenging long-held tenets. Much as the French Revolution shattered the grip of ancien régime cuisine, the upheaval of 1968 facilitated a direct challenge to the *cuisine classique* that had been perfected and codified by Auguste Escoffier at the turn of the previous century. Six decades later, French chefs were still trained and expected to conform to Escoffier's methods and recipes, with little scope for innovation and experimentation. Nouvelle cuisine represented a radical turn in cooking style, facilitated by the broader social currents that exploded in 1968. Its four fundamental values—truth, lightness, simplicity, imagination—were in many ways also the values of the May 1968 protesters.[6]

In a 1973 article, Gault and Millau popularized the term *nouvelle cuisine* and defined its "ten commandments," capturing the essence of the approach that would become so popular over the following decade. The natural flavors of food should be preserved by using only fresh ingredients from local markets, with much shorter cooking times, and enhanced by fresh herbs rather than heavy sauces and marinades. This resulted in a more delicate and healthy style of cooking, presented in newly formalized ways. Chefs should be constantly inventive but not overcomplicated. Regional dishes and foreign flavors, especially those of Asia, could be drawn upon in creating innovative dishes, and modern time-saving devices like food processors and microwaves were no longer sacrilegious. If some of this sounds familiar, you are not mistaken: nouvelle cuisine, as Waverley Root noted in the *New York Times* at the time, was more restoration than revolution, an attempt to return to the more natural culinary traditions that predated Escoffier's opulent transformation of French haute cuisine.[7]

Many chefs and critics disparaged nouvelle cuisine, but it became a popular food trend not only in France but in the United States well into the 1980s, when it succumbed to caricature and cliché itself. Its influence was not wholly lost, however, as its most important principles were absorbed into new styles of cooking, on both sides of the Atlantic, that continued to emphasize fresh regional products and a lighter touch. In the United States, the "New American cuisine" that emerged in California in the 1980s and 1990s drew upon the nouvelle cuisine approach and was sometimes referred to as "California-French cuisine." Nouvelle cuisine also helped inspire "fusion cuisine" of many different varieties around the world.

It is perhaps fitting that the 1970s were the decade of both McDonald's and nouvelle cuisine, two trends that crossed the Atlantic in opposite directions. Much is made of the fundamental differences between our two countries, of the robust anti-Americanism that emerged in France with the ascendancy of American hegemony, and the reflexive anti-French attitudes among many in the United States. The vast gulf between nouvelle cuisine and a McDonald's meal seemingly epitomizes an unbridgeable civilizational divide. Yet the popularity of McDonald's in France, and the French roots of modern American cooking, suggest a different implication, one of shared humanity and habit, of convergence rather than distance. Indeed, the history of Franco-American relations since World War II suggests more affinity than commonly recognized, a mirroring of political and cultural anxieties in an ever-changing world. We alternately admire and despise each other; we celebrate our shared history of revolution and democracy while competing to best represent that tradition to the world. Each country is infused with the cultural by-products of the other, even as fear of contamination—whether by French bacteria or American consumerism—pollutes gastronomic exchange. We each feel superior to the other, but it is an arrogance inflected with respect for what the other has achieved, however grudgingly it may be admitted.

France and the United States are both countries of great passion—usually for entirely different things, it is true, but there is enough shared fervor and appreciation to overcome even the darkest stretches of our relationship. Even as our political administrations clash amid the tragedies and uncertainties afflicting the world today, there are glimmers of amity in the realm of gastronomy: artisanal food movements in the United States have much in common with French regional traditions, and there is a greater appreciation of our respective cuisines outside the rarefied confines of Paris and New York. While food can never be completely divorced from its broader social and political context, it offers a space for peoples across borders to interact and converse, to come to some understanding of each other outside the boundaries of crude propaganda and lazy stereotypes. It is to this form of cultural exchange that we hope our book has contributed, in some small way.

52

Conclusion

Is it possible to deromanticize one of the most romantic lands on Earth? Perhaps not, and yet we hope that our book might help puncture some of the enduring myths about France and its people. Yes, many French people buy regionally sourced foods at their local markets, but they are just as likely to stock up at the *hypermarché* behemoths out in the suburbs (which, by the way, will include long aisles of junk food just like anywhere else). The French may not have hit American levels of obesity and ill-health, but they may be on their way: more than half of French people over thirty are over-weight, and as we have seen, fast food and processed meals have made giant inroads into the French diet. And while of course it is possible to enjoy exquisite meals in Paris, the capital is also full of purely awful restaurants serving reheated slop, coasting on the gas-tronomic reputation built up by the city over the centuries. In short, while there are many French habits and preferences that justify a sense of exceptionalism—the French do genuinely care more about their cuisine and their dining habits than many other peoples, and it is one of the finest gastronomic traditions in the world—we must also acknowledge that there are many ways in which the French are not so very different from anyone else.

For example, one of the recurring themes we have explored is the substantial gulf that usually exists between the diets of the rich and the poor. The Celtic elites drank Roman wines instead of *cervoise*, and prosperous monks found innovative ways to satisfy both God and their stomachs. Nobles feasted on roasted meats while peasants scrabbled for vegetables—at least, until Catherine de' Medici and Louis XIV elevated vegetables to a more exalted perch. Exotic spices and sugar were the preserve of the wealthy until relatively recently, and even during times of siege and war, the richest citizens continued to enjoy their delicacies. It is much the same today, and not only in France. Much attention is devoted to the greatest chefs and the finest restaurants, and the eating habits of the upper classes are sometimes assumed to define an entire national cuisine. Everyday eating by ordi-nary people does not elicit much interest—unless foodie trendsetters unearth an interesting dish or ingredient and bestow upon it a sort of modern-day "nobility," or worthiness.

In short, what we eat can reveal a great deal about the divisions and inequalities that fracture our societies. By examining "foodways"—the political, economic, and social practices related to food in a par-ticular region or era—we can learn much about who holds the most power in a society, what sorts of values they prioritize, and how they sustain their elevated position. We can also learn about the most deprived communities, the constraints and limitations they face in simply trying to feed themselves and survive, and what this indi-cates about the broader society in which they live. And we can see how all these dynamics change over time, thanks to evolving tastes or innovation, restless exploration or wartime devastation. "Tell me what you eat, and I will tell you what you are," said Brillat-Savarin, presaging the creation of a robust field of study.[1]

The notion of foodways also helps in exploring a second theme that runs throughout this book: the tension between Paris and the provinces. Anyone who has ever visited the various regions of France outside the capital will find it difficult to believe that regional cuisines were so long disparaged within France, and largely unknown outside its borders. Some of the most classic French foods and some of its most divine wines were mostly local favorites until relatively recently. The food scene in Paris continues to command the most attention internationally, yet most French people outside of Paris are scornful of the capital's provisions, much preferring their own regional cuisines. And indeed, if you spend some time in Lyon, Marseille, La Rochelle, Nantes, or many other French towns and cities, you will probably find a mind-blowingly good array of local dishes, served up with minimal fanfare but a great deal of local pride.

The idea of terroir is central to these regional dishes and the affection they inspire, and indeed we have seen throughout this book the almost religious devotion that French people have to the concept: the Roquefort cheese that can only be aged in a particular network of caves, the cognac aged in barrels that can only be made with a specific kind of wood, the minuscule wine *domaines* of Burgundy. Terroir is the foundation for the innumerable varieties of honey and oysters and salt, all taking on the flavors of their home in a process that can seem more alchemy than pure science, however rigorous the AOC system tries to be.

While the concept of terroir is limited to the realm of food and wine, our historical narrative shows that similar precepts of localism underlie the regional identities that continue to be strong within France today. A Breton, for example, is someone from the region of Brittany, who may perhaps speak some of the Breton language (a Celtic language, more similar to Welsh or Gaelic) and enjoy the rollicking strains of Breton chansons. They will almost certainly be convinced that Breton cuisine is the best cuisine in France. They may feel that their primary identity is Breton, not French, even five hundred years after Brittany was politically absorbed into France. Similar dynamics can be found in many other parts of France—in the Basque region and the Languedoc, in the cities of Marseille and Strasbourg. This is not to say that French nationalism is weak—the French can be exceedingly patriotic—but rather that identities and loyalties are layered, and in a contest between one's locality and Paris, the capital will often lose. In this sense, the maintenance of regional cuisines, and the sheer variety of cuisines throughout France, is a useful illustration of the fact that French identity is not monolithic, nor static.

We hope our book has demonstrated that French cuisine is not monolithic either, and not only because of its regional variations. The benefit of this long historical exploration is that it reveals the enormous influence of foreign cuisines within French gastronomy. Many elements believed to be ineffably French—the wines and liqueurs, the pastries and chocolates, the flavors of Provence—are not native to France but arrived upon its shores over the centuries and were gradually absorbed. It is a process often described more benignly than it deserves, as in many cases these foreign imports were the result of invasion, conquest, and colonization—a process not yet concluded, as the colonial cuisines of the nineteenth and twentieth centuries continue their slow assimilation into French gastronomy, with still uncertain outcomes.

We believe this extended historical narrative helps present far-right groups like the Front National as—to be blunt—even more ridiculous than they at first appear. Their use of food and culinary traditions to uphold a pure and monolithic French culture looks even more idiotic when you consider that everything from croissants to vineyards, from tomatoes to potatoes, from sugar to chocolate have been imports. There is no pure French gastronomy: it has always accepted ingredients and ideas from around the world, and in the process it became the world's greatest cuisine for centuries. There is no reason to think that this dynamic should be any different today, and thus it must be said that the real roots of the FN's culinary crusades are simple xenophobia. Their recent popularity is worrisome, and it may be that keeping an eye on the success of their anti-Islamic food campaigns can provide some indications of how the movement is faring.

In the end, it is perhaps predictable that food can explain so much about a country that cares so much about it. As France wrestles with the serious challenges of the twenty-first century, with its own identity on the world stage, and with its social conflicts at home, we can perhaps gain a different understanding of its people and its politics by exploring their gastronomic habits and trends. In doing so, we may discover new ways in which our societies have more in common than we think, which can only help encourage the kinds of cooperation necessary to adequately address the epic global challenges we all face. And along the way, we can take the opportunity to sample new dishes and drinks, to enjoy some of the most delicious cuisine ever fashioned, with perhaps a new appreciation for the centuries of events and exchanges—some epochal, some ordinary—that produced the foods and wines gracing our tables today. *Bon appétit.*

Acknowledgments

After writing a book of origin tales, it is hard not to notice that most of them feature a central character—a Catherine de' Medici, a Dom Pérignon, a Napoleon, or a Canon Kir—without whom we may never have heard of our favorite foods and wines. The protagonist in our own origin story must surely be our editor, Carl Bromley, who transformed a casual comment about a book idea into an actual published work. We can never thank him enough for his optimistic faith in our project and for his consistently excellent advice and commentary. This book literally would not exist without him.

We would also like to thank everyone at The New Press who brought our manuscript to life, and especially Benjamin Woodward, Emily Albarillo, and Michael O'Connor. We must also give thanks to our wonderful agent, Gary Morris, and his colleagues at the David Black Agency. Gary was an early enthusiast of our book idea, and we are grateful for his enduring support and encouragement.

Assembling illustrations for the book was not always a simple task, and we are very grateful to those who made it easier. In particular, we would like to thank David Nathan-Maister of the Musée Virtuel de l'Absinthe for allowing us to include the vivid poster celebrating the defeat of the Green Fairy, and Alain Cestari of Les Amis de Benjamin Rabier for granting permission to include Rabier's early illustration of the cow that laughed. We are also highly appreciative of the digital archives of the Bibliothèque Nationale de France, the Bibliothèque Municipale de Lyon, the New York Public Library, and Stanford University.

There are not many people willing to read hundreds of pages of rough drafts for free. We are extremely grateful to our collective parentage—Greg Mitchell and Barbara Bedway, Linda Grace-Kobas and George Kobas, and Anna and Alain Hénaut—for donating so much time to our efforts and for supporting us in such a wide variety of ways. Greg, Barbara, and Linda read our first draft and offered many astute comments and suggestions. Greg came up with the title of the book, while Barbara sent a steady supply of books and articles that proved enormously useful. Linda and George shared a treasure trove of World War II mementos from Jeni's grandfather Victor Kobas, which inspired the closing chapters of the book. Anna's masterful French cooking—you will never taste a more exquisite chocolate mousse—imparted a love of food to Stéphane from an early age and introduced Jeni to the exacting requirements of French cuisine when she joined the family. To all our parents, we offer our heartfelt thanks for helping us complete what once seemed like an impossible task.

We have both been blessed with marvelous colleagues in our respective lines of work, whose tutelage enabled us to write with any semblance of knowledge on food, wine, and war. Stéphane would like to thank the irrepressible trio of French chefs in the City of London who introduced him to the exhausting yet exhilarating world of the professional kitchen: Jean Deillon, Erwan Puel, and Eric Langé. Special thanks also to Zac Fingal-Rock Innes, who gave Stéphane his first proper cheese job, and to Ivo and Kathy Knippenberg for generously allowing him time off from the Knippenbergs *fromagerie* to travel and write.

Jeni would like to thank her colleagues in the Department of War Studies at King's College London, surely one of the best environments in the world for thinking broadly and deeply about humankind's propensity for conflict over the centuries. Its founder, Sir Michael Howard, has long encouraged academics to produce "readable history," and she hopes that this book might make some small contribution in this regard. In particular, she'd like to thank David Betz, David Easter, Marcus Faulkner, Menisha Gor, Mark Hawkins-Dady, Rachel Kerr, Peter Neumann, Anne-Lucie Norton, and Michael Rainsborough for their generous mentorship, inspiration, and congenial support. It has been an incredible privilege to be a member of the War Studies community these many years.

Finally, a special thanks to the lovely Michaela Poppe, who not only read the entire manuscript but highlighted all the bits that made her chuckle, and to Lillian Hueber and Karine Hénaut for their dear friendship and excellent photographs. And we'd like to thank all of our friends and family who kept us going throughout the writing of this book—those who kept us sane, kept us laughing, and kept us convinced that this was all a good idea, especially Monica and Keir Allen; Aicha Diakite, Johnny Kortlever, and Sonja Vilč; Lena and Aglaya Figurkina; Louise, Tim, and Florence Fuller; Adam and Renee Gibbs; John and Bronagh Heaney; Christophe and Betty Hénaut; Philippe Hénaut and Anne-Sophie Guimard; Muraguri Murungi; Kristina Stevens; Tim and Eline Sweijs; and Max Watson. You will never know how much you've encouraged and inspired us over the years, and we cannot quite believe our luck to have so many clever and convivial people in our lives. Here's to all of our adventures, wherever they may lead.

Bibliography

A number of books on French history and gastronomy were useful throughout the writing of this book; they are listed here. Additional sources and recommended reading on specific topics are listed with the endnotes for each chapter.

Bloch-Dano, Évelyne. *La fabuleuse histoire des légumes*. Paris: Le Livre de Poche, 2011.

Brillat-Savarin, Jean-Anthelme. *Physiologie du goût, ou Méditations de gastronomie transcendante*. Paris: Charpentier, 1860.

Conklin, Alice, Sarah Fishman, and Robert Zaretsky. *France and Its Empire Since 1870*. New York: Oxford University Press, 2015.

de l'Aulnoit, Béatrix, and Philippe Alexandre. *Des fourchettes dans les étoiles: brève histoire de la gastronomie française*. Paris: Fayard, 2010.

Dumas, Alexandre. *Grand dictionnaire de cuisine*. Paris: A. Lemerre, 1873.

Favre, Joseph. *Dictionnaire universel de cuisine et d'hygiène alimentaire: modification de l'homme par l'alimentation*. Vol. 1. Paris: Librairie imprimerie des Halles et de la Bourse du Commerce, 1889.

Fernández-Armesto, Felipe. *Near a Thousand Tables: A History of Food*. New York: Free Press, 2002.

Flandrin, Jean-Louis, and Massimo Montanari, eds. *Food: A Culinary History from Antiquity to the Present*. New York: Columbia University Press, 1999.

Guy, Christian. *Almanach historique de la gastronomie française.* Paris: Hachette, 1981.

Librairie Larousse. *Larousse Gastronomique.* London: Hamlyn, 2009.

Marty-Dufaut, Josy. *Cuisiniers et ouvrages culinaires du Moyen Âge.* Rennes: Éditions Ouest-France, 2016.

Pinkard, Susan. *A Revolution in Taste: The Rise of French Cuisine, 1650–1800.* New York: Cambridge University Press, 2009.

Pitte, Jean-Robert. *Gastronomie française: histoire et géographie d'une passion.* Paris: Fayard, 2005.

Rambourg, Patrick. *Histoire de la cuisine et de la gastronomie françaises: du Moyen Âge au XXe siècle.* Paris: Perrin, 2011.

Robb, Graham. *The Discovery of France.* London: Picador, 2007.

Robinson, Jancis, ed. *The Oxford Companion to Wine*, 4th ed. Oxford, England: Oxford University Press, 2015.

Terrier Robert, Valérie. *Il était une fois . . . L'histoire de nos plats.* Lyon: Éditions Stéphane Bachès, 2011.

Toussaint-Samat, Maguelonne. *A History of Food.* 2nd ed. Chichester, England: Wiley-Blackwell, 2009.

Vitaux, Jean, and Benoît France. *Dictionnaire du gastronome.* Paris: Presses Universitaires de France, 2008.

Wellman, Kathleen. *Queens and Mistresses of Renaissance France.* New Haven, CT: Yale University Press, 2013.

Notes

1. Our Ancestors, the Gauls

Brun, Jean-Pierre, and Fanette Laubenheimer, eds. *La viticulture en Gaule*. Special edition of *Gallia* 58, no. 1 (2001).

Laubenheimer, Fanette. "Le vin gaulois." *Revue des Études Anciennes* 91, nos. 3–4 (1989): 5–22.

1. *"Et de vin, divin on devient."* From François Rabelais, *Les songes drolatiques de Pantagruel: nouvelle edition augmentée* (St. Julien en Genevois: Arvensa Editions, 2015), 388.

2. Diodorus of Sicily, a Greek historian of the first century B.C.E., wrote in his epic *Library of History* (book V, chapter 26.3): "The Gauls are exceedingly addicted to the use of wine and fill themselves with the wine which is brought into their country by merchants, drinking it unmixed, and since they partake of this drink without moderation by reason of their craving for it, when they are drunken they fall into a stupor or a state of madness. Consequently, many of the Italian traders, induced by the love of money which characterizes them, believe that the love of wine of these Gauls is their own godsend. For these transport the wine on the navigable rivers by means of boats and through the level plain on wagons, and receive for it an incredible price; for in exchange for a jar of wine they receive a slave, getting a servant in return for the drink."

3. It is estimated that wine imports from Italy may have reached 2.6 million gallons a year, shipped to the ports of Marseille and Narbonne and transported into the interior along France's many navigable rivers. Jancis Robinson, ed., *The Oxford Companion to Wine*, 4th ed. (Oxford, England: Oxford University Press, 2015), 151.

4. Livy, *History of Rome*, trans. Canon Roberts (New York: E. P. Dutton and Co., 1912), vol. 5, chapter 33.

5. Rod Phillips offers an excellent overview of this evolution in "Wine and Adulteration," *History Today* 50, no. 7 (2000): 31–37.

2. The Virgin of the Kidney

Tallon, Alain, and Catherine Vincent. *Histoire du christianisme en France*. Paris: Armand Colin, 2014.

1. There is scant historical evidence of this practice, but in Limoges this is the conventional explanation for why baby Jesus is gnawing on a kidney.

3. Barbarians at the Plate

Heather, Peter. *Empires and Barbarians*. London: Macmillan, 2009.

Lebecq, Stéphane. "Vivent les Mérovingiens!" *French Historical Studies* 19, no. 3 (1996): 765–77.

Scully, D. Eleanor, and Terence Scully. *Early French Cookery*. Ann Arbor: University of Michigan Press, 2002.

Wood, Ian. *The Merovingian Kingdoms, 450–751*. New York: Routledge, 2014.

1. On the use of food in distinguishing classical civilizations from barbarians, see Massimo Montanari, "Food Systems and Models of Civilization," in *Food: A Culinary History from Antiquity to the Present*, ed. Jean-Louis Flandrin and Massimo Montanari (New York: Columbia University Press, 1999), 69–78.

2. The Eastern Roman Empire, later known as the Byzantine Empire, survived for another thousand years.

3. Excerpted in Scully and Scully, *Early French Cookery*, 4. From a standard translation by Shirley Howard Weber, 1924.

4. Ode to Gluttony

Le Jan, Régine. *Les Mérovingiens*. Paris: Presses Universitaires de France, 2015.

Moulinier, Laurence. "Un témoin supplémentaire du rayonnement de sainte Radegonde au Moyen Age? La Vita domnae Juttae (XIIᵉ siécle)." *Bulletin de la Société des Antiquaires de l'Ouest* 15, nos. 3–4 (2001): 181–97.

Nisard, Charles. "Des rapports d'intimité entre Fortunat, sainte Radegonde et l'abbesse Agnès." *Comptes Rendus des Séances de l'Académie des Inscriptions et Belles-Lettres* 33, no. 1 (1889): 30–49.

Venantius Fortunatus. *Poems to Friends.* Translated by Joseph Pucci. Indianapolis: Hackett Publishing, 2010.

1. Venantius Fortunatus, *Poems to Friends*, 95.

2. Le Jan, *Les Mérovingiens*.

3. Venantius Fortunatus, *Poems to Friends*, 101.

4. Ibid., 98.

5. Ibid., 95–96.

5. Left Behind: The Goats of Poitou

Blanc, William, and Christophe Naudin. *Charles Martel et la Bataille de Poitiers: de l'histoire au mythe identitaire.* Paris: Libertalia, 2015.

Hoyland, Robert. *In God's Path: The Arab Conquests and the Creation of an Islamic Empire.* New York: Oxford University Press, 2017.

1. Statistic from the French Ministry of Food, Agriculture and Fishing, Regional Directorate for Food, Agriculture and Forests, "Poitou-Charentes: premier pôle français de production de fromage de chèvre," July 2010, agreste.agriculture.gouv.fr/IMG/pdf_R5410A14.pdf.

2. On this paradox of division and union, see Massimo Montanari, "Food Models and Cultural Identity," in *Food: A Culinary History from Antiquity to the Present*, ed. Jean-Louis Flandrin and Massimo Montanari (New York: Columbia University Press, 1999), 191.

3. FranceAgriMer, *La filière lait de chèvre 2008–2013: une difficile adaptation de l'offre à la demande* (Montreuil: FranceAgriMer, 2014).

6. The Sweetest King

Einhard and Notker the Stammerer. *Two Lives of Charlemagne.* Translated by David Ganz. London: Penguin, 2008.

Toussaint-Samat, Maguelonne. *A History of Food.* 2nd ed. Chichester, England: Wiley-Blackwell, 2009. See esp. chapter 1, "Collecting Honey."

1. Terroir is a quintessentially French concept with no exact English equivalent. It is an attempt to capture the ways in which the natural environment influences the characteristics and taste of a particular product, and serves as the basis for the French AOC system of geographical delimitation. Key

elements of terroir include climate, average rainfall and sunlight, topography, and soil geology. Skeptics of the concept do exist, especially outside Europe. Jancis Robinson, ed., *The Oxford Companion to Wine*, 4th ed. (Oxford, England: Oxford University Press, 2015), 737.

2. The University of Leicester's School of Historical Studies offers a useful translation of the *Capitulare de villis*: www.le.ac.uk/hi/polyptyques/capitulare /latin2english.html.

3. Statistics from Union Nationale de l'Apiculture Française, www.unaf -apiculture.info.

7. They Came from the Sea

Brownworth, Lars. *The Normans: From Raiders to Kings*. London: Crux Publishing, 2014.

Lafont, Olivier. "Le rôle du port de Rouen dans le commerce des drogues et des médicaments avec les Amériques." *Revue d'Histoire de la Pharmacie* 95, no. 359 (2008): 305–10.

1. "Bénédictine: de l'élixir de santé à la liqueur," *Ouest France*, September 27, 2013.

8. Feudal Fare

Birlouez, Eric. *À la table des seigneurs, des moines et des paysans du Moyen Âge*. Rennes: Éditions Ouest-France, 2015.

Montanari, Massimo. "Peasants, Warriors, Priests: Images of Society and Styles of Diet." In *Food: A Culinary History from Antiquity to the Present*, ed. Jean-Louis Flandrin and Massimo Montanari, 178–85. New York: Columbia University Press, 1999.

1. A lack of precise data for the feudal era means that exact breakdowns of population by class are not definitive, but the percentages used in this chapter are those conventionally accepted by historians.

2. On this symbolic role of meat, see Montanari, "Peasants, Warriors, Priests," 180. The association of a carnivorous diet with power would reemerge in the heyday of French imperialism in the nineteenth and twentieth centuries, as discussed in Deborah Neill, "Finding the 'Ideal Diet': Nutrition, Culture and Dietary Practices in France and French Equatorial Africa, c. 1890s to 1920s," *Food and Foodways* 17, no. 1 (2009): 1–28.

9. Of Monks and Men

Jotischky, Andrew. *A Hermit's Cookbook: Monks, Food and Fasting in the Middle Ages*. London: Bloomsbury Academic, 2011.

Racinet, Philippe. *Moines et monastères en Occident au Moyen Âge.* Paris: Ellipses, 2007.

1. "Chapter 40: On the Measure of Drink," *The Rule of Saint Benedict,* http://www.osb.org/rb/text/rbemjo2.html#40.

2. From the annual reports of APPED (Association de Promotion des Poissons des Etangs de la Dombes), available at www.poissonsdedombes.fr/qsn/apped-association-de-promotion-du-poisson-des-etangs-de-dombes-8.php.

3. Catherine Jacquemard and Marie-Agnès Lucas-Avenel, "Des poissons, des mots et des signes: les signes monastiques des noms de poissons au xie siècle," *Annales de Normandie* 62, no. 2 (2012): 140.

4. Michael Casey, ed. and trans., *Cistercians and Cluniacs: St Bernard's Apologia to Abbot William* (Collegeville, MN: Cistercian Publications, 1970), 55.

5. Ibid., 56.

10. Fighting for Plums

Barber, Malcolm. *The Trial of the Templars.* Cambridge, England: Cambridge University Press, 1978.

Barber, Malcolm, and Keith Bate, eds. and trans. *The Templars: Selected Sources* (Manchester, England: Manchester University Press, 2002.

Nicholson, Helen. *The Knights Templar: A New History.* Gloucestershire, England: Sutton Publishing, 2004.

1. FranceAgriMer, *Les filières des fruits et legumes, Données 2014.* Montreuil: FranceAgriMer, 2016.

2. Nirmal Dass, ed. and trans., *The Deeds of the Franks and Other Jerusalem-Bound Pilgrims: The Earliest Chronicle of the First Crusades* (Lanham, MD: Rowman & Littlefield Publishers, 2011), 103.

3. Francesco Franceschi et al., "The Diet of Templar Knights: Their Secret to Longevity?" *Digestive and Liver Disease* 46, no. 7 (2014): 577–78.

11. The Wine That Got Away

Johnson, Hugh. *The Story of Wine.* London: Mandarin, 1991.

Pernoud, Régine. *Aliénor d'Aquitaine.* Paris: Le Grand Livre du Mois, 1994.

Pitte, Jean-Robert. *Bordeaux/Burgundy: A Vintage Rivalry.* Berkeley: University of California Press, 2008.

Soyez, Jean-Marc. *Quand les Anglais vendangeaient l'Aquitaine: d'Aliénor à Jeanne d'Arc.* Bordeaux: Les Dossiers d'Aquitaine, 2013.

1. Jean-Anthelme Brillat-Savarin, *Physiologie du goût, ou Méditations de gastronomie transcendante* (Paris: Charpentier, 1860), 363. Translation by authors.

2. Yves Renouard, "Les conséquences de la conquête de la Guienne par le roi de France pour le commerce des vins de Gascogne," *Annales du Midi: Revue Archéologique, Historique et Philologique de la France Méridionale* 61, no. 1 (1948): 18.

3. This frequently related anecdote is usually attributed to Walter Map, a twelfth-century English courtier, whose *De nugis curialium* is a rich source of courtly lore, of varying reliability. Walter Map, *De nugis curialium* V, ed. and trans. M. R. James, C. N. L. Brooke, and R. A. B. Mynors (Oxford, England: Clarendon Press, 1983), p. 450.

4. From the *Diary of Samuel Pepys*, April 10, 1663, available online at: www.pepysdiary.com/diary/1663/04/10/.

5. Jancis Robinson, ed., *The Oxford Companion to Wine*, 4th ed. (Oxford, England: Oxford University Press, 2015), 89.

12. The Vegetarian Heresy

Aué, Michele. *The Cathars*. Translated by Alison Hebborn and Juliette Freyche. Vic-en-Bigorre: Societé MSM, 2006.

Fernand, Niel. *Albigeois et Cathares*. Paris: Presses Universitaires de France, 2010.

O'Shea, Stephen. *The Perfect Heresy: The Revolutionary Life and Death of the Medieval Cathars*. New York: Walker and Company, 2000.

1. For a detailed look at the practices and questions typical in the Inquisition, see Caterina Bruschi and Peter Biller, eds., *Texts and the Repression of Medieval Heresy* (Suffolk, England: Boydell and Brewer, 2003), especially chapter 6 by Mark Pegg ("Questions About Questions: Toulouse 609 and the Great Inquisition of 1245–6") and chapter 7 by Peter Biller ("Why No Food? Waldensian Followers in Bernard Gui's *Practica inquisitionis* and *culpe*"). The latter shows that Waldensians, another heretical sect, were not asked questions about food because they were known to eat a normal diet.

13. A Papal Red

Lefranc, Renée. *À la table du Pape d'Avignon*. Avignon: Editions RMG-Palais des Papes, 2005.

Renouard, Yves. *La papauté à Avignon*. Paris: J.-P. Gisserot, 2004.

1. In fact, the AOC system was partly based on a prototype for wine-

production rules introduced by Châteauneuf-du-Pape producers in the 1920s, which established standards for the wine based on geographical delimitation, grape varieties, and pruning methods.

2. In the preface to *La Farandoulo*, a short book by a fellow poet from Avignon, Anselme Mathieu.

3. Such extravagant table settings required extraordinary precautions: guests were only allowed to depart the palace when the keeper of the dishware verified that all the settings had been retrieved. Lefranc, *À la table du Pape d'Avignon*, 49.

14. The White Gold of Guérande

de Person, Françoise. *Bateliers contrebandiers du sel*. Rennes: Éditions Ouest-France, 1999.

Huvet-Martinet, Micheline, "Faux-saunage et faux-sauniers dans la France de l'Ouest et du Centre à la fin de l'Ancien Régime (1764–1789)." *Annales de Bretagne et des Pays de l'Ouest* 85, no. 3 (1978).

Kurlansky, Mark. *Salt: A World History*. New York: Walker and Company, 2002.

1. French Ministry of Agriculture and Food, "Le sel de Guérande," June 15, 2016, agriculture.gouv.fr/alimentation/le-sel-de-guerande-label-rouge.

2. Maguelonne Toussaint-Samat, *A History of Food*, 2nd ed. (Chichester, England: Wiley-Blackwell, 2009), 414–20.

3. Kurlansky, *Salt*, 231.

4. Huvet-Martinet, "Faux-saunage et faux-sauniers dans la France de l'Ouest," 383.

15. Legacy of a Black Prince

Contamine, Philippe. *La Guerre de Cent Ans*. Paris: Presses Universitaires de France, 1968.

Mullot, Henry, and Joseph Poux. "Nouvelles recherches sur l'itinéraire du Prince Noir à travers les pays de l'Aude." *Annales du Midi: Revue Archéologique, Historique et Philologique de la France Méridionale* 21, no. 83 (1909): 297–311.

Tuchman, Barbara. *A Distant Mirror: The Calamitous 14th Century*. New York: Random House, 1978.

1. Jeanne Barondeau, ed., *Curnonsky et ses recettes d'autrefois* (Munich: Édition Curnonska, 2013), in the chapter titled "Un cassoulet mémorable" (Kindle location 351 of 1591).

2. George Payne Rainsford James, *A History of the Life of Edward the Black Prince*, vol. 2 (London: Longman, Rees, Orme, Brown, Green, & Longman, 1836), 18.

3. Prosper Montagné, *Le Festin occitan* (Carcassonne: Éditions d'Art Jordy, 1930).

16. The Vinegar of the Four Thieves

Cantor, Norman. *In the Wake of the Plague: The Black Death and the World It Made*. New York: Perennial, 2002.

Carpentier, Élisabeth. "Autour de la peste noir: famines et épidémies dans l'histoire du XIVᵉ siècle." *Annales. Économies, Sociétés, Civilisations* 17, no. 6 (1962): 1062–92.

Ziegler, Philip. *The Black Death*. New York: John Day Company, 1969.

1. Over the years, estimates of the total death toll have ranged from one-third to one-half of the population, an endeavor complicated by a lack of data and the fact that there was significant regional variation.

2. Ziegler, *The Black Death*, 64. Ziegler acknowledges that the figure seems "improbably high" but notes that mortality rates were much higher in the port cities where the plague first arrived than farther inland.

3. For a translation of contemporary accounts of the massacre at Strasbourg, see Fordham University's Jewish History Sourcebook, "The Black Death and the Jews 1348–1349 C.E.," available at sourcebooks.fordham.edu/jewish/1348-jewsblackdeath.asp.

4. For a fascinating look at theriac and other plague remedies, see Christiane Nockels Fabbri, "Treating Medieval Plague: The Wonderful Virtues of Theriac," *Early Science and Medicine* 12, no. 3 (2007): 247–83.

5. For a contemporary explanation of the causes of the plague, including the dangers of the "hot and moist" body, see "The Special Challenges of Plague (1): The Report of the Paris Medical Faculty, October 1348," *Medieval Medicine: A Reader*, ed. Faith Wallis (Toronto: University of Toronto Press, 2010), 414–19.

6. Jean-Anthelme Brillat-Savarin, *Physiologie du goût, ou Méditations de gastronomie transcendante* (Paris: Charpentier, 1860), 344–46.

17. The Cheese of Emperors and Mad Kings

Guenée, Bernard. *La folie de Charles VI, roi bien-aimé*. Paris: CNRS, 2016.

Marre, Eugène. *Le Roquefort*. Rodez: Carrère, 1906.

1. Interestingly, this "glass delusion" was somewhat fashionable at the time, afflicting a number of French nobles in the fifteenth and sixteenth centuries. Descartes mentioned it in his *Meditations on First Philosophy* (1641), saying that to deny his own bodily existence would make him as mad as those who "imagine that they have an earthenware head or are nothing but pumpkins or are made of glass."

18. La Dame de Beauté and the Mushroom Mystery

Duquesne, Robert. *Agnès Sorel: 'La Dame de Beaulté.'* Paris: Michel, 1909.

Tuchman, Barbara. *A Distant Mirror: The Calamitous 14th Century*. New York: Random House, 1978.

Wellman, Kathleen. *Queens and Mistresses of Renaissance France*. New Haven, CT: Yale University Press, 2013.

1. Wellman, *Queens and Mistresses of Renaissance France*, 25.

2. The town of Castillon lends its name to the delightful AOC red wine Castillon Côtes de Bordeaux. In the twentieth century, the town renamed itself Castillon-la-Bataille (the Battle of Castillon).

3. At that time, mercury was often used to treat the kind of parasitic infections that Agnès apparently suffered from.

19. Fruits of the Renaissance

MacDonald, Stewart. "Why Did the Habsburg-Valois Conflict Last So Long?" *History Review* 33 (1999).

McPhee, John. "Oranges." *New Yorker*, May 7, 1966.

Saint Bris, François. "'Nel palazzo del Clu': 500 Years of History." In Leonardo da Vinci & France: Chateau du Clos Lucé, Parc Leonardo da Vinci, Amboise, exhibition catalog, edited by Carlo Pedretti, 19–26. Available at www.vinci-closluce.com/file/francois-saint-bris-nel-palazzo-del-clu-gb.pdf.

Salmon, J. H. M. "Francis the First of France: Le Roi Chevalier." *History Today* 8, no. 5 (1958).

1. François Rabelais, *La vie de Gargantua et de Pantagruel*, book 1, chapter 17 (Paris: Chez Dalibon, 1823), 328–29.

2. Maguelonne Toussaint-Samat, *A History of Food*, 2nd ed. (Chichester, England: Wiley-Blackwell, 2009), 513.

20. The Mother Sauces

Ferguson, Priscilla Parkhurst. "Writing Out of the Kitchen: Carême and the Invention of French Cuisine." *Gastronomica* 3, no. 3 (2003): 40–51.

Flandrin, Jean-Louis. "Seasoning, Cooking, and Dietetics in the Late Middle Ages." In *Food: A Culinary History from Antiquity to the Present*, edited by Jean-Louis Flandrin and Massimo Montanari, 313–27. New York: Columbia University Press, 1999.

1. Marie-Hélène Baylac, *Dictionnaire gourmand: du canard d'Apicius à la purée de Joël Robuchon* (Paris: Omnibus, 2014).

2. Flandrin, "Seasoning, Cooking, and Dietetics in the Late Middle Ages," 314.

3. Jean-Louis Flandrin, "Le goût et la nécessité: sur l'usage des graisses dans les cuisines d'Europe occidentale (XIVᵉ–XVIIIᵉ siècle)," *Annales. Économies, Sociétés, Civilisations* 38, no. 2 (1983): 376.

4. Bonnefons's cookbook *Les délices de la campagne* (1654) was enormously influential for early modern cooking. Susan Pinkard, *A Revolution in Taste: The Rise of French Cuisine, 1650–1800* (New York: Cambridge University Press, 2009), 60–63.

5. These factors are explained in more depth in Jean-Louis Flandrin, "From Dietetics to Gastronomy: The Liberation of the Gourmet," in *Food: A Culinary History from Antiquity to the Present*, ed. Jean-Louis Flandrin and Massimo Montanari (New York: Columbia University Press, 1999), 418–32; and Pinkard, *A Revolution in Taste*, chapter 3.

6. Like many of Talleyrand's best bons mots, the quip has been attributed to him without citation for decades, so may be apocryphal.

7. Jean Vitaux, *Les petits plats de l'histoire* (Paris: Presses Universitaires de France, 2012), 92.

21. Conquest and Chocolate

Coe, Sophie D., and Michael D. Coe. *The True History of Chocolate*. London: Thames & Hudson, 2013.

Huyghe, Edith, and François-Bernard Huyghe. *Les coureurs d'épices*. Paris: Editions Payot & Rivages, 2002.

Norton, Marcy. *Sacred Gifts, Profane Pleasures: A History of Tobacco and Chocolate in the Atlantic World*. Ithaca, NY: Cornell University Press, 2008.

Patemotte, Stephanie, and Pierre Labrude. "Le chocolat dans quelques ouvrages français de pharmacie et de médecine des XVIIᵉ, XVIIIᵉ et XIXᵉ siècles: ses effets fastes et néfastes avérés ou supposés." *Revue d'histoire de la pharmacie* 91, no. 338 (2003): 197–210.

1. In fact, France's most notable achievement in the centuries-long European spice competition was its breach of the powerful Dutch monopoly in the late eighteenth century, when the aptly named colonial administrator Pierre Poivre covertly acquired clove, nutmeg, and cinnamon plants from the Dutch East Indies and established spice crops on the French territories of Mauritius, Réunion, and the Seychelles.

2. Conventional food folklore often states that the Spanish radically transformed Mesoamerican chocolate from bitter to sweet, but in fact local populations already sometimes sweetened their cacao drinks with honey, so the addition of sugar was more of a substitution than a transformation. See Marcy Norton, "Tasting Empire: Chocolate and the European Internalization of Mesoamerican Aesthetics," *American Historical Review* 111, no. 3 (2006): 684.

3. Honoré de Balzac, *Pathologie de la vie sociale* (Paris: Éditions Bossard, 1822), 230. Balzac argued here that "the destiny of a people depends on its food and diet," noting that eau-de-vie destroyed the American Indians, tobacco eventually brought low the Turks and the Dutch, and Russia was "an aristocracy sustained by alcohol." Translations by authors.

4. For a sense of the broader social meaning of this chocolate debate, see Beth Marie Forrest and April L. Najjaj, "Is Sipping Sin Breaking Fast? The Catholic Chocolate Controversy and the Changing World of Early Modern Spain," *Food and Foodways* 15, no. 1–2 (2007): 31–52.

5. Syndicat du Chocolat, "Chiffres clés 2016 des industries de la chocolaterie," March 15, 2017, www.syndicatduchocolat.fr/conference-de-presse-du-syndicat-du-chocolat.

6. For an in-depth report, see Brian O'Keefe, "Inside Big Chocolate's Child Labor Problem," *Fortune*, March 1, 2016, fortune.com/big-chocolate-child-labor. The NGO Slave Free Chocolate, a coalition of organizations working to end child labor on West African cocoa farms, publishes a list of chocolate firms that do not depend on child labor.

22. The Culinary Contributions of Madame Serpent

Cloulas, Ivan. *Catherine de Médicis*. Paris: Fayard, 1979.

Wellman, Kathleen. *Queens and Mistresses of Renaissance France*. New Haven, CT: Yale University Press, 2013.

1. Like many food legends, this quote may be too good to be true: it is possible that Luther was asking to be saved from the hay fork, a formidable weapon at that time.

2. Susan Pinkard suggests that this mythology surrounding Catherine may have originated in the eighteenth century, when Enlightenment thinkers attempted to discredit an overly extravagant noble cuisine by associating its Italian influences with her notorious historical reputation. Susan Pinkard, *A Revolution in Taste: The Rise of French Cuisine, 1650–1800* (New York: Cambridge University Press, 2009), 189.

23. A Chicken in Every Pot

Gandilhon, René. "Henri IV et le vin." *Bibliothèque de l'École des Chartes* 145, no. 2 (1987): 383–406.

Tierchant, Hélène. *Henri IV: roi de Navarre et de France.* Bordeaux: Editions Sud Ouest, 2010.

1. Bernard Lonjon, *Colette, la passion du vin* (Paris: Éditions du Moment, 2013), 15.

2. Béthune, Maximilien de, duc de Sully, *Economies royales*, ed. Joseph Chailley (Paris: Guillaumin & Cie., 1820), 26.

3. For a sublime firsthand account of the Salon International de l'Agriculture, see Lauren Collins, "Come to the Fair," *New Yorker*, April 4, 2016.

4. Letter from Henry IV to Monsieur de Batz, in *Recueil des lettres missives de Henri IV* (Paris: Berger de Xivrey, Imprimerie Royale, 1843), 122.

24. The Chestnut Insurgency

Bruneton-Governatori, Ariane. "Alimentation et idéologie: le cas de la châtaigne." *Annales. Économies, Sociétés, Civilisations* 39, no. 6 (1984): 1161–89.

Crackanthorpe, David. *The Camisard Uprising: War and Religion in the Cévennes.* Oxford, England: Signal Books, 2016.

Jouhaud, Christian. "'Camisards! We Were Camisards!': Remembrance and the Ruining of Remembrance Through the Production of Historical Absences." *History & Memory* 21, no. 1 (2009): 5–24.

Monahan, W. Gregory. "Between Two Thieves: The Protestant Nobility and the War of the Camisards." *French Historical Studies* 30, no. 4 (2007): 537–58.

1. From "An Open Letter to the Christian Nobility of the German Nation Concerning the Reform of the Christian Estate, 1520: Proposals for Reform, Part II," section 19. In C. M. Jacobs, trans., *Works of Martin Luther* (Philadelphia: A. J. Holman Company, 1915).

2. Centre National Interprofessionnel de l'Economie Laitière (CNIEL), *L'économie laitière en chiffres* (Paris: 2017), 184.

3. It is not clear whether the name *Camisard* was derived from their practice of night attacks *(camisades)* or the fact that they fought in plain shirts *(camisoles)*. The rebel fighters themselves, most of them devout young men, preferred to be known as *les enfants de Dieu* (the children of God). Crackanthorpe, *The Camisard Uprising*, 99–103.

4. Bruneton-Governatori, "Alimentation et idéologie," 1161.

5. Jean-Baptiste Lavialle, *Le châtaignier: Étude scientifique du châtaignier* (Paris: Vigot Frères, 1906), 34.

6. Bruneton-Governatori, "Alimentation et idéologie"; French Ministry of Agriculture and Food, *Statistique Agricole*, December 2013, agreste. agriculture.gouv.fr/IMG/pdf/memo13_integral.pdf.

7. Robert Louis Stevenson, *Travels with a Donkey in the Cévennes* (New York: Scribner, 1910), 144. This is not only one of Stevenson's earliest works, first published in 1879, but one of the first books to describe hiking through the countryside as an activity of leisure, not necessity.

25. The Bitter Roots of Sugar

Blackburn, Robin. "Anti-Slavery and the French Revolution." *History Today* 41, no. 11 (1991): 19–25.

Mintz, Sidney W. *Sweetness and Power: The Place of Sugar in Modern History*. New York: Viking Penguin, 1985.

Stein, Robert Louis. *The French Sugar Business in the Eighteenth Century*. Baton Rouge: Louisiana State University Press, 1988.

Viles, Perry. "The Slaving Interest in the Atlantic Ports, 1763–1792." *French Historical Studies* 7, no. 4 (1972): 529–43.

1. Voyages: The Trans-Atlantic Slave Trade Database (www.slavevoyages.org/assessment/estimates); Stein, *The French Sugar Business in the Eighteenth Century*, 20.

2. Scholars continue to assemble detailed statistics about the slave trade, with new documents continuing to come to light today. See Stein, *The French Sugar Business in the Eighteenth Century*, 23; David Geggus, "The French Slave Trade: An Overview," *William and Mary Quarterly* 58, no. 1 (2001): 119–38.

3. Stein, *The French Sugar Business in the Eighteenth Century*, 107.

4. Voltaire, *Candide, ou L'optimisme* (Paris: G. Boudet, 1893), 94. Translation by authors.

5. Today, the Institut Benjamin Delessert continues his legacy by awarding prizes for research in nutrition.

6. Maguelonne Toussaint-Samat, *A History of Food*, 2nd ed. (Chichester, England: Wiley-Blackwell, 2009), 503.

26. The Liquor of the Gods

Delamain, Robert. *Histoire du cognac*. Paris: Delamain & Boutelleau, 1935.

Jarrard, Kyle. *Cognac: The Seductive Saga of the World's Most Coveted Spirit*. Hoboken, NJ: John Wiley & Sons, 2005.

Prioton, Henri, and Prosper Gervais. *La culture de la vigne dans les Charentes et la production du cognac*. Paris: Librairie J.-B. Baillière et fils, 1929.

1. Hugo's quote may be apocryphal, as the original source is difficult to verify, but it was attributed to him as early as 1896, in the newspaper *L'Avenir d'Arcachon*.

2. Whisky consumption statistics from Euromonitor (2015).

3. Brian Primack et al., "Alcohol Brand Appearances in US Popular Music," *Addiction* 107, no. 3 (2012): 557–66. Ironically, Busta Rhymes's manager later confessed to the *New York Times* that "Busta actually drinks Hennessy." Lynette Holloway, "Hip-Hop Sales Pop: Pass the Courvoisier and Count the Cash," *New York Times*, September 2, 2002.

27. The Crescent Controversy

Chevallier, Jim. *August Zang and the French Croissant: How Viennoiserie Came to France*. Chez Jim Books: 2009.

Isom-Verhaaren, Christine. *Allies with the Infidel: The Ottoman and French Alliance in the Sixteenth Century*. London: I. B. Tauris, 2011.

1. Gilbert Pytel, "Comment reconnaître une viennoiserie industrielle d'une artisanale?" *L'Express*, October 6, 2016.

2. Laurent Binet, "'Touche pas à mon pain au chocolat!' The Theme of Food in Current French Political Discourses," *Modern & Contemporary France* 24, no. 3 (2016): 247–48.

28. War and Peas

Cobban, Alfred, "The Art of Kingship: Louis XIV, A Reconsideration," *History Today* 4, no. 3 (1954): 149–158.

De Courtois, Stephanie. *Le potager du Roi*. Versailles: Ecole Nationale Supérieure de Paysage, 2003.

1. Susan Pinkard, *A Revolution in Taste: The Rise of French Cuisine, 1650–1800* (New York: Cambridge University Press, 2009), 130.

2. *Correspondance complète de Madame duchesse d'Orléans née Princesse Palatine, mère du régent*, vol. 2 (Paris: Charpentier, 1857), 37. Translation by authors.

3. Original quote from his *Premiers Lundis*, vol. 2 (Paris: Calm-ann-Lévy, 1883); cited from the 2016 electronic version produced by the Université Paris-Sorbonne (obvil.paris-sorbonne.fr/corpus/critique/sainte-beuve_nouveaux-lundis-02/body-20).

4. Madame de Maintenon, *Lettres de Madame de Maintenon à Monsieur le Cardinal de Noailles*, vol. 4 (Amsterdam: Pierre Erialed, 1757), 60. Translation by authors.

29. The Devil's Wine

Mervaud, Christiane. "Du nectar pour Voltaire." *Dix-huitième Siècle* 29 (1997): 137–45.

Epstein, Becky Sue. *Champagne: A Global History*. London: Reaktion Books, 2011.

1. Jean-Louis Flandrin, "From Dietetics to Gastronomy: The Liberation of the Gourmet," in *Food: A Culinary History from Antiquity to the Present*, ed. Jean-Louis Flandrin and Massimo Montanari (New York: Columbia University Press, 1999), 418–32.

2. Jancis Robinson, ed., *The Oxford Companion to Wine*, 4th ed. (Oxford, England: Oxford University Press, 2015), 156, claims that up until the nineteenth century, up to half of the champagne bottles produced each year would burst.

3. Voltaire, *Le mondain* (Paris: 1736), 5. Translation by authors.

4. Robinson, ed., *The Oxford Companion to Wine*, 156. Two-thirds of champagne sales are in France.

30. An Enlightened Approach to Food

Pinkard, Susan. *A Revolution in Taste: The Rise of French Cuisine, 1650–1800*. New York: Cambridge University Press, 2009.

Roche, Daniel. *France in the Enlightenment*. Translated by Arthur Goldhammer (Cambridge, MA: Harvard University Press, 1998). See esp. chapter 19.

Spary, E. C. *Eating the Enlightenment: Food and the Sciences in Paris, 1670–1760*. Chicago: University of Chicago Press, 2012.

Vasseur, Jean-Marc. *Jean-Jacques Rousseau dans son assiette: les plaisirs de la table au temps des Lumières*. Paris: La Lettre Active, 2012.

1. Jean-Jacques Rousseau, *Emile, or On Education*, trans. Allan Bloom (New York: Basic Books, 1979), 346.

2. Ibid., 153.

3. Ibid., 346.

4. Quoted in Michèle Crogiez, "L'éloge du vin chez Rousseau: Entre franchise et salubrité," *Dix-huitième Siècle* 29 (1997): 186–87. Translation by authors.

5. Ibid., 187.

6. For an in-depth examination of Rousseau's stance on food and broader trends at the time, see Pinkard, *A Revolution in Taste*, chapter 6.

7. Denis Diderot and Jean Le Rond d'Alembert, *Encyclopédie, ou Dictionnaire raisonné des sciences, des arts et des métiers*, vol. 4 (Paris: 1751), 538. Translation by authors.

8. Chad Denton, *Decadence, Radicalism, and the Early Modern French Nobility: The Enlightened and Depraved* (New York: Rowman & Littlefield, 2016), 114.

31. Revolution in the Cafés

Lenotre, G. *La vie à Paris pendant la Révolution*. Paris: Calmann-Levy, 1949.

Lepage, Auguste. *Les cafés politiques et littéraires de Paris*. Paris: E. Dentu, 1874.

Mercier, Louis-Sébastien. *Le nouveau Paris par le cit. Mercier*. Vol. 6. Paris: Fuchs, C. Pougens & C.F. Cramer, 1797.

Weinberg, Bennett Alan, and Bonnie K. Bealer. *The World of Caffeine: The Science and Culture of the World's Most Popular Drug*. London: Routledge, 2004.

1. A very interesting pamphlet written for British servicemen participating in the Allied invasion of France in 1944 explained the revolution thus: "The French Revolution was not, of course, a Communist revolution or even mainly a revolution of the poor against the rich. It was a revolution of the prosperous middle-classes who have led France ever since against an aristocracy which had already ceased to lead." *Instructions for British Servicemen in France 1944*, reprinted by the Bodleian Library, Oxford University (Cambridge, England: University Press, 2005), 17.

2. From his *Qu'est-ce-que le Tiers-État*, available online through the Biblio-

thèque Nationale de France (gallica.bnf.fr).

3. As in most revolutions, the spontaneous popular uprising was channeled and managed by elites and professional revolutionaries striving to overturn the status quo. Some evidence of this can be found in the fact that the two *barriéres* not burned during the revolt belonged to the Duke of Orléans, a supporter of the revolutionary forces. George Rudé, "The Fall of the Bastille," *History Today* 4, no. 7 (1954): 452.

4. *Dictionnaire de la conversation et de la lecture*, vol. 9 (Paris: Belin-Mandar, 1833), 427–28. Quotes translated by authors.

5. Mercier, *Le nouveau Paris*, 72.

32. Pain d'Égalité

Campion-Vincent, Veronique, and Christine Shojaei Kawan. "Marie-Antoinette et son célèbre dire." *Annales Historiques de la Révolution Française* 327 (2002): 29–56.

Kaplan, Steven Laurence. *The Bakers of Paris and the Bread Question, 1700–1775*. Durham, NC: Duke University Press, 1996.

1. Thomas Carlyle, *The French Revolution: A History in Three Volumes*, vol. 3, *The Guillotine* (London: James Fraser, 1837), 420.

2. Olwen H. Hufton, *The Poor of Eighteenth-Century France, 1750–1789* (Oxford, England: Oxford University Press, 1974), 44–46.

3. Quoted and translated in Adrian Velicu, *Civic Catechisms and Reason in the French Revolution* (London: Routledge, 2016), 117.

4. Decree published in *Gazette Nationale, ou Le Moniteur Universel*, November 26, 1793, 57. Translation by authors.

5. The 2015 figure is a reported by the National Association of French Millers, cited in Eric de La Chesnais "On consomme toujours moins de pain en France," *Le Figaro*, June 17, 2016.

6. The idea that wine, cheese, and bread constitute a "holy trinity of the table" is often attributed to the Renaissance humanist writer François Rabelais, perhaps because it sounds like the kind of thing he would have said. But this specific phrase does not appear in his writings, and the actual originator of the phrase appears to be Michel Tournier, a celebrated twentieth-century novelist and philosopher.

33. The Potato Propagandist

Andrews, George Gordon. "Making the Revolutionary Calendar." *American Historical Review* 36, no. 3 (1931): 515–32.

Kennedy, Emmet. *A Cultural History of the French Revolution*. New Haven, CT: Yale University Press, 1989.

Salaman, Redcliffe. *The History and Social Influence of the Potato.* 2nd ed. Cambridge, England: Cambridge University Press, 1985.

Spary, E. C. *Feeding France: New Sciences of Food, 1760–1815.* Cambridge, England: Cambridge University Press, 2014. See esp. chapter 5, "The Potato Republic."

1. Translation by Steven Kaplan; quoted in his *The Stakes of Regulation: Perspectives on "Bread, Politics and Political Economy" Forty Years Later* (New York: Anthem Press, 2015), 358.

2. Spary, *Feeding France*, 177–80.

3. Madame Mérigot, *La Cuisinière républicaine* (Paris: 1794), 16–17.

4. France Agroalimentaire, "French Potatoes: As Many Qualities as Varieties," April 6, 2017, www.franceagroalimentaire.com/en/thematiques/all -products/articles/french-potatoes-quality.

34. The Pyramid Provocation

Howard, Michael. *War in European History.* Oxford, England: Oxford University Press, 1976.

LeMay, G. H. L. "Napoleonic Warfare." *History Today* 1, no. 8 (1951): 24–32.

1. Talleyrand was neither the first, nor the last, to deploy France's gastronomic soft power for political advantage. In July 2017, French president Emmanuel Macron hosted U.S. president Donald Trump at an elegant dinner atop the Eiffel Tower, prepared by the legendary chef Alain Ducasse—a superb Talleyrandian maneuver.

2. From a letter to Madame de Rémusat, translated and quoted in David G. Chandler, *The Campaigns of Napoleon*, vol. 1 (New York: Simon and Schuster, 2009), 248.

3. This profound shift in the character of European warfare is nicely captured in a short and engaging book by one of the founders of the modern academic discipline of war studies, Sir Michael Howard, titled *War in European History.*

35. The Man Who Abolished the Seasons

Appert, Nicolas. *The Art of Preserving All Kinds of Animal and Vegetable Substances for Several Years.* London: Black, Parry and Kingsbury, 1812.

Capatti, Alberto. "The Taste for Canned and Preserved Food." In *Food: A Culinary History from Antiquity to the Present*, edited by

Jean-Louis Flandrin and Massimo Montanari, 492–99. New York: Columbia University Press, 1999.

Pedrocco, Giorgio. "The Food Industry and New Preservation Techniques." In *Food: A Culinary History from Antiquity to the Present*, edited by Jean-Louis Flandrin and Massimo Montanari, 481–91. New York: Columbia University Press, 1999.

Picot, Olivier. *L'avenir est dans la boîte*. Paris: Calmann-Levy, 2002.

1. From the *Courrier de l'Europe*, February 10, 1809; translated and quoted in Maguelonne Toussaint-Samat, *A History of Food*, 2nd ed. (Chichester, England: Wiley-Blackwell, 2009), 665.

36. The Fifth Crêpe

Lieven, Dominic. *Russia Against Napoleon: The Battle for Europe, 1807 to 1814*. London: Penguin, 2016.

Zamoyski, Adam. *1812: Napoleon's Fatal March on Moscow*. London: HarperCollins, 2005.

1. The historical debate over the causes of the fire is well summarized in the introduction to Alexander Mikaberidze's *The Burning of Moscow: Napoleon's Trial by Fire 1812* (Barnsley, England: Pen and Sword: 2014).

37. The King of Cheeses

Jarrett, Mark. *The Congress of Vienna and Its Legacy: War and Great Power Diplomacy After Napoleon*. London: I. B. Tauris, 2013.

Vick, Brian E. *The Congress of Vienna: Power and Politics After Napoleon*. Cambridge, MA: Harvard University Press, 2014.

1. Waterloo was not only the end of Napoleon but the end of nearly eight centuries of frequent warfare between Britain and France: after 1815, the two countries never fought one another again (excluding British operations against Vichy France during World War II).

2. Jean-Anthelme Brillat-Savarin, *Physiologie du goût, ou Méditations de gastronomie transcendante* (Paris: Charpentier, 1860), 134. Translation by authors.

38. A Revolutionary Banquet

Ihl, Olivier. "De bouche à oreille: sur les pratiques de commensalité dans la tradition républicaine du cérémonial de table," *Revue française de science politique* 48, nos. 3–4 (1998).

Louis, Jêrome. "Les banquets républicains sous la monarchie de juillet," in Christiane Demeulenaere-Douyère, ed., *Tous à table! Repas et convivialité, Les banquets républicains sous la monarchie de juillet* (Rennes: 138th Congrès national des sociétés historiques et scientifiques, 2013).

de Tocqueville, Alexis. *The Recollections of Alexis de Tocqueville.* Translated by Alexander Teixeira de Mattos (New York: The Macmillan Co., 1896).

1. This is well summarized in Massimo Montanari, "Food Systems and Models of Civilization," in *Food: A Culinary History from Antiquity to the Present*, ed. Jean-Louis Flandrin and Massimo Montanari (New York: Columbia University Press, 1999), 69–70.

2. Louis-Sebastien Mercier, *Paris pendant la révolution, ou Le nouveau Paris* (Paris: Poulet-Malassis, 1862), 244. Translation by authors.

3. Grimod de La Reynière and C. P. Coste d'Arnobat, *Almanach des gourmands, ou Calendrier nutritif . . . par un vieux amateur* (Paris: Chez Maradan, 1804), 61–62. Translation by authors.

4. In an interesting historical twist, Abd al-Qadir became one of the only insurgent leaders in history to be honored by the government he resisted for so many years. After his defeat, he resided in Damascus, where he saved more than a thousand Christians during a civil war in 1860. For this, the French government awarded him the Legion of Honour.

5. Louis, "Les banquets républicains sous la monarchie de Juillet," 152.

6. Ihl, "De bouche à oreille," 390.

7. Alexis de Tocqueville, *The Recollections of Alexis de Tocqueville*, 19.

8. Ibid., 21.

9. Quoted in Alfred-Auguste Cuvillier-Fleury, *Portraits politiques et révolutionnaires* (Paris: Michel Lévy Frères, 1852), 70. Translation by authors.

39. The End of the Oyster Express

Rambourg, Patrick. "Entre le cuit et le cru: la cuisine de l'huître, en France, de la fin du Moyen Âge au XXᵉ siècle." In *Les nourritures de la mer, de la criée à l'assiette*, 211–20. Caen: Centre de Recherche d'Histoire Quantitative, 2007.

Robert, Sandrine. "De la Manche à Paris: les routes de la marée dans le Val-d'Oise de l'Antiquité au XVIIIᵉ siècle." In *De l'assiette à la Mer*, exhibition catalog, 87–93. Milan: Silvana Editoriale, 2013.

Smith, Drew. *Oyster: A Gastronomic History.* New York: Abrams, 2015.

1. Maguelonne Toussaint-Samat, *A History of Food*, 2nd ed. (Chichester, England: Wiley-Blackwell, 2009), 353–55.

2. It is not clear when the first *chasse-marrée* emerged—possibly as early as the fourteenth century—but by the seventeenth century, a highly organized and efficient delivery system was in place.

3. Robert, "De la Manche à Paris," 87.

4. Jancis Robinson, ed., *The Oxford Companion to Wine*, 4th ed. (Oxford, England: Oxford University Press, 2015), 411.

40. Revelation in a Bottle

Besson, André. *Louis Pasteur: un aventurier de la science.* Monaco: Editions du Rocher, 2013.

Debré, Patrice. *Louis Pasteur.* Johns Hopkins University Press, 2000. See esp. chapter 9.

Hellman, Hal. *Great Feuds in Medicine: Ten of the Liveliest Disputes Ever.* New York: Wiley, 2001.

1. It should be said that not all French drinkers enjoy Jura wines; it is very much a "love it or hate it" wine region.

2. Louis Pasteur, *Oeuvres de Pasteur*, vol. 7, ed. Louis-Pasteur Vallery-Radot (Paris: Masson et Cie, 1939), 130.

3. Debré, *Louis Pasteur*, 227–28.

41. The Curse of the Green Fairy

Adams, Jad. *Hideous Absinthe: A History of the Devil in a Bottle.* Madison: University of Wisconsin Press, 2004.

Baker, Phil. *The Book of Absinthe: A Cultural History.* New York: Grove Press, 2001.

Blocker, Jack S., Ian R. Tyrell, and David M. Fahey, eds. *Alcohol and Temperance in Modern History: An International Encyclopedia.* Santa Barbara, CA: ABC-Clio, 2003.

Cargill, Kima. "The Myth of the Green Fairy: Distilling the Scientific Truth About Absinthe." *Food, Culture & Society* 11, no. 1 (2008): 87–99.

Delahaye, Marie-Claude, "Grandeur et décadence de la fée verte." *Histoire, Économie et Société* 7, no. 4 (1988): 475–89.

Prestwich, P. E. "French Workers and the Temperance Movement." *International Review of Social History* 25, no. 1 (1980): 35–52.

1. Delahaye, "Grandeur et décadence de la fée verte," 479.

2. Jancis Robinson, ed., *The Oxford Companion to Wine*, 4th ed. (Oxford: Oxford University Press, 2015), 555.

3. Didier Nourrisson, *Le buveur du XIXe siècle* (Paris: L'Aventure Humaine, 1990), 321.

4. Quoted in Delahaye, "Grandeur et décadence de la fée verte," 483. Translation by authors.

42. Siege Gastronomy

Decraene, Jean-François, and Bertrand Tillier. *La nourriture pendant le siège de Paris, 1870–1871*. Saint-Denis: Musée d'Art et d'Histoire Saint-Denis, 2004.

Merriman, John. *Massacre: The Life and Death of the Paris Commune of 1871*. New Haven, CT: Yale University Press, 2014.

Pascal, Edmond. *Journal d'un petit Parisien pendant le siège (1870–1871)*. Paris: A. Picard et Kaan, 1893.

Richardson, Joanna. "The Siege of Paris." *History Today* 19, no. 9 (1969): 593–99.

1. Alice Conklin, Sarah Fishman, and Robert Zaretsky, *France and Its Empire Since 1870* (New York: Oxford University Press, 2015), 38–40.

2. Jean Vitaux, *Les Petits Plats de l'Histoire* (Paris: Presses Universitaires de France, 2012), 34–35.

3. Decraene and Tillier, *La nourriture pendant le siège de Paris*, 11. Translation by authors.

4. Pascal. *Journal d'un petit Parisien*, 264. Translation by authors.

5. Ibid., 283.

6. This evolution is well described in Suzanne Citron, *Le mythe national: L'histoire de France revisitée* (Paris: Les Éditions de l'Atelier, 2017).

7. Merriman, *Massacre*, 252.

43. The Peanut Patrimony

Brooks, George E. "Peanuts and Colonialism: Consequences of the Commercialization of Peanuts in West Africa." *Journal of African History* 16, no. 1 (1975): 29–54.

Péhaut, Yves. "The Invasion of Foreign Foods." In *Food: A Culinary History from Antiquity to the Present*, edited by Jean-Louis Flandrin and Massimo Montanari, 457–70. New York: Columbia University Press, 1999.

Wikte, Thomas, and Dale Lightfoot. "Landscapes of the Slave Trade in Senegal and the Gambia." *Focus on Geography* 57, no. 1 (2014): 14–24.

1. Statista Market Forecast, "Peanut Butter," 2017, www.statista.com/outlook/40090400/102/peanut-butter/europe#market-global.

2. Brooks, "Peanuts and Colonialism," 39.

44. Gastronomads on the Sun Road

Csergo, Julia. "The Emergence of Regional Cuisines." In *Food: A Culinary History from Antiquity to the Present*, edited by Jean-Louis Flandrin and Massimo Montanari, 500–515. New York: Columbia University Press, 1999.

Donnaint, Clémentine, and Élodie Ravaux. *Nationale 7: 50 recettes sur la route mythique de Paris à Menton*. Paris: Hachette Livre, 2013.

Lottman, Herbert R. *The Michelin Men: Driving an Empire*. New York: I. B. Tauris, 2003.

Trubek, Amy B. *The Taste of Place: A Cultural Journey into Terroir*. Berkeley: University of California Press, 2009.

1. Menton today hosts only a few lemon suppliers; most of the citrus fruits used in Menton's surreal Fête du Citron, celebrating the end of winter each February with gigantic sculptures made of lemons and oranges, are imported from Morocco and Spain.

2. The *canuts* actually staged one of the first workers revolts, unsuccessfully, in 1831 (their motto: *Vivre libre en travaillant ou mourir en combattant!* or Live Free Working or Die Fighting!)

3. J.-A. Lesourd, "Routes et trafic automobile en France," *L'Information Géographique* 11, no. 1 (1947): 23–27.

4. Curnonsky, *Souvenirs littéraires et gastronomiques* (Paris: Albin Michel, 1958), 53–54. Translation by authors.

5. Jeanne Barondeau, ed., *Cur non . . . bibendum? ou Du PNEU Michelin au guide gastronomique* (Munich: Édition Curnonska, 2014), Kindle location 808 of 3675.

45. A Friend in Difficult Hours

Boisard, Pierre. *Camembert: A National Myth*. Translated by Richard Miller. Berkeley: University of California Press, 2003.

Pourcher, Yves. *Les jours de guerre: la vie des Francais au jour lejour 1914–1918*. Paris: Hachette, 2008.

1. There is also a dessert called a *café liégeois*, which includes coffee-flavor ice cream.

2. It is not entirely clear where this nickname came from. Some say it reminded soldiers who had previously served in the colonies of the monkey meat they sometimes had to resort to eating, but a more likely source for the nickname is the fact that the can openers used at the front were made by a company called Le Singe (The Monkey).

3. Boisard, *Camembert*, 107.

4. Ibid., 113.

5. This remark, purportedly uttered by the prime minister during a speech to former servicemen near Verdun in 1919, has become a veritable French proverb, despite a lack of documentary evidence for it.

46. A Mutiny and a Laughing Cow

La vache qui rit: sa vie, ses recettes. Neuilly-sur-Seine: Éditions Michel Lafon, 2006.

Villemot, Guillaume, and Vincent Vidal. *La chevauchée de la Vache qui rit*. Paris: Editions Hoëbeke, 1991.

1. The first full investigation into the mutinies, made possible after the opening of French military archives, appeared in Guy Pedroncini's *Les Mutineries de 1917* (Paris: Presses Universitaires de France, 1967).

2. According to the association Les Amis de Benjamin Rabier, Bel initially used Rabier's illustration without the latter's permission and only asked him to create a new logo when rival cheesemakers began using the same image.

3. *La vache qui rit*, 43. Translation by authors.

47. "Bread, Peace, and Liberty": The Socialist Baguette

Bertaux-Wiame, Isabelle. "L'apprentissage en boulangerie dans les années 20 et 30: une enquête d'histoire orale," Rapport Final, vol. 2, *Convention CORDES* no. 53/74 (1976).

Vigreux, Jean. *Histoire du Front Populaire: l'échappée belle*. Paris: Tallandier, 2016.

1. George Orwell, *Down and Out in Paris and London* (London: Penguin, 2003), 62, 67.

2. Stephanie Strom, "A Baker's Crusade: Rescuing the Famed French Boulangerie," *New York Times*, July 11, 2017.

48. Couscous: The Assimilation (or Not) of Empire

Béji-Bécheur, Amina, Nacima Ourahhmoune, and Nil Özçağlar-Toulouse. "The Polysemic Meanings of Couscous Consumption in France." *Journal of Consumer Behaviour* 13, no. 3 (2014): 196–203.

Binet, Laurent. " '*Touche pas à mon pain au chocolat!*' The Theme of Food in Current French Political Discourses." *Modern & Contemporary France* 24, no. 3 (2016): 239–52.

Buettner, Elizabeth. *Europe After Empire: Decolonization, Society, and Culture.* Cambridge, England: Cambridge University Press, 2016.

Grange, Henri, and Florence Barriol. "Le marché de la graine de couscous en Europe." In *Couscous, boulgour et polenta: transformer et consommer les céréales dans le monde*, ed. Hélène Franconie, Monique Chastanet, and François Sigaut, 83–92. Paris: Éditions Karthala, 2010.

Janes, Lauren. *Colonial Food in Interwar Paris: The Taste of Empire.* London: Bloomsbury Academic, 2015.

1. The *Maghreb* ("west" in Arabic) conventionally refers to the countries of northwestern Africa: Libya, Tunisia, Algeria, Morocco, and Mauritania. For the purposes of this chapter, the most relevant countries are Algeria, Tunisia, and Morocco, which France occupied in the nineteenth and early twentiethth centuries.

2. TNS SOFRES, "Les plats préférés des Français," August 2011, www.tns-sofres.com/sites/default/files/2011.10.21-plats.pdf.

3. The arid interior of the country was administered by the French armed forces.

4. This era is expertly described by Lauren Janes in *Colonial Food in Interwar Paris*. She argues that the French rejection of colonial food products was a manifestation of a broader reluctance to incorporate the colonies into the French nation.

5. The Third Republic ended with the Nazi occupation of France, and the Fourth Republic was launched in 1946.

6. Béji-Bécheur et al., 197.

7. Buettner, *Europe After Empire*, 236.

8. Ibid., 242.

9. Sylvie Durmelat, "Tasting Displacement: Couscous and Culinary Citizenship in Maghrebi-French Diasporic Cinema," *Food and Foodways* 23, nos. 1–2 (2015): 108.

49. The Forgotten Vegetables

Drake, David. "*Du rutabaga et encore du rutabaga:* Daily Life in Vichy France." *Modern & Contemporary France* 15, no. 3 (2007): 351–56.

Mouré, Kenneth, and Paula Schwartz. "*On vit mal:* Food Shortages and Popular Culture in Occupied France, 1940–1944." *Food, Culture & Society* 10, no. 2 (2007): 261–95.

Schwartz, Paula. "The Politics of Food and Gender in Occupied Paris." *Modern & Contemporary France* 7, no. 1 (1999): 35–45.

1. Elizabeth Kier, "Culture and Military Doctrine: France Between the Wars," *International Security* 19, no. 4 (1995): 65–93.

2. Statistics from Yad Vashem—The World Holocaust Remembrance Center.

3. Regions with a tradition of agricultural self-sufficiency, such as the Loire, Normandy, and Brittany, suffered much less than some of the southern regions and the major urban centers.

4. Bernard Frizell, "Gastronomy: Good Eating Has Survived Both War and Politics as France's Finest Art," *Life*, December 9, 1946, 60.

5. Information and Education Division of the US Occupation Forces, Paris, *112 Gripes About the French* (Oxford, England: Bodleian Library, 2013), 73.

6. The diverse experiences of urban and rural residents are noted in a number of wartime memoirs, such as those by Colette, Simone de Beauvoir, Gertrude Stein, and Alice B. Toklas.

7. *Instructions for British Servicemen in France 1944*, reprinted by the Bodleian Library, Oxford University (Cambridge, England: University Press, 2005), 5.

8. Jean-Louis Flandrin, "The Early Modern Period," in *Food: A Culinary History from Antiquity to the Present*, ed. Jean-Louis Flandrin and Massimo Montanari (New York: Columbia University Press, 1999), 358.

50. Canon Kir Joins the Resistance

Gildea, Robert. *Fighters in the Shadows: A New History of the French Resistance*. Cambridge, MA: Belknap Press, 2015.

Lormier, Dominique. *Histoires extraordinaires de la résistance française*. Paris: Cherche Midi, 2013.

Muron, Louis. *Le chanoine Kir.* Paris: Presses de la Renaissance, 2004.

1. *Instructions for British Servicemen in France 1944*, reprinted by the Bodleian Library, Oxford University (Cambridge, England: University Press, 2005), 32.

2. Nikita Khrushchev, *Memoirs of Nikita Khrushchev*, ed. Sergei Khrushchev, vol. 3, *Statesman, 1953–1964* (University Park: Pennsylvania State University Press, 2007), 200–1.

51. France and the United States: From Liberation to Exasperation

Gordon, Bertram M. "The Decline of a Cultural Icon: France in American Perspective." *French Historical Studies* 22, no. 4 (1999): 625–51.

Kuisel, Richard F. "Coca-Cola and the Cold War: The French Face Americanization, 1948–1953." *French Historical Studies* 17, no. 1 (1991): 96–116.

1. *112 Gripes About the French*, first published in 1945 by the Information and Education Division of the US Occupation Forces, Paris; reprinted in 2013 by the Bodleian Library, University of Oxford.

2. Farley was also a longtime political adviser to President Franklin D. Roosevelt. J. C. Louis and Harvey Z. Yazijian, *The Cola Wars* (New York: Everest House, 1980), 76.

3. Quoted in Kuisel, "Coca-Cola and the Cold War," 110.

4. "Cheese-eating surrender monkey" entered the American lexicon of insulting terms for French people in 1995, thanks to an episode of *The Simpsons* ("'Round Springfield").

5. This is a subjective category to be sure, but it usually includes things like frozen dinners, processed chicken nuggets, cookies, sugary cereals, and fast food generally.

6. Hayagreeva Rao, *Market Rebels: How Activists Make or Break Radical Innovations* (Princeton, NJ: Princeton University Press, 2008), 86.

7. Waverley Root, "The Restoration of French Cooking," *New York Times*, December 17, 1972.

52. Conclusion

1. *Dis-moi ce que tu manges, je te dirai ce que tu es* is the fourth of Brillat-Savarin's famous twenty aphorisms, listed at the beginning of *The Physiology of Taste*.

Index

14th of July (Bastille Day), 163,
    169
Aachen, 29, 193
Abd al-Qadir, 198, 312
Abd al-Rahman, 24–25
Abondance, 44
absinthe, 215–21
Acre, 51, 53
Africa, 23–24, 34, 100, 106,
    111, 114–15, 136, 150, 216,
    229–32, 241, 254–61
Agincourt, 92
agriculture, 3, 28–30, 38, 41, 45,
    52, 89, 125–27, 174, 177, 212,
    217, 242, 250, 257, 279
Aix-en-Provence, 233
Al-Andalus, 24, 113
Albi, 64
Alexander I (Tsar), 191–92
Alexander the Great, 27, 182
Algeria, 198, 216, 218–19, 229,
    235, 255–62
allemande sauce, 108–9
Alsace (region), 16, 33, 44, 48,
    150, 213, 224, 226–27, 240
Alsace (wine), 8, 226
Amboise, 100–103
anarchism, 228
anchovies, 234, 254
angelica, 31, 34
Anjou, 57, 76, 96
Anne of Austria, 149
Anne of Brittany, 102
Anthimus, 17
Apicius, 14
Appellation d'origine controlee
    (AOC), 23, 60, 68, 92–93, 110,
    144, 159, 180, 193, 210, 214,
    243, 270, 275, 284
Appert, Nicolas, 4, 186–89, 213
apples, 49, 203, 274
Aquitaine, 24, 56–60, 80, 83
Arab empire, 23–24, 34, 51, 135
Arbois, 210–12, 214
Arcachon, 208–9
Arles, 9, 217
Armagnac, 50
Armenia, 144, 163

artichokes, 57, 121, 124, 254, 263
Asia, 16, 24, 27, 34, 86, 100, 106, 111, 135, 141, 182, 216, 229, 253, 259, 281
asparagus, 121, 152
Asterix, Obelix, and Getafix, 6–7
Attila the Hun, 15–16
Augustus (Roman emperor), 10, 169
Ausonius, 8
Austria and Austria-Hungary, 3, 145–47, 150, 158, 160, 162, 170, 172, 183–84, 190–91, 194, 223, 240, 263
automobiles, 233–38
Auvergne, 56
Avignon and the Avignon papacy, 68–72, 89
Aztecs, 112

bacteria, 28, 85, 93, 187, 211–14, 243, 278, 282
baguette, 249–54, 256, 279
Balzac, Honoré de, 78, 112
Ban des Vendanges, 37, 42–43
banquets, 17, 71, 151, 195, 197–98, 201–3
barrels, 8, 140, 142, 154, 274, 284
Basques, 65, 110, 113, 284
Bastille prison, 163, 166, 170
Battles of: Austerlitz, 190; Berezina River, 192; Borodino, 192; Castillon, 97; Catalaunian Fields, 15; Crécy, 81; Friedland, 190; Hattin, 53; Marengo, 184; Marignano, 102; Poitiers (732), 23–25; Poitiers (1356), 82; Sedan, 224; Tolbiac, 16; Trafalgar, 140, 188; Vertières, 138; Waterloo, 140, 195
Baudelaire, Charles, 1, 216
Bayonne, 110–11, 113
béarnaise sauce, 105, 109
béchamel sauce, 105, 108–9
Beck, Simone, 35
beef, 13, 17, 40–41, 93, 102, 178, 279
beekeeping, 27–30
beer, 15, 40, 47, 158, 213, 218, 226

Bel, Léon, 246–48
Belgium, 16, 31, 47, 179, 240–41
Belle Époque, 35, 216, 228
Bénédictine (liqueur), 31, 34–36
Berbers, 24, 255–256
Berlin Conference (1884–85), 231
Bernard of Clairvaux, 46
Berry, 76
beurre blanc, 105
Béziers, 64
Bismarck, Otto von, 222, 226
bistro, 16, 18, 196, 257
black currants, 270
Black Death, 82, 85–89, 91
black market, 35, 76–77, 266–67
Blum, Léon, 253
Bocuse, Paul, 280
Bonnefons, Nicolas de, 107
Bordeaux (city), 50, 55, 58–60, 69, 80, 82, 85, 97, 136, 140, 231
Bordeaux (wine), 8, 11, 55, 58–60, 69, 155, 209, 217
bordelaise sauce, 109
bouillabaisse, 237, 254
boulangerie, 130, 145, 147–48, 173, 249–50, 253
Bourbon dynasty, 125, 150, 194, 198
Bourges, 92, 95, 101
Bové, José, 279
brandy, 22, 44, 109, 140–44, 184, 274
brasserie, 16, 226, 240
bread, 2, 40–41, 58, 74, 87, 89, 119, 161, 169–71, 173, 176, 201, 226, 241, 249–54, 257, 267
Breton, André, 134
Breton sauce, 109
Brie, 17, 172, 193–96, 242
Brillat-Savarin, Jean Anthelme, 55, 88, 168, 196, 237, 284
Britain, 112, 138, 159, 162, 173, 175, 182–83, 188–89, 190–91, 194–95, 197, 206, 228–31, 240, 263–64, 266, 269, 272, 274. See also England
Brittany, 27, 73–78, 91, 203–4, 208–9, 239, 242, 273, 284

broccoli, 121
Burgundy (region), 33, 44, 46, 91–92, 95–96, 237, 269–72
Burgundy (wine), 8, 11, 46, 55, 71, 154, 217, 269–71, 284
butchers, 12–13
butter, 14–15, 41, 107, 109, 116, 129–30, 145, 147–48, 169, 177, 225, 253, 268
Butter Tower (Rouen), 129
Byzantine Empire, 23, 50, 57, 99

cafés, 3, 147, 162, 163–69, 224, 252, 280; Café de la Régence, 164, 199; Café du Croissant, 240; Café du Foy, 163–66; Café Maugis, 164; Café Parnasse, 164; Café Procope, 164
café liégeois (beverage), 241
café viennois (beverage), 240
Cahors, 70
Calais, 81–82, 85, 97
calissons, 233
Calvados, 274–75
Calvin, John, 103, 118
Camembert, 208, 239–44, 248, 278
Camisard rebellion, 130–34
Canada, 111, 131, 162, 274
Cancale, 204, 239
Candlemas, 189–91
Cantal, 242
Cap Fréhel, 203
Capet, Hugh, 38
Capetian dynasty, 38, 42, 54, 60
Capitulare de villis, 28
capons, 14, 127
Carcassonne, 65, 79, 83
Cardinal Mazarin, Jules Raymond, 149
Cardinal Richelieu (Armand-Jean du Plessis), 128
Carême, Marie-Antonin, 108–9, 185, 195
Caribbean, 111, 114, 135–38, 141
Carolingian dynasty, 28–34, 37–38, 44
Carolingian Renaissance, 29
carrots, 40, 225
cassoulet, 79–84, 237

Castelnaudary, 79, 82–83
Cathars, 62–67
Catherine de' Medici, 116–22, 123–24, 283
cauliflower, 162, 225
Cavaillon, 233
Celts, 7, 10, 283
cervelle de canut, 234
cervoise, 5, 6, 8, 283
Cévennes, 130–34
Chabichou, 22–26
Chablis, 47, 208
champagne, 140, 154–59, 187, 209, 217
champignons de Paris, 94
Charlemagne, 27–31, 90, 125
Charles IV, 81
Charles V (Holy Roman Emperor), 103
Charles V (the Wise), 75, 83, 91
Charles VI (the Mad), 83, 91–92
Charles VII (the Victorious), 92, 95–98, 101
Charles VIII, 101–2
Charles IX, 117, 119, 124
Charles X, 198
Charles Martel, 24–28
Charles Martel Group, 25
Charles the Bad, 75
Charles the Bald, 31–33
Charles the Fat, 33
Charles the Simple, 33
Chartres, 33
chasse-marrée, 205–6
Château Ausone, 8
Château Pape Clément, 69
Châteauneuf-du-Pape, 68, 70, 72
cheese, 1–2, 25–26, 40–41, 43–48, 68, 69, 74, 93, 104, 116, 127, 173, 193, 195–96, 214, 234, 237, 241–42, 247, 250, 256, 278–79. See also Abondance, Brie, Camembert, Cantal, Chabichou, Comté, Crottin de Chavignol, Époisses, Fourme de Montbrison, goat cheese, Gruyère, Maroilles, Morbier, Munster, Ossau-Iraty, parmesan, Roquefort, Saint-Marcellin,

Saint-Nectaire, Tomme de
   Savoie, Valençay
chestnuts, 22, 131–34
chicken, 95, 98, 123, 125–26,
   184, 210, 225, 267, 279
Child, Julia, 35, 116
Childeric III, 28, 33
China, 85, 144, 232, 255, 259
Chinon, 101
Chirac, Jacques, 127
Chlothar, 22
chocolate, 3, 101, 110–15, 135,
   147, 164, 285
Chouannerie uprising, 78
choucroute (sauerkraut), 16, 226
Christianity in France, 10–13,
   17, 20–22, 30, 34, 37, 39, 41,
   43–48, 50–54, 62–66, 68–73,
   89, 96, 103, 118–19, 171,
   189–90, 261
cider, 15, 40, 203, 218, 273–74
cinnamon, 31, 57, 113, 303
Cîteaux, 45, 64
class differences, expressed in
   food, 3–4, 5, 39–42, 89, 101,
   106–8, 112, 115, 121, 123,
   125, 135, 143, 161–62, 170,
   173, 176, 188, 194, 204, 208,
   218, 222, 225, 265, 283–84
Claude (Queen of France), 50, 104
Clemenceau, Georges, 243
Clement V, 68–69
Clermont, 50
Clos de Vougeot, 47
cloves, 17, 106, 303
Clovis, 16–20
Cluny, 46
Coca-Cola, 275–78
coffee, 3, 112, 135–37, 141, 147,
   163–64, 240
cognac, 8, 50, 98, 136, 139–44,
   217, 284
Colbert, Jean-Baptiste, 76
Colette, 123
colonialism and imperialism, 4,
   108, 111–15, 135–39, 150, 198,
   216, 218, 228–32, 255–62, 285
Columbian Exchange, 111–12
Comité Régional d'Action
   Viticole, 221

communists, 199, 240, 252, 264,
   269, 271, 275, 277–78, 308
Comté, 90, 210, 214, 246
Congress of Vienna, 181, 194–96,
   222
Constantine (Roman emperor), 13
Constantinople, 57, 85, 99
Consulate (1799–1804), 183
cookbooks, 107, 205; L'art de
   bien traiter, 107; La Cuisinière
   bourgeoise, 107, 205; La
   Cuisinière républicaine, 177;
   Le Cuisinier françois, 205; Le
   Ménagier du Paris, 107; Le
   Viandier, 83, 107; Mastering
   the Art of French Cooking, 35
coq au vin, 237
coriander, 57
corn, 112, 126
Corsica, 132, 182, 190
Cortés, Hernán, 112
Côte d'Azur, 233, 272
Côte d'Ivoire, 115
Côtes du Rhône, 68, 70–73
Cotignac d'Orléans, 104
Courvoisier, 140, 144
couscous, 255–62
crayfish, 109, 184
cream, 98, 106–9, 116, 177
crème de cassis, 270, 273
crêpes, 73, 189–92
Crimean War, 189
croissant, 145, 147–48, 279, 285
Crottin de Chavignol, 234
Crusades, 34, 46, 50–55, 57, 62,
   64–66, 135
Curnonsky, 79, 237, 265
Czechoslovakia, 263

Dakar, 230
Daladier, Édouard, 253, 263
Damascus, 24, 54
Danton, Georges, 164, 167
Daudet, Léon, 219, 240
De Gaulle, Charles, 2, 260, 264,
   271, 280
De Molay, Jacques, 54
De Montfort, Simon, 65
Declaration of the Rights of Man,
   167

Degas, Edgar, 216
Delessert, Benjamin, 139
Depardieu, Gérard, 7
Descartes, René, 153, 175, 301
Desmoulins, Camille, 163,
    165–67
Diane de Poitiers, 117, 121
Diderot, Denis, 161, 164
dietetics (classical), 17, 41, 87, 95,
    108, 154
Dijon, 106, 269–273
Directory (1795–99), 181–82, 186
Dom Pérignon, 155–56, 179
Dombes plateau, 45
Dordogne, 60–61
Ducasse, Alain, 110, 310
Dumas, Alexandre, 71, 128, 198,
    233

Edward II (King of England), 80
Edward III (King of England),
    80–81
Edward, the Black Prince of
    England, 79, 82–83
eels, 102
eggplant, 24, 57, 70
eggs, 40–41, 46, 109, 116, 130,
    161, 184, 267
Egypt, 147, 182–83, 185
Elba, 193–95
Eleanor of Aquitaine, 56–61, 141
elephant, 222–23
Elizabeth I, 124
Encyclopédie, 161, 164
England, 31, 32, 38, 54, 55,
    57–61, 71, 75, 79–84, 85, 86,
    88, 91–92, 95–97, 109, 111,
    115, 118, 124, 136, 141–43,
    150, 154–55, 207, 222. See also
    Britain
Enlightenment, 108, 137, 156,
    160–62, 164–65, 167
environmental challenges, 30, 62,
    209
Époisses, 44
escargot, 2, 149
Escoffier, Auguste, 22, 95, 98,
    109, 280–81
espagnole sauce, 108–9
Estates (First, Second, Third),

39–42, 47, 77, 89, 165
Estates General, 76–77, 165
Eudes, 33

famine and food scarcity, 28,
    41, 89, 132, 164, 170, 175–77,
    188–89, 201, 242, 247, 265–67
Fécamp, 31, 34–36
Fermat, Pierre de, 153
fermentation, 27, 106, 154–55,
    158, 211–12
Fête de la Fédération, 163, 197
feudalism, 29, 37–44, 47, 56, 63,
    89, 153, 167
figs, 49, 152
fish, 8, 27, 41, 45–46, 53, 64,
    66, 69, 87, 106, 116, 121, 179,
    205–8, 224
Flanders, 75, 80
fleur de sel, 73–74
foie gras, 14, 17, 50, 127, 237, 279
food and wine marketing, 8,
    35–36, 37, 48, 144, 176, 242,
    247–48, 275
food and wine preservation, 8, 74,
    92, 142, 186–89, 212–13
food as identity marker, 7–8,
    14–18, 24, 39–42, 45–46, 53,
    62–66, 89, 106–8, 123, 125,
    129–30, 132, 134, 161–62,
    197, 219, 240, 255–62, 267,
    275–82, 283–85. See also class
    differences (expressed in food)
food etiquette, 17–18, 49, 145,
    250
food hygiene, 28, 187, 211–12,
    214
food politics, 2–4, 93, 115,
    127–28, 148, 215, 218–21, 253,
    261–62, 275–82, 285
food proverbs, 2, 5, 17–18, 29, 49,
    71, 75, 109, 121, 125, 127, 179,
    186, 199, 250
foodways, 3, 283–84
fork, 57, 121–122
Fortunat (Venantius Fortunatus),
    19–22, 45
Fouquet, Jean, 97
Fourme de Montbrison, 234
Francis I, 50, 102–4, 116, 146

Francis II, 117
Franklin, Benjamin, 164, 176
Franks, 15–33
Franco-American relations, 4, 93, 179, 244, 274–82
Franco-Prussian War, 207, 213, 221–27
Frederick the Great, 175, 186
French Empire: First Empire, 185, 190; Second Empire, 203, 216, 222–23, 228–32
French far right, 3, 25, 128, 148, 253, 261–62, 285
French fry, 179, 228
French identity, 2–3, 62, 67, 103, 128, 173, 215, 255, 261–62, 267, 277, 280–82
French language, 7, 34, 63, 256, 267
French presidents and presidential elections, 25, 127–28, 203, 215, 220, 260–61, 280
French Republic: First Republic, 172, 174, 185; Second Republic, 139, 202; Third Republic, 224, 227, 264, 317; Fourth Republic, 260, 317; Fifth Republic, 260
French resistance, 25, 268–73
French Revolution, 35, 39, 43, 47–48, 70, 77, 131, 138, 150, 160, 163–67, 169–73, 174, 177, 181–82, 184, 185, 194, 197, 212, 216, 242, 280, 282
French schools, 5, 29, 62, 227, 262
Front de Libération Nationale, 259–60
Front National, 25, 128, 261–62, 285
fruit, 24, 41, 49, 53, 58, 64, 84, 87, 100–102, 104, 139, 152–53, 159, 161, 174, 187, 196, 208, 257. *See also* apples, black currants, figs, grapes, lemons, melons, olives, oranges, pears, plums, prunes, quince, tomatoes

gabelous, 76–77
galangal, 106

Gallo-Romans, 7–15, 70, 197, 227
Galois, Évariste, 198
gardens, 28–29, 40, 100, 107, 132, 149, 152–53, 187
Gare du Nord, 207
garlic, 29, 41, 84, 87–88, 106–7, 123, 125, 185, 254, 275
garum, 106, 109
Gascony, 60, 80–81, 96–97, 141
gastronomic tourism, 208, 233–38
gâteau nantais, 134, 137, 139
Gaul, 5–17, 24, 27, 62, 90, 140, 204
Gault, Henri, 280–81
Germany, 16, 20, 28, 31–32, 109, 115, 142, 143, 175, 206–7, 213, 221–27, 235, 238–41, 245–47, 251, 259, 263–73, 275
Gesta Francorum, 51
Ghana, 115
ginger, 17, 51, 106
gingerbread, 27, 98
goat cheese, 22–26, 180, 185
Godard, Jean-Luc, 278
grains of paradise, 106
grapes, 11, 28, 49, 70, 106, 140, 143, 155, 158
Greeks (ancient), 5, 15, 17, 27, 41, 87
Grimod de la Reynière, Alexandre Balthazar Laurent, 168, 187, 197, 237
Gruyère, 109, 196, 222, 225, 242, 246
Guadeloupe, 135, 138
Guérande, 73–78
guilds, 11–12, 88, 167–68, 171
Guises, 124–25

Haiti (Saint-Domingue), 135–38, 229
Hapsburgs, 145–46, 150, 160, 190
haricot beans, 79, 83, 121
Haussmann, Georges-Eugène, 223
Haut-Brion, 60
Henry II (King of England), 57–60

Henry II (King of France), 34, 116–17
Henry III, 117, 121, 124–25
Henry IV (Henry of Navarre), 119, 123–28, 141, 193
Henry V (King of England), 91–92
herbs, 8, 22, 31, 34, 73, 84, 87–88, 106–9, 125, 142, 177, 216, 234, 281. *See also* angelica, coriander, lavender, rosemary
heresy and heretics, 62–67, 70, 103, 118, 130
Holland and the Netherlands, 31, 58, 75, 111–12, 141–43, 150, 160, 229
hollandaise sauce, 105, 109
Hollande, François, 127–28
Holocaust, 113, 264–65
Holy Roman Empire, 30, 190
honey, 8, 21, 26–30, 284
Hoover, Herbert, 122
Hugo, Victor, 140, 199
Huguenots, 118–20, 124–25, 128–31, 141, 143
Hundred Years' War, 54, 60, 71, 75, 79–83, 91–92, 95–98, 99, 101
Huns, 15–16
hypermarchés, 26, 282

Île de France, 38
Île de la Cité, 33
Île d'Oléron, 27
India, 150, 162, 182, 232
Indochina, 257, 259
industrialization, 8, 114–15, 186, 197, 199, 205–8, 211–12, 218, 230, 237, 247, 256, 261
Inquisition, 62, 65–66, 70, 113
Ireland, 111, 143, 150
Isabella (Queen of England), 80–81
Italy, 5, 7, 9, 16, 22, 31, 34, 69, 71, 99, 101–4, 105, 111, 116, 119–22, 151, 175, 182, 184, 204, 234, 240, 251, 254, 278

Jarnac, 140

Jaurès, Jean, 240
Jefferson, Thomas, 179
Jerusalem, 50–53, 57
Jerusalem artichoke, 262, 267–68
Jewish communities in France, 86, 113, 264–65, 271
Joan of Arc, 25, 95–96, 104
John II (the Good), 81–82, 91
John XXII, 69–71
Julius Caesar, 7, 8, 90
July Revolution, 198–99
Jura, 138, 210, 212, 215, 246
Jurançon wine, 123

Khrushchev, Nikita, 273
Kir, 269–73
Knights Templar, 42, 52–55, 70, 75, 80
kouign-amann, 203

La Couvertoirade, 52–53
la France profonde, 126, 215, 237
"La Marseillaise," 168
La Quintinie, Jean-Baptiste, 152–53
La Rochelle, 118, 128–29, 136, 140–41, 143, 208, 284
La vache qui rit (Laughing Cow), 247–48
Lafayette, Marquis de (Gilbert du Motier), 166
Languedoc, 63–66, 78–83, 85, 130–34, 208, 215, 219, 221, 284
Larzac plateau, 52, 90
lavender, 27, 88
Le Grand, Alexandre, 31, 35
Le Havre, 31, 136
Le Pen, Jean-Marie, 25, 261
Le Pen, Marine, 3, 25, 261
leeks, 40, 109
Legislative Assembly, 172
lemons, 49, 106, 209, 234, 315
Lenin, Vladimir, 227
Leonardo da Vinci, 99–100, 102–3
Levant, 23, 50–53, 107, 135
Lille, 211
Limoges, 10–13, 83
Limousin, 10, 13, 60, 140

Liverpool, 136
Livy, 7
Loire Valley, 20, 24, 56, 82, 94–95, 100–101, 134, 137, 180–81, 205, 206, 209, 234
London, 58, 88, 155, 164, 249, 264
Lorraine, 213, 224, 226–27, 240
Lothar, 31
Louis VI, 56
Louis VII, 56–58
Louis IX (Saint Louis), 42
Louis X, 81
Louis XI, 98, 101, 233
Louis XII, 102
Louis XIII, 114, 128–29, 149
Louis XIV, 76, 95, 100, 105, 114, 129, 130, 143, 146–47, 148–53, 156, 205–6, 233, 283
Louis XV, 114, 147, 156, 159–62, 206
Louis XVI, 162, 165, 169–72, 176, 193, 199, 200
Louis XVIII, 194, 195, 198
Louis-Philippe, 197–202
Louis the German, 31
Louis the Pious, 31
Louis the Stammerer, 33
Luther, Martin, 122, 129–30
Lyon, 11, 18, 45, 64, 85, 206, 233–37, 256, 284

macarons, 121
Machiavelli, Niccolò, 102, 117, 146
Macron, Emmanuel, 260, 310
Madagascar, 31, 257
Madame de Maintenon, 151
Madame de Pompadour, 156, 162
Madame du Barry, 147, 162
Maghrebi cuisine, 254–62. See also Algeria, North Africa
magret de canard, 255
Mai 1968, 280
Malquisinat (Street of Bad Cooking), 51
Mamluk dynasty, 53, 182
Manet, Édouard, 216
Marc de Bourgogne, 44
Margaret of Navarre, 103

Marie Antoinette, 147, 169–72, 176
Marie de' Medici, 128
Marie of Anjou, 96
Maroilles, 43, 47–48
marrons glacés, 132
Marseille, 5, 34, 85, 168, 204, 230–31, 254, 256, 260–61, 284
Martinique, 135
Marx, Karl, 199, 227, 278
Mary, Queen of Scots, 117
mayonnaise, 109
McDonald's, 3, 179, 279–81
mead, 27
meat, as symbol, 15, 41, 64, 87, 90, 130, 160
medicinal use of food and wine, 17, 27, 29, 34, 87, 98, 108, 114, 123, 142, 162, 216, 218, 243
Médoc, 58, 204
melons, 102, 233
Menton, 234, 315
Merovingian dynasty, 16–28
Metz, 15, 20, 160, 172, 224
Mexico, 3, 112
Michelin, 234–37
milk, 25, 41, 43, 46, 64, 69, 93, 113, 213–14, 243, 244, 278
Millau, Christian, 280–81
Mistral, Frederic, 70
Mitterrand, François, 127
Mongols, 16, 85
monks and monasteries, 29, 32, 34–35, 43–48, 131, 171, 283; Benedictines, 34, 44–49, 155; Cistercians, 45–46, 55, 64; Dominicans, 47, 65–66; Franciscans, 47, 71; Templars, 42, 52–55; Trappists, 47
Mont-Saint-Michel, 203
Montagné, Prosper, 83
Montélimar, 233
Montesquieu, 137, 156
Montezuma, 112
Montmartre, 37
Montségur, 65–67
Morbier, 278
Mornay sauce, 109
Morocco, 256, 259–60
Mucha, Alphonse, 35

mulberries, 126
Munster, 44, 48
Muscadet, 273
mushrooms, 94–95, 98, 107, 109, 177
Muslim communities in France, 3, 23–25, 255–62
mussels, 203, 254, 255
mustard, 71, 84, 88, 106, 241, 270
mutton, 79, 83, 130

Nantes, 1, 26, 32, 134–39, 249, 268, 273, 284
Nantes, Edict of, 125, 128, 130–31
Nantua sauce, 109
Naples, 101, 185
Napoleon, 78, 138–40, 147, 158–59, 167, 177, 181–86, 188, 190–96, 199, 233
Napoleon III, 203, 212, 222–24, 229
Napoleonic Wars, 139, 183–84, 186, 188–89, 190–95
Narbonne, 27, 63, 82, 293
National Assembly, 138, 165, 167–68, 171–72
National Convention, 172, 182
Navarre, 118–19, 123–24
New York City, 129, 282
New Rochelle, 129
Nice, 233
Nine Years' War, 150
Normandy, 8, 31, 34–35, 38, 57, 59, 92, 96–97, 129, 201, 205, 208–9, 237, 239, 242–44, 272, 273, 274, 278
North Africa, 23–24, 229, 254–61, 262
Nostradamus, 87
nougat, 121, 233
nouvelle cuisine, 280–81
nutmeg, 31, 106, 303

oats, 20, 22, 40
offal, 12–13
olive oil, 14, 15, 109, 129, 228, 230, 254
olives, 68, 234, 254
onions, 40–41, 234

oranges, 100–102, 111, 164
Orientalism, 147
Orléans, 91–92, 96, 104, 137
ortolans, 127
Orwell, George, 252
Ossau-Iraty, 110
Ottoman Empire, 135, 145–47, 163, 182, 240–41, 256
oysters, 68, 127, 157, 203–9, 254, 284

pain au chocolat, 111, 147–48
Palais-Royal, 156, 164, 166, 199
Pantagruel, 104
papeton d'aubergines, 70
Paris, 15, 17, 32–33, 37, 38, 54, 56, 71, 75, 77, 92, 94, 95–96, 101, 103, 119, 123, 125–26, 134, 137, 144, 147, 149, 156, 160, 162, 163–72, 176–79, 182, 187, 193–94, 195, 196, 197, 199, 201–2, 205, 206–8, 215, 216, 221–28, 233, 235, 237, 240, 241, 251–53, 256–58, 264–67, 270, 276–77, 280, 282, 283–85
Paris Commune, 227–28, 251
Parmentier, Antoine-Augustin, 174–78
parmesan, 102
partridge, 79, 151
Pascal, Blaise, 153
pasta, 102, 255, 257
Pasteur, Louis, 4, 158, 187, 210–15
pasteurization, 193, 212–14, 243, 278
pastis, 219
patron saints, 11–13, 22
peanut butter, 228
peanut oil, 228, 230–32
peanuts, 230–32
pears, 49, 152, 199–200
peas, 151–52, 187–88
peasant rebellions, 39, 43, 76, 78, 89, 130–32
peasants, 11, 38–43, 47, 76, 78, 82, 89, 125, 131–32, 170, 172, 178, 283
Pepin III (Pepin the Short), 28

pepper, 17, 51, 106, 177, 222
Pepys, Samuel, 60
Pernod, Henri-Louis, 216
Persian Empire, 23, 135
Pétain, Philippe, 245, 264, 270–71
petits ventres, 12
Philip II (Philip Augustus), 42, 59–60
Philip III (the Bold), 81
Philip IV (the Fair), 42, 53–54, 68, 75, 80–81
Philip V, 81
Philip VI, 80–82
phylloxera, 158, 217, 226
Picasso, Pablo, 216
pièce montée, 108
pieds-noirs, 255–56, 260–61
piment d'Espelette, 110, 112
pissaladière, 234
Pliny the Elder, 7
plums, 49–50, 54–55, 104
poison, 70, 86, 98, 117, 119, 161
Poitiers, 20, 22, 23–25, 56
Poitou-Charentes region, 23, 29, 140–43
Poland, 117, 121, 191, 263, 268
Pontarlier, 216, 219
popes and papacy, 28, 30, 50, 52–54, 57, 63–66, 68–73, 96, 116
Popular Front, 252–53
pork, 3, 8, 16, 17–18, 24, 40, 79, 83, 110, 167, 172, 262
Portugal, 34, 111, 113, 135–36, 209, 230
potatoes, 111–12, 174–79, 241, 267–68, 285
poule au pot, 125
poulet de Bresse, 210
poulet Marengo, 184
prohibition, 159, 219
Protestant Reformation, 72, 89, 99, 103, 107, 118–19, 122, 124–26, 128–31, 146, 153
Proust, Marcel, 216
Provence, 9, 27, 63, 68, 69, 70, 168, 234, 237, 242, 254, 285
prunes, 49–50
Prussia, 158, 160, 172, 175, 190,

194–95, 207, 213, 221–26
Pyrenees, 24, 56–57, 63, 65, 110, 113, 118, 123

quenelle de brochet, 45
quince, 104

Rabelais, François, 5, 101, 103, 104, 122
Radegund, 20–22
railways, 92, 199, 206–8, 212, 217, 224, 230, 270, 271
Ravitaillement en Viande Fraîche, 246–47
Reconquista of Spain, 113
Regency, 156, 159
Reign of Terror, 162, 173, 197
Reims, 17, 96, 154
Renaissance, 5, 27, 89, 99–105, 153, 204
restaurants, 167–68, 198, 222, 225, 226, 233, 235
Revolution of 1848, 201–3
Rhône Valley, 7, 68–71, 85, 234, 272
rice, 255, 257
Richard I (Lionheart), 58, 60
Rimbaud, Arthur, 216
river transport, 32, 206–7
Robert, Duke of Normandy (Rollo the Walker), 33–34
Robespierre, Maximilien, 164, 167, 173, 197
Rome, 69, 71–72
Roman Empire, 3, 5–17, 24, 27, 44, 46, 51, 63, 70, 73, 74, 100, 106, 112, 140, 169, 189, 204, 206, 233, 283
Roquefort, 50, 90, 92–93, 278–79, 284
rosemary, 27, 88
Rouen, 32–34, 96, 129, 206
Rousseau, Jean-Jacques, 156, 159–61, 164
Route du Chabichou, 23, 215
Route Nationale 7, 233, 238
rum, 134–37
Russia and the Soviet Union, 32, 140, 144, 158, 183, 190–92, 194, 196, 219, 240–41, 245,

247, 251, 263, 273, 277, 269, 303
rutabaga, 267
rye, 40, 173

saffron, 51, 71, 106
Saint Aurélien, 12
Saint Bartholomew's Day Massacre, 118–20
Saint Blandina, 11
Saint-Émilion, 8
Saint-Etienne, 206
Saint Helena, 140, 195
Saint Lawrence, 11
Saint-Malo, 203
Saint-Marcellin, 234
Saint Martial, 12
Saint Martin of Tours, 11
Saint-Nectaire, 278
salad, 17, 88, 106
Salah ad-Din, 53
Salon International de l'Agriculture, 127, 215
salt, 52, 73–78, 177, 187, 215, 250, 268, 284
Sancerre, 209
Sarkozy, Nicolas, 3, 127
sauces, 57, 87, 95, 98, 105–10, 230, 250, 254, 257, 270, 281
sausages, 12, 16, 22, 79, 167, 270
sauvignon blanc, 26, 180, 209
Savoy, 8, 242
Scandinavia, 31, 34
scientific revolution, 108, 153–54
Scotland, 144
Seine River, 33, 160, 193, 224
Senegal, 229–32
Serres, Olivier de, 95, 126, 139
Seven Weeks' War (1866), 223
Seven Years' War, 162, 175
shallots, 84, 107, 109, 177, 209, 234
shellfish, 203–4, 205, 254. See also mussels, oysters
Sicily, 32, 34, 51, 135, 164
siege of Paris (885), 33
siege of Paris (1870–71), 221–27
silk, 126, 213, 234
slavery and the slave trade, 32, 135–39, 229
socialism and socialists, 199,

202–3, 218, 223, 225, 227, 240, 245, 251–53
Société des Amis des Noirs, 138
Sorel, Agnès, 95–98, 101
South America, 83, 112, 135, 175, 230
Spain, 23–24, 51, 90, 104, 110–14, 123, 125, 135, 141, 150, 175, 190–91, 221, 253
spices, 17, 31, 34, 51, 74, 87–88, 106–8, 111–13, 121, 141, 283. See also cinnamon, cloves, coriander, galangal, ginger, grains of paradise, nutmeg, pepper, piment d'Espelette, saffron
spinach, 40, 116, 121
Stevenson, Robert Louis, 132–34
Strasbourg, 16, 86, 284
sugar, 24, 27, 51, 104, 111–13, 121, 134–39, 155, 158, 187, 211–12, 216, 249, 283, 285
sugar beets, 139
Switzerland, 31, 103, 115, 210, 216, 247

Taillevent, 83, 107
Talleyrand-Périgord, Charles Maurice de, 108–9, 181, 183, 185–86, 191, 193, 194–96, 310
taxes, 29, 39, 42, 47–48, 54, 58, 74–78, 82, 93, 98, 143, 150, 165, 256; bee tax (abeillage), 29; religious tax (tithe), 39, 165, 171; salt tax (gabelle), 75–78, 165
tea, 135, 141
temperance movement, 218–20
terroir, 8, 27, 58, 68, 73, 140, 209, 210, 214, 237, 284, 295
terrorism, 25, 221, 228
Theodoric, 17, 20
Theriac, 87
Thirty Years' War, 141
Toleration, Edict of, 131
Tocqueville, Alexis de, 201–2
tomatoes, 3, 109, 111, 168, 185, 254, 285
Tomme de Savoie, 278
Toulon, 182, 255, 261

Toulouse, 49, 63, 65, 79, 83
Toulouse-Lautrec, 216
Touraine, 11
Tours, 23–24
Toussaint-Louverture, 138
trade in food and wine, 5, 8, 24,
    34–35, 51, 55, 58–60, 75, 85,
    89, 93, 108, 111–15, 135–37,
    141, 208, 214, 230–32, 278–79
Treaty of Brétigny (1360), 82
Treaty of Paris (1259), 80
Treaty of Troyes (1420), 92
Treaty of Verdun (843), 31
truffles, 98, 162, 222, 279
Tunisia, 235, 256, 259–60
turkeys, 112, 132
turnips, 83
Turquerie, 146

Umayyad caliphate, 23–25
United States, 35, 93, 143–44,
    148, 159, 160, 164, 166, 179,
    193, 199, 214, 217–19, 228,
    229, 233, 240–41, 244, 245,
    247–48, 249, 259, 270, 272,
    274–82

Valençay, 180–81, 185
Valois dynasty, 54, 80–81, 104,
    117, 123–25
Van Gogh, Vincent, 216
vanilla, 31, 112–13, 134, 137
Varenne, François-Pierre de la, 105
Vatel, François, 205
vegetables, 40–41, 49, 62, 64, 66,
    107, 119, 121, 125, 132, 149,
    151–53, 159, 161, 170, 174,
    186–88, 208, 224–25, 234,
    255, 261, 262, 267–68, 283
vegetarian, 61–67, 100, 161
velouté, 95, 109
Vendée, 209
Venice, 104, 121, 135
Verdun, 238
verjuice, 106–7
Verlaine, Paul-Marie, 216
Verne, Jules, 134
Versailles, 100, 147, 149–53, 156,
    160–62, 170–71, 186, 205, 226
Veuve Clicquot, 158

Vichy regime, 25, 166, 264–67,
    269–72
Vienna, 145–47, 190
Vienne, 7, 235
viennoiserie, 147
Vietnam, 259, 280
Vikings, 31–34
Vimoutiers, 243–44
vin jaune, 210–11
vinaigrette, 88, 209, 228
vinegar, 9, 84, 87–89, 106–7, 177,
    211–12
vineyards, 5, 7–8, 28, 37, 42–43,
    46–47, 69–70, 140, 143,
    154–55, 158–59, 208, 217–18,
    234, 285
Virgin of the Kidney, 10–13
Vitré, 76
Voltaire, 137, 156, 164, 176

War of the Austrian Succession,
    160
War of the Spanish Succession,
    150
War of the Three Henrys, 124
Wars of Religion, 118–20,
    124–25, 128–29, 130–31, 141,
    146
Washington, George, 166, 202
West Africa, 106, 114–15, 136,
    150, 229–32
Western Schism, 72
wheat, 40, 89, 111, 170, 173, 176,
    250
whisky, 8, 143
wine, 5–9, 15, 18, 28, 37, 40,
    42–43, 45–47, 52, 55, 58–60,
    64, 70–72, 98, 100, 106, 109,
    125, 127, 140–42, 154–55,
    161, 163–64, 173, 185, 208,
    209, 210–13, 217–21, 222, 226,
    234, 237, 241, 252, 267, 277,
    279, 283–85; experimentation,
    8, 46–47, 154–58, 212–13.
    See also Bordeaux (wine),
    Burgundy (wine), Chablis,
    Champagne, Château Ausone,
    Château Pape Clément,
    Châteauneuf-du-Pape, Côtes du
    Rhône, Haut-Brion, Jurançon,

Muscadet, Saint-Émilion,
Sancerre, sauvignon blanc,
Veuve Clicquot, vin jaune,
vineyards
women in France, 5, 19–20, 48,
63–64, 65, 73, 80–81, 101,
118, 170, 201, 202–3, 257,
260, 267

World War I, 16, 47, 158, 179,
219–20, 227, 234–36, 238–48,
251, 256, 263, 264
World War II, 25, 35, 143,
234–35, 243, 253, 259, 260,
262–75

Zang, August, 147, 250

Publishing in the Public Interest

Thank you for reading this book published by The New Press. The New Press is a nonprofit, public interest publisher. New Press books and authors play a crucial role in sparking conversations about the key political and social issues of our day.

We hope you enjoyed this book and that you will stay in touch with The New Press. Here are a few ways to stay up to date with our books, events, and the issues we cover:

- Sign up at www.thenewpress.com/subscribe to receive updates on New Press authors and issues and to be notified about local events
- Like us on Facebook: www.facebook.com/newpressbooks
- Follow us on Twitter: www.twitter.com/thenewpress

Please consider buying New Press books for yourself; for friends and family; or to donate to schools, libraries, community centers, prison libraries, and other organizations involved with the issues our authors write about.

The New Press is a 501(c)(3) nonprofit organization. You can also support our work with a tax-deductible gift by visiting www.thenewpress.com/donate.